MW01124138

The Changing & Unchanging Face of U.S. Civil Society

Marcella Ridlen Ray

The Changing & Unchanging Face of U.S. Civil Society

with a foreword by Francis Fukuyama

Transaction Publishers
New Brunswick (U.S.A.) and London (U.K.)

This book is printed on acid-free paper that meets the American National Standard for Permanence of Paper for Printed Library Materials.

Library of Congress Catalog Number: 2001058305
ISBN: 0-7658-0139-6
Printed in the United States of America

Library of Congress Cataloging-in-Publication Data

Ray, Marcella Ridlen.
The changing and unchanging face of U.S. civil society / Marcella Ridlen Ray; with a foreword by Francis Fukuyama.
p. cm.
Includes bibliographical references and index.
ISBN 0-7658-0139-6 (cloth: alk. paper)
1. Political participation—United States. 2. Civil society—United States. I. Title.

JK1764.R39 2002
300'973—dc21

2001058305

To Charles
and
to most Americans who,
wittingly or unwittingly,
produce civil society each day

Contents

List of Tables

List of Figures

Acknowledgments

The author gratefully acknowledges the Brookings Institution Press for permission to use previously published material that appeared in *Civic Engagement in American Democracy*, edited by Theda Skocpol and Morris Fiorina.

I am indebted to many for assistance in the research and writing of this book. Support was outstanding from sources within George Mason University: the School of Public Policy, the Department of Sociology and Anthropology, the Department of Public and International Affairs, and Fenwick Library. The Joseph L. Fisher Doctoral Award in recognition of this research symbolizes the encouragement I received.

The researcher's obsession is access to data and there are many who made this possible. I thank busy editors of the *Encyclopedia of Associations* who answered questions about the compilation of their reference work, Census Bureau researchers who shared unpublished data, always responsive researchers at the Independent Sector, editors of the Standard Directory of Periodicals who supplied data with which to construct trends, American Business Directories who furnished annual sales lists enumerating membership groups listed in yellow page directories, and the American Society of Association Executives who shared some of their own research results. Staff from Harris Polls, Gallup, Pew Research Center, Hart Teeter and the Roper Organization helped with searches of survey databases. Invitations from the Independent Sector, the Internal Revenue Service, and National Association of Latino Elected and Appointed Officials to make use of their in-house collections were so helpful. My gratitude to librarians at the Library of Congress, George Mason University, the Internal Revenue Service, the Oxford Union, and the Social Studies Library at Oxford is immense.

Marty Lipset tops the list of people whom I must thank. Marty patiently and dispassionately read and critiqued drafts of this work as it unfolded. I am indebted to Frank Fukuyama for his interest in my work and his thoughtful support of an emergent scholar. Tim Conlan and Hugh Heclo were beyond generous with their encouragement and suggestions. John Stone's review of my analysis of Tocqueville was important. A small working conference on "Civic Engagement in American Democracy" brought thoughtful suggestions from Stephen Brint, Theda Skocpol, Mo Fiorina, Robert Putnam, and Jeff Berry in regard to technological aspects of associational life. I warmly acknowledge contributions of Ingrid Sandole-Staroste, Amy Bunger, Gwen Halford, Gerard Maas, Susan Roche, Miriam Riskind, Reza Banakar, Laura Matthews, Sandra Doyle, Lisa Bodgwick, and Mark Almond. Without the family and friends who sacrificed on its behalf, this project would not have come to fruition. And what would one do without a masterful editor like Anne Schneider, who like a symphony conductor brings it all together? Finally, I thank my life partner for his infinite patience, his always enthusiastic backing of this project, and for caring about the public interest.

Foreword

One of the key features of the debate over the state of democracy at the end of the twentieth century and the beginning of the twenty-first has been the centrality of civil society to the discussion. The idea that intermediary groups standing between the individual and the state should be key to the success of liberal democracy has been around since Tocqueville. But the need to build civil society as a practical project arose in an acute way with the collapse of the Soviet empire in 1989 and the rise of a number of new democracies in former communist countries. The notion that civil society could not be taken for granted, that it was stronger in some societies than in others, and that it could actually disappear, became questions not just of theoretical but of immense practical importance.

Consonant with Alexis de Tocqueville's observation of the importance of voluntary associations to American democracy, some of the greatest worriers about the state of civil society have been Americans. Scholars like Edward Banfield, Gabriel Almond, and Robert Putnam have been important in laying out a theory of the relationship of civil society to other democratic institutions, while various pollsters, social scientists, and observers of all stripes have been busy over the years gathering empirical evidence about the relative health of intermediary institutions both in the United States and abroad. The debate over the health of American democracy in the 1990s was strongly shaped by Putnam's article, "Bowling Alone," later turned into a book, which asserted that American civil society had gone into a generation-long decline in the postwar period as a result of civic disengagement on the part of the baby boom generation.

The Changing and Unchanging Face of U.S. Civil Society constitutes an important contribution to this ongoing debate. Using data sources untapped by Putnam, as well as reinterpreting existing data in different ways, Marcella Ridlen Ray contests his central finding that American social capital has been in decline. She argues instead that the types and forms of civic association have changed over times in a flexible manner that adapts to changing conditions. In particular, they have adapted to the requirements for greater inclusiveness that have changed the character of how and with whom Americans associate. She argues that the ability of American civil society to reinvigorate itself is undiminished.

America's response to the terrorist attacks of September 11, 2001, reinforces her point. In the face of an unprecedented external threat, Americans have suddenly found new sources of community and mutual support that had little precedent in the preceding economic boom years that formed the backdrop to Putnam's analysis. Patriotism came back in fashion (as evidenced by the ubiquitous flags following the attacks), there was an enormous outpouring of concern and active help to the victims, and, at least anecdotally, a greater interest in public service and public issues more generally. Even if Putnam were clearly right that American social capital had been in decline, it could well turn out that the single day of September 11 was sufficient to reverse some of the most important of the negative trends he chronicled.

In retrospect, it would seem that the high level of civic engagement and trust that characterized the United States in the 1950s was not some kind of "normal" baseline for the society, but was itself a somewhat abnormal period shaped by external events. The Great Depression, World War II, and emerging Cold War were traumatic events that reinforced an American sense of community and identity. The fact that the U.S. government was perceived as dealing competently and effectively with these large problems also added to a general trust of the state and of society's major institutions. The period that followed was not one of great success for public enterprises, and despite the ongoing Cold War, did not produce the kind of acute trauma that is often needed to cement bonds of social solidarity. By this account, the underlying story is not long-term decline of social capital, but regression to the mean in a society that periodically rejuvenates itself.

The debate set off by Putnam has been a healthy one, since we cannot take the American art of association for granted. But before we come to final conclusions about U.S. social capital, it is extremely useful to have a book that examines civil society's variability, both over time and in the forms that it has taken. This is something that *The Changing and Unchanging Face of U. S. Civil Society* does with fresh insight, while pointing hopefully to the new forms of community that will come to be in the future.

FRANCIS FUKUYAMA
Bernard L. Schwartz Professor of International Political Economy
Paul H. Nitze School of Advanced International Studies
Johns Hopkins University

1

Democratic Civil Society: What is It and Why is It Important?

You and I cannot see democratic civil society. Anthropologist Mary Douglas explains that institutions, once created, fade from view to work automatically on our behalf. Our first challenge, when wishing to evaluate or to change an institution, is to bring this automatically functioning phenomenon into focus.[1] The demise of communist regimes and subsequent democratization efforts provide a particular incentive to learn more about democratic civil society. As attention turns toward the experience of mature democracies, such as the United States, a second incentive appears, as maturity has its own challenges.

Older, as well as new, democracies continue to face an uncharted future. Social scientist Michael Walzer warns that all advanced democracies, including the United States, have neglected their pluralist institutions and their "networks through which civility is produced and reproduced."[2] Political philosopher John Gray cautions that Western democracies must discover how to perpetuate civil society in order to safeguard cultural freedom and the liberty of the individual. Competition for state resources and group rights policies has weakened the autonomy of civil society institutions.[3] From French political sociologist Guy Hermet, we hear that citizens in older democracies lack participative passion and rely on a legitimacy that is fragile.[4] British political philosopher David Selbourne observes that the "flux of the social order," obeisance to the market order, and our "ubiquitous transfer of individual moral responsibility" all contribute to "increasingly random forms of human association." Within the context of a liberal civil order permeated with "claims to dutiless right, demand-satisfaction and self-realization through unimpeded freedom of action," Selbourne concludes that too few have a sense of civic order, that too many are strangers who share no bond of civic obligation.[5] Unfortunately, although these observations resonate with collective concerns, they fail to provide the substance and form necessary for empirical analysis of democratic civil society.

My own awareness of the shadowy institution of democratic civil society began to form in the 1970s. It was while directing Comprehensive Employment and Training Act programs for a county commission that I first experienced the tensions that exist between the many stakeholders in a democracy. The needs of individual citizens, citizen advisory groups, local community groups and businesses, professional staff members, and officials from local, state, and federal levels of government were all important parts of the production. Each group had its own agenda(s) for federal monies. Agendas were sometimes compatible, frequently at odds. Unprepared for this raw experience with democracy, I often felt caught in the middle.

Intuitively, I hoped to safeguard that mix of agendas, despite the resulting tension. Individuals in similar situations often choose to sidestep this tension by adopting the objectives of the primary funding entity, usually state or federal levels of government.[6] Some of my own colleagues in other communities made that very choice. Certainly, the influx of dollars from the federal level into our local communities ran into the millions, giving federal representatives a strong, overweening sense of ownership of the dollars that flowed into local areas. In my judgment, it was important to maintain and mediate the resulting tension rather than to resolve it by sacrificing local interests. Such decisions were made each day, on the front lines, without the benefit of theoretical and empirical guidance. Most participants in the process did their part in articulating and promoting their interests, but few appreciated the full value of a complete panorama of conflicting or competing interests. Too often, perhaps, the tendency was to try to resolve or to circumvent strain, instead of seeking a healthy, democratic tension among all views.

The lesson I took from this experience is that the complex, indistinct institution of civil society deserves greater scrutiny. It must be brought into sharper focus for those who wish to be effective in democratic self-governance. To this end, we must understand the basic tenets of democratic civil society and think institutionally. We must envision democratic civil society, in theory and in fact.

Democratic Civil Society Defined

Democratic civil society is that intermediate part of the social order which is not the state, not commerce, and not private life.[7] In general, it is a cluster of institutions, organizations, and practices comprised of both social structure and process. Structurally, civil society is a pluralistic mix of institutions and relational networks comprised, in turn, of associations, citizen groups, social movements, mass media, intellectual currents and centers, ideologies, and local entities. Civil society as a process consists of talking, meeting, reasoning, and acting together on varied matters that may pertain to family, faith, interest, or ideology. It might be spontaneous or customary, formal or informal, but it is necessarily voluntary and autonomous. [8]

What Does Civil Society Do for Democracy?

A pluralist democratic system supports cooperation and competition of interests under an overarching shared sense of justice, moral progress, and economic advancement.[9] The unique contribution of civil society stems from its potential to combine and consolidate diverse citizens in an intermediate, autonomous network of relationships located between state and nonstate entities. The result enhances the state and makes a democratic system more democratic by several means. The flow of information increases. Isolation is reduced and that which citizens share expands. Common objectives are reached. Private and public institutions communicate. Citizens influence political decisions. Political institutions are more responsive and accountable to the public. Power is broadly distributed. Monopolization of truth is countered. Individual freedom and liberty are safeguarded. Liberty and the general good are integrated.[10]

Significantly, political sociologist Seymour Martin Lipset finds that the complex, dynamic cluster of practices and institutions comprising democratic civil society is noticeably absent in nondemocratic systems.[11] Power is less diffused and more concentrated in the hands of those who govern in nondemocratic, mass society conditions. Totalitarianism has its opportunity when a society is atomized, a population alienated and without community. It is under these circumstances that those in governing positions are able to dominate and manipulate the governed.[12] Tocqueville graphically described such conditions:

> After having thus successively taken each member of the community in its powerful grasp and fashioned him at will, the supreme power then extends its arm over the whole community. It covers the surface of society with a network of small complicated rules, minute and uniform, through which the most original minds and the most energetic characters cannot penetrate, to rise above the crowd. The will of man is not shattered, but softened, bent and guided; men are seldom forced by it to act, but they are constantly restrained from acting. Such a power does not destroy, but it prevents existence; it does not tyrannize, but it compresses, enervates, extinguishes, and stupefies a people, till each nation is reduced to nothing better than a flock of timid and industrious animals, of which the government is the shepherd.[13]

Civil society stands in the way of total concentration of power and complete mobilization of the population by the elite.[14] When sociologist William Kornhauser contrasted pluralist, communal, totalitarian and mass societies, he found the pluralist system unique with its buffer of strong intermediate groups that filtered and modulated the interactions between elites and nonelites. Elites were indirectly accessible but accountable to the rest of the population. Nonelites held close attachments to intermediate groups that kept loyalties local, personal, and less vulnerable to manipulation.[15]

A fundamental goal of totalitarianism is to eradicate individual liberty and to control citizens in all aspects of life. Signs of civil society must either be destroyed or co-opted as an instrument of control.[16] This was documented in a well-known study conducted by Lipset, Trow, and Coleman of a large typographical union where conditions of weakness or the lack of intermediate groups within the political system led to mass society-like conditions. In authoritarian chapters of the union, union leaders suborned existent intermediate groups as vehicles for political indoctrination and control. In other locales, intermediate groups that functioned independently, autonomously, and in appreciable numbers enhanced the democratic process by mediating between individuals and authority *and* by heightening the involvement of individuals in union politics.[17]

Whether in a union organization or in the above example from Tocqueville, a concentration of power draws disproportionate attention and response toward remote, rather than immediate affairs, social relations, and power sources.[18] Without the moderating effect of close intermediate associations, social and political attachments that are distant and impersonal are ineffective in constraining fickle, impulsive, and excessively intense attention and behavior. This gives opportunity to extra-constitutional and anti-democratic social movements.[19] Indeed, Tocqueville saw the complete lack of exchange between the governed and the governing as a contributing factor to the French Revolution. Prior to the Revolution, the aristocracy grew more exclusive and the gap between the noblemen and the bourgeois widened to almost no contact. There was no mediation, no cooperative effort between the classes—the nobility, bourgeoisie, the common people, the townsfolk, and the rural folk. None thought beyond themselves.[20]

Such concentration of power and homogeneity of interests makes a less stable system. It is analogous, political scientist Karl Deutsch explained, to loading all of the power at the apex of a pyramid. This makes it vulnerable to overload, imbalance, and unexpected power shifts.[21] These conditions for instability do not flourish in a pluralist state that is decentralized and diversified in order to meet citizen needs.[22] Such developments are prevented in contemporary democratic society, Kornhauser found, by buffered relations in which those with superordinate roles and responsibilities for governing and those who are governed attempt to block the efforts of each to dominate the other.[23] The founding fathers understood this and sought to balance the tension by design. As James Madison wrote in *The Federalist Papers*, it is necessary "to guard one part of society against the injustice of the other parts."[24] The best conditions for stability exist, as David Truman said, when "pluralistic structure is a central fact of the distribution of power... a structure that is intervening between government at the national level and the rank and file of the population."[25] Civil society, with its intermediate relational network, is thus the means to stability, liberty, and an improving democracy.

The Idea of the Intermediary and of Flexible Tension

Fundamental to the role of democratic civil society is the idea of an intermediate, flexible tension that stabilizes the system. A stable democracy, political scientist Harry Eckstein once explained, requires balances of contradictory behavior patterns so as to avoid "undue strain and intolerable anomie."[26] Balances are needed between a sense of civic obligation and actual civic participation, between too much and too little citizen activity, and between conflict and consensus.[27] Almond submits that with time and experience we have learned about sustaining a balanced tension between opposing influences.[28] The lessons to be found in failures and successes in achieving political stability actually caught the attention of early political analysts like Aristotle and Machiavelli, both of whom collected empirical data that documented and described institutional and social arrangements and their outcomes. Each sought to identify the conditions for a peaceful and contented community life, regardless of its characteristics and its members.

The vocabulary used to discuss the concept of political equilibrium—tension, balance, intermediary, mediate—has origins traceable at least to the Middle Ages, according to *The New Oxford Dictionary of English*. Balance denotes a condition in which elements are equal, in proportion, in symmetry, on a moderate course, or in compromise. In its early usage, balance referred mostly to that between two elements. The modern perception of balance often dichotomizes, as well, but we have learned to expect multiple factors to be involved. *Tension*, in medieval terminology, denoted a condition or feeling of being physically stretched or strained, while we also think of it in psychological and sociological terms today. The term *intermediary* comes from medieval Latin *intermediatus* and *intermedius* (inter "between" and medius "middle") and *mediate* is derived from late Latin *mediatus,* which means placed in the middle.

The application of this terminology to political order grew with experience. As historian Paul Rahe points out, the citizenry of the ancient city was relatively homogeneous.[29] The concept of balance was not largely applicable to the internal political order, but awareness grew that internal faction, unless managed effectively, destroys a political society. Both Plato and Aristotle sought solutions for the political discord between the poor and wealthy classes.[30] Modern theorists continue to recognize the importance of keeping inherent contradictions from producing what Eckstein once called "insupportable strains" within a political community.[31]

A dynamic sort of balance is pertinent to the mediating role of a democratic civil society, but there is a balance of another kind. Static balance is inherently brittle and lacks capacity to accommodate, in contrast to a dynamic one that adjusts to changes in stresses and strains without breaking apart. Democratic civil society, as an intermediate institution, allows this adjustment by holding different contingents of a social order in a flexible relationship of tension. The tensile strength derived from the ability to flex is potentially a stabilizing factor within a democratic framework.

The roots of this insight are buried in the writings of early political thinkers who grasped the importance of institutionalizing political equilibrium. Aristotle, Machiavelli, Locke, Burke, and Tocqueville were significant contributors to the idea that intermediate institutions and principles were important to political stability. Yet, the idea of intermediate elements used to bring about balance has not always been entertained in the same way. Aristotle recognized the contribution of the intermediate to political balance, but it was a static balance reached by constitutional design. Machiavelli, on the other hand, sought the elasticity that comes with dynamic balance. Later in Anglo-American and French thought, as seen in the work of John Locke, Edmund Burke, and Alexis de Tocqueville, intermediate elements in managing political tensions also appear. The contributions these thinkers made to this particular idea are discussed below. Each thinker obviously appreciated two sorts of intermediaries. The mediating institutional structure is one; the mediating principle is another (table 1.1).

Table 1.1

Intermediate Institutions and Principles

Political Thinker	**Mediating Institution**	**Mediating Principle**
Aristotle (384-322 BC)	Mixed constitution; Large middle class	Doctrine of the mean
Niccolò Machiavelli (1469-1527)	Mixed government	*Virtù* and adaptability
John Locke (1632-1704)	Voluntary political society; Public opinion	Rule of reason
Edmund Burke (1729-1797)	Formal political party system	Prudence
Alexis de Tocqueville (1805-1859)	Autonomous voluntary associations	Self-interest rightly understood

Aristotle: The Mean, the Middle Class, and a Relationship in Tension

Within the context of a Greek ethic that sought order and balance, Aristotle sought "a proper equilibrium for the forces in the state."[32] Pertinent to the concept of a mediated tension was Aristotle's thesis concerning the utility of the mean for stabilizing a governance system. He argued that choosing a middle way, via an appropriately designed constitution that contained important elements of the extremes—in the *Politics* it was between democratic and oligarchic constitutions—led to the most stable political community.[33] The stability of a mixed constitution could be derived from an intermediate or best balance between extreme and opposing views and forces.[34] The "mean" was one of "three kinds of disposition"; the other two were excess and deficiency. Aristotle explained that

> all are in a sense opposed to all; for the extreme states are contrary both to the intermediate state and to each other, and the intermediate to the extremes...the greatest contrariety is that of the extremes to each other, rather than to the intermediate; for these are further from each other than from the intermediate...the extremes show the greatest unlikeness to each other....[35]

The doctrine of the mean, when manifested in constitutional form, thus bound extremes in a relationship of static tension. This principle also enabled a large middle class to be the best "mediator and arbitrator between contending factions," or the extremes of rich and poor, because it contained and "share[d] in the interest of both."[36] The effective way to find the mean, and to sustain it, was through consideration of a full range of views, Aristotle suggested. The substantive quality of debate and its outcome relied upon the number and diversity of the deliberators: "Each individual may indeed, be a worse judge than the experts, but all, when they meet together, are either better than experts or at any rate no worse." There was, in the polis, "a difference of capacities among its members, which enables them to serve as complements to one another, and to attain a higher and better life by the mutual exchange of their different services."[37] Aristotle thus defended a constitutional form based on diversity, exchange, and moderation. As long as the distribution of power was congruent with community interests he believed it could remain stable.[38] Too much unity of thinking, political conflict that became too severe and excessive, or dissension that reflected real or perceived inequality among the citizens—all were signs to Aristotle of a need for a change in constitutional design that would effect a best balance among the extremes.[39]

Machiavelli: Virtù, Adaptability, and Mixed Government

Those who study classical works debate the extent of the influence of Aristotle's thought upon Machiavelli.[40] We do know that each, in his own way, appreciated the value-added contributions of mixed government and citizen participation to community stability. Political scientist Bernard Crick, in an introduction to an edited volume of *The Discourses*, found Machiavelli thoroughly "golden meanish" in defending a mix of principles and governmental forms that is not inconsistent with Aristotle's idea of the mean.[41] Yet Aristotle's model of political community was static, whereas Machiavelli was unique in his search for stability and positive ends to social conflict within the dynamics of politics and inevitable change.

The idea of governing with the flexibility to mitigate the impact of chance, the unexpected, and the negative forces that had previously seemed inevitable took shape with Machiavelli. Inhabitants of fifteenth-century Northern Italy were only just beginning to recognize connections between the particulars of daily life and the grander, more universal understandings unbound by time and space. While earlier forms of society had simply followed ritual and custom, it now seemed feasible to use past experience to shape the present. Resignation to fate no longer was the sole contingency. Instead, human societies could exert control over fate with the manner in which they responded to the unexpected or the unpredictable, especially in politics.[42]

In this context, Machiavelli sensed the possibility of accommodating the multiple needs held by a population: of the people to be happy and free, rulers to retain power, competitors to access authority, young men to seek office and fame, the "have nots" to have, and the "haves" to retain what they most value.[43] Yet, the balance necessary to stabilize a political system so that all of these interests could flourish seemed illusive. Machiavelli sought answers in historical experience. His *History of Florence* stands as a timeless documentation of instability due to (a) cleavages insufficiently mediated and (b) of too much disparity between levels of private and public interest. The consequences of civil dissension and internal conflict frequently ended in the loss of liberty.[44]

Machiavelli found numerous imbalances of power. Many regimes were relatively short-lived due to defects in constitutional forms and structures.[45] Institutions were often inadequate in correcting them, such as the church's ineffective attempt to reconcile disputes between the nobility and the people.[46] In what seemed to be an absence of provisions for effective reconciliation among factions, Machiavelli described the difficulty in achieving stability: "it is impossible, so I hold, to adjust the balance so nicely as to keep things exactly to this middle course...for to find a middle way between the two extremes I do not think possible."[47] He thus rejected the utility of a static balance, although constitutions were an important element of equilibrium. Machiavelli observed "if due weight be given to both sides...it still remains doubtful which to select as the guardians of liberty, for it is impossible to tell which of the two dispositions we find in men is more harmful in a republic, that which seeks to maintain an established position or that which has none but seeks to acquire it."[48]

In one instance, Machiavelli described a period in which the people of Florence were successful over time in excluding the nobility from power. It illustrates what so easily happened without an effective mechanism for balancing power:

> The nobility were deprived of all participation in the government; and in order to regain a portion of it, it became necessary for them not only to seem like the people, but to be like them in behaviour, mind, and mode of living....military virtue and generosity of feeling became extinguished in them; the people not possessing these qualities, they could not appreciate them, and Florence became by degrees more and more depressed and humiliated.[49]

In this case, the aristocracy retained too little influence upon the affairs of the day to the detriment of the whole political society. This imbalance might have occurred in the opposite direction, as well.

Machiavelli described in the *Discourses* the positive effect of a flexible, intermediate institution once tried by the Romans. In this experiment, an overbearing Roman nobility and the populace were at such odds that the nobility feared they would lose everything they valued.[50] The impasse was surmounted with the appointment of tribunes of the plebs which helped to stabilize the government with three groups blended into a commonwealth—the people, the nobility, and a middle range of men upon whose active participation a republic depended.[51] The mix was important,

> not that it should restrain the other elements, but that it should push them all into the most effective and concerted direction...the state that can integrate its population into public life is far stronger than those traditional autocracies who have to rely either on the passivity or the fear of the people.[52]

The populace thus shared in governing while the senate and consuls kept sufficient authority to retain a position of influence. The appointed tribunes were invested with enough status and authority to "mediate between the plebs and the senate and curb the arrogance of the nobility."[53] On the advantage of this institutionalized mediation within a legal framework, Machiavelli remarked:

> it is easy to see what benefit a republic derives when there is an authority that can bring charges in court, which was among the powers vested in the tribunes... nothing does so much to stabilize and strengthen a republic as some institution whereby the changeful humours which agitate it are afforded a proper outlet by way of the laws.[54]

This republican form of government, with its mix of participating citizens, successfully held disparate population elements in a relationship of tension.

It concentrated the attention, energies, and *virtù* of more than just a few.[55] *Virtù*, a dynamic "idea of strength, efficiency, power, or efficacy in particular circumstances for particular purposes" leading to less extreme outcomes, mitigated the impact of *fortunà* upon the social order.[56] *Fortunà* was the term for the "many events…and many misfortunes [that] come about, against which the heavens have not been willing that any provision at all should be made (Book II.28-31)."[57]

The diversity and *virtù* of those involved in republican self-governance was a rich source of the adaptability necessary to counter the impact of *fortunà*. "The citizen will show his *virtù* in the style in which he performs his tasks, the way he executes his civic obligations, and dedicates himself to the common good. Such a citizen is not one who blindly obeys, but who demonstrates initiative by using his discretionary powers in certain ways and not in others."[58] This helped to make a community robust and resistant to misfortune. It was best, Machiavelli reiterated, that each citizen benefit from public service, thus ensuring that the greatness of individual citizens would be helpful to the city and its liberties.[59] A mixed, republican form of government, Machiavelli concluded, "has a fuller life and enjoys good fortune for a longer time than a principality, since it is better able to adapt itself to diverse circumstances owing to the diversity found among its citizens…."[60]

Diversity implied adaptability, which increased the probability of political stability since "all human affairs are ever in a state of flux and cannot stand still, either there will be improvement or decline, and necessity will lead you to do many things which reason does not recommend." If a political entity were to survive the fickleness of *fortunà*, an agility of response was essential. "A Republic that would preserve its Freedom, ought daily to make Fresh Provisions to this End," Machiavelli decided; "[T]he downfall of cities also comes about because institutions in republics do not change with the times…."[61]

John Locke: Voluntary Political Community, Public Opinion, and the Rule of Reason

The intermediary function of a commitment to voluntary political community, itself, is appreciated in Locke's work. The individual in a state of nature and without political society enjoyed freedom and equality but had no assurance of being able to protect and defend those advantages.[62] Due to this vulnerability, political society was voluntarily entered for "no other end, but the *Peace, Safety,* and *publick good* of the People (II §131)." Yet, the only unanimity likely to occur, thought Locke, would be around the decision to form a political community. The force of this voluntary community, in the form of collective political power invested in a magistrature to make and enforce laws, would then mediate between the "contrariety of Interests (II §§97, 222)."

The ultimate mediating institution in Locke's vision of political society was public opinion. The commitment to political society could hold diverse interests together in tension, but the final arbitrar of conflicting views, as long as a voluntary political society endured, would necessarily be majority opinion (II §§96-99, 212, 243). Additionally, an important mediating principle that modulated majority opinion was the rule of reason (II §§17-19). Locke felt the majority could be trusted to decide things fairly and do no harm to a minority since the majority consisted of the rational individuals who had voluntarily initiated the political community (II §§166, 98). He argued that those who constructed societies would work to preserve their investment of reasoning and labor. Hence, the motivation existed to act reasonably on behalf of their own interest and that of others at the same time (II §§96, 98). Although reason was imperfect, it was an innate capability that developed and guided the actions of men toward the positive ends of cooperation, mutual respect, freedom, and the use of resources to life's best advantage, convenience, and enjoyment (II §§8, 61).[63] In this implied "doctrine of natural political virtue" Locke saw grounds for assuming that a minority could expect to be treated responsibly by the majority who grasped that the interests of all were intertwined.[64] Diverse elements of political society could thus be bound together in workable tension.

Edmund Burke: Mixed Government, Prudence, and Parties

A dynamic Constitution that grew and changed was at the core of Burke's understanding of good government. He described its mixed form of government as holding extremes in a dynamic relationship to one another:

> to prevent any one of its principles from being carried as far as, taken by itself, and theoretically, it would go.... To avoid the perfections of extreme, all its several parts are so constituted as not alone to answer their own several ends...in the British Constitution there is a perpetual treaty and compromise going on....[65]

A governing principle in sustaining this relationship among different interests was prudence, Burke believed. Prudence, "the director, the regulator, the standard [of all virtues political and moral]" held "entire dominion over every exercise of power."[66] "The rules and definitions of prudence can rarely be exact, never universal," said Burke.[67] Sensible thought and action meant giving a morally obligated consideration to differences and varied circumstances.[68] "The situations in which men relatively stand produce the rules and principles of that responsibility, and afford directions to prudence in exacting it."[69] "We never can say," cautioned Burke, "what may or may not happen, without a view to all the actual circumstances. Experience, upon other data than those, is of all things the most delusive."[70]

A practitioner, not a theorist, Burke was committed to preserving and enhancing the political system from within the context of the Constitution. His idea of prudence was practical in that it attended to particular grievances and to feasible governmental actions.[71] It was even applicable to situations in which it was *im*prudent to follow the usual rules of prudence.[72] "[I]n every measure of moral and political prudence it is the choice of the moment which renders the measure serviceable or useless, noxious or salutory!"[73]

The principle of prudence, applied to the problems of factious politics, suggested mediation between opposing views and forces. This was Burke's recommendation, in discussing the relationship between Great Britain and the American colonies, for example. Thus, "[t]roublesome discussions are brought to some sort of adjustment, and every hot controversy is not a civil war."[74] That Burke favored a flexible tension between extremes is apparent in his observation that neither should have their demands fully met; "it is not by deciding the suit, but by compromising the difference that peace can be restored or kept." "[E]xtremes, as we all know, in every point which relates either to our duties or satisfactions in life," Burke said, "are destructive both to virtue and enjoyment."[75] At one point, Burke elaborated on the intermediate piece that provides elasticity in relationships between factions, noting

> The world is governed by go-betweens...[that] carry on the intercourse, by stating their own sense to each...as the sense of the other...a middle sort of men, a sort of equestrian order, who, by the spirit of that middle situation, are the fittest for preventing things from running to excess.[76]

Burke's initiation of political party reform was based upon what he perceived as a need for an intermediate, connecting institution between the royal Court and the public.[77] Burke was an energetic partisan and strongly "favored the harmony of discordant powers that tested ideas through incessant and vigorous opposition."[78] But "'Formed opposition' was considered disreputable, even unconstitutional, in Burke's day because it seemed to imply disloyalty to the King."[79] Parties, during this time, were cliques of friends and associates imbued with party spirit, but not necessarily infused with public spirit.[80] The thought of party often evoked images of corruption, favoritism, unbridled ambition, and inconsistency.[81] Representation of the people rarely existed. If it occurred, its base was particularly narrow and not truly representative.[82] Burke raised his alarm publicly, arguing that this state of affairs undermined free government and the Constitution.[83] He thought a party should consist of a "body of men united, for promoting by their joint endeavors, the national interest, upon some particular principle in which they are all agreed."[84] An effective party would be an intermediate institution working from within the House of Commons to link government more closely with public opinion, thus strengthening the relationship between the public and its representatives.[85] Party members had a duty to sustain a balance of political tensions for the good of government. Burke cautioned that they were not to "suffer themselves to be led, or to be controlled, or to be overbalanced, in office or in council...."[86]

Tocqueville: Voluntary Intermediate Association and Self-Interest Rightly Understood

Tocqueville's analysis of historical developments that culminated in the French Revolution details an overly centralized government insufficiently counterbalanced by local autonomy and self-governance. Tocqueville described the distance between the ordinary citizen and the government run by the aristocracy as a "vast gulf" from which most intermediate interactions and bodies were eliminated.[87] Classes were too segregated to be able to cooperate and the middle class was not an effective intermediary, co-opted as it was as a pseudo-aristocracy (107, 132, 115). In Tocqueville's assessment, this lack of intermediate bodies and an imbalance of power and privilege that favored both the monarchy and the nobility resulted in a public ignorant of public affairs, no avenues for developing political thought, no political mobilization by groups or organized parties, and no opportunities for developing skills in working collectively (77-81). Not only did these conditions help to destabilize the French regime, but when pre-revolutionary administrative reforms were precipitously imposed, based upon collective powers of assemblies, the French people and their institutions were ill-equipped and disinclined to make such reforms work (193-203).

The tragedy in the unfolding of the French Revolution, in Tocqueville's view, was that the goal of liberty was sacrificed to aspirations for equality (x-xi). Some type of rapprochement seemed necessary between the two sets of conditions. Liberty is necessary in that it counters the problems inherent in conditions of equality, the desire for which is natural and unstoppable.[88] Equality places people at the same level and aside of one another without the traditional bonds, such as social class and family, which once held them together in society. With this reorganization of social connectedness, Tocqueville reasoned that people are less disposed, less obligated to consider one another. It is easier to be indifferent and focused only on selfish interests, without the traditional social constraints. In Tocqueville's words, "When men are no longer bound together by caste, class, corporate or family ties, they are only too prone to give their whole thoughts to their private interest and to wrap themselves up in a narrow individuality in which public virtue is stifled."[89] If men become too indifferent to common affairs, the danger of despotism grows. Despotism finds the disinterest of individuals in common affairs advantageous and reinforces it however it can; "it isolates them. They [look] coldly on each other: it freezes their souls."[90] In this manner, despotism discourages social connectedness, self-governance, cooperation, and interdependence. It strangles freedom.[91]

The observations Tocqueville made of America in the 1830s helped him to crystallize his thinking about the necessary conditions for democracy.

It seemed to Tocqueville that Americans uniquely held equality and freedom in working balance by using voluntary, intermediate institutions to counter the disadvantages of equality. Citizens freely combined for a wide variety of reasons and interests. These varied associations could mediate a balanced relationship between the weak individual and a disproportionately powerful state for several reasons. First, associations aggregated power and influence that extended to individuals: "they are no longer isolated men, but a power seen from afar, whose actions serve for an example and whose language is listened to (II:117-118, 330)." Second, associations stimulated relational networks that generated energy, information, communication, and self-governance. "[T]he reciprocal influence of men upon one another...accomplished by associations" makes possible a "vast multitude of lesser undertakings which American citizens perform every day.... A government can no more be competent to keep alive and to renew the circulation of opinions and feelings among a great people than to manage all the speculations of productive industry (II:116-117)." Political associations, in particular, "stimulate competition and...discover those arguments that are most fitted to act upon the majority; for they always entertain hopes of drawing over the majority to their own side and then controlling the supreme power in its name (I:203)."

Finally, voluntary associations discourage liberty carried to an extreme, that is, excessive amounts of individuality and independence. The American citizen, Tocqueville observed, "is taught from infancy to rely upon his exertions...he looks upon the social authority with an eye of mistrust and anxiety, and he claims its assistance only when he is unable to do without it (I:198)." Yet, complete independence is analogous to having no power at all (II:311). People involved in common affairs realize they need others; they have regard for one another; and they cooperate. The approval and esteem of one's compatriots provides an incentive to restrain the pride, disdain, and selfishness that might curry disfavor (II:109-110).

Tocqueville remarked on the commitment of Americans to the mediating principle of "self-interest rightly understood," a force that countered excessive individualism and withdrawal into private interests. Americans "almost always manage to combine their own advantage with that of their fellow citizens (II:129)." Adherence to this principle of "self-interest rightly understood" meant no great or remarkable acts, but a willingness to sacrifice some part of one's own well-being for the benefit of all (II:129-132). Alone, it did not "make a man virtuous; but it disciplines a number of persons in habits of regularity, temperance, moderation, foresight, self-command" that mediate between public and private interests (II:131).

Summary

Each of these thinkers applied, in some manner, the idea that intermediate structures and principles could hold opposing or contradictory forces in a relationship of tension that prevented a concentration of power and facilitated the process of politics. Aristotle thought to effect political equilibrium with a well-considered constitutional design that accurately reflected and held a political system steady. Incorporated within this design was the built-in capacity to accommodate opposing forces. Machiavelli thought it was nearly impossible to arrive at a constitutional design that could, on its own, be well enough considered to stand the test of factious times and events. Static balance could too easily be upset by the unexpected. Machiavelli saw the necessity of a dynamic balance brought about by mixed government and citizens whose diversity and *virtù* constituted readiness and an ability to respond to developments with flexibility and agility. In Locke's paradigm, voluntary commitment to political society held disparate groups in a working relationship-of-tension while public opinion, moderated by an innate rule of reason, ultimately mediated differences. Like Aristotle, Burke envisioned a constitution that brought extremes together in a workable relationship. In contrast to Aristotle's static constitution, Burke perceived a dynamic constitution made workable through consistent application, in all decisions, of the principle of prudence—similar to Machiavelli's understanding of *virtù* and not inconsistent with Locke's rule of reason. Prudence inserted flexibility into the political process, which in turn supported the stability of the Constitution over the long term. Tocqueville elaborated on the capacity of voluntary association to promote the principle of "self interest rightly understood" that moderates excesses of liberty and of equality—excessive individualism, isolation, and disinterest in the common welfare—that foster conditions for despotism.

How Healthy is Civil Society in the United States?

It is one thing to understand, in theory, what civil society is and how it serves democracy. It is another to understand how this institution works, in fact. Tocqueville foresaw, in the mid-1800s, how difficult it would be for Americans to maintain a proper balance between the objectives of liberty and equality, or rather, between their private and public interests.[92] Vulnerability to nondemocratic conditions seemed particularly poignant in the decades surrounding World War II, especially with the rise of totalitarian movements at the time. It was feared that the institutional order would fail to counter irrational social movements during a time of profound social change.[93] The social impact of modernization, or the progressive march of industrialization, urbanization, democratization, mass communication, popular education, and bureaucratization, meant that Americans were increasingly treated en masse as they grew more alike in affluence, available free time, and patterns of leisure.

These developments raised the fearsome specter of a "mass society."[94] Kornhauser explains the term mass society as vulnerability of democratic institutions to totalitarianism—characterized by loss of community, absence of intermediate groups, atomization, and alienation of the population. These conditions permit total concentration of power with those in governing positions and allow manipulation of the masses.[95] The depersonalizing effect of modernization upon relationships and institutions led to the question of what would prevent individuals from becoming too alienated, detached, manipulated, and mobilized toward totalitarian ends. Historian C. E. Black concluded in a mid-1960s comparative study that a society's response to modernization depended upon its political traditions, its safeguards for individual liberties and representative institutions, the character of its leaders, and the circumstances under which these leaders had gained power. Sets of social ties, such as religious and ethnic attachments, seemed to enable modern societies to survive the crisis with reasonable stability.[96] Indeed, social ties and association are recognized, even in nondemocratic systems, as valuable agents in the adaptation and integration of societal change.[97]

The United States entered the decade of the sixties with an assessment from preeminent social scientists that its civil society was healthy. Retrospectively, sociologist Claude Fischer examined leisure activities in three California towns for the period between 1890 and 1940. He found that group and public activities multiplied, that participatory events increased, and that informal association probably did not decline as a result of modernization.[98] Political sociologist Daniel Bell found no compelling evidence in the 1950s that modern advancements, and the ensuing massification of culture, were leading to mass society conditions in the United States. Broken primary group ties, estranged individuals, and a loss of unifying values did exist. Nevertheless, Bell found a continuing vitality in intermediate organizations and institutions. It was significant, he thought, that Americans were joining voluntary organizations at high rates, consuming cultural activities at increasing rates, and subdividing and diversifying their interests. Concurrently, indicators of social disorganization and conformity showed no dramatic change. Bell concluded that concerns about the impact of massification were originating from an "ideology of romantic protest against contemporary society."[99] Sociologist Talcott Parsons, in the 1950s, also looked for and did not find, evidence that Americans were alienated and easily manipulated within a mass culture. Instead, Parsons found that educational and cultural content was more widely distributed and more diverse than ever. The diverse forms of mass media, none of which had the same audiences, were an example. The quality of communications had improved, probably stimulated by greater competition. Yet another development of even greater importance was that of a growing complexity of structural networks, "of crisscrossing solidarities (290)," suggesting that Americans' associational life was flourishing.[100]

Scholarly attention to the topic subsided until the 1990s. Broad interest in civil society was renewed in 1989 by the fall of totalitarian regimes in the former Soviet Union and eastern and central Europe.[101] Again attention turned to Tocqueville's prediction that a democracy would increasingly be confronted with a loss of cohesiveness as progress toward the democratic objective of equality accrued. To reiterate his concern, equality places individuals at the same level, no longer obligated by family or social class to look after one another's welfare. Free and equal individuals, unconstrained by traditional social ties and controls, can grow extremely indifferent to common affairs, allowing despotism to grow unchecked.[102] Certainly, by the end of the century, it seemed that this risk should be considered once again. Sociologist Phillip Selznick wrote that with modern society came a segmented and fragmented social life that meant looser social ties.[103] Social relationships were not necessarily bound by what social scientist Ernest Gellner refers to as the demanding and stifling "tyranny of cousins, and of ritual."[104]

Debate on the status of social connectedness in the United States grew lively when Harvard political scientist Robert Putnam decried the neglect of bowling leagues in favor of metaphorically "bowling alone." Putnam claims that quantitative and qualitative shifts in patterns of voluntary association result in too little involvement in matters of public interest. He contends that Americans increasingly equate civic engagement with dues-paying memberships in remote organizations, with association that fails to elicit deliberation, and with affiliation that does not require personal investment and commitment. This, he argues, has produced a downward spiraling of interpersonal trust, cohesion, and solidarity.[105]

Not proven, argued the late political scientist Everett Carll Ladd, who summoned an impressive amount of evidence to show that civic engagement in the U.S. is not only renewing itself continuously, but is clearly on the rise. Although a predominant strain of individualism is well recognized in this country, Ladd posited that we misunderstand the individualistic tendencies of Americans. He suggested "the drift and consequences of American individualism are collectivist, though certainly not of a state-centered variety. It's a collectivism of *citizenship*" that melds private and public interests.[106] In a similar vein, American political scientist Jayne Mansbridge says that self-interest is too narrowly understood. She points to evidence that people, more often than not, are committed to moral principle, to the interest of others, to self-interest rightly understood. Indeed, she insists, our own interests are defined and influenced by the interest of others. Mansbridge defends self-interest's utility for the common good when it helps people to better understand their own interests.[107]

Some who have joined the "bowling alone" debate urge us not to overlook the nature of contemporary civic engagement, which includes a strong

American tradition of "pitching in" and new sorts of collective activities and relationships like self-help groups, Internet affiliations, and class action suits.[108] It is also noted that our perceptions and judgments about 'acceptable' forms of community and connectedness must be carefully scrutinized.[109] One reviewer questions, "why should we expect one generation's community to mirror another's? To expect any society to maintain the level *and* form of social interaction that obtained at one specific, and highly unusual, movement of history, seems a cramped and ahistorical way of approaching social change."[110] Political sociologist Theda Skocpol and other scholars remind us that different social activities have been salient at different times in the nation's history for a variety of reasons. Changing needs, economic strain, the context of politics, joint private-public enterprises, race and gender relations, shifts in generational focus, class, and organizational dynamics all have their imprint on civic engagement.[111] Such arguments are consistent with a model of a flexible and resilient institution.

Others enjoin us not to forget how we are trying to live together, pointing to change in the democratic nature of associational life. It is feasible, as political scientist Paul Rich posits, that we may yet be judging civicness by obsolete standards that emanate from "stuffy white male bastions."[112] National columnist Robert Samuelson observes that with its segregation of women and minorities, the "'community' of yesterday was more compartmentalized and less compassionate than today's."[113] Scholar David Steiner reassuringly calls "[p]ostmodernism's scepticism...a natural ally of democratic thinking" because the absence of only *one* truth intensifies the necessity for all views to emerge in "public conversation...without excluding anyone from speaking."[114] Greater inclusion implies progress towards a better democracy, yet it is obviously a challenge. German social scientist Klaus von Beyme notes the difficulty in finding an adequate consensus within a democracy when rationality is rule-based and a single "Truth" is sought. Modern pluralism implies multiple truths, less consensus, and rationality based upon situational factors, in addition to principles and rules.[115]

Reservations about the framing of the Putnam argument and/or how it is substantiated continue to appear in the literature, suggesting that the discourse about the status of civic engagement is just beginning.[116] As Francis Fukuyama reminds us, we do not know if "democracy is necessarily healthiest when large numbers of citizens are perpetually eager to strike, demonstrate or pressure...."[117] *If* neglect of civic matters were to be established beyond question, others suggest, it might not be attributable to the ordinary citizen. It might be the privileged, elite American who is withdrawing from the public arena.[118] Some have suggested that the focus on civic engagement is too narrow, that the health of democratic community depends on other important conditions.[119]

These contributions to the public conversation attest to the complexity of what is involved in pondering the institutional health of U.S. civil society. Democracy scholar Larry Diamond provides one of the most helpful tools for such study with his caution not to confuse civic community with civil society. Yes, he agrees with Putnam, civic community is essential to the health of a democracy because it does consist of strong horizontal bonds generally characterized by trust, cooperation, shared norms, and mutual reciprocity. Civil society, on the other hand, also encompasses vertical relationships, structures, and processes. And notably, it is not always "democratic, noble, decent, and good." It may contain much that is "undemocratic, paternalistic, and particularistic in its internal structure and norms but also distrustful, unreliable, domineering, exploitative, and cynical....To the extent that such organizations characterize civil society, it will be less effective and liberal, and so will democracy."[120]

An Empirical Basis for Analysis

This work attempts to give U.S. civil society greater visibility to determine how it changed during the twentieth century. The flurry of argument about the status of civic community and its effect on the health of civil society cannot be satisfied until we have made the institution more accessible to analysis. My goal is to give empirical substance to each of five theoretical components of democratic civil society—voluntary association, diversity of association, communication, autonomy of voluntary association, and mediation of democratic tension. I drew upon Tocqueville and pluralist theory to identify these major components that constitute a conceptual model of U.S. civil society. The model is synergistic in that each component is interdependent with the others.

I used data from surveys, opinion polls, government reports, commercial sources, histories, and case studies to give factual substance to these five key components of civil society. Historical and trend data allowed comparisons across a span of time. My intent was to avoid the pitfalls of a short-term perspective and to produce an analysis that benefits from a century of experience. Although the United States remains a relatively new country, its history must continually be revisited to reach new understandings of old data. The reader will see that empirical observations from single points in time are also tools with which I confirmed data and added depth to the empirical description.[121] I used multiple sources of information to verify facts or to discover contradictions. Certainly, despite my extensive collection of data, this bas-relief of U.S. civil society can only improve with additional research and attention to its detail.

Change in gross numbers of voluntary associations, their rates of growth, and behavioral evidence of association as seen over the sweep of a century is the focus of chapters 2 and 3. This study examines the familiar activities of voluntary association membership, volunteerism and charitable giving, civic activity, and informal association. I consider, as well, practical constraints and possibilities that help to shape the associational life of Americans—leisure time, discretionary income, and transportation technology. Chapter 4 is a study of diversity and the crossing of divisive barriers in significant collective endeavors. Communication and its technologies used to maintain social connectedness is explored in chapter 5. Chapter 6 traces an evolution in the meaning of autonomy for local entities and the subsequent, difficult demands for sustaining autonomy. The evidence evaluated in chapters 5 and 6 confirms the preservation of tension between forces of localism and centralism. Finally, the roles and performance of political parties and of the United States Supreme Court in service to civil society-sustaining mediation are scrutinized in chapter 7. The final chapter weighs these findings on whole. The picture that emerges is one of a complex, multidimensional, and very dynamic institution with important strengths and weaknesses. The results are significant for our assessment of, and for our initiatives to strengthen, the health of U.S. civil society. It is on both the changing *and* unchanging face of civil society, with all of its dynamic features, that the student of this institution must concentrate.

Notes

1. Mary Douglas, *How Institutions Think* (Syracuse, NY: Syracuse University Press, 1986), 63, 92-111.
2. Michael Walzer, "The Idea of Civil Society: A Path to Social Reconstruction," *Dissent* 38 (Spring 1991): 294.
3. John Gray, *Post-Liberalism: Studies in Political Thought* (New York: Routledge, 1993), 202-215.
4. Guy Hermet, "The Disenchantment of the Old Democracies," *International Social Science Journal* 129 (August 1991): 451-461.
5. David Selbourne, *The Principle of Duty* (London: Little, Brown, 1997), 5-6.
6. See Paul E. Peterson, Barry G. Rabe, and Kenneth K. Wong, *When Federalism Works* (Washington, DC: Brookings Institution, 1986), 189-190.
7. William Kornhauser, *The Politics of Mass Society* (Glencoe, IL: Free Press, 1959), 74. Kornhauser defines intermediate association as social relations that bridge individual or local and state or national levels of relations. It is not limited to organized voluntary groups, but includes any type of mediating structure such as local government or the press.
8. Jean L. Cohen and Andrew Arato, *Civil Society and Political Theory* (Cambridge, MA: MIT Press, 1994), 18-20, 564; Ernest Gellner, *Conditions of Liberty: Civil Society and Its Rivals* (New York: Allan Lane, Penguin, 1994), 100; Larry Diamond, "Economic Development and Democracy Reconsidered" in Gary Marx and Larry Diamond, eds., *Reexamining Democracy* (Newbury Park, CA: Sage Publications, 1992), 134; Larry Diamond, "Civil Society and the Construction of Democracy," speech delivered at Harvard University, December 7, 1993; Larry Diamond, "Rethinking Civil Society: Toward Democratic Consolidation," *Journal*

of Democracy 5 (July 1994): 5-7; Seymour Martin Lipset, "The Social Requisites of Democracy Revisited," *American Sociological Review* 59 (February 1994):12-15; Luis Roniger, "Civil Society, Patronage and Democracy," *International Journal of Comparative Sociology* 35 (September-December 1994): 207-220; Walzer, "The Idea of Civil Society," 293-304; Benjamin R. Barber, "The Search for Civil Society," *The New Democrat* 7 (March/April 1995): 13-17; Antony Black, "Civil Society," in David Miller, ed., *The Blackwell Encyclopaedia of Political Thought* (New York: B. Blackwell, 1987), 77; Stuart N. Eisenstadt, "Civil Society" in Seymour Martin Lipset, ed., *The Encyclopedia of Democracy* (Washington, DC: Congressional Quarterly, 1995), 240-242; Roger Scruton, *A Dictionary of Political Thought* (New York: Harper and Row, 1982), 66, 199; Larry Diamond, *Developing Democracy: Toward Consolidation* (Baltimore, MD: Johns Hopkins University Press, 1999), 221-227.

9. See comprehensive definition of a democratic system in Fred I. Greenstein and Nelson W. Polsby, eds., *Handbook of Political Science* (Reading, MA: Addison-Wesley, 1975), 183. Also John W. Chapman, "Voluntary Association and the Political Theory of Pluralism," in J. Roland Pennock and John W. Chapman, *Voluntary Associations* (New York: Atherton, 1969), 87-118; Kornhauser, *The Politics of Mass Society*, 131-141, 229-231; Robert A. Dahl, "Pluralism" in Joel Krieger, ed., *The Oxford Companion to Politics of the World* (New York: Oxford University Press, 1993), 705-707; Seymour Martin Lipset, *Political Man: The Social Bases of Politics* (New York: Doubleday, 1963), 51-52; Robert Nisbet, *The Quest for Community: A Study in the Ethics of Order & Freedom* (San Francisco, CA: Institute for Contemporary Studies Press, [1953] 1990), 235-247.
10. Barber, "The Search for Civil Society"; Cohen and Arato, *Civil Society and Political Theory*; Eisenstadt, "Civil Society"; Gellner, *Conditions of Liberty*, 100; Lipset, "The Social Requisites of Democracy Revisited."
11. Lipset, "The Social Requisites of Democracy Revisited." Also see Robert A. Dahl, "Thinking about Democratic Constitutions: Conclusions from Democrat Experience" in Ian Shapiro and Russell Hardin, eds., *Political Order* (New York: New York University Press, 1996), 178.
12. Kornhauser, *The Politics of Mass Society*, 16, 33-34, 41, 122-123.
13. Alexis de Tocqueville, *Democracy in America* (New York: Vintage Books, 1945), II:337.
14. Kornhauser, *The Politics of Mass Society*, 16, 33, 40-41; Seymour Martin Lipset, Martin A. Trow, and James S. Coleman, *Union Democracy: The Internal Politics of the International Typographical Union* (New York: Free Press, [1956] 1977); Nisbet, *The Quest for Community*, 235-246; Alex Inkeles, "The Totalitarian Mystique: Some Impressions of the Dynamics of Totalitarian Society" in Carl J. Friedrich, ed., *Totalitarianism* (New York: Grosset and Dunlap, [1954] 1964), 90; 99-105.
15. There were other qualities that a pluralist society had, as well: high levels of communication, contacts between diverse groups that made cultural standards more fluid, individuals less susceptible to mass appeal, limited government, and a strong rule of law. Kornhauser, *The Politics of Mass Society*, 39-42, 63-64.
16. Hannah Arendt, *Totalitarianism* (New York: Harcourt, Brace and World, [1951] 1968), 3-38, 171-173; Gray, *Post-Liberalism*, 156-195, 202-215; James Q. Wilson, *The Moral Sense* (New York: Free Press, 1993), 246; Franz Neumann, *Behemoth: The Structure and Practice of National Socialism 1933-1944* (New York: Octagon, [1942]1963), 428-431; 464-467.
17. Lipset, Trow, and Coleman, *Union Democracy*, 69-105.

18. Emil Lederer, *State of the Masses: The Threat of the Classless Society* (New York: Howard Fertig, [1940]1967), 31; Kornhauser, *The Politics of Mass Society,* 32-33.
19. Kornhauser, *The Politics of Mass Society*, 46-51; Nisbet, *The Quest for Community*, 182-187.
20. Alexis de Tocqueville, *The Old Regime and the Revolution*, trans. John Bonner (New York: Harper, 1856), 106-136.
21. Karl W. Deutsch, "Cracks in the Monolith: Possibilities and Patterns of Disintegration in Totalitarian Systems," in Friedrich, *Totalitarianism*, 321-323.
22. Nisbet, *The Quest for Community*, 251.
23. Kornhauser, *The Politics of Mass Society*, 39-42, 63-64.
24. James Madison, "No. 51," in Alexander Hamilton, James Madison, and John Jay, *The Federalist Papers* (New York: New American Library, 1961), 323.
25. David B. Truman, "The American System in Crisis," *Political Science Quarterly* 74 (December 1959): 488.
26. Harry Eckstein, *Division and Cohesion in Democracy* (Princeton, NJ: Princeton University Press, 1966), 281, 285.
27. Gabriel A. Almond, "Civic Culture," in Vernon Bogdanor, ed., *The Blackwell Encyclopaedia of Political Institutions* (Oxford: Blackwell, 1987), 98-99.
28. Ibid.; also see Eckstein, *Division and Cohesion*, 248-253.
29. Paul Rahe, *Republics Ancient and Modern* (Chapel Hill, NC: North Carolina University Press, 1992), 30, 114.
30. Ernest Barker, *The Political Thought of Plato and Aristotle* (New York: Dover, 1959), 12-13.
31. Eckstein, *Division and Cohesion in Democracy*.
32. Barker, *The Political Thought of Plato and Aristotle*, 472-490; Max Lerner, "Introduction" in Aristotle, *On Politics,* trans. Benjamin Jowett (New York: Random House, 1943), 22-23.
33. Aristotle, *The Politics* (Oxford: Clarendon, [1946] 1952), Book IV, chapters 8-9.
34. Aristotle, *The Nicomachean Ethics*, trans. David Ross (Oxford: Oxford University Press, [1980] 1998), Book V.5, Book II.6-8.
35. Ibid., Book II.8.
36. Barker, *The Political Thought of Plato and Aristotle*, 13; also see 474-475 for discussion of the influence of the middle class. Barker found earlier proponents of the "middle" in the social order that include Phocyclides, Euripedes, and Theramenes, 475-476.
37. Aristotle, *The Politics*, Book II, chapters 2-3; Book III, chapter 11.
38. R. G. Mulgan, *Aristotle's Political Theory* (Oxford: Clarendon, 1977), 116-138.
39. Aristotle, *The Politics*, Book V, chapter 1; Book II, chapter 2.
40. See Harvey C. Mansfield, *Machiavelli's Virtue* (Chicago, IL: University of Chicago Press, 1966), 11-24; Neal Wood, "Niccolò Machiavelli," in *International Encyclopedia of the Social Sciences*, ed. David L. Sills (Toronto: Crowell Collier and Macmillan, 1968), 507-508; Anthony J. Perel,"Mansfield on Machiavelli," *The Review of Politics* 59:2 (1997): 404-407; J. G. A. Pocock, *The Machiavellian Moment* (Princeton, NJ: Princeton University Press, 1975), 164, 211-218; Vickie B. Sullivan, "Machiavelli's Momentary 'Machiavellian Moment': A Reconsideration of Pocock's Treatment of the Discourses," *Political Theory* 20 (May 1992): 309-318; Barker, *The Political Thought of Plato and Aristotle*, 515-517; Leslie J. Walker, "Introduction," in Niccolò Machiavelli, *The Discourses of Niccolò Machiavelli* (London: Routledge and Kegan Paul, 1950), 80-100; Quentin Skinner, *The Foundations of Modern Political Thought* (Cambridge: Cambridge University Press, 1978), xiv, 47-50, 158-159.

41. Bernard Crick, "Introduction," in Niccolò Machiavelli, *The Discourses,* trans. Leslie J. Walker (London: Penguin, 1970), 539.
42. Pocock, *The Machiavellian Moment*, viii, 3-5, 48, 156-167; Bruce James Smith, *Politics and Remembrances: Republican Themes in Machiavelli, Burke, and Tocqueville* (Princeton, NJ: Princeton University Press, 1985), 3-25.
43. Walker, "Introduction," 118-128.
44. Niccolò Machiavelli, *The History of Florence, and of The Affairs of Italy, From the Earliest Times to the Death of Lorenzo the Magnificent; Together with The Prince* (London: Henry G. Bohn, 1851), Book II, chapter III.
45. Machiavelli, *Discourses*, Book I.2, Book I.7.
46. Machiavelli, *History of Florence*, Book II, chapter IX.
47. Machiavelli, *Discourses*, Book I.6.
48. Ibid., Book I.5.
49. Machiavelli, *History of Florence*, Book III, chapter I.
50. Machiavelli, *Discourses*, Book I.2.
51. Skinner, *Foundations of Modern Political Thought*, 157-160; Crick, "Introduction," 24-27; Machiavelli, *Discourses*, Book I.47.
52. Crick, "Introduction," 32.
53. Machiavelli, *Discourses*, Books I.2-3.
54. Ibid., Book I.7.
55. Ibid., Book II 2.2, Book I.3-4, Book III.9.
56. Sydney Anglo, *Machiavelli: A Dissection* (London: Victor Gollancz, 1969), 233.
57. Machiavelli, *Discourses*, Book II 2.2, Book I.3-4, Book III.9.
58. Neal Wood, "Machiavelli's Concept of Virtù Reconsidered," *Political Studies* XV:2 (1967): 201.
59. Machiavelli, *Discourses*, Book I.4, Book I.5.
60. Ibid., Book III.9; Skinner, *Foundations of Modern Political Thought*, 181-182.
61. Machiavelli, *Discourses*, Book I.4-6, Book III.9, Book III.49.
62. John Locke, *Two Treatises of Government*, ed. Peter Laslett (Cambridge: Cambridge University Press, 1988), II § 123.
63. Ibid., II §§ 52, 181; II §§ 32, 56, 63; II §§ 6, 26, 31, 60.
64. Peter Laslett, "Introduction," in Locke, *Two Treatises of Government*, 110.
65. Edmund Burke, "Appeal from the New to the Old Whigs," *The Works of the Right Honorable Edmund Burke*, 6th ed. (Boston, MA: Little, Brown, 1880), IV:207-208.
66. Ibid., IV:81; Burke, "Letter to the Sheriffs of Bristol, on the Affairs of America, April 3, 1777," *The Works*, II:226.
67. Burke, "Three Letters to a Member of Parliament on the Proposals for Peace with the Regicide Directory of France. Letter I," *The Works*, V:241.
68. Peter J. Stanlis, *Edmund Burke and the Natural Law* (Shreveport, LA: Huntington House, 1986), 111; Burke, "Letter to Sir Hercules Langrishe, on the Subject of the Roman Catholics of Ireland," *The Works*, IV:251.
69. Burke, "Three Letters to a Member of Parliament on the Proposals for Peace with the Regicide Directory of France. Letter I," *The Works*, V:321.
70. Burke, "Thoughts on French Affairs," *The Works*, IV:349. In this spirit, Gerald W. Chapman, *Edmund Burke: the Practical Imagination* (Cambridge, MA: Harvard University Press, 1967), 122, concluded that prudence is "a vigorous dialectic of experience and situation."
71. This guiding principle permeated Edmund Burke's writings, speeches, the expectations he held for his colleagues, and his own practice as a politician. He hoped "to preserve consistency by varying his means to secure the unity of his end; and, when the equipoise of the vessel in which he sails may be endangered by overload-

ing it upon one side, is desirous of carrying the small weight of his reasons to that which may preserve its equipoise." Burke, "Reflections on the Recent Revolution in France (1790)," *The Works,* III:563.

72. Harvey C. Mansfield, Jr., *Statesmanship and Party Government* (Chicago, IL: University of Chicago Press, 1965), 228, 240-241, 244.
73. Burke, "Second Letter to Sir Hercules Langrishe, on the Catholic Question (May 26, 1795)," *The Works*, VI:378.
74. Burke, "Letter to Sheriffs of Bristol," *The Works*, II:217.
75. Ibid., II:229-231.
76. Burke, "Appeal from the New to the Old Whigs," *The Works*, IV:188-191.
77. Burke, "Thoughts on the Cause of the Present Discontents," *The Works*, I:444, 446, 460, 471, 491, 536.
78. Stanlis, *Edmund Burke and the Natural Law*, 124. Also see Alfred Cobban, *Edmund Burke and the Revolt Against the Eighteenth Century* (London: George Allen and Unwin, 1960), 38.
79. Harvey C. Mansfield, Jr., ed., *Selected Letters of Edmund Burke* (Chicago, IL: University of Chicago Press, 1984), 160.
80. Burke, "Letter to Richard Burke, Esq., on Protestant Ascendency in Ireland (1793)," *The Works*, VI:389; Burke, "Thoughts on the Cause of the Present Discontents," *The Works*, I:469.
81. Burke, "Letter to Richard Burke, Esq., on Protestant Ascendency in Ireland (1793)," *The Works*, VI:389. Burke shares his analysis of the historical circumstances and the abuses of power that led to these impressions in "Thoughts on the Cause of the Present Discontents," *The Works*, I:444-475.
82. Burke believed, despite hopes for the House of Commons as an intended check upon executive power, this had gone awry due to the subversion of Parliament's autonomy by the court cabal. Burke, "Thoughts on the Cause of the Present Discontents," *The Works,* I:490-499, 508. Also see Ian Crowe, ed., *Edmund Burke: His Life and Legacy* (Dublin, Ireland: Four Courts, 1997), 16; Mansfield, *Statesmanship and Party Government*, 17.
83. Burke, "Observations on a Late Publication, Intituled, 'The Present State of the Nation,'" *The Works,* I:271; Burke, "Thoughts on the Cause of the Present Discontents," *The Works*, I:435-537.
84. An unresolved question exists among scholars about whether Burke was referring to a single party as a means of "applying true principles to politics" (and possibly taking a doctrinal position on behalf of his own party, the Whigs) or if he really believed a plurality of parties was desirable. Mansfield in *Statesmanship and Party Government*, 181-186, thinks that it was the latter as Burke appeared to welcome a plurality of principles and would have seen no inconsistency between independent thought and choosing a party. This view appears to be supported by Burke when he speaks of the need for good men to associate to counter combinations of bad men and again when he suggests that if one cannot agree much of the time with his selected party, he "ought to...have chosen some other, more conformable to his opinions" in Burke, "Thoughts on the Cause of the Present Discontents," *The Works*, I:530, 533, 526.
85. Burke, "Thoughts on the Cause of the Present Discontents," *The Works*, I:502-503, 516-531, 535-536; M. Morton Auerbach, "Edmund Burke," in David L. Sills, ed., *International Encyclopedia of the Social Sciences*, 224; Crowe, *Edmund Burke: His Life and Legacy*, 15; Mansfield, *Statesmanship and Party Government*, 4-6, 11, and 7-13 for other theses on how party government originated in Britain; B. W. Hill, ed., *Edmund Burke On Government, Politics and Society* (Sussex, England: Harvester, 1975), 17-21.

86. Burke, "Thoughts on the Cause of the Present Discontents," *The Works*, I:530.
87. Tocqueville, *The Old Regime and the Revolution*, 68.
88. Tocqueville, *Democracy in America*, I:208; II:147, 99, 113.
89. Tocqueville, *The Old Regime and the Revolution*, viii; Tocqueville, *Democracy in America*, II:109-113, 336-339.
90. Tocqueville, *The Old Regime and the Revolution*, ix.
91. Tocqueville, *Democracy in America*, II:109-113.
92. Tocqueville, *The Old Regime and the Revolution*, viii, x-xi; Tocqueville, *Democracy in America*, I:208; II:147, 99, 109-113, 336-339.
93. Arendt, *Totalitarianism*, v-xxii, 39-86; Daniel Bell, "The Theory of Mass Society," *Commentary* 22 (July 1956): 75-83; Lederer, *State of the Masses*, 31; Walter Lippman, *The Public Philosophy* (New Brunswick, NJ: Transaction, [1955] 1992), 1-15; 58-62; Cohen and Arato, *Civil Society and Political Theory*, 495-496.
94. Daniel Bell, *The Coming of Post-Industrial Society* (New York: Basic Books, [1973] 1976), 12-13, 313-320; C. E. Black, *The Dynamics of Modernization: A Study in Comparative History* (New York: Harper and Row, 1966), 80-89, 112-113.
95. Kornhauser, *The Politics of Mass Society*, 16, 33, 41. Also see Philip Selznick, *The Moral Commonwealth: Social Theory and the Promise of Community* (Berkeley: University of California Press, 1992), 188-189, 371, 522-523, for theoretical description of mass society.
96. Black, *The Dynamics of Modernization*.
97. See Kenneth L. Little, *West African Urbanization: A Study of Voluntary Associations in Social Change* (Cambridge, MA: Cambridge University Press, 1965), 85-167; David L. Sills, "Voluntary Associations: Instruments and Objects of Change," *Human Organization* 18 (Spring 1959):17-21; James Nwannukwu Kerri, "Studying Voluntary Associations as Adaptive Mechanisms: A Review of Anthropological Perspectives," *Current Anthropology* 17 (March 1976): 23-47.
98. Claude S. Fischer, "Changes in Leisure Activities, 1890-1940," *Journal of Social History* 27:3 (Spring 1994):453-475.
99. Bell, "The Theory of Mass Society," 213.
100. Talcott Parsons with Winston White, "The Mass Media and the Structure of American Society" in Leon H. Mayhew, ed., *Talcott Parsons on Institutions and Social Evolution* (Chicago, IL: University of Chicago Press, 1960), 277-290.
101. Increases in listings for "civil society" between 1990 and 1996 in the literature reveal the surge of interest. Of all "civil society" entries made in the *Social Science Citation Index* for a quarter of a century between 1972 and 1996, 83 percent were after 1989. This was true for 50 percent of listings for "civil society" in the *Dissertation Abstracts* database (1861-1996), for 72 percent of "civil society" entries in *Sociofile* (1973 to 1996), and for 46 percent of the listings in *Sociological Abstracts* (1963 to 1996). Popular media references to the subject, as indicated by *UMI Newspaper Abstracts*, the *EBSCO Masterfile* of periodicals, and *Readers' Guide Abstracts* also grew more numerous, doubling or tripling between 1990 and 1996. The *Dissertation Abstracts Online* (Ann Arbor, MI: UMI, 1861-1997); *Social Science Citation Index* (Bronx, NY: UMI, 1972-1997); *Sociological Abstracts* (San Diego, CA: Sociological Abstracts, 1963-1997); *Sociofile* (San Diego, CA: Sociological Abstracts, 1973-1997). The latter two databases were made available by electronic presentation and platform in *FirstSearch* (Dublin, OH: Online Computer Library Center, 1992-1997).
102. Alexis de Tocqueville, *The Old Regime and the French Revolution*, trans. Stuart Gilbert (New York: Doubleday, 1983), viii; Tocqueville, *Democracy in America*, II:109-113, 336-339.

103. Selznick, *The Moral Commonwealth*, 5.
104. Gellner, *Conditions of Liberty*, 7-8. Gellner was referring to the prescription of modes of relations, roles, and behavior by such social mechanisms as tradition, convention, and status.
105. Robert D. Putnam, "Bowling Alone: America's Declining Social Capital," *Journal of Democracy* 6 (January 1995): 65-78; Robert D. Putnam, "Tuning In, Tuning Out: The Strange Disappearance of Social Capital in America," *PS: Political Science and Politics* 28 (December 1995): 664-683; Robert D. Putnam, "Robert Putnam Responds," *The American Prospect* (March-April 1996): 26-28; Robert D. Putnam, *Bowling Alone* (New York: Simon and Schuster, 2000).
106. Everett Carll Ladd, *The Ladd Report* (New York: Free Press, 1999); Everett Carll Ladd, "The Data Just Don't Show Erosion of America's 'Social Capital,'" *The Public Perspective* (June/July 1996): 1, 5-6.
107. Jayne J. Mansbridge, ed., *Beyond Self-Interest* (Chicago, IL: University of Chicago Press, 1990), 3-22, 133-143, 305-315, 322-326.
108. John Wilson, "Dr. Putnam's Social Lubricant," *Contemporary Sociology* 30:3 (May 2001): 225-227; Garry Wills, "Putnam's America," *The American Prospect* (17 July 2000): 34-37; Paul Rich, "American Voluntarism, Social Capital, and Political Culture," *ANNALS* 565 (September 1999): 15-34; Rebecca G. Adams, "The Demise of Territorial Determinism: Online Friendships," in Rebecca G. Adams and Graham Allan, eds., *Placing Friendship in Context* (Cambridge: Cambridge University Press, 1998), 153-182; Andrew Greeley, "The Other Civic America: Religion and Social Capital," *The American Prospect* (May-June 1997): 68-73; Richard Stengel, "Bowling Together," *Time* (22 July 1996): 35-36; Michael Schudson, "What If Civic Life Didn't Die?" *The American Prospect* (March-April 1996): 17-20; Nicholas Lemann, "Kicking in Groups," *Atlantic Monthly* 277 (April 1996): 22-26;"The Solitary Bowler," *The Economist* (18 February 1995): 21-22; William F. Powers, "The Lane Less Traveled," *Washington Post* (3 February 1995): D1-D2.
109. Corey Robin, "Missing the Point," *Dissent* 63 (Spring 2001): 108-111; Richard John Neuhaus, *First Things* (January 2001): 68-69; Wilfred M. McClay, "Community and the Social Scientist," *The Public Interest* 143 (Spring 2001): 105-110; Francis Fukuyama, "Community Matters," *Washington Post Book World* (28 May 2000): 5; L. Lynne Kiesling, "Book Reviews: Bowling Alone," *Cato Journal* 20 (Spring/Summer 2000): 131-133.
110. Andrew R. Murphy, "In a League of its Own," *The Review of Politics* 63:2 (2001): 408-411.
111. Theda Skocpol, "Unravelling From Above," *The American Prospect* (March-April 1996): 20-25; Richard M. Valelly, "Couch-Potato Democracy?" *The American Prospect* (March-April 1996): 25-26; Robert J. Samuelson, "'Bowling Alone' is Bunk," *Washington Post* (10 April 1996): A19; Powers, "The Lane Less Traveled"; Rich, "American Voluntarism, Social Capital, and Political Culture."
112. Rich, "American Voluntarism, Social Capital, and Political Culture," 20.
113. Samuelson, "'Bowling Alone' is Bunk."
114. David M. Steiner, "Postmodernism," in Seymour Martin Lipset, ed., *The Encyclopedia of Democracy* (Washington, DC: Congressional Quarterly, 1995), 992-993.
115. Klaus von Beyme, "Post-Modernity, Postmaterialism and Political Theory," in K. Reif and R. Inglehart, eds., *Eurobarometer* (New York: St. Martin's, 1991), 324-325.
116. Bob Edwards and Michael W. Foley, "Much Ado about Social Capital," *Contemporary Sociology* 30:3 (May 2001): 227-230; Douglas Baer, James Curtis, and

Edward Grabb, "Has Voluntary Association Activity Declined? A Cross-National Perspective," paper presented at annual meeting of the American Sociological Association, August 2000; Pippa Norris, *A Virtuous Circle* (Cambridge: Cambridge University Press, 2000), 293-306; Leslie Lenkowsky, "Still 'Bowling Alone'?" *Commentary* 110 (October 2000): 57-60; Margaret Talbot, "Who Wants to be a Legionnaire?" *New York Times Book Review* (25 June 2000): 11-12; Pamela Paxton, "Is Social Capital Declining in the United States? A Multiple Indicator Assessment," *American Journal of Sociology* 105 (July 1999): 88-127; Thomas Rotolo, "Trends in Voluntary Association Participation," *Nonprofit and Voluntary Sector Quarterly* 28 (June 1999): 199-212; Robert W. Jackman and Ross A. Miller, "Social Capital and Politics," in Nelson W. Polsby, ed., *Annual Review of Political Science* (Palo Alto, CA: Annual Reviews, 1998), 47-73; Alejandro Portes, "Social Capital: Its Origins and Applications in Modern Sociology," in John Hagan and Karen S. Cook, eds., *Annual Review of Sociology* (Palo Alto, CA: Annual Reviews, 1998), 1-24; Tom W. Smith, "Factors Relating to Misanthropy in Contemporary American Society," *Social Science Research* 26 (1997):170-196.

117. Fukuyama, "Community Matters."
118. Carl Boggs, "Social Capital and Political Fantasy: Robert Putnam's Bowling Alone," *Theory and Society* 30:2 (2001): 281-297; Wills, "Putnam's America."
119. Boggs, "Social Capital and Political Fantasy"; Amitai Etzioni, "Is Bowling Together Sociologically Lite?" *Contemporary Sociology* 30:3 (May 2001): 223-224; James Davison Hunter, "Bowling with the Social Scientists," *The Weekly Standard* (August 28/September 4, 2000): 31-35; Wills, "Putnam's America."
120. Diamond, *Developing Democracy*, 225-227.
121. For more detail on method, see Marcella Ridlen Ray, "Out of the Shadows: An Empirical Analysis of How Civil Society in the United States Changed During the 20th Century." Ph. D. dissertation, George Mason University, Fairfax, VA, 2000, 39-41.

2

Organized Voluntary Association: Pervasive and Elastic

Detailed record keeping of associational life simply does not have a high priority in an open, decentralized society such as the United States. In contrast, this differs markedly from what Putnam et al. found in Italy, where "a census of all associations...local as well as national, enables us to specify precisely the number of amateur soccer clubs, choral societies, hiking clubs, bird-watching groups, literary circles, hunters' associations, Lions Clubs, and the like in each community and region of Italy."[1] The indicators of associational life examined in this chapter are of an organized and quantifiable form. Without comprehensive records, we must gain a sense of the volume of organized associational initiatives by examining case studies, attempts to estimate the numbers of voluntary associations, and databases that make it feasible to count some kinds of voluntary associations over time. The rates of growth and decline of such groups, compared to population growth also enhance an understanding of the dynamics of this organized aspect of social connectedness. These changes are examined in this chapter.

Insight from the Case Study

One source of data is the case study. Archival materials specific to a community sometimes contain early accounts of voluntary groups that proliferated to build and transform community. For example, such groups multiplied rapidly in the fifteen years it took for Grand Junction, Colorado, to transition from a pioneer settlement to a frontier town. Fourteen voluntary associations and five churches existed in Grand Junction in 1885. Three additional churches and seventy voluntary associations were active fifteen years later in 1900. Some groups met only a few times, others endured, and still others reorganized several times during this period. Six of the original organizations remained active in 1900. Two had already changed form. The Mesa County Fair was transformed into Peach Day Celebration and the Volunteer

Firefighters became the municipal Volunteer Fire Department.[2] Similarly, the transition of "Middletown," Indiana from an agricultural to a manufacturing economy in the late 1800s was accompanied by a significant multiplication of organized clubs that sustained and transformed the community; by 1924, there were five times as many clubs than there were in 1890.[3]

Decades later in the state of New Jersey, when the planned community of Levittown was established in 1958, the role for voluntary associations was evident. Community building and integration with the larger world outside of Levittown were both catalysts for association. Fourteen associations were organized in the first nine months, thirty-six in the following nine months, and in just six years, by 1964, there were 100 voluntary associations and churches. The largest proportion of these groups, 45 percent, rose in tandem with the specific needs of community members, such as the formation of a babysitting cooperative. Organizations external to the community, mostly national, reached into this new community. Groups that were external to the community of Levittown initiated nearly one-third of new associations. Community members initiated another 24 percent of the groups that affiliated with national organizations.[4] It is important to note this two-way process for bringing about integration of the local community with the larger community.

Growth is also mirrored in a 1925 study of five rural Wisconsin counties in which 351 voluntary organizations were counted, a number that increased 60 percent by 1940.[5] But in other instances, the population of voluntary associations grows slowly or not at all. This is evident in a poor and isolated farming community in "Plainville," Missouri where, for a thirteen-year time period between 1941 and 1954, only a slight increase in the number of organized groups occurred along with the demise of two youth and church-affiliated women's groups.[6]

That a pattern of association might fluctuate is demonstrated in yet another case study that documents growth, followed by decline in number of associations during a twelve-year period, 1924 to 1936, in a national sample of 140 American agricultural villages. This case demonstrates the dynamic nature of the voluntary association picture quite well. Social organizations rose and fell in number by 3 percent in these communities between 1924 and 1936, while churches and cooperatives simply declined. But the story is not in the quantity of groups; it is in the turnover. Sixty percent of the groups active at the beginning of the study were no longer active by 1936; the remaining two-fifths endured. New ones outnumbered associations that expired or became inactive during the first six years of observation. This pattern was reversed in the last half of the observation period when 975 associations became inactive or disbanded and only 730 new ones were formed or reorganized.[7] The researchers commented on the turnover: "[t]he outstanding characteristic of local social organizations is their instability."[8]

A similar turnover situation was found in "Yankee City," a New England community of 17,000, in the 1930s. Just 40 percent of the 899 voluntary organizations identified by the research team were stable and enduring. The continuous disappearance and generation of voluntary associations and the differences in their longevity was so notable that researchers referred to some groups as "ephemeral."[9] This quality of association, at once short-lived but stable, challenges every attempt, including the present one, to analyze this sector of society. Political scientist David Truman explained:

> When a single association is formed, it serves to stabilize the relations among the participants in the institutionalized groups involved. At the same time...it may cause disturbances in the equilibriums of other groups or accentuate cleavages among them. These are likely to evoke associations in turn to correct the secondary disturbances.... a natural consequence of what is understood as interaction in a highly complex social situation.[10]

Estimation

Singular attempts have been made to estimate numbers of associations nationwide, although the change and turnover in the population of voluntary associations remains largely undocumented. None of these attempts are entirely comprehensive, but they highlight awareness of and the presence of the intermediate institution of civil society. In 1933, a report was issued by the Research Committee on Social Trends appointed by President Herbert Hoover to examine "the feasibility of a national survey of social trends in the United States" as a basis for developing national policy.[11] The Committee subsequently gathered numerous research results for a view of social life in the nation as a whole. Statistics on associations from a variety of sources appear throughout the text of this extensive report–which, if listed, comprises a nationwide approximation of at least 685,000 known and recognized associations in 1930 (table 2.1). Other groups were mentioned but not enumerated in this work, confirming that this is a conservative representation. It attests to a presence of an extensive web of social connectedness, even before several technological advancements made it possible to affiliate in new ways and at a faster rate.

Less comprehensive counts were recorded two decades later. A handbook published in 1949 by the United States Department of Commerce described 4,000 national associations. It estimated that there were an additional 201,000 nonprofit voluntary trade and business organizations, women's groups, labor unions, civic service groups, luncheon clubs, and professional groups at national, local, and branch levels.[12] W. Lloyd Warner, in his introduction to *The Emergent American Society*, estimated that in 1960 there existed several million small social, civic, and voluntary associations plus

Table 2.1

Counts of Voluntary Associations in the United States c. 1930

Group	*Pre-c. 1930*	c. 1930	Year
academic sororities		150	1927
Altrusa		109	1931
American Association of University Women branches		586	1930
American Association of Social Worker chapters		43	1931
American Legion Auxiliaries		9,130	1930
art societies		800	1931
Association of Business and Professional Women		1,146	1930
Association of Junior Leagues		109	1930
Boy and Girl Scout, Campfire Girl camps		1,052	1929
community houses		660	1924
consumer coops	*est. 3,000 (1920)*	1,800	1932
churches, synagogues	*210,000 (1906)*	232,000	1926
Daughters of American Revolution chapters		2,377	1930
Farm Bureau Federation clubs	*210,560 (1922)*	403,602	1929
farmer cooperatives	*5,524 (1915)*	11,950	1931
Garden Clubs of America	*13 (1915)*	94	1930
Jewish Community Centers		102	1929
local community church federations		1,800	1930
local Knights of Columbus Lodges		2,500	1929
luncheon club federations		25	1930
museums	*92 (1900)*	151	1929
National Association of College Women branches		8	1930
National Council of Catholic Women diocese councils, state and local		1,756	1930
National Council of Colored Women, state		42	1930
National Council of Social Work, national and local agencies	*422 (1900)*	495	1930
National Council of Women, state chapters		38	1928
National Consumer Leagues, state and local		17	1930
National sororities		44	1927
National Youth Service organizations		15	1930

Group	***Pre-c. 1930***	**c. 1930**	**Year**
Nursing professional organizations		3	1930
Overseas Service Leagues		50	1930
PTA state branches		15	1930
public official professional organizations, national, state, regional		1,299	1931
Quota International		30	1931
Rotary, Kiwanis, Lions clubs	*388 (1917)*	6,839	1929
social service exchanges		194	1930
trade associations		1,000-1,800	1933
U.S. Lawn Tennis Association clubs	*294 (1920)*	800	1930
Young Men and Women's Christian Associations*		1,954	1930
Young Men and Women's Hebrew Associations		160	1929
Zonta		108	1930
	approximate total = 685, 053		

Source: Compiled from Research Committee on Social Trends, *Recent Social Trends in the United States.*
* includes Canada

thousands of small local governments, and thousands of small religious sects and churches, not to mention extended clusters of friends, cliques, and informal relationships.[13] A 1962 exploration of the large organization as a catalyst for an emerging national society produced a tally of 8,000 national associations with a guess that the actual number was closer to 12,000. This project also acknowledged the presence of another set of groups:

> Not even an approximately complete compilation of local and state associations exists; their number must greatly exceed 200,000, the majority purely local groups, few linked together by any formal ties, and most short-lived.[14]

In 1974, sociologist Morris Janowitz also called attention to an expansion of a national stratum of voluntary associations, commenting on a "definite trend toward the development of roof organizations, federations, and even "regional" alliances to link the local units to the realities of large-scale administrative organization...the emergence of a hierarchical structure in community organization."[15]

More recently, in 1989, Lester Salamon used Internal Revenue Service (IRS) data to reach an estimate of 1.14 million associations in the United States that were nongovernmental, nonprofit, and self-governing. This work reflected 400,000 member-serving associations (social clubs, business associations, labor unions, political parties, and cooperatives) and 740,000 public-serving organizations (political action agencies, service providers, religious congregations, and funding intermediaries).[16] Salamon revised the latter number of public-serving organizations in 1995 to 1.2 million, raising the total to 1.6 million.[17] In a different effort, David Horton Smith used Internal Revenue Service and Independent Sector data to conclude that 786,000 member benefit organizations and 572,000 public organizations, a total of 1.358 million, were in existence in 1990.[18] Smith also argues that 90 percent of grassroots associations are missing from prevailing estimates.[19] Among those groups that go uncounted are many that thrive in poor and minority communities. As Benjamin Barber recently observed to an interviewer, "the educated middle class is often unable to perceive the organizational forms of the poor."[20] In illustration, when sociologist Albert Hunter broadened his definition of local voluntary organizations in 1967-68 to include block clubs, he found no difference in the degree to which black and white communities in the Chicago area were organized.[21]

These recent, but imperfect, estimates confirm an extensive and persistent presence of voluntary associations in the United States, consistent with the picture proffered by the work of the Research Committee on Social Trends in 1930 (table 2.1).[22] If the accounting of the number of known groups provided by the Committee is as accurate as Smith's 1990 estimate, there is little per capita difference in the ratio of groups to population size, from .00556 in 1930 to .00543 in 1990. Salamon's 1995 estimate yields a per capita rate of .0061.

Trends as Indicators of Quantitative Change

Estimates give a sense of the volume and the enduring quality of the intermediate sector. Case studies highlight the sector's dynamic nature. Trends are informative about the nature of long-term changes. In general, changes in the total number of a variety of voluntary groups—national nonprofit membership associations, tax exempt organizations, membership groups recognized in the Standard Industrial Classification system, religious congregations, and local government entities—are positive. These databases exist for various purposes, use different definitions, follow different criteria for inclusion, and, in some instances, they overlap. Each allows a comparison of longitudinal patterns; each contributes to an empirical description of how organized association changes. The following confirms the dynamic nature of the organized elements of voluntary association as demonstrated above in the case studies discussed.

Nonprofit Membership Groups

In 1956, associations at the national level became the subject of a reference guide to trade, business, professional, labor, scientific, educational, fraternal and social organizations of the United States.[23] The total number of *national* nonprofit membership associations that appeared in the fifth edition (1968) of the *Encyclopedia of Associations* was 10,299; by 1999, those entries doubled to 22,500.[24] This database was recently extended to include an additional 143,200 associations of two sorts, one international and one predominantly local. The first includes 19,600 nonprofit membership organizations whose scope, membership, or interests are international. This list continues to develop. The 1995 edition, for example, contained special efforts to locate development organizations, an initiative that resulted in 1,400 new entries. The following year's focus was on improving coverage of scientific and technical organizations. The second sort of association—regional, state, and local nonprofit membership organizations—is the focus of a new, rapidly growing database that numbers 124,000.[25]

When the years of origin are charted for groups that appear in the *Encyclopedia of Associations,* it is clear that new associations have gradually proliferated since at least the eighteenth century. Many membership associations listed in this reference do not report their founding dates. However, the dates were available online for a large portion (97 percent) of the national groups in 1996.[26] Figure 2.1 shows an accelerated founding rate for national associations after 1960.[27] The trend is consistent with the phenomenon of emerging national groups to which Nall called attention in 1967.[28] Until that point in time, national, international, and regional/state/local groups organized at a similar rate, as shown. Overall, the trend lines reflect an expansion of social space throughout the century. Increasingly, social space reflects national and international ties, but not at the expense of the most local of groups, whose number also continued to climb.

Tax-Exempt Organizations

Another trend, constructed from Internal Revenue Service (IRS) annual reports, enumerates the active, nonprofit, tax-exempt organizations on this federal agency's master file. In 1970, there were 475,000 such organizations. Four years later, 673,000 organizations were listed, with much of the increase attributed to a Tax Reform Act of 1969 clause requiring heretofore exempt units under group rulings to register with the IRS.[29] The base year from which change is measurable, therefore, is 1974. Tax exempt organizations on file steadily increased to a total of 1.3 million by 1999, an increase of 95 percent in twenty-five years.[30] This count is akin to the recent estimates by Salamon and by Smith, noted above.

Figure 2.1

Nonprofit Membership Associations Formed in 20th Century

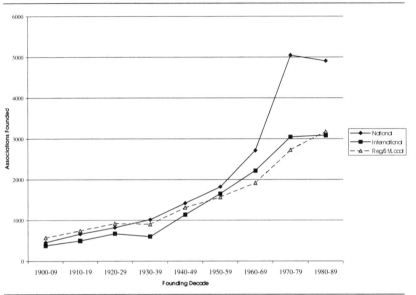

Source: Gale Research Group, "Associations Unlimited," 2001.

This IRS file contains membership and nonmembership groups at the local, state, regional, and national levels.[31] It is noteworthy that a majority of these groups are *not* national ones. In 1969, the IRS estimated that over one-half of the organizations on the list were local, while less than one-fourth of a 1992 national sample of tax-exempt organizations surveyed by the Independent Sector had any national affiliation.[32] The IRS master file, because it includes local associations, may provide the most comprehensive count but it, too, has its omissions. Groups with annual revenues under $25,000 are generally excluded, as are church congregations.[33] Salamon estimated that the total would increase by another 25 percent if these excluded agencies were counted.[34] Smith figures the IRS data capture only 10 percent of the entire nonprofit group population when grassroots associations are included.[35]

Between 1989 and 1994, the Urban Institute documented the growth of eight types of public charities classified by the IRS as tax exempts. These were groups organized around the causes described as environment and animals, education, public and societal benefit, human services, international, religion related, arts and culture, and health. The total number of these groups grew from 120,300 to 161,700 during this six-year period, an increase of 34 percent. Although some types of groups grew faster than others, each held the same proportionate share of the total in 1994 as it had in 1989. The data, therefore, inadvertently reveal that some groups were more volatile than others. Those with the higher growth rates also had higher turnover; those with the slowest growth rates were the most stable during this period.[36] At one extreme, environmental and animal groups increased in number by 56 percent, but continued to make up only 3 percent of the total. At the other extreme, the slower growing category of health groups grew by 20 percent. It accounted for 19 percent of the total in 1989, 17 percent of the total in 1994, and obviously had the least turnover activity of the eight categories.

Standard Industrial Code Classifications

Several commercial enterprises compile entries from yellow page directories. The sales lists from one such enterprise are organized according to the Standard Industrial Codes (SIC), which contains a cluster of nonprofit membership organizations.[37] Active status of listings is confirmed before being transferred from 4,800 different yellow page directories that, in aggregate, provide national coverage. The accuracy of the SIC classification as a nonprofit membership group is not verified, however.[38] Nor do many such organizations choose to appear in the Yellow Pages, *if* they have a telephone. With these limitations in mind, listings for membership groups increased by 21 percent during this time, while those for churches and synagogues grew by 28 percent between 1987 and 1996.[39] Whether the increase is attributable to the birth of new groups or simply to added listings is unknown. Either explanation recognizes the presence and expansion of voluntary organized group life. Reliance on one cluster of SIC codes, as used in the Yellow Pages, results in a conservative count since nonprofit associations are found throughout the classification system. Indeed, Rudney and Weitzman, in a review of service industries, found nonprofits scattered across twenty-nine different SIC codes.[40] Growth in these particular groups has also been documented. The Independent Sector measured an increase of 31 percent between 1977 and 1982 in this class of service nonprofits; Salamon documented a 66 percent growth by 1987.[41]

Religious Congregations

In 1926, the number of religious congregations in the country was estimated at 232,000 (see table 2.1). The Independent Sector has maintained data on the number of religious congregations in the United States since 1974. These groups, generally considered separately from other types of membership groups, increased by 6.6 percent—from 332,000 in 1974 to 354,000 in 1998.[42]

Local Governments

Tocqueville classified voluntary associations in the United States as civil or political. The latter included local governmental units established by law, as distinct from a centralized government, to run local affairs.[43] Core units of local government—municipalities, townships, and counties—have remained relatively stable in number, 39,044 in 1997, a 2 percent increase over the last half-century. But the appearance of local government has changed markedly since 1942. School districts then were predominant in local government, accounting for 70 percent of all local entities. Core units accounted for 24 percent of local governing units; special districts only 5 percent (figure 2.2).

Figure 2.2

Mix of Local General Purpose Units, School Districts, and Special Districts, 1942-1997

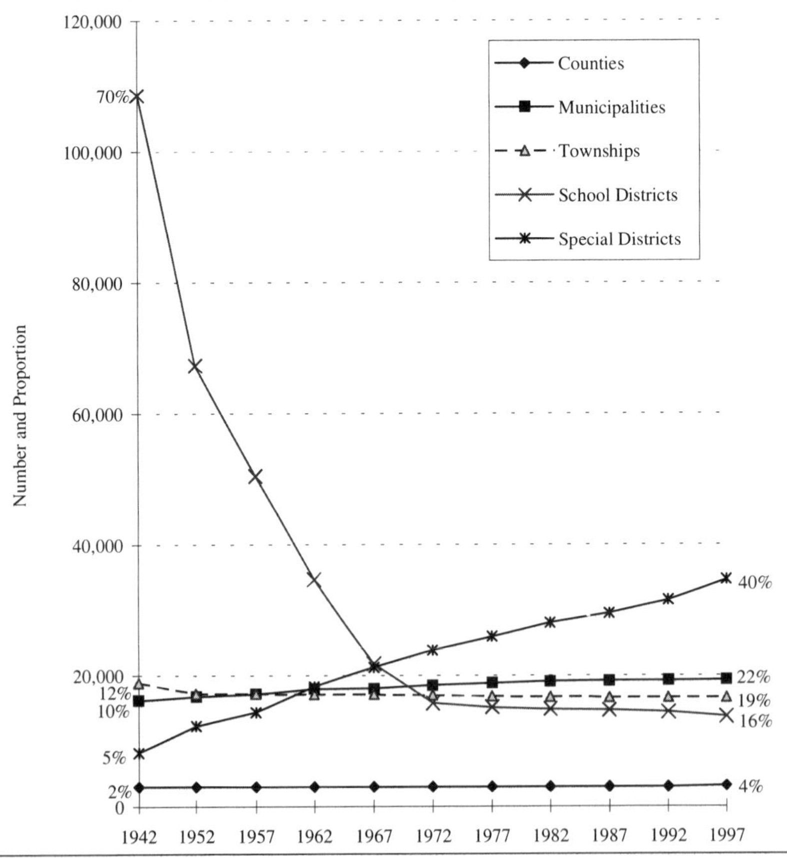

Source: *The Municipal Yearbook* and *Census of Governments*, serial editions.

This profile has altered significantly. In 1997, fifty-five years later, the total of local governmental units, 87,453, was 44 percent smaller, largely due to the consolidation and annexation of schools that leveled off in the early 1970s. The decline in school districts, the multiplication of special districts, and the stability of core governmental units resulted in a markedly different picture of local government in 1997. Core units of municipalities, townships, and counties constituted 45 percent of the total; special districts made up 40 percent of local entities and school districts only 16 percent.[44]

Proliferation Rates

Population growth provides a common standard with which to evaluate the rate at which these different varieties of voluntary organizations changed in number (table 2.2). The growth of most of the databases examined here—national nonprofit membership groups, tax exempt organizations, yellow page listings of nonprofit membership groups and places of worship, Standard Industrial Classification service groups, local special districts—exceeds the rate of population growth in comparable time periods. There are three

Table 2.2

Association Growth Referenced to Population Growth (in rounded percentages)

Database	Time Period	Population Growth	% Change
National Nonprofit Membership Groups	1968-1999	36	120
Tax Exempt Organizations	1974-1999	26	95
Yellow Page Listings	1987-1996	9	
• nonprofit membership			21
• churches, synagogues			28
SIC Nonprofit Service Groups	1977-1987	10	66
Religious Congregations	1974-1998	26	7
Local Governmental Entities	1942-1997	99	
• townships, counties, municipalities			3
• school districts			- 87
• special districts			318

Source: Compiled from annual editions of United States Bureau of the Census, *Statistical Abstract of the United States*; United States Bureau of the Census, *Historical Statistics of the United States: Colonial Times to 1970 Part I* (United States Department of Commerce, 1975); United States Bureau of the Census, *Census of Governments* and International City Management Association, *The Municipal Yearbook*, various editions; and sources noted in the text.

exceptions. The population grew faster than core local governmental units, school districts, and religious congregations.

Religious congregations have long shown a tendency to grow more slowly than the population. Historical data on religious congregations compiled by the Independent Sector, when scrutinized in relation to the growth of population between 1974 and 1997, indicate a lag similar to one recognized early in this century. Fry, of the Institute of Social and Religious Research, reported in 1933 that

> since 1906 the number of churches in this country has not increased in proportion to the growth of the population.... The 1926 total of 232,000 Christian churches and Jewish synagogues compares with slightly more than 210,000 in 1906, representing a net increase of less than 11 percent in twenty years.... Between 1906 and 1916 the number of churches grew 7.6 percent or less than half as fast as the population; while during the decade from 1916 to 1926 the increase was only 1.7 percent or one tenth of the rate of population increase....[45]

The lag pattern of growth of religious congregations in the last two decades is consistent with this early observation.

The overall negative growth of local government is attributable to the decline in school districts, which implies a narrower opportunity for participation in local self-governance. This, however, has been partially offset by the rise in numbers of special districts (shown in figure 2.2).

Summary and Discussion of Findings

This focus on organized efforts to sustain social connectedness highlights some important characteristics and functions of voluntary associations. Voluntary organizations have an extensive and enduring presence in the United States. These groups meet pragmatic need, build community, work as change agents, and help to integrate distinct communities vertically and horizontally. Broadly, this is a cluster of groups that sustains a continuous presence and remains elastic and dynamic in nature. Early case studies document the potential for rapid build-up, turnover, and persistence in total numbers of voluntary associations. Historical trends document varying patterns of growth, both fast and slow, of fluctuation, and of decline in numbers of associations. Local government, with its fifty-year profile of core units, special districts, and school districts, demonstrates the capacity to flex, change, and survive.

Referenced to population growth, organized association is strong. Certain segments of organized association, such as the national nonprofit membership groups and the tax-exempt organizations, grew in number at a faster rate than that of the nation's population during the last several decades. Religious congregations multiply, but at a notably slower pace than the population, in accordance with a phenomenon first observed early in this century.

Finally, a feature of note is the multi-dimensionality of organized association. With progress in quantifying organized association comes a clearer picture of associational life that operates at grassroots levels, at regional and state levels, in the national domain, and that reaches beyond national borders. Certainly, organized association is increasingly visible and expands with the social space.

Notes

1. Robert D. Putnam with Robert Leonardi and Raffaella Y. Nanetti, *Making Democracy Work: Civic Traditions in Modern Italy* (Princeton, NJ: Princeton University Press, 1993), 91.
2. Kathleen Hill Underwood, "Town Building on the Frontier: Grand Junction, Colorado, 1880-1900." Ph.D. dissertation, University of California, Los Angeles, 1983.
3. Robert S. Lynd and Helen Merrell Lynd, *Middletown: A Study in American Culture* (New York: Harcourt Brace, 1929), 13-17, 527.
4. Herbert J. Gans, *The Levittowners: Ways of Life and Politics in a New Suburban Community* (New York: Pantheon, 1967), 52-68.
5. J. H. Kolb and Edmund deS. Brunner, *A Study of Rural Society* (Boston, MA: Houghton Mifflin, 1946), 332-334, citing J. H. Kolb and A. F. Wileden, "Special Interest Groups in Rural Society," Research Bulletin 84 (Madison, WI: Agricultural Experiment Station, University of Wisconsin, December 1927).
6. Art Gallaler, Jr., *Plainville Fifteen Years Later* (New York: Columbia University Press, 1961).
7. J. H. Kolb and Edmund deS. Brunner, *A Study of Rural Society: Its Organization and Changes* (Boston, MA: Houghton Mifflin, 1935), 528-535; Kolb and Brunner, *A Study of Rural Society* (1946), 558-563.
8. Kolb and Brunner, *A Study of Rural Society: Its Organization and Changes* (1935), 529.
9. W. Lloyd Warner and Paul S. Lunt, *The Social Life of a Modern Community* (New Haven, CT: Yale University Press, 1941).
10. David B. Truman, *The Governmental Process* (New York: Alfred A. Knopf, [1951] 1971), 59.
11. Research Committee on Social Trends, *Recent Social Trends in the United States: Report of the President's Research Committee on Social Trends* (New York: McGraw-Hill, 1933), v.
12. Calvert Jay Judkins, *National Associations of the United States* (Washington, DC: United States Department of Commerce, 1949). This was based on 1940 census data.
13. W. Lloyd Warner, ed., *The Emergent American Society* (New Haven, CT: Yale University Press, 1967).
14. Frank C. Nall, II, "National Associations," in Warner, *The Emergent American Society*, 276-313.
15. Morris Janowitz, "Foreword," in Albert Hunter, *Symbolic Communities: The Persistence and Change of Chicago's Local Communities* (Chicago, IL: University of Chicago Press, 1974), xiv.
16. Lester M. Salamon, *America's Nonprofit Sector* (New York: Foundation Center, 1992).

17. Lester M. Salamon, *America's Nonprofit Sector: A Primer*, 2d ed. (New York: Foundation Center, 1999), 22.
18. David Horton Smith, "Public Benefit and Member Benefit Nonprofit, Voluntary Groups," *Nonprofit and Voluntary Sector Quarterly* 22 (Spring 1993): 53-68.
19. David Horton Smith, "The Rest of the Nonprofit Sector: Grassroots Associations as the Dark Matter Ignored in Prevailing 'Flat Earth' Maps of the Sector," *Nonprofit and Voluntary Sector Quarterly* 26 (June 1997): 114-131; David Horton Smith, *Grassroots Associations* (Thousand Oaks, CA: Sage Publications, 2000), 36-41. Smith describes grassroots organizations as local, autonomous, run by volunteers, formally organized, nonprofit, membership, and altruistic.
20. Uwe Jean Heuser and Gero von Randow, "Try Cleaning Things Up," *Die Zeit* (29 October 1998): 58. Translated by Ingrid Sandole-Staroste.
21. Hunter, *Symbolic Communities*, 144-145.
22. Research Committee, *Recent Social Trends in the United States*.
23. This was first published as the *Encyclopedia of American Associations* (Detroit, MI: Gale Research Company, 1956) and retitled as the *Encyclopedia of Associations* with the 1961, or third, edition. Initial collection of data began by compiling information from local phone directories, newspapers, magazines, periodicals, chambers of commerce, and other national organizations. Subsequently, questionnaires were mailed to organizations with follow-up by written correspondence, telephone, and reliable secondary source confirmations. There is a period of several years, generally three, before an inactive or defunct status of an organization is confirmed and the entry is dropped. Lag time also occurs between the founding date of an association and when it first enters the encyclopedia.
24. Gale Research Group, "Associations Unlimited," 1999, website: http://galenet.gale.com.
25. Ken Karges, ed., *Encyclopedia of Associations: Regional, State, and Local Organizations* (Farmington Hills, MI: Gale Group, 2001); Editions of *Encyclopedia of Associations: International Organizations* (Farmington Hills, MI: Gale Group); Gale Research Group, "Associations Unlimited."
26. Marcella Ridlen Ray, "Pieces to the Association Puzzle." Paper presented at annual meeting of the Association for Research on Nonprofit Organizations and Voluntary Action, New York, 1996.
27. The picture for the twentieth century is incomplete. Once past the lag time for identification of groups organized in the latter part of the decade, we will learn if group organizing kept pace, slowed, or accelerated as the century ended.
28. Nall, "National Associations."
29. United States Internal Revenue Service, "Annual Report 1974," Washington, DC: United States Department of the Treasury, 32.
30. From the United States Internal Revenue Service, "1971 Annual Report /Commissioner of Internal Revenue," Washington, DC: United States Department of the Treasury, 20; United States Internal Revenue Service, *Data Book, 1993-94* (Washington, DC: United States Department of the Treasury, 1994), 62, 105; United States Internal Revenue Service, "IRS Data Book, 1996-99," no. 55B, website http://www.irs.gov. According to a March 1996 conversation with an IRS spokesman, the Internal Revenue Service does relatively little auditing that would remove the tax-exempt status of ineligible organizations in the master file. This is also noted in Virginia Ann Hodgkinson and Murray S. Weitzman, *Dimensions of the Independent Sector: A Statistical Profile*, 3d ed. (Washington, DC: Independent Sector, 1989), 209.

31. From a national survey of charitable organizations, which constitutes over half of the tax-exempt group considered here, the Independent Sector has estimated that 40 percent are membership organizations. See Virginia A. Hodgkinson, Murray S. Weitzman, Stephen M. Noga, and Heather A. Gorski, *A Portrait of the Independent Sector: The Activities and Finances of Charitable Organizations* (Washington, DC: Independent Sector, 1993), 2.
32. United States Internal Revenue Service, "Annual Report 1969," Washington, DC: United States Department of the Treasury, 14; Hodgkinson et al., *A Portrait of the Independent Sector*, 2.
33. United States Internal Revenue Service, "Tax-Exempt Status for Your Organization," Publication 557, Department of the Treasury, January 1995.
34. Lester M. Salamon, *Partners in Public Service: Government-Nonprofit Relations in the Modern Welfare State* (Baltimore, MD: Johns Hopkins University Press, 1995), 274.
35. Smith, *Grassroots Associations*, 44.
36. Carol J. De Vita, "Viewing Nonprofits Across the States," August 1997, the first in a series of papers on "Charting Civil Society" published by the Urban Institute. I calculated growth rates by using the number of new groups added during the time period, divided by the 1989 total and multiplied by 100.
37. The 8,600 cluster of codes used by this particular enterprise includes the categories of business and trade, chambers of commerce, professional, labor, veterans' and military, clubs, fraternal, fraternities and sororities, environmental/ conservation, political, religious, athletic, other, churches and synagogues.
38. Per telephone interview with manager of American Business Directories, Omaha, Nebraska, in January 1996.
39. From annual sales lists of the *American Business Directories* (Omaha, NE: American Business Lists). Some particular types of groups were not consistently organized. Other types of groups were treated uniformly throughout the period and can be examined in terms of growth or decline. Listings for labor groups and fraternities and sororities declined. Listings for veterans' and military groups, churches and synagogues, Chambers of Commerce, and fraternal organizations increased.
40. Gabriel Rudney and Murray Weitzman, "Significance of Employment and Earnings in the Philanthropic Sector, 1972-1982," Working Paper No. 77 (New Haven, CT: Program on Non-Profit Organizations, Yale University, 1983) as cited in Hodgkinson and Weitzman, *Dimensions* (1989), 207-208.
41. Salamon, *Partners in Public Service*, 236-237.
42. Virginia Ann Hodgkinson, Murray S. Weitzman, Christopher M. Toppe, and Stephen M. Noga, *Nonprofit Almanac 1992-1993: Dimensions of the Independent Sector* (San Francisco, CA: Jossey-Bass, 1992), 23-24; Hodgkinson and Weitzman, *Dimensions* (1989), 27-28; Hodgkinson and Weitzman, et al., *Nonprofit Almanac 1996-1997: Dimensions of the Independent Sector* (San Francisco, CA: Jossey-Bass, 1996), 39; Salamon, *America's Nonprofit Sector: A Primer*, 151, 157; Independent Sector, "America's Religious Congregations: Measuring Their Contributions to Society," November 2000, website http://independentsector.org; Independent Sector, "The Nonprofit Almanac in Brief," 2001, website http://independentsector.org.
43. Alexis de Tocqueville, *Democracy in America* (New York: Vintage Books, 1945), I:198.
44. Core units of local government totaled 38,189 in 1942 and 39,044 in 1997. School districts totaled 108,579 in 1942 and 13,726 in 1997. Special districts totaled 8,299 in 1942 and 34,683 in 1997. These figures are from serial editions of *The Munici-*

pal Yearbook and the *Census of Government*, published respectively by the International City Management Association and the United States Bureau of the Census, and from preliminary unpublished data provided by the United States Bureau of the Census.

45. C. Luther Fry, "Changes in Religious Organizations," in Research Committee, *Recent Social Trends in the United States*, 1019.

3

Attachment and Involvement: How Much and What Kind?

A democracy relies on the sovereignty of its people who must necessarily take care of public matters. There is no aristocratic class in the United States expected to do the governing, nor do members of the working class have unlimited time to devote to civic matters. Nevertheless, self-governance "must go forward and accelerate the union of private with public interests, since the period of disinterested patriotism is gone by forever." It is necessary to sacrifice time and energy needed for the "discharge of political duties...a troublesome impediment."[1]

Political scientists Verba, Schlozman, and Brady have used survey data to project how the contemporary American public involves itself in voluntary political, religious, and secular non-political activities. Their projection suggests that 95 percent of Americans are active to the extent that they vote, attend church, and/or contribute to charitable and religious causes. "The activity may be intermittent and peripheral to Americans' basic concerns, but it is activity nonetheless (82)."[2] In other words, only a small portion of citizens seem *completely* detached from society at any particular point in time.

This chapter examines behavioral characteristics of associational life—resource dedication and constraints, membership, civic participation, political and social activism, voluntarism and charitable giving, and informal association. Historical data permit us to see how voluntary association has changed over time.

Practical Constraints and Resource Dedication

The nature of associational life is partly predicated upon available time and money. This was clear in a cross-national survey of human values conducted in 1979 by the Leisure Development Center of Tokyo/Gallup. Survey participants included Canada, France, the United Kingdom, the United States, and West Germany—all Western, democratic, industrialized nations that share similar interest aggregation profiles.[3] Samples from each of these nations reported that limits on time and money were the biggest barriers to a satisfactory leisure life, underscoring the importance of the allocation of these precious resources.[4] A third resource with a remarkable impact on the nature of the associational life of Americans is transportation technology. The convenience of the automobile, applied to associational life, converges with a tradition of embracing opportunities to move out and onwards.[5] And it converges with a tendency of Americans to form attachments for multitudinous reasons, tailored by choice and pragmatic factors.[6]

Leisure Time: Solitude or Society?

Employment, sleep, personal and family care, household maintenance, and travel time consume the greatest portion of adult Americans' time each week. Leisure, or free, time is that which remains after meeting these demands. How much free time do Americans generally have? Two case studies on time budgeting in the 1930s, one in 1954, two in 1965, one in 1975, and one in 1985 produced estimates that fell within a range of 33 to 40 hours per week.[7] More recent estimates from time diary research suggest that the average amount of free time per week in America averages close to 39 hours per week.[8] There are methodological differences in these studies, but results are not markedly varied.[9] Free time, of course, varies with such factors as life-cycle stage, gender, race, parental situation, employment status, and lifestyle. But the amount of free time available to Americans is presently in contention. Varied approaches in determining the length of the workweek, blurred distinctions between work and pleasure, differences in gender experience of free time, and different perceptions of time make it a complex issue that cannot be resolved easily.[10]

Edmund Burke observed, "We are creatures designed for contemplation as well as action; since solitude as well as society has its pleasures."[11] Thus, we ask how much of free time is dedicated to society, in contrast to solitude? Between 1930 and 1985, case studies and national samples suggest that the average American adult devoted from ten to eleven hours in a week's time to organizational, religious, and social activities.[12] Much of leisure-time activity offers at least some potential for association and connection. Sorokin and Berger provided evidence of this in a time-budget study conducted in 1935 in which participants reported 38 types of leisure activities in their time diaries and made note of their co-participants. *If* an activity that involved at least two other individuals is designated as social, 53 percent of the reported leisure activities were solitary and 47 percent were social.[13] When Almond and Verba asked survey respondents in 1960 what activities they preferred or engaged in during their leisure time, these researchers drew a distinction between pursuits that were individual and those that would bring people into social contact. Forty percent of Americans said they took part or would like to engage in activities that were social in nature, as opposed to the 60 percent who preferred individual pursuits.[14] Both studies reveal an apportionment of social and solitary activity that favors the latter slightly.

Almond and Verba did not classify sports, spectator amusements, and cultural events as social activities. Such activities do mobilize socialization, discussion, and sharing of common interests, however, as demonstrated in Sorokin and Berger's time-budget study. These researchers found that 62 percent of their subjects observed games and spectacles together with at least three other persons, and sometimes with as many as ten to twenty. This was also the case in 53 percent of the amusements attended, in 80 percent of organized indoor sports, in 50 percent of organized outdoor sports, and in 47 percent of unorganized outdoor sports.[15] Clearly, in Sorokin and Berger's nonrepresentative sample, a significant portion of what Almond and Verba labeled "individual pursuits" entailed social connectedness.

Yet, the discovery that a larger portion of leisure time is dedicated to solitary pursuits is a pattern consistent with other research:

- Reports of urban Americans who completed time diaries in 1965 show that approximately 34 percent of their free time was allocated to outgoing, social activity and 66 percent to more solitary pursuits.[16]
- Respondents in the 1975 Americans' Use of Time study reported that 27 percent of their free time went to socially oriented activity, leaving the larger portion for individual activity.[17]
- When a 1979 Leisure Development Center/Gallup poll asked respondents "How do you spend your free time? Please name as many as you like on this card," 33 percent mentioned activities that required social interaction, although no mention was made of religious observance in any of the twenty-four response choices.[18]
- A 1982 survey sponsored by United Media Enterprises asked participants about their participation in a list of 39 leisure activities. Thirty-seven percent reported having been engaged in outgoing, socially oriented activity "every day or almost every day" *or* "about once or twice a week."[19]
- And, finally, in the 1985 Americans' Use of Time study, at least 26 percent of leisure time was dedicated to social, in contrast to individual, enterprise.[20]

In each case, it is apparent that the larger portion of free time is devoted to individual pursuits. Accordingly, "Getting relaxed at home such as TV-watching, listening to radio or records, playing with children, just doing nothing, etc." was the top ranked choice for use of free time in the 1979 Leisure Development Center/Gallup survey.[21] Recent surveys by Louis Harris and Associates and by Gallup confirm that reading, watching television, spending time with family, gardening, and fishing are preferred ways of spending free time.[22]

The vitality of civil society thus rests on a very small amount of temporal investment in associational activity that must compete with private time. The average American adult has from 33 to 40 hours of free time per week. Ten to eleven of those hours, on average, are spent in outgoing, social activities while individual pursuits absorb the other two-thirds of available leisure time. This seems to be the pattern at least since the 1930s. It is this general and persistent configuration of individual and social pursuits within which American associational life is produced.

Money

We also find clues to associational practices in gross consumer leisure spending patterns, although associational life is less dependent upon fiscal resources than upon free time. Not all of associational life entails expenditure of monies, nor, admittedly, do all leisure activities necessarily command spending at equal rates but discretionary spending possibilities help to shape social connectedness. The Middletown studies, for example, tell us that the Great Depression was the backdrop for an informal social life.[23] Upon their return to Middletown in 1935, the Lynds found a change in the focal point of entertaining. In lieu of the country club setting of 1925, the backyards became a center of social life with the accompanying grills, furniture, vegetable gardens, and "a mild mania for flower gardening."[24]

In the national accounts, five types of expenditures often related to social connectedness hold a small, but important, place in the national scheme of personal spending: dues and fees for clubs and fraternal organizations, spending on religious and welfare activities, spectator pastimes, commercial participant amusements, and playthings (such as toys, sports gear, and pleasure craft).[25] The share of personal consumption attributable to these five categories accounted for 6.2 percent of personal spending in 1998, up from 4.1 percent in 1929.[26] This 1929 figure is similar to what Warner and Lunt found in Yankee City in the early 1930s. The rate of spending there on six similar activities—associations, charity, amusements, sporting equipment, photography, and vacation travel—varied by social class but averaged 4.3 percent per family budget.[27] The expansion of the association dollar over the last seven decades occurred within an expanding context of total leisure and recreation spending that increased from 5 percent of total personal consumption in 1929 to 11.2 percent in 1998.[28] The distribution of spending across the aforementioned five categories perceptibly shifted between 1929 and 1998 (figure 3.1). In both years, the largest portion of the associational dollar went to religion and welfare, but its share of that dollar increased from 38 percent to 45 percent.

The next largest portion of the 1929 dollar, 29 percent, was spent on spectator amusements, which fell to 7 percent in 1998. The technologies of play—

Figure 3.1

Allocation of the Associational Dollar, 1929 and 1998

	1929	1998
Religion, Welfare	38	45
Clubs, Fraternal Organizations	10	4
Commercial Participant Amusements	7	15
Toys, Sports Equipment	17	29
Spectator Amusements	29	7

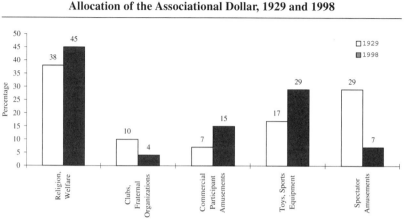

Source: U.S. Bureau of Census, *Statistical Abstract*, various editions.

toys, sports and recreational paraphernalia—rose from 17 percent in 1929 to 29 percent in 1998. Clubs and fraternal organizations received proportionately less of the associational dollar in 1998, dropping from 10 to 4 percent. Spending on commercial participant amusements, such as dancing, golf, and sightseeing, rose from 7 to 15 percent.[29] These spending changes denote a move toward more participatory leisure activity that fosters social connectedness. This, undoubtedly, is fueled by transportation technologies that increase daily mobility.

Transportation

Adaptation of the automobile was rapid in the United States, as was its remarkable impact upon associational life. The Research Committee on Social Trends established that in the eighteen-year period from 1913 to 1931, private motor vehicle registrations multiplied twenty times while the motor vehicle and gas tax became one of three major sources of government revenue.[30] First seen in Middletown early in the century, the automobile was an integral part of the life and leisure style of the community by 1925.[31] Middletowners of the 1930s viewed the car as a necessity, a view that persisted despite slowed sales and replacements during the Great Depression.[32]

This new technology radically altered patterns of social life. Americans, with the freedom the personal vehicle provided, revised their social space by expanding its boundaries and changing its composition. One of the early offshoots of this new mobility was the spread of the suburban residential division.[33] Although the automobile cut into the isolation of many people and intensified local contacts, it also had the capacity to detract from local community involvement. Those with greater mobility could, if they chose, more easily detach themselves from civic matters.[34] This was a matter of wide concern as it related to church attendance in Middletown. The local paper once estimated that "10,000 persons leave Middletown by automobile for other towns and resorts every fine Sunday."[35] One pillar of the church interviewed in the original study acknowledged a decision to forego worship services to embark on an eighty-mile trip to a lake he had never seen. His comments reflect a personal interest in expanding experience, on one hand, and a sense of social responsibility on the other.

> It's a fine thing for people to get out that way on Sundays. No question about it. They see different things and get a larger outlook.... you can't do both. I never missed church or Sunday School for thirteen years and I kind of feel as if I'd done my share. The ministers ought not to rail against people's driving on Sunday. They ought just to realize that they won't be there...during the summer, and make church interesting enough so they'll want to come.[36]

The locus of association activity, its flavor, and its reach shifted with the automobile. Sunday dinners and get-togethers became less popular.[37] Visiting in the parlor and courting rituals, once centered in the home, faded as activities increasingly relied upon the automobile.[38] It was not unusual for a drive or an event accessible by wheel to replace an evening gathering on the porch.[39] A dampening effect on neighboring occurred, even as neighborhoods became voluntary in a truer sense.[40] Old neighborhoods, town celebrations of holidays, and church attendance competed with the day trip, the vacation, and access to resources from an ever-widening social space.[41] What happened is what Gellner so aptly describes as liberation from the "tyranny of cousins, and of ritual," a freedom readily embraced by many Americans.[42]

Additional options for who, how, and when people got together evolved around the car. It became a focal point of socializing for small groups and made larger gatherings a more frequent occurrence. Motoring, for instance, was a popular social activity and drives often included groups of friends.[43] Social events, once occasional, became regular occurrences with access by car.[44] Middletown residents attended gatherings more frequently, organized impromptu affairs such as picnics, and followed high school ball games at home and away.[45] Visits to relatives living at some distance became more frequent.[46]

The pattern continues today. In 1995, only 8 percent of all households were without a vehicle, according to the Federal Highway Administration, while 60 percent had two or more vehicles.[47] Most respondents (93 percent) polled in 1996 by *Washington Post*/Kaiser/Harvard considered the automobile a necessity.[48] Contemporary physical arrangements of communities rely upon the personal vehicle as an important linchpin for many aspects of American life outside of the home. The coordination of work, chores, and leisure made possible by the automobile gives rise to innovative ideas like drive-in movies, drive-in worship services, and drive-through funeral home visitations. Travel time for organizational, religious, and social events amounted to more than one-fifth (22 percent) of total commuting time in 1985, slightly more than in 1965.[49] National Personal Transportation Surveys show the number of trips Americans reported for social and recreational reasons grew by 12 percent between 1969 and 1990. At the same time, the length of these trips grew shorter by 10 percent and the total number of miles traveled per household remained about the same, suggesting an increase in the density of peoples' associational lives.[50]

Often combined with spending time with friends and family, tourism and travel for pleasure became a new variant of association. Today, the most frequent reason for pleasure travel is to visit friends and family—the means for getting there is by automobile over three-fourths of the time.[51] The automobile is also its own catalyst for association and recreation in its own right. Auto racing, for example, is a sport that interests a third of Americans. Louis Harris and Associates found that 6 percent of respondents in a 1993 poll named auto racing as their favorite sport, while another 26 percent said it was a sport they followed.[52] Associations such as the United States Auto Club and the National Association for Stock Car Auto Racing (NASCAR) who coordinate racing activities are among the nonprofit membership organizations with interests related in some way to the automobile. In 2001, the *Encyclopedia of Associations* listed online 1,900 automobile hobby and recreational groups at local, state, regional, national, and international levels.[53] Other voluntary groups such as the American Automobile Association were influential early on in shaping public policy towards improving streets and roads.[54]

Voluntary Association Membership

Tocqueville observed that the United States seemed to have much higher rates of voluntary association than England and his own country of France.[55] This observation has since been confirmed empirically.[56] Recently, Putnam pointed to a decline in membership levels in thirty-two national nonprofit membership groups with chapters around the country, including the PTA, that have traditionally played important roles in the United States.[57] Other scholars, especially Ladd, just as easily point to organizations that have had tremendous boosts in membership rosters. Parent-teacher organizations (PTOs), Ladd argues, are an example of why one should not look too narrowly at particular groups. He calls attention to the results of surveys of random 10 percent samples of all accredited private and public schools in two states, Connecticut and Kansas. While chapters in the national PTA constituted but one-fourth of the total, Ladd found a wide array of parent-teacher groups in each state that extended beyond PTA and PTOs. Both Ladd and Rotolo have called attention to an upswing in membership in school service groups from 1984 to 1994, as shown in the General Social Survey. And Ladd further cites surveys conducted by Gallup for Phi Delta Kappa in 1983, 1991, and 1994 that indicate a rise in the portion of parents of public school students who attended a PTA meeting and met with teachers or administrators about their child.[58]

Groups diversify. People can and do participate without formally joining an organization. Although the described drop in proportion of the association dollar that goes to clubs and fraternal organizations could support an argument that "joining" has declined, it is not clear that membership subscription changed much in the long term. The most appropriate interpretation of these various bits of data, when taken together, is that we are simply glimpsing the dynamic nature of voluntary association. Such observations are fragments of a relatively stable, but extremely dynamic, pattern. Evidence found in case studies or discrete national surveys prior to the early 1970s suggest that this is the case. A sampling of membership rates produced by area studies between 1924 and 1968, all conducted prior to the development of national trend data, varies widely from 32 to 86 percent (table 3.1). This array attests to the varied and dynamic nature of organized voluntary association, even though these studies are unique in their samples, research questions, methods, definitions, demographics, and points in time.

For twenty years, the General Social Survey (GSS) regularly monitored levels of self-reported membership in sixteen categories of voluntary organizations. This instrument registered a small increase in the number of respondents who reported *no* memberships at all—from 25 percent in 1974 to 30 percent in 1994. The portion of respondents who belonged to at least one voluntary association ranged from a low of 65 percent in 1991 to a high of 75 percent in 1974, averaging 70 percent. A fluctuation of five percentage points occurred in several instances between 1978 and 1989. The latest rate for belonging to at least one association, 70 percent in 1994, coincides with the average for the entire period.[59] Such narrow fluctuation around a mean does not support the thesis that membership in these types of groups declined. From a different perspective, Rotolo's curvilinear analysis of GSS trends shows an overall drop in membership levels from 1974 to 1984, followed by an increase after 1985.[60] Indeed, it seems that voluntary association membership remained relatively stable between 1974 and 1994, considering the dynamic quality of association.

GSS results are consistent with, or lower than, the measures taken at two discrete points in time by the World Values Survey. This survey found in 1981 that 72 percent of Americans said they belonged to at least one of ten kinds of voluntary associations. In 1990, 82 percent claimed membership in at least one of sixteen kinds of voluntary groups. Consistent with these findings,

Table 3.1

An Array of Voluntary Association Membership Rates (in rounded percentages)

One or More Memberships	Location/Year	Source
58%	Muncie, IN (1924)	Lynd and Lynd, *Middletown: A Study in American Culture,* 285-286, 527-528.
40	Yankee City, MA (1930-35)	W. Lloyd Warner, J. O. Low, Paul S. Lunt, and Leo Srole, *Yankee City* (New Haven, CT: Yale University Press, 1963), 107.
38	Westchester Co., NY (1931-32)	Lundberg et al., *Leisure: A Suburban Study,* 128-129, 136.
48	New York, NY (1934-35)	Mirra Komarovsky, "The Voluntary Associations of Urban Dwellers," *American Sociological Review* (December): 686-698.
52	Boulder, CO (1939)	Frederick A. Bushee, "Social Organization in a Small City," *American Journal of Sociology* 51 (1945): 217-226. (When church membership was included, it was 71%.)
50	Jonesville, IL (1940)	W. Lloyd Warner, *Democracy in Jonesville: A Study in Quality and Inequality* (New York: Harper and Row, 1949), 115-117.
64	New York (1944)	Harold Kaufman, "Prestige Classes in a New York Rural Community," in *Class, Status and Power,* edited by Reinhard Bendix and Seymour Martin Lipset (New York: Free Press, 1953), 190-203.
65	Bennington, VT (1947)	John C. Scott, Jr., "Membership and Participation in Voluntary Associations," *American Sociological Review* 22 (June 1957): 315-326.
64	Denver, CO (1949)	NORC reported in David L. Sills, "Voluntary Associations: Sociological Aspects," in *The International Encyclopedia of the Social Sciences* (New York: Macmillan and Free Press, 1968), 365.

One or More Memberships	Location/Year	Source
63%	Detroit, MI (1951)	Morris Axelrod, "Urban Structure and Social Participation," *American Sociological Review* 21 (February 1956): 13-18.
43	National (1952)	National Election Study (1952) cited in Frank R. Baumgartner and Jack L. Walker, "Survey Research and Membership in Voluntary Associations," *American Journal of Political Science* 32:4 (November 1988): 908-928.
64	National Survey Research Center (1952)	Murray Hausknecht, *The Joiners: A Sociological Description of Voluntary Association Membership in the United States* (New York: Bedminster, 1962), 21.
82	San Francisco, CA (1953)	Wendell Bell and Maryanne T. Force, "Social Structure and Participation in Different Types of Formal Associations," *Social Forces* 34:4 (May 1956): 345-350; Bell and Force, "Urban Neighborhood Types and Participation in Formal Associations," *American Sociological Review* 21 (February 1956): 25-34.
55	National AIPO (1954)	Hausknecht, *The Joiners,* 23.
36	National NORC (1955)	Hausknecht, *The Joiners,* 23.
32	Flint, MI (1957)	Basil G. Zimmer and Amos H. Hawley, "The Significance of Membership in Associations," *American Journal of Sociology* 65:2 (September 1959): 196-201.
73	Levittown, NJ (1958-60)	Herbert J. Gans, *The Levittowners: Ways of Life and Politics in a New Suburban Community* (New York: Pantheon, 1967), 52-68.
57	National (1959-60)	Almond and Verba, *The Civic Culture,* 264.

One or More Memberships	Location/Year	Source
80%	Nebraska (1961, 1965)	Nicholas Babchuk and Alan Booth, "Voluntary Association Membership: A Longitudinal Analysis," *American Sociological Review* 34 (February 1969): 31-45.
43	National NORC (1962)	Herbert H. Hyman and Charles R. Wright, "Trends in Voluntary Association Memberships of American Adults: Replication Based on Secondary Analysis of National Sample Surveys," *American Sociological Review* 36:2 (April 1971): 191-206.
62	National (1967)	Sidney Verba and Norman H. Nie, *Participation in America: Political Democracy and Social Equality* (Chicago, IL: University of Chicago Press, 1972), 41.
86	Benson, MN (1967)	Don Martindale and R. Galen Hanson, *Small Town and the Nation: The Conflict of Local and Translocal Forces* (Westport, CT: Greenwood, 1969), 76.
61	Indianapolis, IN (1968)	Marvin E. Olsen, *Participatory Pluralism: Political Participation and Influence in the United States and Sweden* (Chicago, IL: Nelson-Hall, 1982), 129.
82 (women) 90 (men)	Muncie, IN (1976)	Caplow et al., *Middletown Families,* 83-84.

AIPO = American Institute of Public Opinion
NORC = National Opinion Research Corporation

Wolfe found that 74 percent of a diverse sample of middle-class Americans in the mid-1990s belonged to at least one such group.[61] Seventy-nine percent of a sample of 3,000 from forty communities in twenty-nine states recently reported involvement in at least one of eighteen kinds of groups in the past year.[62] So it seems that at least seven of every ten adults hold at least one membership in a voluntary association.

It is important to note that the level of membership involvement in the United States is greatly enhanced by religious-related activities. Curtis et al. demonstrated this influence by removing the effect of religious organization memberships on the overall level of "belonging" to voluntary associations in the 1981 World Values Survey. The adjusted level of voluntary association membership went from 72 percent to 47 percent.[63] A similar difference exists in the 1990 World Values Survey in which the gross membership level of 82 percent fell to an adjusted 57 percent with the removal of the religious influence.[64]

Church Membership

The above reports, in which seven out of ten Americans belong to at least one voluntary organization, do not include membership in churches. In the United States, churches are also voluntary associations but are often treated separately.[65] The role of religion is historically identified with an exceptional demonstration of vitality in the United States.[66] Edmund Burke recognized it in the character of the American colonists:

> Religion, always a principle of energy, in this new people is no way worn out or impaired; and their mode of professing it is also one main cause of this free spirit. The people are Protestants, and of that kind which is the most adverse to all implicit submission of mind and opinion. This is a persuasion not only favorable to liberty, but built upon it.[67]

When Tocqueville visited mid-nineteenth-century American society he, too, found the role of religion forceful with its curious melding of national custom, patriotism, and individual practices.[68] "It must never be forgotten," he stressed, "that religion gave birth to Anglo-American society. In the United States, religion is therefore mingled with all the habits of the nation and all the feelings of patriotism, whence it derives a peculiar force." So deeply embedded was religion within the custom, values, opinion, law, and loyalties of Americans that it seemed to reign "by universal consent." It influenced the "manners.... [and the] intelligence of the people" due either to actual belief or from fear of being known as a nonbeliever.[69]

Statistics about religious observance began to appear around the time of Tocqueville's visit. From those early estimates, Lipset concluded there was "almost universal religious adherence by Americans in the 1830's."[70] Church membership was a different thing. McLoughlin estimated that 20 percent of the total population belonged to a church in the early 1800s.[71] Indeed, as Lipset remarks, "reasons why men might attend church and support a given denomination without becoming a member are not difficult to understand, given the conditions for membership which existed for most of the nineteenth century." These conditions included things like formal admission, a conversion experience, good works, an exemplary life, outreach work, and a successful probationary period.[72]

Finke and Stark's construction of a history of religious adherence throughout the nation's history suggests that religious influence grew greater as it became more embedded, more institutionalized. Their use of the term "religious adherence" combines standardized measures of church membership, attendance, Bureau of Census reports of numbers and seating capacities supplied by denominations, values of church properties, and reports from religious bodies. These articulated adherence rates rose from 17 percent in 1776 to 59 percent in 1952, slowing to 62 percent by 1980, a higher rate than contemporary church attendance statistics but lower than church membership figures based on self-reports.[73]

Membership numbers were elusive at the beginning of the twentieth century. In 1930, President Hoover's Research Committee on Social Trends estimated that, from 1906 to 1926, 55 percent of the population aged thirteen and above were enrolled in a church.[74] An early trend in church membership compiled from *Christian Herald* surveys for the period of 1926 through 1939-40 indicated that of those aged thirteen years and over, more than one-half belonged to church congregations.[75] At about the same time, Kolb and Brunner found, in their national sample of 140 agricultural villages, that 35 percent of the population in 1924, and 33 percent in years 1930 and 1936 were members of churches in these communities.[76] A 1926 estimate by C. Luther Fry of the Institute of Social and Religious Research was that 55 percent of American adults nationwide had joined a congregation, an overall estimate that absorbed regional differences of from 40 to 90 percent.[77] *The Yearbook of American Churches* estimated that 47 percent of the population belonged to a church in 1930, 49 percent in 1940, 57 percent in 1950, and 64 percent in 1960.[78]

In any attempt to assess church membership there is a persistent problem of church rosters that carry "inactives," of differences in definition of membership, and of exaggerated self-reports by church groups and survey respondents.[79] A fine example of the inflation of membership rolls comes from a case study of one small town where the tally of church membership rolls was higher than the official census count, which also has its problems.[80] These measuring difficulties are not resolved, but may be somewhat mitigated by nationwide data collection. Gallup implemented the first national survey on church membership in 1937. Seventy-three percent of respondents in that initial poll said they belonged to a church or synagogue. We have since learned that Gallup samples in the 1930s and 1940s were not strictly national due to underrepresentation of nonvoters, the less educated, and the lower socioeconomic groups.[81] Improved sampling techniques in the 1950s and 1960s coincide with some deflation in the Gallup trend and from 1976 to 2000 the membership rate averages 68 percent with only minor variation.[82] In yet another national survey repeated five times since 1987 by the Independent Sector and Gallup, results are consistent with the lengthier Gallup trend data. Sixty-five percent of participants in this survey reported belonging to a church or synagogue in 1987. Then, the percentage rose to 70 percent in 1989, stayed the same in 1991, held at 71 percent in 1993 and 1995, and dropped to 67 percent in 1999.[83] These self-reports suggest, as with other voluntary associations, that 7 out of 10 adults belong to a church congregation. World Values Survey findings suggest slightly higher membership rates of 77 percent in 1990 and 78 percent in 1995.[84]

Active Voluntary Association Membership

One dimension of voluntary association membership is the degree to which those who join an organization also actively participate. The discrepancy between membership and active participation was noted at least as early as 1923-25 in the study of 140 agricultural villages across the nation where the average attendance for social organizations was 34.3 percent of the membership.[85] A nationwide study by Almond and Verba in 1959-60 used having held an officer's position in a voluntary organization as a measure of active membership. Forty-six percent of Americans reported they had served in this way.[86] In 1967, Verba and Nie found that 40 percent of their nationwide survey of adults were active members in a voluntary association, in contrast to the 62 percent who merely joined without becoming active.[87]

The World Values Survey membership question also addresses this distinction between nominal and active membership in organizations. Thirty-one percent of Americans who reported membership in a voluntary association in the 1981 World Values Survey said they were active, in that they worked (unpaid) for an organization. In 1990, 46 percent reported active membership in voluntary associations. Although this appears to be an increase, the two years are not comparable due to variation in the wording of the question. The data do confirm, however, that the majority of members are inactive in their voluntary associations at any point in time. Baer et al. (2000) examined active membership in six types of groups that were included in both the 1981 and 1990 World Values Surveys—trade unions, religious or church organizations, professional, education/arts/music or cultural activities, political parties or groups, and youth work. Counting the number of nominal (inactive) and working (active) memberships in fifteen countries combined, there was no significant change in either one in these six kinds of groups. In the United States, which had the highest count of active memberships *and* of nominal memberships, the proportion of active memberships grew while nominal membership fell.[88] This analysis refutes the argument that active participation in groups declined.

Active Church Membership

Church attendance is an indicator of active membership in religious congregations. In 1930, the Research Committee on Social Trends discussed the questionable accuracy of church membership and attendance figures, due to reporting variations and the potential for inflated reporting. The Committee's unease about the reliability of self-reported church attendance was noted, but its conclusion was that "the proportion of the adult population belonging to church is a significant social index."[89] The lack of good information was a problem. Benson Landis, of the Federal Council of the Churches of Christ in America, remarked on the scarcity of good data and on low church attendance in 1935: "Only one body, the Congregational and Christian churches, has available systematic studies of church attendance covering a period of years...the figures indicate that 70 per cent of the seats in churches are *not* being used on Sunday morning...."[90] In a case study in Westchester County, New York, in the early 1930s, only 43 percent of families attended services each week yet Protestant church membership far exceeded church attendance: "So general is nonattendance that nineteen out of forty-five churches (42 percent) on which data were available had a larger adult membership than seating capacity.... The average membership of a church was 650 and the average seating capacity was 406. In one instance, a church counted 722 members and had room in the church for only 250."[91] These rates of church attendance from the 1930s are similar to current measures reporting that only three or four out of every ten American adults attend worship services each week (see below).

Lingering doubt about the veracity of the attendance data recently led Hadaway et al. to explore discrepancies in self-reported and actual church attendance. Using the case study method in which churchgoers, as well as the number of cars in the parking lot, were counted, these researchers concluded that actual attendance is probably half of what the Gallup national samples report, which averages 42 percent.[92] Gallup posits that this discrepancy is due to a wide range of regional variation and seasonal fluctuations in attendance, all of which is absorbed in nationwide sampling.[93] This seems a reasonable thesis, given the dynamic nature of association. One glimpse of this dynamic nature is seen in the rapid change in church attendance within a very short time frame found in Kolb and Brunner's longitudinal study of agricultural villages. In a brief six-year period between 1924 and 1930, researchers estimated that the average attendance per worship service fell roughly by 30 percent.[94] The decline occurred during a time in which rural churches experienced membership turnover, competition from town churches, and demise.[95]

Two sets of trend data, in addition to that of Gallup, report on attendance at worship services. Gallup has regularly monitored self-reported church attendance since 1939. The National Election Studies (NES) has tracked it since 1952, as has the National Opinion Research Center (NORC) since 1972. Between 1939 and 2000, an average of 42 percent of Americans told Gallup they had attended services within the past week.[96] Between 1972 and 1998, an average of 30 percent told NORC they had been to religious services

"Every week" or "Several times a week." However, only 24 percent in 1996 and 25 percent in 1998 reported this frequency of church attendance.[97] The question asked in the National Election Studies was changed after 1970, producing two separate, briefer trends. From 1952 to 1968 the question was "Would you say you go to church regularly, often, seldom, or never?" to which an average of 42 percent replied "regularly." After 1970, the question was changed to "Would you say you go to church/synagogue every week, almost every week, once or twice a month, a few times a year, or never?" Between 1972 and 1998, an average of 26 percent of respondents said "every week."[98] Notably, after 1970, the NES results are similar in stability to the NORC or Gallup attendance patterns, although it shows lower attendance levels than the other two.

Independent measures reinforce this profile of worship service attendance:

- The International Social Survey Program (ISSP), conducted by NORC in the United States, reported a rate of weekly church attendance by Americans in 1991 that, at 34 percent, fell between the NORC rate of 29 percent and the Gallup rate of 42 percent for that year.[99]
- The World Values Survey indicated that weekly or more frequent religious service attendance remained stable during the 1980s and 1990s. Forty-three percent in 1981, 44 percent in 1990, and 44 percent in 1997 said they attended church one or more times per week.[100]
- In 1999 and in 2000, 37 percent of participants in *Wall Street Journal*/NBC News polls reported attending worship services once a week or more often.
- Thirty-six of respondents to the Social Capital Community Benchmark Survey (2000) reported weekly or more frequent attendance at religious services.[101]

In summary, case studies reflect a wide array of local "joining" patterns, while national studies provide a general picture in which 7 out of 10 adults join voluntary associations. Self-reports are the same for churches, although the influence of religion in the United States makes it socially appropriate to claim that one is a church member. The active component of membership in voluntary groups and churches, however, is much smaller. Only three to four of these joiners claim to be active members of voluntary associations; this is also true for religious congregations. It is a relatively enduring profile of membership.

Volunteerism and Charitable Giving

Volunteering and charitable giving imply personal investments in the welfare of others, thereby reflecting Tocqueville's concept of "self-interest rightly understood."[102] As such they signal the health of civil society. A decline would suggest diminishing mutual concern on the part of Americans and, perhaps, indifference to the maintenance of democracy. For these reasons, any marked change in levels of volunteerism and charitable giving is important to note.

Volunteerism

Membership in voluntary groups and volunteerism are, at least in some respect, complementary. They blur in distinction in that taking part freely in an enterprise may or may not be the same as active membership in a group. Nevertheless, researchers recognize that volunteerism is associated with a broad spectrum of social activities, from which it is reasonable to infer that association stimulates association.[103] The leading way that volunteers learn about their subsequent activities is from someone asking them to volunteer, according to Independent Sector surveys. Most often the invitation comes from a friend; learning about volunteering activities through participation in an organization is a close second.[104] The Independent Sector research group finds that survey respondents who say they belong to organizations also volunteer more frequently:

> In 1995, over half of members of religious organizations volunteered compared with slightly more than one-third of nonmembers. Among the population reporting membership in another organization, more than seven out of ten volunteered compared to less than three out of ten among nonmembers.[105]

This same pattern was observed in the 1993 survey; and for members and nonmembers of religious organizations the same pattern has held since 1987 across five surveys. Moreover, the Independent Sector found the highest rates of church attendance and participation in socializing activities among those who spend the most hours doing volunteer work.[106]

The historical information on volunteerism levels in the United States is sketchy with a number of survey questions phrased differently at discrete points in time. I found at least eighteen of these questions about volunteering, usually asked only once or twice within the last thirty years by eight different polling firms. Three Current Population Surveys (CPS) conducted by the Bureau of Labor Statistics also asked unique questions about volunteering during the same time period; in comparison to most other surveys the resultant rates of volunteerism in the CPS were quite low, between 18 percent in 1965 and 24 percent in 1974.[107] Surveys that were taken as part of an Independent Sector Americans Volunteer project in 1981 and 1985 found rates of 52 and 48 percent, respectively.[108]

Three survey questions repeated over time imply growth in the percentage of the population that tells surveyors that it volunteers:

- Gallup and Princeton Survey Research Associates, in asking "Do you, yourself, happen to be involved in any charity or social service activities, such as helping the poor, the sick, or the elderly?" found an increase in affirmative responses from 26 percent in 1977 to 54 percent in 1995.[109]
- The same positive directional change was evident when 55 percent responded affirmatively to a question asked by ABC News/*Washington Post* in 1997: "In the last year or so I've done volunteer work for a church, charity, or community group," whereas only 44 percent gave a positive response when the same question was asked by CBS/*New York Times* in 1984.[110]
- Based on answers to Independent Sector/Gallup biennial surveys, the adult volunteer rate increased from 45 percent in 1987 to 56 percent in 1998.[111]

The Independent Sector report provides additional information for the period of 1987 to 1998 that underscores the dynamic quality of volunteerism. First, the number of volunteers increased by 36 percent—from 80 to 109 million volunteers. Second, there was a 1.8 percent rise in the total annual number of hours volunteered—from 19.55 to 19.9 million hours. Third, the average amount of time dedicated by one volunteer declined 1.2 hours per week from 4.7 to 3.5 hours per week.[112] In essence, during this brief twelve-year period, an increasing number of Americans produced an expanding output of volunteering, even though individual output dropped.

This vitality is consistent with the preference reflected in responses to a nationwide survey question asked by Maricopa Research in 1997. At that time, 69 percent thought that if someone wants to help the community it is better to volunteer for civic activities while only 19 percent felt it was better to get involved in politics and government.[113] This report is also consistent with the preferences that Almond and Verba found in 1959-60 when only 2 percent of a national sample of American adults preferred civic and political activities to other kinds of pursuits.[114] Similarly, 1998 GSS respondents were less likely to volunteer for political activity than for charitable, religious and church-related, and other kinds of work.[115]

If the volunteering activity by over half of the American adult population is captured in these data, there are other acts of caring behavior not systematically captured by survey questions. Ellis and Noyes suggest that volunteering is such a part of life in the United States that it goes unseen, yet "mobilizes enormous energy." Examples cited by these authors include donating blood, caroling the infirm, and appearing on fund-raising telethons.[116] Wuthnow found in a nationwide survey that many respondents who had acted compassionately toward someone in the previous year did not volunteer for an organization. This was true for 57 percent of those who had cared for an elderly relative in their home, 61 percent of those who stopped to help someone with car trouble, 64 percent who had visited an ill person in the hospital, et cetera.[117]

Charitable Giving

The Independent Sector/Gallup surveys administered biennially between 1987 and 1998 also allow closer scrutiny of charitable giving. They show that people are most likely to give to charity, as they are to volunteer, when in contact with one another for other reasons. For example, those who volunteer give more than nonvolunteers do to charity and those who belong to religious and secular groups give more than do nonjoiners.[118] In 1998, 70 percent of American households gave an average of $1,017, which amounts to 2.1 percent of household income. For the twelve-year period, an average of 72 percent of households gave an average of 2.2 percent of their income to charity. During this time, the portion of contributor households ranged from 69 to 75 percent and the percentage of household income ranged from 1.9 to 2.5.[119] Concurrently, the number of American households expanded more rapidly—by 16 percent between 1985 and 1998.[120] Thus, the pool of contributions to charity continues to grow due to the sheer number of households. We should also consider that the Independent Sector's reported average size of household contributions might be too conservative. The actual dollar amounts might be a third larger than reported each year.[121]

Long-term reports on charitable giving suggest that individual Americans habitually make this a priority, with some flex in the pattern. This is inferred from the following four perspectives. First, the climb in per capita contributions to charity has not faltered, increasing each decade between 1930 and 1990. The 1995 per capita contribution was $522 (in constant 1993 dollars), which was nearly six times greater than the 1930 per capita contribution of $88 (also in constant 1993 dollars).[122] Second, individuals continue to provide the largest share of giving. Between 1960 and 2000, private individuals accounted for 80 percent of all charitable contributions, according to the American Association of Fund-Raising Counsel.[123] Third, the percentage of personal income devoted to charitable giving between 1960 and 1990 ranged from 2.29 (in 1963) to 1.77 (in 1978) and averaged 2.0 percent, showing both elasticity and constancy. Fourth, levels of private contributions as a portion of national income ranged narrowly between 2.77 percent in 1990 and 2.07 percent in 1978 and 1979, again demonstrating some elasticity within a narrow band of constancy.[124]

Sociologist Christopher Jencks concluded on the basis of his research on philanthropy that none of the elements of giving are fixed. The elasticity of giving generally reflects the perception of needs—of one's own family and of the need of others—and the moral judgments about how to make tradeoffs between them.[125] It seems that Americans remain faithful to this practice and process.

Citizen Participation and Activism

Civic-political participation is not popular among Americans. It came last in the leisure time preferences reported in a 1959-60 study of political culture when respondents were asked an open-ended question about preferences in leisure-time activity apart from family and work-related pursuits. Participation in civic and political pursuits were preferred by only 2 percent of Americans—preceded in popularity by hobbies and sports (70 percent), cultural (33 percent), religious (20 percent), social (18 percent), charitable and welfare (8 percent), other group interest activity (3 percent) or doing nothing (3 percent).[126] This low preference increases the significance of efforts that are made to communicate, to join forces, and/or to achieve an end through participation in community and public affairs. In this section, I have looked for change in three kinds of citizen involvement—electoral behavior, community participation, and activism.

Electoral Behavior

National Election Studies (NES) have monitored self-reports of activities related to the presidential and midterm election processes since 1952. The intent of these studies is to learn about expectations, attitudes, interests, perceptions, opinions, ways of getting information, and levels of awareness that Americans maintain about politics, elections, and government. This continuous research, fiscally underwritten and designated by the National Science Foundation as a national resource, attempts to improve the measurement of these phenomena while remaining sensitive to change and continuity.[127]

NES respondents are asked how interested they are in and how much they care about election matters. Those who professed the highest level of interest in political campaigns shrank from 37 percent to 21 percent between 1952 and 1998, while the ranks of the somewhat interested expanded by 14 percent.[128] A majority claims to care a good deal which party wins the presidential election. This majority grew from 67 to 78 percent during the latter half of the century. Fewer cared very much or pretty much about the outcome of Congressional elections in 1998 (52 percent) than they did in 1970 (65 percent), however.[129] Thus, sentiment about electoral politics is somewhat less avid and more focused on presidential campaigns today than earlier in the century.

Making an effort to influence others about how to vote in presidential election years is one activity that has consistently engaged the largest portion of NES respondents, ranging from 27 to 37 percent between 1952 and 1996, but differs not at all between the two discrete points in time (see table 3.2). The same effort to influence persisted in midterm election years, as well, ranging more widely between 15 and 27 percent, but the positive difference

Table 3.2

Involvement in Civic Activities (in percentages)

From Verba et al., *Voice and Equality*			
	1967	**1987**	**absolute change**
Voted regularly in presidential elections	66	58	- 8
Voted in local elections	47	35	- 12
Contacted local official about issue	14	24	10
Contributed to party, candidate	13	23	10
Contacted state, national official about issue	11	22	11
Worked on local problem with others	30	34	4
Persuaded others how to vote	28	32	4
Belonged to a political club	8	4	- 4
Belonged actively to community problem-solving group	31	34	3
Worked for party, candidate	26	27	1
Attended political meeting or rally	19	19	0
Formed group to help solve local problem	14	17	3
Contacted local official, particularized	7	10	3
Contacted state and national official, particularized	6	7	1
			Total = +26
From National Election Studies			
in presidential years . . .	**1952**	**1996**	
Tried to influence others how to vote	27	27	0
Gave money to help campaign	4	7	3
Attended political meeting	7	5	- 2
Worked for party or candidate	3	2	1
			Total = 0
in midterm years . . .	**1962**	**1998**	
Tried to influence others how to vote	18	19	1
Gave money to help campaign	9	7	- 2
Attended political meeting	8	5	- 3
Worked for party or candidate	4	2	- 2
			Total = - 6

	1956	**1996**	
Wore campaign button or put sticker on car	16	10	-6
From Roper Organization			
	1973	**1995-96***	
Wrote congressman or senator	15	15	0
Attended political rally or speech	10	7	-3
Attended public meeting on town or school affairs	23	17	-6
Held or ran for political office	1	1	0
Served on committee for local organization	10	8	-2
Served as officer of club or organization	10	8	-2
Wrote letter to newspaper	5	8	3
Signed petition	34	31	-3
Worked for political party	6	3	-3
Made speech	5	5	0
Wrote article for magazine or newspaper	2	3	1
Served as group member	4	6	2
			Total = -13
No—None of these	50	56	+6

Source: Compiled from Verba et al., *Voice and Equality*, 72; National Election Studies; Roper Center at University of Connecticut, Public Opinion Online and data provided courtesy of Roper Starch Worldwide.

* average of ten measures taken from July through June.

between 1962 and 1998 is insignificant. The percentage of Americans who proclaimed their presidential candidate preference by wearing a button or displaying a bumper sticker or a sign fell from 16 percent in 1956 to 10 percent in 1996. The remaining three behaviors—giving money to a party or a candidate, attending political meetings, and working for a party or candidate—are used by less than 10 percent of the population in any given election year.[130] This pattern has been the same for four decades.

Voting turnout, per self-report in National Election Studies, averaged 74 percent during presidential and 56 percent in midterm election years between 1952 and 1996, with little variation. However, self-reports on voting are generally higher than the actual turnout to vote and the NES rates are especially exaggerated.[131] Between 1967 and 1987, Verba and Nie found that self-reports on voting declined in both local (47 to 35 percent) and presidential (66 to 58 percent) elections.[132] A similar trend in self-reporting is confirmed in Current Population Reports where the portion of the eligible population that reported voting in presidential years between 1964 and 1996 declined from 69 to 54 percent and from 49 to 45 percent in midterm election years.[133]

Although the discrepancy narrows, actual voter turnout rates remain still lower than these declining self-reports. Voter turnout for the presidential election was 62 percent in 1952 and fell to 50 percent in 2000. Even lower, the midterm election turnout dropped from 42 percent in 1954 to 33 percent in 1998.[134]

In sum, these data suggest generally that one-half of Americans vote and less than one-third attempt to sway others in how to vote during presidential election years. Furthermore, the decline in voting that occurred over a period of forty-four years is the only large change in electoral behaviors. A consistently small portion of the population, 15 percent, engages in other miscellaneous electoral behaviors.

Community Participation

In a comparison between 1967 and 1987 of ways that citizens participate, five changes are particularly notable: growth in working collectively on community problems; increased contact of public officials; a rise in issue-related contacts of public officials in contrast to particularized reasons; marked growth of contributions to parties and candidates; and decline in the already small percentage who belonged to a political club (table 3.2).[135] The increases in collective effort and contact with officials at all levels of authority, particularly of an issue-related nature, surely have greater salience for civil society than the growth in dollar contributions. Most important, the gross positive change implies a citizenry more engaged in these civic matters in 1987 than two decades earlier (table 3.2).

Roper Organization surveys from 1973 until the mid-1990s repeatedly inquired about participation in twelve kinds of civic activities (table 3.2). One-half (50 percent) of Americans consistently reported at least one such activity through 1991; that subsequently began to fall between 1992 and 1995. The decision by a weighty number of Americans to eschew these activities is consistent with Almond and Verba's earlier findings that civic activity is a very low-order preference. Nevertheless, actual civic participation was much higher than might be predicted from the ordering of leisure activity preferences.

The most remarkable change in the Roper trend was a drop in attending a public meeting on town or school affairs—23 to 17 percent. Attending a political rally or speech, working for a political party, and signing petitions waned. No significant difference occurred in writing one's representative or senator, making a speech, and in having held or run for political office. Small increases occurred among those who sent a letter to the paper, wrote an article for a magazine or newspaper, or belonged to some group interested in better government. Among the activities inquired about, three were clearly preferred. One was signing a petition, which one-third of the respondents reported doing (34 percent in 1973; 31 percent in 1995-96). A second was attending a public meeting on town or school affairs, which declined. A third was writing one's legislative representatives, engaged in by 15 percent of American adults without variation. Ten percent or less of the survey respondents engaged in each of the remaining nine activities.[136]

Subsequent, independent measures of these or similar activities reflect no decline in civic-political involvement. Of seven independent surveys administered between 1995 and 2000, six expressly ask about attendance at a "public meeting on town or school affairs" and one asks about attending a "public meeting." Each survey registers equivalent or higher rates of participation than did the Roper data for two decades. The same vitality shines through recent independent inquiries about contacting elected officials, serving on committees for a local organization, serving as an officer of a club or organization, belonging to a group interested in better government, attending a political rally or speech, holding or running for political office, working for a political party, signing a petition, writing a letter to the paper, and making a speech.[137] This most recent information about civic participation confirms that it is sustained, rather than declining.

In sifting through this evidence, the important point is that Americans continue to get involved in community affairs despite a long-standing ambivalence about the costs of time and effort. About one-half of the adult population *did* involve themselves in public affairs, despite clear preferences for nonpolitical leisure pursuits. Obviously, much resistance to citizen duty and obligation was overcome throughout the two decades, with only a slight decrease in this behavior. Americans continue to be the pragmatists, described by Tocqueville, who understand the nation's well being is inextricably linked to the welfare of the individual. Americans need not stop exhorting each other to be good citizens, but can also celebrate their will to sustain public-spiritedness.

Holding Local Elective Office

Of the many ways to take part in local affairs, an important one is to hold elective office. Due to the diminished number of school districts, the total number of local elective offices fell between 1957 and 1992 by 4 percent—from 514,200 to 493,800. Although there was an increase in general purpose offices by 11 percent and a 137 percent increase in offices generated by special districts, the bottom line is that in 1992 fewer Americans were involved as locally elected officials. However, the downward trend halted after 1977 and the number has since risen.[138] For every local elected official, there are others also participating as contending candidates, campaigners, and supporters. In a 1962 study of city council and mayoral elections in cities of 25,000, for example, an average of 2.3 candidates ran for each of 3,000 seats,

Figure 3.2

Three Kinds of U.S. Political Activism, 1948-1982

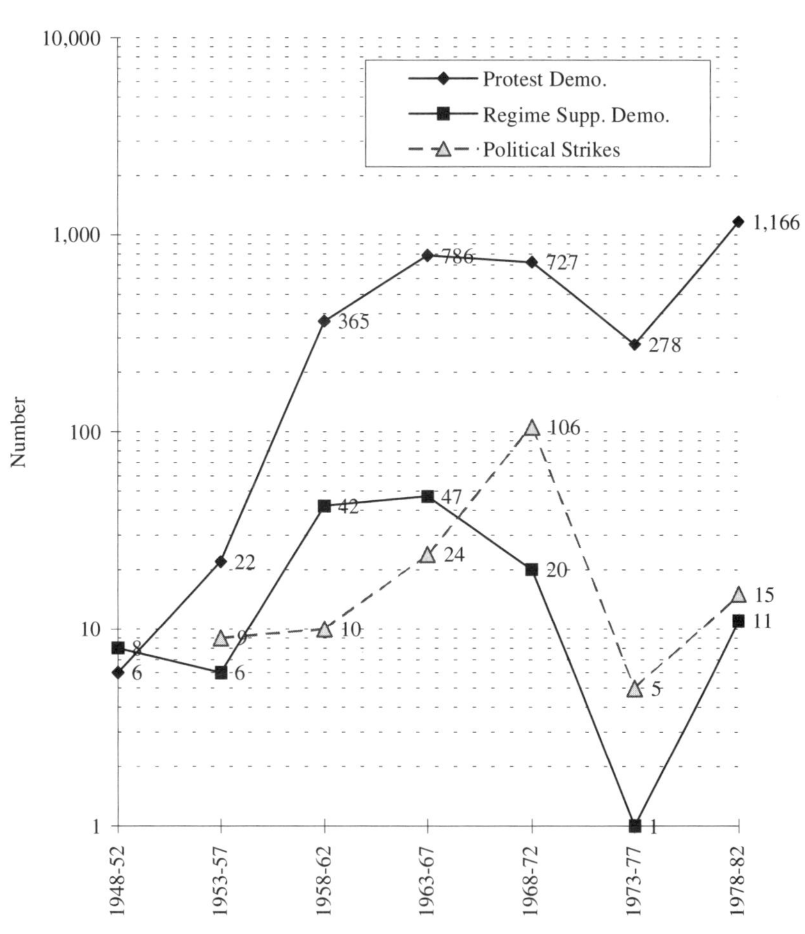

Source: Taylor and Jodice, *World Handbook of Political and Social Indicators.*

which means that over one-fourth of the affected population made themselves available to hold public office.[139]

Activism

The appearance of citizen initiatives on state ballots, although state laws vary, is yet another way to gauge change in citizen involvement. The initiatives filed between 1904 and 1998 total 1,900. Thirty-nine percent of these were filed during the first thirty-six years (1904-39); 23 percent were filed in the next thirty-six-year period (1940-75), and 38 percent were filed in the last twenty-four years (1976-98). The post-1976 acceleration has slowed in the past six years. Outside influences that affect this rate include fiscal backing by interest groups, state laws that make the process more difficult to use, fear of litigation, and election targeting strategies.[140]

Table 3.3

Activism in the United States, 1974 through 1995 (in rounded percentages)

Have . . .		Year	Percentage	Would Never Do That
Signed a Petition				
	Political Action Study	1974	58	-
	World Values Survey	1981	61	12
	World Values Survey	1990	70	4
	World Values Survey	1995	73	8
Joined in a Boycott				
	Political Action Study	1974	15	-
	World Values Survey	1981	14	45
	World Values Survey	1990	17	34
	World Values Survey	1995	19	37
Attended a Lawful Demonstration				
	Political Action Study	1974	11	-
	World Values Survey	1981	12	44
	World Values Survey	1990	15	38
	World Values Survey	1995	16	41
Joined an Unofficial Strike				
	Political Action Study	1974	2	-
	World Values Survey	1981	3	74
	World Values Survey	1990	4	62
	World Values Survey	1995	4	69
Occupied a Building or Factory				
	Political Action Study	1974	2	-
	World Values Survey	1981	2	83
	World Values Survey	1990	2	77
	World Values Survey	1995	2	83

Source: Compiled from Barnes et al., *Political Action*, 1979, 537-596 for 1974 data; World Values Study Group. WORLD VALUES SURVEY. N in 1974 = 1,719; N in 1981 = 2,325; N in 1990 = 1,839; N in 1995 = 1,542.

Among less conventional political acts documented by Taylor and Jodice for thirty-five years, from 1948 through 1982, protest demonstrations were the dominant mode of action (figure 3.2). After an increase in incidence of protests, regime support demonstrations, and political strikes in the 1950s and 1960s, support demonstrations and strikes subsided. Protest demonstrations also slowed only to rebound between 1978 and 1982 to reach their highest rate of occurrence.[141]

Signing petitions and influencing policy and decision making by taking part in boycotts, lawful demonstrations, unofficial strikes, and sit-ins were similar in a 1974 Political Action Study to the rates of participation reported in the 1981 World Values Survey (table 3.3).[142] During the 1980s, the only significant change in reported behavior from the first World Values Survey measure was the increase in those who had signed a petition, from 61 percent in 1981 to 70 percent in 1990. Shifts in attitude about these actions were the most noticeable. Those who believed they would *never* sign a petition, join in a boycott, attend a lawful demonstration, join an unofficial strike, or occupy a building or factory declined in number, indicating a tapering off of resistance to these actions during the 1980s.[143]

Informal Association

Informal aspects of association are less visible, but powerful and omnipresent. Lundberg and Lawsing wrote in 1937 that these "least tangible social units because of their informal, transitory, private and frequently secret character, as well as their occasionally illicit and sometimes illegal nature," have a "profound influence in determining especially the functioning of the more formal structures" and are "quite basic both to understanding and intelligent control of the community."[144]

One of the more observable characteristics of associational life accented by case study is the capacity to shift between formality and informality. In contrast to the late 1890s, researchers in Middletown found that "leisure was becoming more passive, more formal, more organized, more mechanized, and more commercialized" in 1925.[145] "This trend toward greater organization appearing in so many leisure pursuits culminates in the proliferating system of clubs which touches the life of the city in all its major activities."[146] Upon revisiting Middletown during the Great Depression, the Lynds found associational life reminiscent of the late 1800s, with "more informality and less expenditure in their social life."[147] Again, when researchers returned to Middletown forty years later, in 1976, they found associational life much richer and fuller than in 1935. Organized social life was prevalent. The ratio of churches to people had increased, along with attendance. Clubs and associations had proliferated. Eighty-two percent of women and 90 percent of men were members of at least one organization.[148]

An important ethnographic documentation of informal social activity that hints at its ubiquity comes from Yankee City, an old New England community. During a three-year stay there in the 1930s, investigators identified over 22,000 informal associations and cliques in the community of 17,000.[149] Some would fit Smith's definition of grassroots entities (see chapter 2), of which he estimates only 10 percent are detected by researchers. Other gatherings that would be classified as informal social activity include small groups that gather for utilitarian reasons—like the neighbors in the rural area of my childhood who pooled resources to thresh everyone's grain *or* our modern neighbors who "crime watch" for one another *or* those of us who work to clean up the trash that clutters the byways. Also part of this informal facet of association are the friends who bike together, meet over coffee to discuss a book, meet regularly in a chat room, or commute to work together.

Time spent with friends and in socializing is a persistent preference over organized association. For participants in Sorokin and Berger's 1935 time study, 75 percent of association was informal.[150] In the Multinational Comparative Time-Budget Research Project of 1965, 84 percent of time spent by Americans in socially oriented activity was in conversation, visiting with friends, and socializing; the remainder was in organized associational activity. The 1975 Americans' Use of Time study found these informal activities absorbed just 77 percent of socially oriented time; in 1985, the proportion was 83 percent.[151] Clearly, informal voluntary association absorbs a significant part of leisure time spent with others.

Hansen's study of the diaries of 170 working people who lived in pre-Civil War New England found that visiting was not only ubiquitous, but a medium for the "fluidity of activity where friendship and socializing meld into political discussion, which stimulates political action...the means by which people constructed and maintained communities, mobilized social movements, and expressed moral sensibilities." Sociability, Hansen concluded, not only

> spans and mediates the public and private spheres.... It [also] obliterates any notion of their mutual exclusivity because visitors traversed households as well as outdoor common spaces, often cooperated in productive work while socializing, and discussed each other's moral behavior in addition to national and local politics.[152]

Gallaher recorded 400 primary cliques and visiting relationships in Plainville, Missouri, in the mid-1950s. In this small community of 275 households he found that aside from the usual functions of socializing, pursuing common interests, and helping one another, informal association had an impressive record for spreading information: "Plainville clique groups so effectively disseminate rumor and fact that in a matter of hours news literally blankets the community." This seemed especially useful in expressing and enlisting support for one's opposition to change, Gallaher observed.

> [A]ppeal through personal relationships, especially those mediated by kinship, friendship, or religious bonds, [was] the most effective way to register opposition....The importance of personal relationships in the culture change process derives partly from the fact that the most effective communicative channels in the community are intimately linked to informal friendship cliques.[153]

As does Hansen, Gallaher provides a glimpse of how the apolitical and the political are integrated via informal association. Yet another variable, relatively unexplored, is the quality of the relationship, which seemed to be a factor in a study of 541 members of a local unit of the American Contract Bridge League. Erickson and Nosanchuk found that 53 percent frequently or often discussed politics with their regular bridge partners. Due to league rules, however, such discussion occurred away from the bridge table. If the relationship did not carry beyond the game itself, there was no discussion of politics.[154]

The way in which Americans allocate social time across family, friends, and neighbors varies according to place, time, or situation. Visiting with friends has been a persistent, albeit small (from 4 to 10 percent), preference among twelve to fifteen kinds of leisure activity inquired about by Gallup between 1938 and 1998.[155] Of all the social contacts reported by Sorokin and Berger, in 1935, the largest portion, 36 percent, was made with friends. Family members, at 24 percent, were the second most frequent class of contacts made.[156] Axelrod's research of a cross-section of the Detroit area population in 1951 found that people spent most of their visiting time with relatives. At least once a week 49 percent visited with relatives, 28 percent with friends, and 29 percent with neighbors.[157] In the mid-1950s, Reiss also found that samples of urban, rural farm, and rural nonfarm men in Tennessee interacted most often with family members. Friends were in second place for urbanites, but rural participants interacted least often with friends.[158] Gans found a different profile in the planned community of Levittown, first inhabited from 1958 to 1960. Many Levittowners, with the move to this new suburban locale, were distanced from relatives and family. Thus, the people with whom they socialized most were neighbors (33 percent), people they met in organizations (24 percent), and people they met in church (13 percent). Compared to the amount of visiting with neighbors in their previous home, 50 percent said they did more of it in Levittown and 25 percent did just as much visiting with neighbors as before.[159] Among the most primary of social interactions, then, informal patterns may vary according to circumstances.

The General Social Survey (GSS) data show little change in the portion of Americans who engaged in social evenings with friends from "almost daily" to "several times a month"—40 percent in 1974 and 43 percent in 1998, further confirming the persistence of informal association and of the influence of friendship. Socializing this often with neighbors declined from 44 to 32 percent. Instead, Americans who socialized with neighbors "about once a year" or "never" rose from 28 to 38 percent. This is consistent with Fisher's conclusion that the necessity to "neighbor" declines where people no longer must rely on proximity for social interaction.[160] While friends strengthened their position in socializing and neighbors lost theirs, according to GSS trends, relatives held the strongest position across time—attesting to the status of primary relationships. About one-half (52 percent) of the survey participants spent social evenings with relatives "almost daily" or at least "several times a month" in 1998, as did 58 percent in 1974.[161]

Placing the GSS trends in perspective, recent surveys indicate that Americans continue to value and to practice neighboring.

- Seventy-two percent of Social Capital Community Benchmark Survey (SCCBS) respondents reported talking with or visiting neighbors at least several times a month, if not more often. Four out of five said that people in their neighborhood give them a sense of community.[162]
- Majorities in surveys sponsored by Shell feel they personally know their neighbors well.
- Three-fourths of Shell respondents are very or fairly comfortable going to a next-door neighbor for emergency help.
- Children and family, home improvement, local issues, and weather are favorite topics of discussion among neighbors. [163]
- Four out of ten in an NBC News, *Wall Street Journal* Poll feel they live in neighborhoods where people know each other well.[164]
- Sixty-eight percent of those polled by the *New York Times* say it is very important to them to be a good neighbor.[165]
- Asked to look back a hundred years ago, only 14 percent of the NBC News, *Wall Street Journal* respondents wished to revive that previous form of community and ties to neighbors. The largest majority, 38 percent, felt the emphasis should return to a family-centered, in lieu of a work-centered, life.
- Zogby International asked a national sample of adults to look forward to assess how equipped we are to confront problems of a new century with community life, neighbors, and friends. Forty-four percent felt great confidence and 45 percent had some confidence.[166] Reflected through the lens of public opinion, the institution of neighboring appears to be relatively fit even as it makes the adjustments indicated by the General Social Survey.

Sociologist Robert Wuthnow's study of the small group movement in the United States reports that 40 percent of adult Americans participate regularly in support groups, which meet once to four times a month for an average of ninety minutes per session. These small groups flourish in a context of social connectedness. Sixty percent of participants in these small, informal groups are there because someone they knew invited them. Forty-three percent indicated that the reason for being involved came from hearing about it through their place of worship. One-third (33 percent) reported that it was from being in a similar group before. And 11 percent used small groups to get acquainted in their community.[167] Such groups are among those associational phenomena that Putnam thinks may not facilitate the kind of civic engagement that constitutes "people's connections with the life of their communities."[168] There would be reason for this concern if informal association remained fixed and focused only on private matters, rather than extending to matters of broader interest.

Wuthnow acknowledges the concern but recognizes, as Hansen does, that the political and the apolitical tend to merge:

> Even self-help movements concerned primarily with personal addictions have increasingly recognized the relevance of tax laws governing medical claims for mental-health treatment to their objectives, or the value of lobbying for substance-abuse laws, or the necessity of giving legal testimony as expert witnesses.[169]

Tocqueville also recognized this blending of political and nonpolitical when he posited that the civic and political aspects of association were interrelated and that they stimulated one another: "Civil associations...facilitate political association; but, on the other hand, political association singularly strengthens and improves associations for civil purposes."[170] Likewise, the interface of informal and incorporated association has been confirmed. For example, in Providence, Rhode Island, in the late 1800s, men's clubs suddenly multiplied at a great rate. Gilkeson found "[p]ractically all were the products of the formalization of casual, or desultory, patterns of sociability."[171] A positive relationship between formal and informal association was also found in Chicago communities in 1967-68.[172] This is evident, too, in the Detroit Area studies in 1951 where a positive correlation between formal and informal association was identified.[173] The group of friends who originally met to watch *Monday Night Football* but did not wish to disband at season's end, so they formed a successful investment club demonstrates it. Now they "educate themselves and their families about finance while building a growing circle of friends."[174]

The substantive nature of time spent with friends seems to be changing, with the result that politics are discussed more often.

- In 1941, a mere 16 percent of men and 8 percent of women in an American Institute of Public Opinion poll said that politics and government were most often the topic of discussion among their friends and acquaintances.[175]
- When Americans were asked in 1960 by the National Opinion Research Center to what source they would turn to find out more about a complex public issue, 24 percent said they would do so with friends, neighbors, relatives, co-workers, and other named persons.[176]

- Sixty-four percent of Americans in a 1974 Political Action Study discussed politics "often" with friends.[177]
- Forty percent of Americans, in answering questions about local community involvement in 1980, reported they frequently discussed local issues with friends and neighbors.[178] Forty-five percent of interviewees told Hart Teeter in 1999 that there was a fair amount or a great deal of talk at home about government and politics when they were growing up.[179]

Two measures confirm movement toward more frequent discussion of politics with family and friends:

- In the National Election Studies (NES), when asked in 1984 if they ever discuss politics with family or friends, 67 percent of respondents replied "yes," a rate that climbed to 78 percent in 1994. Thirty-four percent said such discussion occurred every day or 3 to 4 times a week in 1994; 31 percent gave the same reply in 1984.
- A World Values Survey question regarding discussion among friends asks, "When you get together with your friends, would you say you discuss political matters frequently, occasionally or never?" A majority, in 1981 (54 percent), 1990 (56 percent), and 1995 (57 percent) said they have such discussions occasionally. The increase in replies of "frequently" between 1981 and 1990, from 11 to 14 percent, was significant, but even more so was the drop in those who said "never"—from 35 percent to 29 percent. This change parallels the one found in the National Election Studies, which shows that only 33 percent of those surveyed did *not* discuss politics with family or friends in 1984; a number that fell to 22 percent in 1994.

Responses to a series of questions asked in the 1987 General Social Survey (GSS) support the picture portrayed by NES and World Values Survey results. Eighty-one percent of respondents surveyed said they had discussed politics, with varying frequency, with those with whom they tended to discuss important matters; 35 percent said this kind of discussion occurred almost daily or at least weekly. Further evidence that public matters have expanded as a topic of discussion since 1941 is found in a 1995 Gallup survey. One-half of the sample was asked where and how often they get their news; 58 percent said it was through discussions with friends or family that occurred very or somewhat regularly. Fifty-three percent of the second half of the sample, that was given different response gradients, said such discussions happened daily or several times a week. This discussion of news and information with friends and family was very or extremely important to 51 percent of all respondents.[180] The 1996 Survey of American Political Culture found that 63 percent often or sometimes discuss "politics and politicians with other people."[181] And finally, 52 percent of national adult parents of children aged 8-17 told Pew Research they regularly or sometimes discuss politics with their progeny.[182]

In sum, informal social interaction is important to Americans. The priority given to socializing and spending time with friends and family does not waver, but flexibly adapts to social conditions. Nor does informal association inevitably lead to isolation from or withdrawal from public matters. On the contrary, its coverage is ubiquitous. Informal interaction can effectively carry information, influence social change, integrate the public and the private, fuse the apolitical and the political, and prompt political action. This makes informal association, as a significant site of attachment and community production, an extremely important element of a self-sustaining civil society.

This conclusion is consistent with that reached by other scholars in regard to informal relationships. Axelrod described them as the points at which common attitudes, norms, and actions are formed and organized.[183] Hunter saw such interactions as significant in creating attachments between the individual and society.[184] Berger and Neuhaus make the poignant point that it is in the ordinary matters that people develop a clear idea of their interests and political will.[185]

Summary and Discussion of Findings

Associational life occurs within the confines of available time and is shaped by discretionary spending. It is further constrained by preference for solitary over nonsolitary leisure pursuits. Roughly, and it varies with life circumstances, Americans dedicated a third of their free time to voluntary association through much of the last century. Discretionary spending on associational activity expanded. Although changes occurred in the way that the growing association dollar is spent, one priority stayed the same. The portion that goes to religious and welfare causes remained the largest. It also expanded from 38¢ to 45¢ of the association dollar over the latter two-thirds of the twentieth century. Americans increasingly invest less in spectator amusements and more in active, participatory kinds of leisure that expand the opportunity for social connectedness. On the other hand, spending on clubs and membership fell.

On a continuum of formal to informal modes of association, membership subscription is a formal act in which shared commitment is affirmed, thus securing resources for an organization as well as meeting whatever needs and motivations for joining that an individual might have. The example of Middletown demonstrates that association varies along the formal-informal continuum to meet societal circumstances. Trends in membership in voluntary groups monitored by the General Social Survey for the two decades that ended in 1994, and confirmed by independent measures, narrowly fluctuated. Our information, however, is too limited to say whether membership as a mode of association is used more or less than twenty-five years ago. Membership roster data have been collected and used to support either argument. Some of what we know about membership has not changed. We know that religious adherence existed long before formal congregational membership became routine and that religion and voluntary association membership is closely intertwined in the history of the United States. We also know that church membership levels gained momentum into the twentieth century and do not seem to have altered appreciably after the mid-1970s. We know from attempts to measure membership levels prior to the collection of nationwide trend data that the organized associational life of Americans is varied and dynamic. And we know that throughout much of this century, at least, it is more likely that an American will join an association or a church than to actively participate in its activities.

Informal association is a crucial, ubiquitous phenomenon that helps to blend the apolitical with the political at a fundamental point where individuals connect and process information. Historically, it is a mode of social connectedness that absorbs a large proportion of socially oriented time. During the last two decades informal association shifted away from neighboring activity. Socializing with relatives remained strong; spending time with friends remained a persistent, and seemingly greater, preference. At the same time, politics were increasingly discussed with family and friends, a locus of strong ties.[186]

Volunteering, charitable giving, and civic activity emanate from either formal group membership or informal affiliation, since association perpetuates itself. Volunteerism is an activity that seems to have become more salient with greater output of volunteer time by an increasing proportion of Americans over the last two decades. As suggested by the expanding portion of the association dollar that goes to religious and welfare causes, charitable giving has been a priority for Americans during the latter two-thirds of this century. Individuals and private households, as opposed to corporations and foundations, do most of the giving. Per capita charitable giving increased with each decade. As a percentage of personal income, charitable contributions fluctuated narrowly around a mean, showing some adjustment to perceived need. The proportion of household income that went to charitable gifts also rose with each decade, although the actual size of the contribution fell slightly, countered by a faster rate of growth in number of households.

Americans usually prefer to do other things with their free time, rather than engage in civic and community affairs. This is not a new development, nor is it unique to this society. After 1952, voting declined, but no other marked change is apparent in the miscellaneous electoral behaviors tracked by the National Election Studies. Two different sets of trend data about civic participation cover different, overlapping periods of time—1967 to 1987 and 1973 to 1995-96. The first reflects an overall enhanced level of citizen involvement; the second shows a small overall decrease in involvement in the activities inquired about. Whether there was significant change in the level of civic and community activity is inconclusive, although additional and more recent information confirms that Americans continue to fulfill public responsibilities. That nearly one-half of Americans participate in the few civic activities recorded is especially significant in light of opposing activity preferences.

The opportunity to hold local elective office shrank after 1952, but recovered somewhat. Filings of citizen petitions grew at varying rates throughout the twentieth century, accelerating after 1976. Between 1948 and 1982, the number of protest demonstrations climbed, outnumbering political strikes and regime support demonstrations whose numbers fell in the 1970s. Overall, from 1974 to 1995, the number of Americans who engaged in political activism increased. The most notable change was the decline during the 1980s of those who adamantly would *not* take part in petitions, boycotts, lawful demonstration, unofficial strikes, and occupations of buildings. Obviously, resistance to activism of this sort lessened.

In conclusion, investments of personal resources in voluntary association appear to be embedded in the American tradition. Americans *do* get involved, despite their resistance to citizen duty and obligation. This is public-spiritedness, for which Tocqueville offers an explanation. It is in keeping with a pragmatic understanding that the nation's well being is inextricably of benefit to the welfare of the individual, who is also aware that the government is of one's own making. In Tocqueville's terminology, it is "self-interest, rightly understood."[187]

Notes

1. Alexis de Tocqueville, *Democracy in America* (New York: Vintage Books, 1945), II:109-111, 149; I:252.
2. Sidney Verba, Kay Lehman Schlozman, and Henry E. Brady, *Voice and Equality: Civic Voluntarism in American Politics* (Cambridge, MA: Harvard University Press, 1995), 81-84, 535-536, 538-549.
3. Contrasted nations share similar interest aggregation profiles as developed by Gabriel A. Almond, G. Bingham Powell, Jr., and Robert J. Mundt, *Comparative Politics: A Theoretical Framework* (New York: HarperCollins, 1993), 135-139, and Gabriel A. Almond and G. Bingham Powell, Jr., *Comparative Politics: System, Process, and Policy*, 2d ed. (Boston, MA: Little, Brown, 1978), 201-213; 233-240. Interest aggregation profiles are rough, the authors caution, and may vary with issues.
4. Elizabeth Hann Hastings and Philip K. Hastings, eds., *Index to International Public Opinion, 1981-1982* (Westport, CT: Greenwood, 1983), 617-620.
5. Albert O. Hirschman, *Exit, Voice, and Loyalty* (Cambridge, MA: Harvard University Press, 1970), 106-112.
6. Kathleen Gerson, C. Ann Stueve, and Claude S. Fischer, "Attachment to Place" in Claude S. Fischer, ed., *Networks and Places* (New York: Free Press, 1977), 139-161.

7. George A. Lundberg, Mirra Komarovsky, and Mary Alice McInerny, *Leisure: A Suburban Study* (New York: Columbia University Press, 1934), 92-101; Pitirim A. Sorokin and Clarence Q. Berger, *Time-Budgets of Human Behavior* (Cambridge, MA: Harvard University Press, 1939), 187-191; J. A. Ward, Inc., "A Nationwide Study of Living Habits," in Sebastian de Grazia, *Of Time Work and Leisure* (New York: Twentieth Century Fund, 1962), 444-445; Susan Ferge, ed.,"Part III: Statistical Appendix," in Alexander Szalai, ed., *The Use of Time: Daily Activities of Urban and Suburban Populations in Twelve Countries* (The Hague: Mouton, 1972), 561-577; John P. Robinson and Geoffrey Godbey, *Time for Life: The Surprising Ways Americans Use Their Time* (University Park: Pennsylvania State University Press, 1997), 322-323.
8. Jim Spring, "Seven Days of Play," *American Demographics* (March 1993): 50; Robinson and Godbey, *Time for Life*, 133-134, 322-323.
9. Differences in method are described by F. Thomas Juster, "A Note on Recent Changes in Time Use," in F. Thomas Juster and Frank P. Stafford, eds., *Time, Goods, and Wellbeing* (Ann Arbor: Institute for Social Research, University of Michigan, 1985), 313-332, 515-518, and John P. Robinson and Ann Bostrom, "The Overestimated Workweek? What Time Diary Measures Suggest," *Monthly Labor Review* (August 1994): 11-23; John P. Robinson, "The Time-Diary Method: Structure and Uses," in W. E. Pentland, A. S. Harvey, M. P. Lawton, and M. A. McColl, eds., *Time Use Research in the Social Sciences* (New York: Kluwer Academic/Plenum, 1999), 47-90.
10. Robinson and Bostrom, "The Overestimated Workweek? What Time Diary Measures Suggest," 11-23; Juliet B. Schor, *The Overworked American* (New York: Basic Books, 1992), 2, 168-169, 176; Arlie Hochschild, *The Time Bind* (New York: Metropolitan Books/Henry Holt, 1997); Joseph A. Tindale, "Variance in the Meaning of Time by Family Cycle, Period, Social Context, and Ethnicity," in Pentland et al., *Time Use Research in the Social Sciences*, 155-168; Jiri Zuzanek and Brian J. S. Smale, "Life-Cycle and Across-the-Week Allocation of Time to Daily Activities," in Pentland et al., *Time Use Research in the Social Sciences*, 127-153.
11. Edmund Burke, "On the Sublime and Beautiful," *The Works of the Right Honorable Edmund Burke*, 6th ed. (Boston, MA: Little, Brown, 1880), I:116.
12. Lundberg et al., *Leisure: A Suburban Study*, 99-101; Sorokin and Berger, *Time-Budgets of Human Behavior*; Ferge, "Part III: Statistical Appendix," 561-577; Grazia, *Of Time Work and Leisure*, 444-445; John P. Robinson and Geoffrey Godbey, "Are Average Americans Really Overworked?" *The American Enterprise* (September/October 1995): 43; Robinson and Godbey, *Time for Life*, 322-323.
13. Sorokin and Berger, *Time-Budgets of Human Behavior*, 148-160, 194-195.
14. The open-ended question: "'We'd like to start out by talking about some of your more general interests. Now aside from your work and your family, what are the activities that interest you most, that you spend your free time on.... Is there anything else?' [For those who say they have no free time:] 'If you had more free time and opportunity, which activities would you like to engage in?'" Gabriel A. Almond and Sidney Verba, *The Civic Culture: Political Attitudes and Democracy in Five Nations* (Newbury Park, CA: Sage Publications, [1963] 1989), 209-211.
15. Sorokin and Berger, *Time-Budgets of Human Behavior*, 148-160, 194-195.
16. Ferge, "Part III: Statistical Appendix," 561-577; Robinson and Godbey, *Time for Life*, 322-323.
17. Robinson and Godbey, *Time for Life*, 322-323.
18. Elizabeth Hann Hastings and Philip K. Hastings, eds., *Index to International Public Opinion, 1980-1981* (Westport, CT: Greenwood, 1982), 483-484, 496.

19. Question: "I'll read you a list of activities and ask how often you engaged in them during the past year. Some activities you may do only in the winter or the summer, for example. When answering how often you participate in those activities, think of how often you did them during that season." United Media Enterprises, *Where Does the Time Go?* (New York: Newspaper Enterprise Association, 1983), 30-32.
20. Robinson and Godbey, *Time for Life*, 322-323.
21. Hastings and Hastings, *Index to International Public Opinion, 1980-1981*, 483-497.
22. Elizabeth Hann Hastings and Philip K. Hastings, eds., *Index to International Public Opinion, 1997-1998* (Westport, CT: Greenwood, 1982), 368-370; George Gallup, Jr., *The Gallup Poll: Public Opinion 1999* (Wilmington, DE: Scholarly Resources, 1999), 252-253; Harris Polls of national adult samples, Roper Center at University of Connecticut, Public Opinion Online, 1998, 1999, 2000. LEXIS, Market Library, RPOLL File.
23. Robert S. Lynd and Helen Merrell Lynd, *Middletown in Transition: A Study in Cultural Conflicts* (New York: Harcourt Brace Jovanovich, [1937]1965), 249-251.
24. Theodore Caplow, Howard M. Bahr, Bruce A. Chadwick, Reuben Hill and Margaret Holmes Williamson, *Middletown Families: Fifty Years of Change and Continuity* (Minneapolis: University of Minnesota Press, 1982), 83-84, 104-106, 362.
25. *Spectator pastimes* include movies, theater, opera, nonprofit entertainments, and sports events. *Commercial participant amusements* include billiard parlors, bowling alleys, dancing, riding, shooting, skating, and swimming, amusement devices and parks, golf courses, sightseeing buses and guides, private flying operations, gambling casinos, and others. *Playthings* also include sport supplies, wheel goods, and photography equipment.
26. Personal consumption records are based on data from the Survey of Current Business and The National Income and Product Accounts of the United States, both produced by the United States Bureau of Economic Analysis and regularly reported by the United States Bureau of the Census. Data from the year 1929 are from Grazia, *Of Time Work and Leisure,* 453-459, in which he consolidated Bureau of Economic Analysis data and Twentieth Century Fund survey information. Also United States Bureau of the Census, *Historical Statistics of the United States, Colonial Times to 1970* (Washington, DC: United States Department of Commerce), 316-320, 401; and United States Bureau of the Census, *Statistical Abstract of the United States 2000* (Washington, DC: United States Government Printing Office), 253, 457.
27. W. Lloyd Warner and Paul S. Lunt, *The Social Life of a Modern Community* (New Haven, CT: Yale University Press, 1941), 295, 203.
28. Four estimates for recreation as a percentage of total personal consumption in 1929 vary by source: (1) Research Committee on Social Trends, *Recent Social Trends in the United States: Report of the President's Research Committee on Social Trends* (New York: McGraw-Hill, 1933), 889, estimated total personal consumption loosely at $85-90 billion with recreation spending at $4.3 billion (5.1 percent); (2) Grazia, *Of Time Work and Leisure*, 453-459, estimated that consumer recreation spending of $3.84 billion was 4.9 percent of the total; (3) the United States Bureau of the Census, *Historical Statistics of the United States*, 319-320, in Series G 470-494 reports that consumer recreation spending was $3.836 billion or 4.7 percent of total personal consumption of $80.761 billion; (4) the United States Bureau of the Census, *Historical Statistics*, 316-318, in Series G 416-469 reports that recreation spending was $4.331 billion, or 5.6 percent of the $77.222 billion total of personal consumption. The difference in recreation spending between the two series is due to different account-

ing methods for items such as clothing, food, shelter, and transportation purchased for recreation purposes. Two-thirds of the difference in totals of personal consumption is due to the reporting of alcoholic beverages only in series G 470-494 while the remaining third of the difference is attributable to smaller variations in accounting. The 1998 figure is compiled from data reported by the United States Bureau of the Census, *Statistical Abstract of the United States 2000*, 253, 457.

29. United States Bureau of the Census, *Statistical Abstract 2000*, 253, 457.
30. Malcolm M. Willey and Stuart A. Rice, "The Agencies of Communication," in Research Committee on Social Trends, *Recent Social Trends in the United States*, 172; Clarence Heer, "Trends in Taxation and Public Finance," in Research Committee on Social Trends, *Recent Social Trends in the United States*, 1366-1367.
31. Robert S. Lynd and Helen Merrell Lynd, *Middletown: A Study in American Culture* (New York: Harcourt, Brace, 1929), 251-253. Middletown (Muncie, Indiana) was a small industrial community studied by sociologists in 1924-1925 and again in 1935 (Lynd and Lynd, *Middletown in Transition: A Study in Cultural Conflicts)*. Later follow-up studies were done between 1976 and 1978 by Caplow et al., *Middletown Families: Fifty Years of Change and Continuity* (Minneapolis: University of Minnesota Press, 1982).
32. Lynd and Lynd, *Middletown in Transition*, 267.
33. R. D. McKenzie, "The Rise of Metropolitan Communities," in Research Committee on Social Trends, *Recent Social Trends in the United States*, 464-465.
34. Willey and Rice, "The Agencies of Communication," 179-180.
35. Lynd and Lynd, *Middletown in Transition*, 307.
36. Lynd and Lynd, *Middletown*, 259-260.
37. Ibid., 153.
38. Caplow et al., *Middletown Families*, 164.
39. Lynd and Lynd, *Middletown*, 254.
40. J. H. Kolb and Edmund deS. Brunner, *A Study of Rural Society* (Westport, CT: Greenwood, 1952), 167-168.
41. Lynd and Lynd, *Middletown*, 260-263; John H. Kolb and Douglas G. Marshall, "Neighborhood-Community Relationships in Rural Society," *Bulletin* 154 (November 1944) Agricultural Experiment Station of the University of Wisconsin, 2; J. H. Kolb and R. A. Polson, "Trends in Town-Country Relations," *Research Bulletin* 117 (September 1933) Agricultural Experiment Station of the University of Wisconsin and United States Department of Agriculture, 27.
42. Ernest Gellner, *Conditions of Liberty: Civil Society and Its Rivals* (New York: Allen Lane, Penguin, 1994), 7-8.
43. J. F. Steiner, "Recreation and Leisure Time Activities," in Research Committee on Social Trends, *Recent Social Trends in the United States*, 922; Sorokin and Berger, *Time-Budgets of Human Behavior*, 69, 104, 191.
44. Lynd and Lynd, *Middletown*, 265.
45. Ibid., 260, 485-487.
46. Caplow et al., *Middletown Families*, 198, 260-262.
47. United States Bureau of Census, *Statistical Abstract of the United States 2000*, 631.
48. *Washington Post*/Kaiser Family Foundation/Harvard University, "Survey of Americans and Economists on the Economy," (Menlo Park, CA: Kaiser Family Foundation, 1996), 13.
49. Robinson and Godbey, *Time For Life*, 322-323.
50. Patricia S. Hu and Jennifer R. Young, *Summary of Travel Trends 1995 Nationwide Personal Transportation Survey* (Washington, DC: Federal Highway Administra-

tion, 1999), 13. A change in methodology in the 1995 survey precludes comparison of the number and length of trips with 1969.

51. United States Travel Data Center, "National Travel Survey," Washington, DC; United States Bureau of Census, *Statistical Abstract of the United States 2000*, 268.
52. Questions: "Please tell me which of these sports you follow" and "If you had to choose, which one of these sports would you say is your favorite?" The list of choices: "Pro football, Baseball, Pro basketball, College football, College basketball, Boxing, Tennis, Golf, Auto racing, Track and field, Horse racing, Hockey, Bowling, Soccer?" Humphrey Taylor, "Fishing, Gardening, Golf and Team Sports Are America's Most Popular Leisure Activities–Apart From Reading, TV Watching, and Spending Time With Family," *The Harris Poll* 31 (7 July 1997).
53. Gale Research Group, "Associations Unlimited," 2001, website http://galenet.gale.com.
54. Ruth Schwartz Cowan, *A Social History of American Technology* (New York: Oxford University Press, 1997), 233.
55. Tocqueville, *Democracy in America*, II:115, 123.
56. World Values Study Group, World Values Survey [computer file]. ICPSR version. Ann Arbor, MI: Institute for Social Research [producer]. Ann Arbor, MI: Interuniversity Consortium for Political and Social Research [distributor], 2000.
57. Robert D. Putnam, *Bowling Alone* (New York: Simon and Schuster, 2000).
58. Everett Carll Ladd, *The Ladd Report* (New York: Free Press, 1999); George Pettinico, "Civic Participation Alive and Well in Today's Environmental Groups," *The Public Perspective* (June/July 1996): 27-30; Andrew Stark, "America, the Gated?" *Wilson Quarterly* (Winter 1998): 58-79; Alissa Quart, "Neo-Counterculture," *Washington Post* (7 June 1998): C1; C4; Thomas Rotolo, "Trends in Voluntary Association Participation," *Nonprofit and Voluntary Sector Quarterly* 28:2 (June 1999): 199-212.
59. Question: "Now we would like to know something about the groups or organizations to which individuals belong. Here is a list of various organizations. Could you tell me whether or not you are a member of each type? Fraternal groups; Service clubs; Veterans groups; Political clubs; Labor unions; Sports groups; Youth groups; School service groups; Hobby or garden groups; School fraternities or sororities; Nationality groups; Farm organizations; Literary, art, discussion or study groups; Professional or academic societies; Church-affiliated groups; Any other groups; Any membership at all?" James Allan Davis and Tom W. Smith, General Social Surveys, 1972-1999. Cumulative Computer File. Chicago, IL: National Opinion Research Center [producer]. Ann Arbor, MI: Interuniversity Consortium for Political and Social Research [distributor], 1999, website http://www.icpsr.umich.edu/GSS.
60. Rotolo, "Trends in Voluntary Association Participation." Rotolo checked for curvilinearity over time using a quadratic model. Total number of memberships was regressed on year.
61. Alan Wolfe, *One Nation, After All: What Middle-Class Americans Really Think* (New York: Penguin, 1998), 253-263.
62. The Social Capital Community Benchmark Survey sponsored by community foundations and designed by the Saguaro Seminar at the John F. Kennedy School of Government, Harvard University, was conducted from July to November, 2000, by TNS Intersearch. Additional information and results are found at website http://cfvs.org/communitysurvey.
63. James E. Curtis, Edward G. Grabb, and Douglas E. Baer, "Voluntary Association Membership in Fifteen Countries: A Comparative Analysis," *American Sociological Review* 57 (April 1992): 139-152.

64. Seymour Martin Lipset and Scott Talkington, unpublished work at The Institute of Public Policy, George Mason University, Fairfax, VA (December 1994).
65. Seymour Martin Lipset, *The First New Nation* (New York: Anchor, Doubleday, [1963]1967), 181-188; Tocqueville, *Democracy in America*, I:310-326.
66. Robert N. Bellah, *Beyond Belief* (New York: Harper and Row, 1970), 168-189; Samuel P. Huntington, *American Politics: The Promise of Disharmony* (Cambridge, MA: Belknap, 1981), 149-166; Lipset, *The First New Nation*, 169-192; Edward A. Tiryakian, "American Religious Exceptionalism: A Reconsideration," *ANNALS* 527 (May 1993): 40-54.
67. Edmund Burke, "Speech on Moving His Resolutions for Conciliation with the Colonies," *The Works*, II:122.
68. Tocqueville, *Democracy in America*, II:6, 7, 10.
69. Ibid., I:315; II:6.
70. Lipset, *The First New Nation*, 162-171.
71. William G. McLoughlin, *Revivals, Awakenings, and Reform: An Essay on Religion and Social Change in America, 1607-1977* (Chicago, IL: University of Chicago Press, 1978), 3.
72. Lipset, *The First New Nation*, 166.
73. Roger Finke and Rodney Stark, *The Churching of America, 1776-1990* (New Brunswick, NJ: Rutgers University Press, 1992), 16, 288. Their method of calculation is detailed in Roger Finke, "Demographics of Religious Participation: An Ecological Approach, 1850-1980," *Journal of the Scientific Study of Religion* 28:1 (1989): 45-58.
74. C. Luther Fry, "Changes in Religious Organizations," in Research Committee on Social Trends, *Recent Social Trends in the United States,* 1020-1021. The author reports that he tried to adjust for variation in definition of church membership to make collected data comparable.
75. Hornell Hart, "Religion," *American Journal of Sociology* (May 1942): 888-897. The Bureau of the Census had compatible figures in 1926; later calculations differed due to incomplete census returns.
76. J. H. Kolb and Edmund deS. Brunner, *A Study of Rural Society: Its Organization and Changes* (Boston, MA: Houghton Mifflin, 1940), 500.
77. C. Luther Fry, *The United States Looks at Its Churches* (New York: Institute of Social and Religious Research, 1930), cited in Frederick A. Bushee, "The Church in a Small City," *American Journal of Sociology* XLIX: 3 (November 1943): 223-232.
78. Annual editions of the *Yearbook of American Churches* (New York: National Council of the Churches of Christ in the U.S.A.).
79. See Lipset, *The First New Nation*, 164-165, for discussion of measurement difficulties.
80. Don Martindale and R. Galen Hanson, *Small Town and the Nation: The Conflict of Local and Translocal Forces* (Westport, CT: Greenwood, 1969), 67.
81. Norval D. Glenn, "Trend Studies with Available Survey Data: Opportunities and Pitfalls," in Jessie C. Southwick, ed., *Survey Data for Trend Analysis: An Index to Repeated Questions in U.S. National Surveys Held by the Roper Public Opinion Research Center* (Washington, DC: Social Science Research Council Center for Social Indicators, 1974), I-6 to I-50; Herbert H. Hyman, *Secondary Analysis of Sample Surveys* (Middletown, CT: Wesleyan University Press, 1972), 218-220.
82. Gallup Organization, website http://www.gallup.com.
83. Question: "Are you or the members of your family or household a member of a church or synagogue?" Independent Sector, "Giving and Volunteering in the United

States 1992," Washington, DC, 327; Independent Sector, "Giving and Volunteering in the United States: Findings From a National Survey, 1994," Washington, DC, I:127, I:69, II:28; Independent Sector, "Giving and Volunteering 1996," Washington, DC, 41. The 1999 prepublication figure was provided by courtesy of the Independent Sector.

84. Question: "Please look carefully at the following list of voluntary organizations and activities and say (a) Which, if any, do you belong to? Social welfare services for elderly, handicapped or deprived people; Religious or church organisations; Education, arts, music or cultural activities; Trade unions; Political parties or groups; Local community action on issues like poverty, employment, housing, racial equality; Third world development or human rights; Conservation, the environment, ecology; Professional associations; Youth work (e.g., Scouts, guides, youth clubs, etc.); Sports or recreation; Women's groups; Peace movement; Animal rights; Voluntary organizations concerned with health; Other groups; None, and (b) Which, if any, are you currently doing unpaid work for?" World Values Study Group, World Values Survey.
85. The kinds of groups included were fraternal, civic, patriotic, economic, social, socio-religious, educational, athletic, and musical. Edmund deS. Brunner, Gwendolyn S. Hughes, and Marjorie Patten, *American Agricultural Villages* (New York: George H. Doran, 1927), 210-213.
86. Almond and Verba, *The Civic Culture*, 256-259.
87. Sidney Verba and Norman H. Nie, *Participation in America: Political Democracy and Social Equality* (Chicago, IL: University of Chicago Press, 1972), 41.
88. Douglas Baer, James Curtis, and Edward Grabb, "Has Voluntary Association Activity Declined? A Cross-National Perspective." Paper presented at American Sociological Association Annual Meeting, 2000.
89. Fry, "Changes in Religious Organizations," 1020-1021.
90. Benson Y. Landis, "The Church and Religious Activity," *American Journal of Sociology* XL (May 1935), 783. Italics added by author.
91. Lundberg et al., *Leisure: A Suburban Study*, 198-199.
92. C. Kirk Hadaway, Penny Long Marler, and Mark Chaves, "What the Polls Don't Show: A Closer Look at U.S. Church Attendance," *American Sociological Review* 58 (December 1993): 741-752.
93. "Do That Many People Really Attend Worship Services?" *Emerging Trends* 16:5 (May 1994): 1-3.
94. J. H. Kolb and Edmund deS. Brunner, *A Study of Rural Society: Its Organization and Changes* (Boston, MA: Houghton Mifflin, 1935), 481. Estimates were based on numbers of churches and average memberships in each of four types of church density communities.
95. J. H. Kolb and Edmund deS. Brunner, *A Study of Rural Society* (Boston, MA: Houghton Mifflin, 1946); Kolb and Brunner, *A Study of Rural Society: Its Organization and Changes* (1935), 496. Four hundred, or 29 percent of the original 1,399 churches open in 1924 were closed by 1936.
96. Question: "Did you, yourself, happen to attend church or synagogue in the last seven days, or not?"
97. Question: "How often do you attend religious services?"
98. David C. Leege, "Religiosity Measures in the National Election Studies: A Guide to Their Use, Part 1," *Votes & Opinions* (October/November 1995): 6-9; 27-30; National Election Studies 1948-1998 Cumulative Data File, Ann Arbor: University of Michigan, Center for Political Studies, 2001, website http://www.umich.edu/~nes.
99. Question: "Now thinking about the present. How often do you attend religious services? Never; Less than once a year; About once or twice a year; Several times

a year; About once a month; 2-3 times a month; Nearly every week; Every week; Several times a week." This is also the question used in the General Social Survey.

100. Question: "Apart from weddings, funerals and christenings, about how often do you attend religious services these days? More than once a week, Once a week, Once a month, Christmas/Easter day, Other specific holy days, Once a year, Less often, Never/practically never."
101. See note 62.
102. Tocqueville, *Democracy in America*, II:129-132.
103. See Independent Sector, "Giving and Volunteering in the United States 1994," 93-94; Verba et al., *Voice and Equality,* 140-142; Robert Wuthnow, *Sharing the Journey: Support Groups and America's New Quest for Community* (New York: Free Press, 1994), 84; Independent Sector, "Giving and Volunteering 1996," 8, 110-111; David Horton Smith, "Determinants of Voluntary Association Participation and Volunteering: A Literature Review," *Nonprofit and Voluntary Sector Quarterly* 23:3 (Fall 1994): 243-263. For a review of the most widely used definitions of volunteering, see Ram A. Cnaan, Femida Handy, and Margaret Wadsworth, "Defining Who is a Volunteer: Conceptual and Empirical Considerations," *Nonprofit and Voluntary Sector Quarterly* 25:3 (September 1996): 364-383.
104. Virginia Ann Hodgkinson and Murray S. Weitzman, *Dimensions of the Independent Sector: A Statistical Profile,* 3d ed. (Washington, DC: Independent Sector, 1989), 105; Independent Sector, "Giving and Volunteering in the United States 1994," I:77-78; Independent Sector, "Giving and Volunteering in the United States 1996," 110-111.
105. Independent Sector, "Giving and Volunteering in the United States 1996," 43.
106. Ibid., 42-44, 130-131.
107. United States Department of Labor, Manpower Administration, "Americans Volunteer," Monograph 10, April 1969; ACTION, "Americans Volunteer 1974," February 1975; Howard V. Hayghe, "Volunteers in the U.S.: Who Donates the Time?" *Monthly Labor Review* 114 (February 1991): 17-23. Also see Hayghe for detail on methodological differences in studies.
108. Hodgkinson and Weitzman, *Dimensions*, 77, 101.
109. "Voluntarism and Philanthropy," *The Public Perspective* (October/November 1997): 15.
110. "Volunteering in America," *The American Enterprise* (July/August 1997): 92.
111. Question: "In which, if any, of the areas listed on this card have you done some volunteer work in the past twelve months? Health; Education; Religious organizations, Human Services, Environment, Public/society benefit; Recreation–adults; Arts, culture, & humanities; Work-related organizations; Political organizations/ *campaigns*; Youth development; Private and community foundations; International/ foreign; Informal—alone—*not for pay*; Other (PLEASE SPECIFY); None of these." [Author's italics show wording added in 1994].
112. Calculated from total population figures in United States Bureau of the Census, *Statistical Abstract 1998*, 8, and data on volunteering from surveys sponsored by Independent Sector.
113. "Volunteering in America," 92.
114. Almond and Verba, *The Civic Culture*, 210.
115. Davis and Smith, General Social Surveys, 1972-1999.
116. Susan J. Ellis and Katherine H. Noyes, *By the People: A History of Americans as Volunteers* (San Francisco, CA: Jossey-Bass, 1990), xii.
117. Robert Wuthnow, *Acts of Compassion: Caring for Others and Helping Ourselves* (Princeton, NJ: Princeton University Press, 1991), 199-200.
118. Independent Sector, "Giving and Volunteering 1996," 4-7.

119. Independent Sector, "Giving and Volunteering 1996," 2; Independent Sector, "Giving and Volunteering in the United States, 1999: Key Findings," October information release.
120. United States Bureau of the Census, *Statistical Abstract 1998* (Washington, DC), 63.
121. Paul G. Schervish and John J. Havens, "Embarking on a Republic of Benevolence? New Survey Findings on Charitable Giving," *Nonprofit and Voluntary Sector Quarterly* 27:2 (June 1998): 237-242.
122. "Real, Per Capita Charitable Giving Has Continued to Rise," *The Public Perspective* (October/November 1997): 15.
123. Annual reports of the American Association of Fund-Raising Counsel Trust for Philanthropy, "Giving USA," New York.
124. Virginia Ann Hodgkinson, Murray S. Weitzman, Christopher M. Toppe, and Stephen M. Noga, *Nonprofit Almanac 1992-1993: Dimensions of the Independent Sector* (San Francisco, CA: Jossey-Bass, 1992), 59-61.
125. Christopher Jencks, "Who Gives to What?" in Walter W. Powell, ed., *The Nonprofit Sector* (New Haven, CT: Yale University Press, 1987), 335.
126. Almond and Verba, *The Civic Culture*, 262-264.
127. National Election Studies, "The Origins of ANES," website http://www.umich.edu/~nes; Interuniversity Consortium for Political and Social Research, *Guide to Resources and Services 1994-1995* (Ann Arbor, MI: ICPSR, 1995), 269.
128. Question: "Some people don't pay much attention to the political campaigns. How about you, would you say that you have been/were very much interested, somewhat interested, or not much interested in following the political campaigns (so far) this year?"
129. Questions: "Generally speaking, would you say that you personally care a good deal which party wins the presidential election this fall, or don't you care very much which party (1992, 1996: who) wins?" and "How much would you say that you personally cared about the way the elections (1996 and later: election) to the U.S. House of Representatives (1970, 1974: to Congress) came out: (1978 and later: Did you care) very much, pretty much, not very much or not at all?"
130. Question: "We would like to find out about some of the things people do to help a party or a candidate win an election. During the campaign, did you talk to any people and try to show why they should vote for or against one of the parties or candidates?; Did you wear a campaign button, put a campaign sticker on your car, or place a sign in your window or in front of your house?; Did you go to any political meetings, rallies, speeches, dinners, or things like that in support of a particular candidate?; Did you do any (other) work for one of the parties or candidates?; During an election year people are often asked to make a contribution to support campaigns. Did you give money to an individual candidate running for public office?; Did you give money to a political party during this election year?"
131. National Election Studies; see Robert F. Belli, M. W. Traugott, M. Young, and K. A. McGonagle, "Reducing Vote Overreporting in Surveys," *Public Opinion Quarterly* 63 (Spring 1999): 90-108, for discussion of two influences upon self-reporting, memory failure and the wish to present one's self favorably. Also see Jerry T. Jennings, "Estimating Voter Turnout in the Current Population Survey," in United States Bureau of the Census, *Studies in the Measurement of Voter Turnout*, Current Population Reports, Series P-23, No. 168 (Washington, DC: United States Government Printing Office, 1990): 21-28.
132. Verba and Nie, *Participation in America*, 350-355, for questions as cited in Verba, et al., *Voice and Equality*, 72.

133. Question: "In any election some people are not able to vote because they are sick or busy or have some other reason, and others do not want to vote. Did you vote in the election held on…?" Jerry T. Jennings, "The Current Population Survey of Voting and Registration: Summary and History," in United States Bureau of the Census, *Studies in the Measurement of Voter Turnout*, 1-20.
134. United States Bureau of the Census, *Statistical Abstract 2000*, 291; Martin P. Wattenberg, "Getting Out the Vote," *Public Perspective* (January/February 2001): 16-17.
135. Verba and Nie, *Participation in America*, 350-355. The 1987 data was from the General Social Survey cited by Verba et al., *Voice and Equality*, 72. The drop in membership in political clubs had to have occurred between 1967 and 1974 since there was no marked changed after 1974 when it was 5 percent; in 1994 it was also 5 percent. The National Election Studies also reflected an increase in campaign contributions during presidential election years.
136. Question: "Now here is a list of things some people do about government or politics. Have you happened to have done any of those things in the past year? (If "Yes") Which ones? Written your Congressman or Senator; Attended a political rally or speech; Attended a public meeting on town or school affairs; Held or run for political office; Served on a committee for some local organization; Served as an officer of some club or organization; Written a letter to the paper; Signed a petition; Worked for a political party; Made a speech; Written an article for a magazine or newspaper; Been a member of some group like the League of Women Voters, or some other group which is interested in better government; No—None of these; Don't know/No answer." Roper Center, Public Opinion Online, 1994. Data for years 1993-1996 were supplied by special courtesy of Roper Starch Worldwide.
137. These surveys include the Kaiser Survey on Americans and AIDS, HIV (1995); a Harris Poll (1996); AARP Civic Involvement Survey (1996); Social Trust and Volunteerism Survey (1997); a Gallup, CNN, *USA Today* Poll (1997); State of the First Amendment Survey (1997); National Philanthropy Survey (1997); the General Social Survey (1998); a CBS News Poll (1999); People and the Press Political Typology Survey (1999); a Gallup Poll (2000); Fox News, Opinion Dynamics Poll (2000); News Interest Index (January 2000); and the U.S. Census Survey (2000).
138. United States Bureau of the Census, *Census of Governments,* published every five years. The 1997 census report does not include the customary volume on popularly elected officials.
139. Eugene C. Lee, "City Elections: A Statistical Profile" in Orin F. Nolting and David S. Arnold, eds., *The Municipal Year Book 1963* (Chicago, IL: International City Management Association, 1963), 75.
140. Lisa Oakley and Thomas H. Neale, "Citizen Initiative Proposals Appearing on State Ballots, 1976-1992," Congressional Research Service, February 15, 1995; M. Dane Waters, "A Century Later—the Experiment with Citizen-Initiated Legislation Continues," *The Public Perspective* (December/January 1999): 123-144. Time periods and percentages of total citizen initiative petitions filed break down as follows: 1904-1921, *19 percent*; 1922-1939, *20 percent*; 1940-1957, *13 percent*; 1958-1975, *10 percent*; 1976-1992, *26 percent*; and 1993-1998, *12 percent.*
141. Charles Lewis Taylor and David A. Jodice, *World Handbook of Political and Social Indicators, Volume 2: Political Protest and Government Change* (New Haven, CT: Yale University Press, 1983), 1-15, 22-32. A protest demonstration is "organized for the announced purpose of protesting against a regime or government or one or more of its leaders; or against its ideology, policy, intended policy,

or lack of policy; or against its previous action or intended action (19)." A regime support demonstration lends "support to a government, its policies and actions, or one or more of its leaders (20)." A political strike is a "work stoppage by a body of industrial or service workers or a stoppage of normal academic life by students to protest a regime and its leaders' policies or actions (20)."

142. The 1974 question from The Political Action Study: "Now I'd like you to look at this card. I'm going to read out some different forms of political action that people can take, and I'd like you to tell me, for each one, whether you have done any of these things, whether you might do it or would never, under any circumstances, do it." Choices in addition to those shown in table 4.3 were: refusal to pay rent or taxes, painting slogans on walls, blocking traffic with a street demonstration, damaging property, using personal violence. Percentages of respondents who engaged in these additional activities ranged from 0 to 2 percent. Samuel H. Barnes and Max Kaase et al., *Political Action: Mass Participation in Five Western Democracies* (Beverly Hills, CA: Sage Publications, 1979), 537-596.
143. Question: "Please place the cards on this scale to show me, first, whether (1) you have actually done any of these things on the cards during the past ten years; (2) you would do any of these things if it were important to you; (3) you might do it in a particular situation or (4) you would never do it under any circumstances." Actions were: Signing a petition; Joining in boycotts; Attending lawful demonstrations; Joining unofficial strikes; Occupying buildings or factories.
144. George A. Lundberg and Margaret Lawsing, "The Sociography of Some Community Relations," in Logan Wilson and William L. Kolb, *Sociological Analysis* (New York: Harcourt, Brace, 1949), 274.
145. Lynd and Lynd, *Middletown in Transition*, 245.
146. Lynd and Lynd, *Middletown*, 281, 285.
147. Lynd and Lynd, *Middletown in Transition*, 249.
148. Caplow et al., *Middletown Families: Fifty Years of Change and Continuity*, 22-25, 83-84, 105.
149. W. Lloyd Warner, J. O. Low, Paul S. Lunt, and Leo Srole, *Yankee City* (New Haven, CT: Yale University Press, 1963), 105-156.
150. Sorokin and Berger, *Time-Budgets of Human Behavior*, 153.
151. These studies are not strictly comparable due to methodological variation. Robinson and Godbey, *Time for Life*, 322-323.
152. Karen V. Hansen, "Rediscovering the Social: Visiting Practices in Antebellum New England and the Limits of the Public/Private Dichotomy," in Jeff Weintraub and Krishan Kumar, eds., *Public and Private in Thought and Practice: Perspectives on a Grand Dichotomy* (Chicago, IL: University of Chicago Press, 1997), 270, 274.
153. Art Gallaher, Jr., *Plainville Fifteen Years Later* (New York: Columbia University Press, 1961), 135-139, 250.
154. Bonnie H. Erickson and T. A. Nosanchuk, "How an Apolitical Association Politicizes," *Canadian Review of Sociology and Anthropology* 27:2 (1990): 206-219.
155. The question "What is your favorite way of spending an evening?" was first asked in 1938 when 4 percent preferred this way of spending an evening. Subsequent surveys were in 1960 (10 percent), 1966 (5 percent), 1974 (8 percent), 1986 (8 percent), 1990 (5 percent), and 1998 (6 percent). A few variations have occurred in the choice of preference activities. The item "Drinking, going to bars," for example, did not appear until after the 1974 survey.
156. Sorokin and Berger, *Time-Budgets of Human Behavior*, 153.
157. Morris Axelrod, "Urban Structure and Social Participation," *American Sociological Review* 21 (February 1956): 13-18.

158. Albert J. Reiss, Jr., "Rural-Urban and Status Differences in Interpersonal Contacts," *American Journal of Sociology* 65 (September 1959): 182-195.
159. Herbert J. Gans, *The Levittowners: Ways of Life and Politics in a New Suburban Community* (New York: Pantheon, 1967), 51-67.
160. Claude S. Fischer, *The Urban Experience* (New York: Harcourt Brace Jovanovich, 1976), 117-121.
161. Question: "Would you use this card and tell me which answer comes closest to how often you do the following things...(A) spend a social evening with relatives? (B) Spend a social evening with someone who lives in your neighborhood? (C) Spend a social evening with friends who live outside the neighborhood? (D) Go to a bar or tavern? (E) Spend a social evening with your parents? (F) Spend a social evening with a brother or sister? Almost every day; Once or twice a week; Several times a month; About once a month; Several times a year; About once a year; Never."
162. See note 62.
163. See Shell Polls of 1,277 and 1,010 national adults conducted by Peter D. Hart Research Associates, Roper Center, Public Opinion Online, 1999 and 2000.
164. See NBC News, *Wall Street Journal* Poll of 2,011 national adults conducted by Hart Teeter Research, Roper Center, Public Opinion Online, 1999.
165. See *New York Times* Poll of 1,178 national adults in 1999, Roper Center, Public Opinion Online, 2000.
166. See the Zogby Real America Poll of 1,008 national adults, Roper Center, Public Opinion Online, 1999.
167. Robert Wuthnow, *Sharing the Journey*, 47-50, 84, 318-321.
168. Robert D. Putnam, "Bowling Alone: America's Declining Social Capital," *Journal of Democracy* 6 (January): 65-78; Robert D. Putnam, "Tuning In, Tuning Out: The Strange Disappearance of Social Capital in America," *PS: Political Science and Politics* 28 (December): 665.
169. Robert Wuthnow, "Tocqueville's Question Reconsidered: Voluntarism and Public Discourse in Advanced Industrial Societies," in Robert Wuthnow, ed., *Between States and Markets* (Princeton, NJ: Princeton University Press, 1991), 296.
170. Tocqueville, *Democracy in America*, II:123-128.
171. John Shanklin Gilkeson, Jr., "A City of Joiners: Voluntary Associations and the Formation of the Middle Class in Providence, 1830-1920." Ph.D. dissertation, Brown University, 1981, 91-96.
172. Albert Hunter, *Symbolic Communities: The Persistence and Change of Chicago's Local Communities* (Chicago, IL: University of Chicago Press, 1974), 151-152.
173. Morris Axelrod, "Urban Structure and Social Participation."
174. Albert B. Crenshaw, "An Investing Club Seeks Funds and Friendship," *Washington Post* (15 October 1995): H1, H6.
175. Question: "In general, what subjects do you think are most often talked about among your men (women) friends and acquaintances these days? War, work and business, politics and government, sports, women, draft, lend-lease aid to Britain, money & cost of living, farming, labor and strikes, family and children, cultural interests, clothing and fashions, household activities, gossip, religion, all others." Men were asked about their male associates and women about their female associates. Hadley Cantril, ed., *Public Opinion 1935-1946* (Princeton, NJ: Princeton University Press, 1951), 496.
176. Question: "Public issues often arise that are complex and hard to understand. Suppose such an issue arose which might affect your own way of life—such as a law concerning taxes or an international crisis that might lead to war—but you

didn't understand this issue fully. What would you do to find out more about it?" Roper Center, Public Opinion Online, 1989.

177. Question: "How often do you discuss politics with other people? Often, sometimes, seldom, never." Barnes and Kaase et al., *Political Action*, 540-542.
178. Question: "Now, I'd like to read a list of activities and feelings related to involvement in your local community. Again, please tell me how frequently you do or feel each and whether you would like to do this more or less often in the future, or about the same...Discussing local issues with friends and neighbors." "American Values in the '80s," survey conducted by Research and Forecasts for Connecticut Mutual Life Insurance, Roper Center, Public Opinion Online, 1989.
179. Hart Teeter, Study 5436 for the Council for Excellence in Government.
180. Question: "Now, I would like to ask you some questions about the media. As you know, people get their news and information from many different sources, and I would like to ask you where you get *your* news and information. I will read a list of sources, and for each one please tell how often you get your news from that source...every day, several times a week, occasionally, or never (for Sample B)...very regularly, somewhat regularly, occasionally, or never (for Sample A)." Question: "Now, apart from how *frequently* you use different sources of news, I would like to know how *important* each of the following is to you personally as a source of news and information—is it extremely important to you, very important, somewhat important, not too important, or not important at all?...Discussions with your friends or family." David W. Moore, "Americans' Most Important Source of Information: Local TV News," *The Gallup Poll Monthly* (September 1995): 2-8.
181. James Davison Hunter and Carl Bowman, *The State of Disunion: 1996 Survey of American Political Culture* (Ivy, VA: In Medias Res Educational Foundation, 1996).
182. People and the Press Poll conducted by Princeton Survey Research Associates in 1998, Roper Center, Public Opinion Online, 1999.
183. Axelrod, "Urban Structure and Social Participation," 41.
184. Hunter, *Symbolic Communities*, 188.
185. Peter L. Berger and Richard John Neuhaus, *To Empower People: The Role of Mediating Structures in Public Policy* (Washington, DC: American Enterprise Institute for Public Policy Research, 1977), 42-43.
186. The sharing of information underpins associational life. Weak ties, or loose connections between people, expedite the traveling of information throughout a network. In contrast, strong ties do not reach as far or carry as much information because they require more attention, greater commitment, and more homogeneity among the participants. Both strong and weak ties are important to the viability of a democratic civil society. Mark Granovetter, "The Strength of Weak Ties," *American Journal of Sociology* 78:6 (1973): 1360-1380.
187. Tocqueville, *Democracy in America*, I:250-253, 258-260; II:129-132, 148-151, 117-118.

4

Association: Diversity and Transcending Difference

Tocqueville, during his visit to America in the 1830s, observed several things that happened when people of numerous viewpoints and circumstances met, talked, and listened. Divisive barriers fell. Ideas, debate, competition, and innovation circulated. Activity generated even more activity. Reciprocal relationships perpetuated a sense of solidarity and equality. Multiple authorities evoked multiple loyalties, spreading authority and commitment broadly. Minorities countered the power of the majority with effective persuasion and by forming coalitions. Diversity increased opportunity for peaceful resolution of conflicts and differences of opinion. Such conditions are the essence of that intermediate element of the democratic social structure called civil society that constrains and binds extremes, and impedes over-centralization. In aggregate, these conditions form a natural deterrent to imbalances of power.

Tocqueville concluded that a democracy relied on both civil and political associations. Political associations were of two types: those permanently established by law to run local affairs as townships, cities, and counties and those organized through the initiatives of private individuals. In this paradigm, each type of association, civil and political, was necessary to the other. Civil associations offered an opportunity to practice and develop skills that made it easier to associate for political reasons. Political association, in turn, encouraged association for civil purposes. A mix of civil and political associations fosters freedom and autonomy. Civil associations alone, without the existence of political association, can distract citizens from intervening in public affairs, allowing government to garner power and to centralize its practices. Tocqueville spoke favorably of a mix, not only of civil and political association, but also of association large and small, general and restricted, serious and futile. He saw that variety brought choice and selective pursuit of interests that united individuals in expressions of freedom. Obviously, freedom was enhanced by diversity, as was the substance of reciprocal influence of people on each other.[1]

Sundry forms and functions of voluntary association constitute a complex pluralism that benefits the individual, social strata, and democratic society in general.[2] Thus, an assessment of U.S. civil society needs to consider how the condition of pluralism fares. How rich and varied is the mix of voluntary associations? Is the nature of its diversity segmented or crosscutting and integrated? This chapter seeks an answer to these questions by exploring (1) trends in rationale for forming voluntary associations and (2) trends in cutting across differences as demonstrated by developments in political party identification, national identity, tolerance, lifestyle, and local self-governance.

Diversity in Rationale and Interests

At the time of Tocqueville's visit to the United States, Americans formed associations for many reasons. Together, they solved problems, fixed inconveniences, promoted causes or morals, resisted threat or evil, organized fun, showed solidarity, and persuaded majorities. The highly varied appearance of associational life seemed consistent with the diversity of public opinion that Tocqueville also found among Americans, who were divided on numerous issues and to many degrees.[3] Many voluntary organizations in the United States at the time were formed for purposes of public safety, entertainment, commerce, industry, morality, and religion.[4] Attempts to classify these initiatives continue to the present day, yet the increasing complexity of the typologies point to dramatic change in the appearance of associational life.

In the 1940s, Kolb and Brunner proposed a general classification scheme to encompass the interests around which voluntary groups formed: athletic, civic, educational, fraternal, musical, patriotic, social, socioeconomic, socioreligious, youth-serving, and informal groups, cliques, or coteries.[5] A National Taxonomy of Exempt Entities, an ongoing cooperative project of scholars and interested nonprofit groups since the early 1980s, has classified "26 major groups collapsible into 10 major categories, and divisible into over 645 subgroups."[6] More recently, Salamon and Anheier developed a typology to use for cross-national comparisons of nonprofit organizations that reflects an even greater elaboration of civil societies. This scheme has eleven broad categories that subsume 146 subvarieties of groups including business and professional associations and unions; religion; philanthropic intermediaries and voluntarism promotion; international activities; law, advocacy, and politics; development and housing; environment; social services; health; culture and recreation; and education and research.[7]

Classifications of voluntary organizations reflect the enterprise of subsocietal venues. One example is seen in the contrast between organized life of urban dwellers in the 1930s and their rural compatriots. Associations in the urban area reflected the greater density and diversity of inhabitants, who might have belonged to the Country Club, to Greek letter societies, the YMCA and the YWCA and their satellite groups, or to groups that focused on minority protection or a particular sport. Associations unique to the rural area were the groups with an agricultural focus, such as the Farm Bureau, the Home Bureau, and farm cooperatives.[8] At the same time, similar interests reached across urban and rural differences. Groups with a focus on religion, youth, fraternal orders, civic improvement, and politics existed in both settings.

Change in Classification, Size, Share-of-total, and in Subcategories

Today, new types of voluntary associations attest to expansion and diversification in interests, concerns and the boundaries of social space. Foreign interests, consumerism, human rights, civil rights, animal welfare, the environment, and anti-nuclear sentiments are just a few of the contemporary catalysts for association that received little or no attention in the first half of this century.[9] Modifications in the *Encyclopedia of Association*'s classification of national nonprofit membership groups, since its genesis in 1959, trace a few twists and turns of interest, emphasis, and meaning that imply diversification:[10]

- In 1961...
  - The category of *national, foreign, economic, and political* groups assumed the encompassing name of *public affairs*;
  - The category of *veteran and patriotic* groups expanded its name to *veterans, hereditary, patriotic*;
  - The category of *athletic* broadened to *athletic and sports.*
- In 1964, the *fraternal* and *foreign interest, nationality, and ethnic* categories combined under a new heading of *fraternal, nationality, and ethnic.*
- In 1972, the category of *horticultural* groups was dropped and its listings were dispersed into the hobby, scientific, and agricultural sections.
- In 1975, *labor unions* became *labor unions, associations, and federations.*
- In 1976, the category of *governmental, public administration, military and legal* groups was renamed to *legal, governmental, public administration and military*;
- In 1979, *Greek letter societies* was extended to include *Greek and Non-Greek Letter Societies, Associations, and Federations*;
- In 1987, a new category was added for *fan clubs*;
- In 1991...
  - *Agricultural organizations and commodity exchanges* changed to *environmental and agricultural.*
  - *Scientific, engineering and technical* became *engineering, technological, and natural and social sciences.*

Delving deeper into this data we discover that shifts in share-of-total actually affirm a broadened base of group interests. Whereas in 1968, *trade, business, and commercial* organizations accounted for 27 percent of the total, that share dropped to 17 percent in 2000, still the largest proportion held by any category. *Religious* groups and *fraternal, nationality, and ethnic* groups also lost in share by 3 and 4 percentage points, respectively. The groups that gained 3 to 5 percentage points in share were *social welfare, public affairs, hobby and avocational, and health and medical* groups.

Further evidence of growing diversity in national nonprofit membership associations is found in the multiplication of subcategories within major types of organizations. Their number reached nearly 1,900 in 1996, evidence of growing diversity in associations. The 1994-95 listings of regional, state, and local associations poignantly highlights variety. With the country divided into five geographical regions in this reference work, each region contained groups that represented up to 600 different interests—with regional variation. That same year, in listings of international groups with which Americans also affiliate, more than 1,100 subtypes of groups were organized under fifteen general subject classifications.

Change in Size and Share of Tax-Exempt Organizations

The extremely broad classifications of tax-exempt organizations mask how these associations diversify—although shifts in emphasis are evident. Between 1977 and 1998, the Internal Revenue Service classification of 501(c)3s, a category comprised of *charitable, educational, religious and scientific* groups, increased its count (see chapter 2) and assumed a larger share-of-total from 35 to 58 percent of all tax exempt groups. A second classification of *fraternal beneficiary societies,* or 501(c)8s, shrank both in size (-40 percent) and in share-of-total from 18 to 7 percent.[11] *Labor, agricultural, and horticultural* groups, called 501(c)5s, decreased in both size and share. *Civic and social welfare advocacy* groups, known as 501(c)4s, increased in number despite a loss-in-share, simply growing at a slower rate than other types of groups or experiencing greater rates of turnover.[12]

Types of Membership in the General Social Survey

Thomas Rotolo's curvilinear analysis of General Social Survey (GSS) trends characterizes the last half of the period between 1974 and 1994 as one of recovery from an overall dip in belonging to a voluntary association that occurred in the first decade. His analysis shows membership levels in six kinds of groups remained steady throughout the entire period. Another six made gains and only four fell.[13] Absolute changes from 1974 to 1994 among the sixteen varieties of membership reported in the GSS denote a decrease in *church-affiliated* group memberships (-9 percentage points), *labor* memberships (-5), and in *fraternal* memberships (-4). Memberships held in *professional and academic* groups (+6) and *sports* associations (+4) increased (table 4.1). Some narrowing in the variety of memberships an individual holds is implied. Indeed, this observation is supported by the slippage in the percentage of those who held from five to sixteen different types of memberships between 1974 and 1994—from 10.4 to 5.8 percent.[14]

Perhaps most important to the health of civil society, however, is the lack of overall change in the proportion of Americans (64.4 percent) who maintained one to four types of memberships in 1974 as well as in 1994. Moreover, the number holding from one to four kinds of memberships during that twenty-

Table 4.1

Change in Types of Voluntary Association Memberships Held, General Social Survey, 1974-1994 (in rounded percentages)

Membership Types	1974	1994	Absolute Change
Decreases			
Church-affiliated	42*	33	- 9
Labor	17	12	- 5
Fraternal	14	10	- 4
School service	18	16	- 2
Youth	11	10	- 1
Veterans	9	8	- 1
Hobby, garden	10	9	- 1
Increases			
Professional, academic	13	19	6
Sports	18	22	4
Other	10	11	1
Service clubs	9	10	1
Literary, art, discussion, study	9	10	1
School fraternities, sororities	5	6	1
No change			
Farm groups	4	4	0
Nationality	4	4	0
Political clubs	5	5	0

Source: Davis and Smith, *General Social Surveys, 1972-1999.*

* This was the high end of the range of reported church-affiliated memberships; the low was 31 percent in 1980. An appreciable amount of fluctuation occurred until the late 1980s, when it subsequently stabilized. The overall mean for church-affiliated memberships was 36 percent. This type of voluntary association consistently drew the largest proportion of membership subscribers.

year period varied narrowly, ranging between 59 and 66 percent. This is a stable base of organized association activity. There is much that the General Social Survey fails to tell us about membership in voluntary associations, however.[15] First, we must be aware that membership interests may never have been fully captured in the survey question. We do not know if the types of membership inquired about grew more internally diverse. Nor did we learn to what extent the typology used in this instrument became outmoded, excluding types of groups that contemporary Americans now join.

Growing Variety of Periodicals

Reading periodicals is an activity in which diversification of shared interests and avocational pursuits are markedly evident. Over the last three decades, the types of periodicals published have proliferated from the ten categories monitored in 1947 by the *United States Census of Manufactures* to 255 categories recorded in the *Standard Periodical Directory* in 1996.[16] In a detailed examination of listings in the latter reference for the six-year period of 1991 to 1996, I found marked expansion of subject categories, turnover, and significant reordering of interests in just this brief period of time. Periodical consumption during this time reflects nineteen new subject categories, rising interest in environmental and ecology matters, politics, and international affairs, and declining interest in reading house organ, genealogy, and ethnic issue magazines.[17]

Cutting Across Diversity

Rationales for association grow increasingly varied, but do not tell us how well Americans cut across their differences to unite. One source of such information is in the loose, symbolic process of political party identification. Other sources lie in shared values and identity, attitudes, and lifestyles.

Political Party Identification

Identification that reflects political orientations cuts across the differences of class and condition and causes citizens from a variety of situations to act or opine collectively. In Tocqueville's view, political association seems an easy way to combine large numbers of quite different people, unacquainted and unable to organize around apolitical issues. Political association entails little risk in that the commitment (fiscal or otherwise) required from its members is clearly delineated, task oriented, and time limited. This, Tocqueville posited, holds special appeal for inexperienced members or those who do not know each other well.[18]

Political party identification is a choice made by most Americans. The choice between two major parties cuts across numerous differences and denotes a generally shared disposition.[19] The result is a loosely maintained, flexible unity that fits Tocqueville's description of political association. Each party attracts numerous individuals unacquainted and unlikely to aggregate for any other reason.[20] The act of identifying with one of the parties is based on an expectation held by Americans that differences must ultimately acquiesce to some degree of consensus. It is this "general set of social attitudes...over and above political differences [that] keeps the affective attachments to political groups from challenging the stability of the system."[21]

The political party identifications of nearly 40,000 respondents pooled from twenty-two American National Election Studies conducted between 1952 and 1994 shows how members of forty-three different demographic groups in the United States transcended social and political differences to align (or not) themselves with one or the other major party.[22] In total, 53 percent of the pooled survey participants identified themselves as Democrats, 36 percent as Republicans, and 11 percent as Independents. The same identification profile is found within most demographic groups. Profiles that mimic this distribution include those for most ages, men, women, whites, white collar workers, farmers, housewives, nonunion members, the upper working class, Americans in the middle income percentile (34th-67th), residents of the Northeast and West, the high-school educated, moderates in ideology, and Protestants. Some demographic groups were divided rather evenly between the parties: residents of the North Central region, professionals, the college-educated, and self-described members of the average middle class.

Those favoring a party in higher than average numbers, thereby departing from the general pattern of identification, highlight the demographic characteristics that seem most associated with separatism: race; the extremes of class, occupation, income, and education; religion; ideology; and region. In particular, Black Americans, Southerners, blue collar and unskilled workers, union members, Catholics and Jews, liberals, and the grade school educated identified at above average rates with the Democratic Party. Conservatives and the eldest Americans, aged 75 and up, identified at greater than average rates with the Republican Party. Republican identifiers grew denser with upward progression on the social ladder from average working class, upper working class, average middle, to upper middle class. A similar distribution occurred across the five income percentiles. Lower income brackets were heavily loaded with Democrat identifiers, the higher income groups with Republican identifiers.

Several shifts in identification during the four decades between 1952 and 1994 demonstrate the dynamic nature of association (table 4.2). Some demographic group identification profiles grew increasingly *balanced* between the Democratic and Republican parties.

Table 4.2

Change in Political Party Identification by Demographic Segments, 1952-1994 (in percentages)

Selected groups that grew more evenly divided	*from. . . 1952*	*to. . . 1994*	*Change in difference between parties*
Southerners	D 75 R 14	49 41	61 ▶ 8
Middle income earners (34-67th %ile)	D 61 R 33	45 44	28 ▶ 1
Blue collar workers	D 66 R 27	51 36	39 ▶ 15
Males	D 58 R 33	41 48	25 ▶ 7
Whites	D 56 R 36	43 46	20 ▶ 3
Selected groups that grew more disparate			
Conservatives	D 34 R 56	21 70	22 ▶ 49
Blacks	D 63 R 17	81 11	46 ▶ 70
Liberals	D 71 R 20	83 12	51 ▶ 71
Groups with largest increases in Independent identifiers			***Difference***
Unskilled	6	23	+17
Grade school educated	6	18	+12
Lowest income earners (0-16th %ile)	4	14	+10
Housewives	5	14	+9

Source: Compiled from National Election Studies.

Among those that grew more evenly divided in their identifications between the two parties were Southerners, those in the middle-income percentile, blue collar workers, males, and white Americans. In each group, Republican identifications increased to lessen the gap in size between the two kinds of identifiers. The *imbalance increased* between numbers of Republican and Democratic identifications in other groups. Conservatives and those in the highest income bracket moved in greater number to identification with the Republican Party. Black Americans, members of the lowest income group, and liberals leaned increasingly towards Democratic Party identification. A third type of change occurred in the form of *fluctuating* identification between the two major parties. Among the college educated, farmers, professionals, white Americans, males, and those from the 68th-95th income percentile, the party that elicited the majority of identifications switched at three or more points in time between 1952 and 1994. Yet another phenomenon was the growth of Independent identifications. Many demographic groups saw an *increase in Independent identifiers* during this time, especially among the unskilled (from 6 to 23 percent), the grade school educated (from 6 to 18 percent), Americans in the lowest income percentile (from 4 to 14 percent), and housewives (from 5 to 14 percent). Just as important to note are those groups whose pattern of party identification did not alter for forty years. Ideological moderates, with a profile that reflected the general breakout, fell into this category of *no change*—as did those in the 17th-33rd income percentile.

The dynamics of party identification between 1952 and 1994, then, included a variety of shifts ending in an overall party identification profile in 1994 that was less skewed between the two major parties. In 1952, 57 percent identified as Democrats, 34 percent as Republicans, and 6 percent as Independents, whereas the 1994 profile reflected a decrease in Democratic identifiers (to 47 percent) and an increase in Republican identifiers (to 41 percent). The increase in Independent identifiers (to 11 percent) implies some weakening of traditional ties between citizens and the political party system.

An Expectation of Unity

When questions about unity and diversity were posed in the 1994 General Social Survey, 58 percent of the total expressed the view that Americans are divided, rather than united.[23] However, when asked if the consideration of social and political issues is carried out in light of one's membership in a particular group or mainly just as an American, a majority of 87 percent reported that it was as an American.[24] Asked how strong their feelings were about whether racial and ethnic groups should maintain their unique cultures or melt into the larger society, the majority (56 percent) chose neither extreme, but selected numbers 3 through 5 on a scale of seven.[25] Most, 86 percent, thought retention of ethnic identity and assimilation should be left up to the groups, themselves—that it was not a responsibility that belonged to government.[26] Such matters, when politicized, grow more difficult according to two-thirds of Americans who agreed that "[P]olitical organizations based on race or ethnicity promote separatism and make it hard for all of us to live together." A national sample of registered voters interviewed by Daniel

Yankelovich Group in 1998 was split on the appropriate response to growing diversity in the United States. Forty-one percent felt strongly that teaching people about each other's cultures, background, and lifestyles needs to be stressed; 43 percent felt strongly that the emphasis should be placed on teaching common American values.[27] The distribution was not as evenly divided in a national sample of adults who were asked a similar question by Peter Hart for Shell in 1999. On this occasion, respondents were asked if they agreed more that the country "needs to appreciate its diversity better" or "needs to focus on what we all have in common." Thirty-eight percent agreed with the first statement while a larger 52 percent thought the needed focus was on what Americans have in common.

Americans value both their common *and* unique identities. Their sense of national unity had different beginnings than in societies where legitimacy derives from ascriptive, religious, and/or military traditions. As a new nation, the formation of a national self-image was challenged by tension between visions of the founding intellectuals and populist, pragmatic, and provincial forces, Lipset explained. The intertwining of national celebrations, political events, and political creed provided ways to affirm national consciousness, yet there was much to counter unity and to reinforce diversity.[28] For one thing, early Americans had the luxury of space and an open frontier that invited separation, rather than accommodation, among those who differed. Vital forces for local conformity and homogeneity, territorial expansion, and economic development meant that unity was elusive, seemingly unnecessary in some ways. Specific and localized loyalties were firmly embedded at the beginning of the twentieth century when frontier development ended. Although political parties provided some sense of a national level of politics, loyalties were compartmentalized and protected.[29]

The political power that emanated from geographic and cultural segments of society was extremely hard to marshal on behalf of broad purposes. "Just beneath the soft assertions of unity lay the hard demands for conformity...Cohesion in a segmented society, therefore, required a high level of abstraction and a low level of implementation."[30] Such abstract cohesion is played out in what Gans calls love of the nation, in contrast to government or politics, a sentiment that seems to be evoked in a variety of circumstances.[31] This loosely constructed sense of national unity stood to be strengthened by the expansion of social space achieved through the use of technology, by the proliferation of national organizations during the 1960s, and by shifts in advertising and preferred news sources that reach beyond local segments of the nation (chapters 2, 3, and 5).

A 1998 cross-national analysis conducted by the National Opinion Research Center (NORC) suggests that national pride is realized in specific achievements: how a democracy works; its political influence in the world; its social security system; scientific and technological achievements; achievements in sports; accomplishments in arts and literature; its armed forces; its history; and its fair and equal treatment of all groups in society. These items were used to construct a scale with a maximum score of 50 for survey respondents who were very proud of their nation's achievements in all ten areas. The United States, with a score of 38.5, ranked second among twenty-three countries. The United States also ranked second with a score of 17.2 out of a maximum of 25 on a five-item scale for general national pride. This was based on the degree to which survey respondents agreed or disagreed that they would rather be a citizen of their own than any other country, whether there are some things about their country that make them feel ashamed, whether the world would be a better place if people elsewhere were more like citizens of their own country, whether theirs was a better country than most others, and whether people should support their country right or wrong. On this instrument, the national pride of Americans is comparatively stronger than most nations, including Great Britain and Germany.[32]

Tolerance

Surveys indicate an increase in tolerance for difference:

- In a follow-up visit to Middletown, researchers found that the percentage of adolescents there who believed conscientious objectors should be prosecuted fell from 55 percent in 1924 to 30 percent in 1999.[33]
- Between 1972 and 1998, Americans increasingly became accepting of community-speaking and teaching in colleges by atheists, homosexuals, communists, and militarists. Declining proportions favored removal of books from libraries that espoused the views of such individuals.
- The proportion of Americans who believe that white people have a right to segregated neighborhoods fell from 31 to 11 percent in 1996.
- Laws prohibiting racial intermarriage lost favor between 1970 and 1998. The percentage that approve of such laws fell from 35 to 11 percent.
- Those who believe that sex between two same-sex adults is always or almost always wrong fell from 76 to 64 percent between 1973 and 1998.
- In 1998, 87 percent believed that homosexuals have the right to equal job opportunities, up from 56 percent in 1977.
- Between 1965 and 1998, a rising number of Americans favored abortion under a variety of special circumstances.
- Those who believe that women's job is to take care of the home while men run the country declined from 34 to 15 percent of the adult population between 1974 to 1998.[34]

Such issues continue to elicit controversy, despite gains in tolerance. Divergent views are not in danger of vanishing, even as an acceptance of equality of conditions progresses. Yet, the majority of Americans are in general agreement about the importance of diversity. Based on in-depth interviews with 200 middle-class Americans from eight suburban communities that vary in location, income, and lifestyle, sociologist Alan Wolfe recently concluded that the largest segment of American society strives to be accepting.

> Reluctant to pass judgment, they are tolerant to a fault, not about everything—they have not come to accept homosexuality as normal and they intensely dislike bilingualism—but about a surprising number of things, including rapid transformations in the family, legal immigration, multicultural education, and the separation of church and state. Above all moderate in their outlook on the world, they believe in the importance of leading a virtuous life but are reluctant to impose values they understand as virtuous for themselves on others....[35]

In national surveys, American adults clearly come down on the side of diversity.

- In 1990, 61 percent told Research and Forcasts that they strongly agreed, and another 30 percent somewhat agreed that diversity of opinion strengthens our democracy.[36]
- In 1991, 57 percent of participants in a *Detroit Free Press* and Tokyo/ *Chunichi Shimbun* survey said racial diversity has made America a stronger society.[37]
- In 1996, 81 percent of adults told the Post-Modernity Project that changes in recent decades toward greater cultural and ethnic diversity were very or mostly good. In the same survey, ethnic diversity was an idea that gave 65 percent of respondents a positive or very positive feeling.[38]
- In 1998, Bruskin, Goldring Research found that 56 percent of adults believed it very or somewhat important that racial, ethnic, cultural, and religious diversity in their neighborhood should expand within the next two to three decades.[39]
- In 1999, 71 percent of Americans interviewed for Pew Research Center identified cultural diversity as a major cause of U.S. success in the past century.[40]

A majority of Americans are aware of the growth in tolerance. According to the Peter Hart for Shell Poll, about six out of ten feel the nation has grown stronger over the last decade, in terms of acceptance of people who are different. Despite greater tolerance, the acceptance of diversity exists in tension with other concerns that Americans also hold. When asked if it is more important to show tolerance for different others *or* to show respect for community standards, 47 percent agreed with the former while a close 41 percent chose the latter. Asked to choose whether protected free speech or racial harmony and equality is more important in a 1994 nationwide study conducted by the Survey Research Center, 54 percent chose free speech; 46 percent chose racial harmony and equality. In the same study, 60 percent felt it more important to promote racial harmony and equality than to promote traditional religious values in politics and society.[41]

Diverse, but Convergent, Ways of Life

Lifestyle typologies, as developed from census data, consumer research, interviews, and political polls illustrate the diversity, segmentation, and the crosscutting of Americans. The market research firm Claritas Corporation used this information to sort all of the zip code areas in the United States by thirty-four lifestyle factors into forty initial classifications of neighborhoods. Weiss, a free-lance journalist who explored the results of this research, found that residents of each type of neighborhood "tend to lead similar lives, driving the same kinds of cars to the same kinds of jobs, discussing similar interests at similar social events...[and share] a perspective from which [they] view the world." This geodemographic segmentation further shows nearly identical lifestyles scattered about the country, with some concentrations located in large metropolitan areas.[42] One passes through sixty neighborhoods while driving the 65-mile stretch along U.S. 50 and Route 7 between Annapolis, MD, and Leesburg, VA. At the time of the 1990 census, this slice of America was comprised of twenty-four varieties of neighborhoods also found scattered throughout the nation. Towards each end of this stretch of road one could drive through "God's Country," a type of neighborhood characterized as upscale frontier boomtowns representative of 2.7 percent of the nation's households—and found as well in places far afield like Woodstock (NY), Albuquerque (NM), Lake Arrowhead (CA), and Clancy (MT).[43]

Geodemographic segmentation further emphasizes the dynamic nature of this diverse picture of Americans at a grassroots level. As Weiss notes, "the map is always changing—through gentrification, urban decay and demographic shifts." Between the 1970 and 1980 censuses, eight neighborhood types replaced eight others, five were renamed, and three underwent significant changes. Eight new neighborhood types were expected to appear with the 1990 census, but the classification system was ultimately expanded from 40 to 62 profiles to reflect developments that occurred during the previous decade.[44]

The 1984 presidential election offers an example of how Americans in these various kinds of neighborhoods cut across ideology and geography to reach a consensus. Thirty-three moderate and conservative kinds of neighborhoods combined forces to elect Ronald Reagan. Of the seven types of neighborhoods that voted for Mondale, the losing candidate, four were liberal and three were moderate in political ideology (table 4.3). Communities in these seven neighborhood clusters, which accounted for 14 percent of U.S. households, came from across the nation and included Watts in Los Angeles,

CA; Galveston, TX; Selma, AL; Newburg in Cleveland, OH; West Dodge, NE; Capital Heights, MD; Haight-Ashbury in San Francisco, CA; Skokie, IL; and Upper East Side in Manhattan, NY. These seven types of neighborhood differed in age, median household income, median home value, housing, education, occupation, and family constitution. The magazines and newspapers, leisure activities, and TV programs prevalent in these neighborhood types varied. Yet, the key election issues were less disparate: trade protection, jobs, nuclear arms, the federal budget, social programs, and poverty.

More recently, a move toward greater convergence in TV viewing habits of black and white Americans signals some important changes between 1996 and 2000. The lists of the twenty most popular TV programs for both groups, compiled by Nielsen Media Research, shared only *Monday Night Football* in 1995. The two lists shared nine programs in common by the end of the 2000/01 season. The common viewing ground now includes *Monday Night Football, E.R., Temptation Island, Survivor II, Millionaire* (Tuesday and Wednesday), *Law and Order*, *The Practice*, and *CSI*. The first three programs are also among the twenty programs frequented most in Hispanic households.[45]

Lack of Diversity in Local Self-Governance

Broad community involvement in self-governance of daily affairs not only encourages investment in and attachment to local community. It also results in government suited to the taste and choice of a locale. For these reasons, the large number of offices at the local level, noted in chapter 3, is desirable for a healthy civil society. Local self-governance in the U.S. is not widely diverse, however, by the profile of its elected officials. Some attempt is customarily made to alleviate fiscal hardship created by serving in local office. Compensation for this civic duty, commensurate with the task, is considered a protection for democracy. As Tocqueville pointed out, "if public officers are unpaid, a class of rich and independent public functionaries will be created who will constitute the basis of an aristocracy; and...the choice can [then] be made only from a certain class of citizens."[46] I find, in a review of the *1992 Census of Governments*, that most duties associated with local elective office are compensated, at least for expenses. Localities usually authorize fees, commissions, salary, or a combination of these for duties performed. I counted only seventy-four, or 4 percent, of an estimated total of 1,728 kinds of local elective offices designated as unpaid in 1992.[47] Expense is not the only barrier to this kind of civic participation. Time is one. Access for women and minorities is another.

Women and minorities have assumed a larger share of local elective offices over the last four decades, resulting in a more representative mix of local officials. This occurred at some sacrifice of local autonomy, via national civil rights legislation. The civil rights initiative that stimulated elective opportu-

Table 4.3

Neighborhood Types That Supported Mondale in 1984 Presidential Election

Neighborhood	Median Income, Home Value	Typical Inhabitants	Education, Occupation	Newspapers, Periodicals	Leisure Activity	Television Programs	Important Issues
1. Urban Gold Coast	$36,838; $200,000+	white; single; 18-24, 65+	college; white collar	*New York; New York Times; Metropolitan Home; Atlantic Monthly*	theatre; tennis	*Nightline; Letterman; Entertainment Tonight; At the Movies*	trade protection; jobs
2. Bohemian Mix	21,916; 110,668	racially mixed; single; 18-34	college; white collar	*Atlantic Monthly; Harper's; Esquire; New Yorker*	environmental organizations; movies	*Nightline; Letterman; At the Movies; Good Morning America*	nuclear arms; federal budget
3. Black Enterprise	33,149; 68,713	black; family; 35-54	some college; white collar	*Essence; Ebony; MS; GQ*	theme restaurants; unions	*Nightline; Hotel; American Bandstand; Miami Vice*	jobs; trade
4. Emergent Minorities	22,029; 45,187	black; single parent family	some high school; blue collar and service	*Esquire; Ebony; Jet; Working Woman*	watch track and field; movies	*Friday Night Videos; Dance Fever; CBS Sports Saturday; Donahue*	jobs; social programs
5. Single City Blues	17,926; 62,351	racially mixed; single; 18-34	some college; white and blue collar	*Atlantic Monthly; Harper's; Modern Bride; Architectural Digest*	watch roller derby; jogging; backgammon; environmental organizations	*Nightline; Miami Vice; Dance Fever; The Young and Restless*	nuclear arms; federal budget
6. Downtown Dixie Style	15,204; 35,301	black; single; single parent family; 18-24, 65+	some high school; blue collar and service	*Ebony; Jet; Soap Opera Digest; Sport*	watch horse racing; health clubs	*General Hospital; As the World Turns; Falcon Crest; Dynasty*	poverty; social programs
7. Public Assistance	10,804; 28,340	black; single; single parent family; 18-24, 65+	grade school; blue collar and service	*Essence; Ebony; GQ; Jet*	salt-water fishing; watch pro-wrestling	*Friday Night Videos; Dance Fever; Ryan's Hope; Loving*	poverty; jobs

Source: Compiled from Weiss, *The Clustering of America*, 278-280, 301-302, 310-311, 350-351, 353-354, 377-378, 390-391.

nities for women and minorities challenged a deeply resistant social structure. Indeed, Burns found that exclusion was not an uncommon rationale for forming local governments in the first place, often on the basis of economic, racial, religious, political, and/or security preferences.[48]

A few women were elected to school committees in Massachusetts in the 1860s-70s, followed by a smattering of females elected mostly to school superintendencies and education-related positions. Not until the 1920s and 1930s did women, in significant numbers, begin to appear as court clerks, recorders, auditors, tax collectors and assessors, treasurers, justices of the peace, constables, and "poor" directors. One small town in Minnesota elected a female mayor in 1920 and Cleveland had three women city council members in 1927.[49] The Center for the American Woman in Politics (CAWP) at Rutgers University concluded that approximately 5 percent of all officials holding elective office in 1975 at local, state, and national levels were women. That estimate grew to 7.8 percent two years later.[50]

Women continue to move into more visible elective leadership roles. At local levels, the CAWP found that the 3 percent of county governing board offices held by women in 1975 grew to 9 percent by 1989 and that the 4 percent of female mayors and members of municipal and township governing boards in 1975 rose to at least 14 percent by 1985.[51] In the more comprehensive *Census of Governments*, 20 percent of local officeholders were women in 1987, a figure that improved to 24 percent by 1992.[52] Slowly, women are filling more elective offices than at any time in American history.

The same is true of racial minorities. In 1964, there were only 184 black state and local elected officials in the United States.[53] Six years later, the Joint Center for Political and Economic Studies (JCPES) identified 1,077 black city, county, and education officials. By 1998, black elected officials in such local offices numbered 8,216.[54] The *Census of Governments* reports that blacks popularly elected to local public office numbered 8,181 in 1987 and 11,441 in 1992, a 40 percent increase within five years.[55]

Most officials listed in the National Association of Latino Elected and Appointed Officials (NALEAO) roster are at the local level, with four-fifths in county, municipal, special district, and education/school board positions. Latino officeholders in these positions doubled between 1983 and 1994. Subsequent changes in reporting methods produce noncomparable numbers but show 4,100 Hispanics holding these local offices in 1997.[56] A more complete coverage of local Hispanic officeholders in the *Census of Governments* reflects an increase from 4,704 in 1987 to 5,859 in 1992, a 25 percent increase in five years.

Two *Census of Governments* taken in 1987 and 1992 provides a window for closer scrutiny of developments in local elective offices. The total number of local elective offices expanded by 3 percent, consistent with a recovery from the decline in school districts that curtailed local participation. Progress made in minority and female representation in these local elective offices is important symbolically, while small statistically. Demographic profiles of local elected officials show that females and minorities are not yet close to being represented in local elective offices relative to their share of the population (table 4.4).[57] In 1992, males comprised 49 percent of the resident popu-

Table 4.4

Women and Minorities in Local Elective Offices: Proportionate Representation and Concentration (in percentages)

	Female	Black	Hispanic	Other
U.S. Resident Population:				
1992	51	12	10	4
Local Elected Officials:				
1987	20	2	1	*
1992	24	3	1	1
Largest Representation:				
1992	school districts 31	school districts 5	school districts 3	*
Largest Concentration:				
1992	municipalities 27; townships 28; school districts 25	municipalities 40; school districts 37	municipalities 29; school districts 42	municipalities 38; school districts 32
Largest Numerical Gain:				
1987-1992	special districts 36; counties 31	school districts 131	school districts 74	special districts 44

Source: Compiled from 1987 and 1992 editions of the United States Census Bureau, *Census of Governments*. Resident population figures are calculated from United States Census Bureau, *Statistical Abstract of the United States* 1997, 14, 19.

* less than 1%

lation, but held 76 percent of the local elective offices. Ninety-five percent of local officeholders were white, descriptive of only three-fourths of the population.[58] Blacks, who constituted 12 percent of the population, held 3 percent of local offices. Hispanics, who accounted for 10 percent of the population, and *other* minorities who comprise 4 percent of the population, each held 1 percent of local offices.

Proportionately, 31 percent of elected school board members were women, while 5 percent were black, 3 percent were Hispanic, and less than 1 percent were other minorities. Four-fifths of female elected officials held municipal, township, and school district offices. Three-fourths of black elected officials were clustered in municipalities and school districts. Among Hispanic local officials, 42 percent filled school district offices and 29 percent were located in municipalities. Seven of every ten local officeholders with American Indian, Alaskan Native, and Asian or Pacific Islander origins were in municipalities and school districts. The greatest gains between 1987 and 1992 were made by blacks and Hispanics moving into school district offices. Women became more visible in special district and county positions, broadening their base of representation. American Indian or Alaskan Native and Asian or Pacific Islanders made inroads into special district offices.

Summary and Discussion of Findings

Early in the nation's history, Tocqueville remarked on the sundry opinions of Americans and the multiple purposes to which voluntary association seemed dedicated. Reasons for association have since multiplied and diversified, as shown by increasingly elaborate and detailed classifications of voluntary association. While some rationales for associations are universal, others are unique to the venue and enterprise of a community. It is clear that fresh concerns and interests continually emerge, meanings are adjusted, priorities are reordered, and subject classifications of voluntary associations become more elaborate.

Race, ethnicity, socioeconomic discrepancies, political ideology, geography, and religious belief are catalysts for partition in the United States. At the same time, tolerance grows and stands beside a developed appreciation for diversity and unity. Americans are free to segment themselves to an excessive extent and are known to have used voluntary associations and communities to that end. Yet, most Americans transcend differences to maintain a modicum of connectedness through shared interests, sentiments, concerns, activities, identifications, and communities. While a variety of circumstances, experiences, and opinions blend in collective effort into a richer mix, it is also evident that gaps and linkages remain to be forged and strengthened.

Notes

1. Alexis de Tocqueville, *Democracy in America* (New York: Vintage Books, 1945), II:114-115, 123-127, 227, 182-195; I:113-114, 117, 198-199, 202-204.
2. Florence Mishnun, "Voluntary Associations," in Edwin R. A. Seligman and Alvin Johnson, *Encyclopedia of the Social Sciences* (New York: Macmillan, 1934), 283-297; C. Wayne Gordon and Nicholas Babchuk, "A Typology of Voluntary Associations," *American Sociological Review* 24:2 (February 1959): 22-29; Arnold M. Rose, *The Power Structure: Political Process in American Society* (New York: Oxford University Press, 1967), 214, 233-252; Michael Banton, "Voluntary Associations: Anthropological Aspects," in David L. Sills, ed., *International Encyclopedia of the Social Sciences* (New York: Macmillan and Free Press, 1968), 357-362; David L. Sills, "Voluntary Associations: Sociological Aspects," in Sills, *International Encyclopedia of the Social Sciences*, 362-379; Constance Smith and Ann Freedman, *Voluntary Associations: Perspectives on the Literature* (Cambridge, MA: Harvard University Press, 1972), 45-47, 92-94; David Horton Smith, "The Impact of the Volunteer Sector on Society," in Brian O'Connell, ed., *America's Voluntary Spirit* (New York: Foundation Center, 1983), 331-344; Donato J. Pugliese, *Voluntary Associations: an Annotated Bibliography* (New York: Garland, 1986), 6-10, 41-121, 177-192; Herbert J. Gans, *Middle American Individualism: The Future of Liberal Democracy* (New York: Free Press, 1988), 44-51; Jon Van Til, *Mapping the Third Sector: Voluntarism in a Changing Social Economy* (New York: Foundation Center, 1988), 57-87; David Horton Smith, "Grassroots Associations are Important: Some Theory and a Review of the Impact Literature," *Nonprofit and Voluntary Sector Quarterly* 26:3 (September 1997): 269-306.
3. Tocqueville, *Democracy in America*, I:199, 203, 181-182, 115.
4. Ibid., I:199; II:114.
5. J. H. Kolb and Edmund deS. Brunner, *A Study of Rural Society* (Boston, MA: Houghton Mifflin, 1946), 246-247.
6. Virginia Ann Hodgkinson, Murray S. Weitzman, with John A. Abrahams, Eric A. Crutchfield, and David R. Stevenson, *Nonprofit Almanac 1996-1997: Dimensions of the Independent Sector* (San Francisco, CA: Jossey-Bass, 1996), 271-309.
7. Lester M. Salamon and Helmut K. Anheier, *The Emerging Nonprofit Sector* (Manchester, UK: Manchester University Press, 1996), 136-140.
8. Mirra Komarovsky, "The Voluntary Associations of Urban Dwellers," *American Sociological Review* (December 1946): 686-698; Kolb and Brunner, *A Study of Rural Society* (1946); Arthur J. Vidich and Joseph Bensman, *Small Town in Mass Society* (Garden City, NY: Anchor, Doubleday, [1958] 1960), 23-29, 83-84.
9. World Values Study Group, World Values, 1981-1984 and 1990-1993 [Computer file]. ICPSR version. Ann Arbor, MI: Institute for Social Research [producer]. Ann Arbor, MI: Interuniversity Consortium for Political and Social Research [distributor], 1994; *Encyclopedia of Associations* (Detroit, MI: Gale Research); Karlheinz Reif and Ronald Inglehart, eds., *Eurobarometer* (New York: St. Martin's Press, 1991), 364-370.
10. Annual editions of the *Encyclopedia of Associations*. This was first published as *Encyclopedia of American Associations* (Detroit, MI: Gale Research, 1956) and retitled the *Encyclopedia of Associations* with the 1961, or third, edition. Initial collection of data began by compiling information from local phone directories, newspapers, magazines, periodicals, chambers of commerce, and other national

organizations. Subsequently, questionnaires are mailed to organizations with follow-up by written correspondence, telephone, and reliable secondary source confirmations. There is a period of several years, generally three, before an inactive or defunct status of an organization is confirmed and the entry is dropped. Lag time occurs between the founding date of an association and when it first enters the reference work.

11. This decline is consistent with the category noted in the *Encyclopedia of Association* that includes fraternal groups.
12. Annual editions of United States Internal Revenue Service, "Commissioner of Internal Revenue Annual Report," Washington, DC. According to a March 1996 interview with an Internal Revenue Service spokesman the agency does relatively little auditing that would glean ineligible organizations from the master file.
13. Thomas Rotolo, "Trends in Voluntary Association Participation," *Nonprofit and Voluntary Sector Quarterly* 28:2 (June 1999): 199-212.
14. Question: "Now we would like to know something about the groups or organizations to which individuals belong. Here is a list of various organizations. Could you tell me whether or not you are a member of each type? Fraternal groups; Service clubs; Veterans groups; Political clubs; Labor unions; Sports groups; Youth groups; School service groups; Hobby or garden groups; School fraternities or sororities; Nationality groups; Farm organizations; Literary, art, discussion or study groups; Professional or academic societies; Church-affiliated groups; Any other groups; Any membership at all?" James Allan Davis and Tom W. Smith. "General Social Surveys, 1972-1999." Cumulative Computer File, Chicago, IL: National Opinion Research Center [producer]. Ann Arbor, MI: Interuniversity Consortium for Political and Social Research [distributor], 1999, website http://www.icpsr.umich.edu/GSS.
15. See Frank R. Baumgartner and Jack L. Walker, "Survey Research and Membership in Voluntary Associations," *American Journal of Political Science* 32:4 (November 1988): 908-928; Tom W. Smith, "Trends in Voluntary Group Membership: Comments on Baumgartner and Walker," *American Journal of Political Science* 34:3 (August 1990): 646-661 for classic discussion of the problem.
16. United States Department of Commerce, *Census of Manufactures* (Washington, DC: United States Department of Commerce, 1947); annual editions of the *Standard Periodical Directory* (New York: Oxford Communications).
17. Marcella Ridlen Ray, "Technological Change and Associational Life," in Theda Skocpol and Morris Fiorina, eds., *Civic Engagement in American Democracy* (Washington, DC: Brookings Institution and Russell Sage Foundation, 1999), 304-306.
18. Tocqueville, *Democracy in America*, II: 123-124. It is noted that Tocqueville has been criticized for not having made a clear distinction between political association and political parties. For discussion, see George Kateb, "Tocqueville's View of Voluntary Associations," in J. Roland Pennock and John W. Chapman, eds., *Voluntary Associations* Nomos XI (New York: Atherton, 1969), 138-144.
19. For discussion of the general interest, see H. S. Harris, "Voluntary Association as a Rational Ideal," in Pennock and Chapman, *Voluntary Associations*, 47-49, who observes that even though group members share a general interest, it cannot be inferred that it will have an overriding influence on an individual member at a particular point in time. Richard Jenkins, *Social Identity* (London: Routledge, 1996), 102, explains that social identity, generally flexible, situational, and negotiable, is generated via processes of interaction and daily living.
20. Tocqueville, *Democracy in America*, I:198-200.

21. Gabriel A. Almond and Sidney Verba, *The Civic Culture: Political Attitudes and Democracy in Five Nations* (Newbury Park, CA: Sage Publications, [1963] 1989), 357.
22. Question: "Generally speaking, do you usually think of yourself as a Republican, a Democrat, an Independent, or what?" National Election Studies, Cumulative Data File, 1948-1998. Ann Arbor: University of Michigan, Center for Political Studies, 1999, website http://www. umich.edu/~anes.
23. Question: "There is a lot of discussion today about whether Americans are divided or united. Some say that Americans are united and in agreement about the most important values. Others think that Americans are greatly divided when it comes to the most important values. What is your view about this?" Davis and Smith, General Social Surveys.
24. Question: "When you think of social and political issues, do you think of yourself mainly as a member of a particular ethnic, racial, or nationality group, or do you think of yourself mainly as just an American?" Ibid.
25. Question: "Some people say that it is better for America if different racial and ethnic groups maintain their distinct cultures. Others say that it is better if groups change so that they blend into the larger society as in the idea of a melting pot. Where do you place yourself on the following scale, from: (1) Racial and ethnic groups should maintain their distinct cultures; to (7) Groups should change so that they blend into the larger society." Twenty percent selected (1) or (2) on the scale; 22 percent chose (6) or (7). Ibid.
26. Questions: "Should it be up to the government to help racial and ethnic groups maintain their distinct cultures, or should this be left up to the groups themselves?" and "Should it be up to the government to help racial and ethnic groups change so that they blend into the larger society, or should this be up to the groups themselves?" Ibid.
27. Roper Center at University of Connecticut, Public Opinion Online, 1999, LEXIS, Market Library, RPOLL File.
28. Seymour Martin Lipset, *The First New Nation* (New York: Anchor, Doubleday, [1963]1967), 83-86.
29. Robert N. Bellah, Richard Madsen, William M. Sullivan, Ann Swidler, and Steven M. Tipton, *Habits of the Heart: Individualism and Commitment in American Life* (New York: Harper and Row, 1985), 250-271; Robert H. Wiebe, *The Segmented Society: An Introduction to the Meaning of America* (New York: Oxford University Press, 1975), 27-30, 59-60, 87-125.
30. Wiebe, *The Segmented Society*, 133, 94.
31. Gans, *Middle American Individualism*, 58-64.
32. Tom W. Smith and Lars Jarkko, "National Pride: A Cross-National Analysis," GSS Cross-National Report No. 19 (Chicago, IL: National Opinion Research Center, 1998).
33. Theodore Caplow, Louis Hicks, and Ben J. Wattenberg, *The First Measured Century* (Washington, DC: AEI Press, 2001), 211.
34. Trends gathered from the National Opinion Research Center, Harris, Gallup, and New York Times surveys by Lee Epstein, Jeffrey A. Segal, Harold J. Spaeth, and Thomas G. Walker, *The Supreme Court Compendium: Data, Decisions, and Developments* (Washington, DC: Congressional Quarterly, 1996), 675-702; Robert J. Blendon, John M. Benson, Mollyann Brodie, Drew E. Altman, Richard Morin, Claudia Deane, and Nina Kjellson, "The 60s and the 90s," *Brookings Review* (Spring 1999): 15-16; Davis and Smith, General Social Surveys. Also see Jeffrey M. Berry, Kent E. Portney, and Ken Thomson, *The Rebirth of Urban*

Democracy (Washington, DC: Brookings Institution, 1993), 214-231 for a discussion of their finding that tolerance increases with citizen participation, not just in the participants themselves, but throughout the community; also see "The Personal Gap Narrows," *Public Perspective* (May/June 2001): 27.

35. Alan Wolfe, *One Nation, After All: What Middle-Class Americans Really Think* (New York: Penguin, 1998), 278.
36. Roper Center, Public Opinion Online, 1990.
37. Ibid., 1992.
38. Ibid., 1997.
39. Ibid., 1998.
40. This survey, conducted by Princeton Survey Research in 1999, is reported in *American Enterprise* (November/December 1999): 90.
41. This was a nationwide study of 1,464 English-speaking adults, aged 18 years and older, in households with telephones. Multi-Investigator Study, website http://sda.berkeley.edu.
42. Michael J. Weiss, *The Clustering of America* (New York: Harper and Row, 1988), 2-3, xi-xiii, 11-14, 268.
43. Susan Mitchell, "Birds of a Feather," *American Demographics* 17:2 (February 1995): 40-48.
44. Weiss, *The Clustering of America*, 6-7, 238-263; Mitchell, "Birds of a Feather," 41; Michael J. Weiss, *The Clustered World* (Boston, MA: Little, Brown, 2000).
45. Stacey Lynn Koerner, "Viewership Update: African Americans and Hispanics," *Initiative Media Research Report* (August 2001), 5-7; Nielsen Media Research, website http://www. nielsenmedia.com.
46. Tocqueville, *Democracy in America*, I:69-71, 215.
47. United States Bureau of the Census, *1992 Census of Governments* (Washington, DC: United States Department of Commerce, Economics and Statistics Administration, 1995), Appendix A, A1-A183.
48. Nancy Burns, *The Formation of American Local Government* (New York: Oxford University Press, 1994), 35-37.
49. Kristi Andersen, *After Suffrage* (Chicago, IL: University of Chicago Press, 1996), 111-130.
50. Center for the American Woman and Politics, *Women in Public Office* (New York: R. R. Bowker, 1976), xv-xxiii; Center for the American Woman and Politics, *Women in Public Office* (Metuchen, NJ: Scarecrow, 1978), xvii-xix.
51. Sara E. Rix, ed., *The American Woman 1988-89: A Status Report* (New York: W. W. Norton, 1988), 90; Center for the American Woman and Politics, "Women in Elective Office 1997 Fact Sheet" issued in September 1997 by National Information Bank on Women in Public Office, Eagleton Institute of Politics, Rutgers University.
52. Overall response rates for the *Census of Governments* surveys were 88.2 percent in 1992 and 87 percent in 1987. County governments were more diligent in reporting sex and race of their officials than other local entities; special districts and townships were least. Nonreport rates for sex and race in 1992 ranged from 4 percent for county officials to 33 percent for township officials. Between 1987 and 1992, the report rate improved for special districts and got worse for townships. This raises an interesting question. Does the rate of nonreporting to a centralized, federal agency say anything about the autonomy of a local entity? If so, counties would have less autonomy compared to other local entities. Improved reporting in 1992 implies that special districts might have experienced some loss of autonomy.

53. James E. Conyers and Walter L. Wallace, *Black Elected Officials: A Study of Black Americans Holding Governmental Office* (New York: Russell Sage Foundation, 1976), 2.
54. Taken from annual editions of United States Bureau of Census, *Statistical Abstract of the United States* (Washington, DC: United States Government Printing Office) and annual editions of Joint Center for Political and Economic Studies, *Black Elected Officials: A National Roster* (Washington, DC).
55. United States Bureau of the Census, *Census of Governments*, 1987 and 1992 editions.
56. Annual editions of the NALEAO Educational Fund, *National Roster of Hispanic Elected Officials* (Washington, DC), now retitled the *Directory of Latino Elected Officials*.
57. Resident population figures used are from the United States Bureau of the Census, *Statistical Abstract of the United States 1996*, 14, 19.
58. Comparison of population with local government profiles is possible with *Census of Government* reports in 1987 and 1992. Sex and race data on local elected officials in these reports were unreported for 13-15 percent of the total.

5

Communication: Circulation, Constraints, and Connections

Public communication in the United States in the 1830s seemed remarkably vibrant to Tocqueville. Americans of all conditions mingled, communicated regularly, exchanged ideas, became more equal, and were more ambitious than he had otherwise seen in France and England. The absence of rigid class divisions facilitated communication in vertical, as well as horizontal, directions. Americans of all socioeconomic conditions shared responsibility for affairs concerning justice, common welfare, and governance and they were schooled in ways that encouraged public interaction. The press, the primary instrument of public communication, effectively enlarged the public discourse and provided linkages necessary for shared behavior and thought.

Newspapers, Tocqueville remarked, were like advisers that talked daily with individuals about the common well being—without causing inconvenience or distraction from private affairs. Voluntary associations were hard to form when those with similar interests and motivations were unacquainted and unlikely to encounter one another. Generally, newspapers made it easier to form associations and to counter extreme individualism. They helped people with like concerns, although widely scattered, to keep each other informed, to sustain public discourse, and to act in concert without meeting face-to-face. Newspapers fostered a sense of connectedness by circulating ideas and information that transcended distance and differences. Thus, a free and sovereign people had the means to marshal mutual assistance, rally community interest around principles, influence one another's thinking, reveal conspiracies, hold one another accountable, and, in general, to stimulate politics.[1]

The press, a term herein used interchangeably with the media, fulfills a mediating function as do all voluntary associations. It is the only voluntary association with such a comprehensive reach into the lives of citizens. This reach into private life appeals to centralized governments who can use the press to shape public opinion. Decentralized governments, as found in the United States, are less able to control the press. Therefore, Tocqueville believed the content of a newspaper seemed an appropriate, if rough, measure of press autonomy and freedom. Unique to American newspapers, for example, relatively little space was devoted at that time to the discussion of politics in contrast to the space devoted to advertising and other immediate information necessary to a self-governing people.[2]

Freedom and autonomy of the press is examined in this chapter as an indicator of a healthy civil society. Free circulation of information and news from diverse and decentralized sources is fundamental to democratic civil society for two important reasons. It supports connectedness and it mediates a balanced tension between Americans and an overweening government. An overriding question is if and how the communication component of civil society has changed during the twentieth century. The United States has the legal basis for a free media, but how well is it working in actual practice? Is there change in how the government, the press, and the public sustain this institution? Are news sources diverse and decentralized? Do Americans use media and communication technology to stay loosely connected? These questions, important to the vitality of a democratic civil society, are examined in this chapter.

A Free Media

Many historical accounts of the relationship between government and the media begin with the 1735 acquittal of the colonial printer John Peter Zenger, who was tried for criticizing the royal governor of New York. It was this landmark case that established truth as a credible defense against prosecution for seditious libel.[3] Thus a foundation was laid for a balanced tension between the two institutions that would require constant maintenance. Furthering the process of institutionalization of a free press in 1791, the First Amendment of the United States Constitution prohibited abridgement of freedom of the press and most state constitutions carried provisions for protecting the liberty of print media.[4] These were soon sorely tested in the midst of the fever of undeclared war with France. Congress passed the Sedition Act of 1798 that made it a criminal offense to publish false and malicious writings about the president or the government. Subsequently several Republican publishers were prosecuted, but the Act was repealed two years later.[5] The inherent tension between freedom of the press and the interests of government was thus exhibited early in the nation's history.

Empirical measures taken in the twentieth century continue to support Tocqueville's impression that the American press was relatively free and independent of governmental control.[6] The media was judged to be comparatively free in the mid-1960s, when the University of Missouri School of Journalism assigned scores for press freedom and critical ability.[7] A nominal classification for this scoring, developed by Almond and Powell, characterized the media in the United States as highly autonomous.[8] The Comparative Survey of Freedom, conducted annually by Freedom House since 1973, has consistently found that the press and broadcast media in the United States are free. This country is among the 37 percent of the world's nations with a free press and broadcast media—an assessment based on freedom from government control and on representation of a full spectrum of opinion.[9] Public opinion in the United States concurs with this assessment. Sixty-nine percent of a national sample of adults told Pew Research Center in 1999 that freedom of the press was a major reason that "America has been successful during this past century," while 22 percent thought it a minor reason and 7 percent thought it was not at all a reason.[10] Americans, however, are ambivalent about the freedom that the press has; at times a majority tell pollsters that the press may have too much freedom.[11]

First Amendment scholar Jeffery Smith says that the government "by withholding information, policing thought, and spreading propaganda, frequently acts as if it is necessary to destroy democracy in order to save it."[12] In 1953, Justice Douglas observed in *United States v. Rumely* that the "finger of government leveled against the press is ominous."[13] Thus it is that keeping the flow of information and ideas free from government intervention is never settled. The relationship between government and the press must be mediated anew with each change in circumstances and each choice presented by new technologies. A working tension has to be maintained by the parties involved, regardless of the Constitutional guarantee of freedom. This continuous negotiation process has an exhaustive history that can only be briefly recognized here. Many of the perceptible challenges to a balanced tension between the needs of government and the freedom of the media have occurred around war, felt threats to national security, and most recently, attempts to regulate the telecommunications industry.

War and National Security

The first censorship of news media during wartime occurred in the Civil War. The telegraph permitted the press to quickly report events and both the Confederacy and the Union tried to censor such reporting. When the voluntary self-restraint requested by the Union failed to work to the satisfaction of government, papers that published information believed to be helpful to the Confederacy were prosecuted, denied access to the mail, and their telegrams were monitored. The *New York Journal of Commerce*, *New York World*, and *Chicago Times* were all temporarily suspended for false reporting and, in the latter case, for attacking the Lincoln administration. Generals in the field barred or kept reporters at a distance. In subsequent wars, the same issues of national security, voluntary self-censorship by the press, government and military field censorship arose. During World Wars I and II the government and the military attempted to use the press as a vehicle for disseminating propaganda and misinformation. As technologies of communication and transportation made direct access to the fighting possible, contentions about war coverage intensified between government and the media. Challenges to the severity of the censorship and questioning about the extent to which the press should cooperate have followed each war.[14] Direct access by the media to the Vietnam war proved problematic to the government, both militarily and politically. At the other extreme, complete blockage of the media from access during the Grenada invasion tipped the balance too far towards censorship. Media frustration was high with the imposition of press pools escorted by the military during the Persian Gulf War; the government clearly prevailed at the time. The participation of public relations firms and expert commentators during the Persian Gulf and Balkan conflicts often substituted clutter and propaganda for real information, further accentuating an imbalance in the free press-government relationship.[15]

Regulation

The United States Supreme Court has been called upon to mediate free press issues (see chapter 7) at numerous points in the nation's history. Two important Court decisions together demonstrate the opposing tenets held in working balance between freedom of the press and government regulation. In a significant reconfirmation of Constitutional protection for a free press, the Supreme Court struck as unconstitutional an attempt by the state of Minnesota to legislatively suppress a weekly newspaper that was highly critical of government officials. Chief Justice Hughes wrote clearly in the decision of *Near v. Minnesota* (1931) that the democratic press must necessarily be free to report on and to criticize the government without fear.[16] When the authority of the Federal Communications Commission (FCC) to regulate chain broadcasting was challenged all the way to the Supreme Court, Justice Frankfurter wrote in *National Broadcasting Company v. United States* (1943) that there *was* a role for government beyond the "engineering and technical aspects of regulation of radio communication" that served the public interest.[17]

Regulatory efforts to control the media delineate an arena of discourse and spell out some of the rules of institutional interaction. The actions of each party therefore have better exposure to scrutiny and public discourse than do unregulated issues. This helps to sustain a workable balance in the long term. An example is the chronic tension between the two institutions that is traceable to the Communications Act of 1934. This legislation provided for regulation of radio broadcasting stations through licensing by the Federal Communications Commission (FCC). The Act explicitly denied the Commission any power of censorship, specifying that the basis for approving licenses could only be the public interest, convenience, or necessity. Yet, the FCC soon found itself at cross-purposes with the media about the meaning of the public interest. The Commission's announcement in 1936 that foreign programs could not be rebroadcast without its written permission seemed to a protesting media to be beyond its scope of authority.[18] In 1938, the FCC charged a network owner with letting his radio stations take sides in a partisan political conflict, maintaining that this was inconsistent with the public interest. The Commission ruled that a station that sells radio time to one political party must do so to all parties. A broader question, of course, was whether a license holder could take an editorial position, such as the newspapers did.[19] The Commission's decision in 1938 to cite or silence radio stations for broadcasting a Eugene O'Neill play, *Beyond the Horizon*, raised another storm of objection.[20]

Controversies like these were catalysts for public opinion, a source of legitimacy for both government and the media. When questioned by Gallup in 1938, 85 percent of radio owners reported having heard a broadcast in the past year that was offensive due to its vulgarity. However, a majority of 59 percent felt that government censorship of programs would be harmful, while a smaller 41 percent believed it would be good.[21] That same year the Federal Council of the Churches of Christ in America said explicitly that government censorship was *not* the solution: "To avoid an increased centralization of cultural activities under the government voluntary associations must function more vigorously and conscientiously in the development of standards to govern broadcasting...(249)."[22] The mediating function offered by other institutions was thus suggested as a way to advance the relationship between media and government. A *New York Daily News* editorial at the time, in criticizing the FCC decision about the O'Neill play, pointed out its pertinence to democracy:

> If we want a totalitarian United States, one way to bring it nearer fast, is for us to take these censorship rulings of the FCC without protest—to let the FCC gradually increase its power over the radio until it runs the radio.... We must keep the FCC within bounds, and narrow bounds at that.[23]

Such boundaries are not easily drawn, but must be revisited with each new technological innovation. Even today, the roles of Congress and the Federal Communications Commission, in their efforts to regulate broadcasting, telecommunications, and, most recently, the Internet, are continuously negotiated.[24]

Self-Regulation

Another facet of balancing the tension between government and the press is the self-regulation by journalism in accordance with its own ethical codes and principles.[25] When, if ever, is it appropriate to withhold or distort information in order to placate or to cooperate with the government? It may be more easily justifiable in times of war or threat to national security, but perhaps not. The dilemma was made clear in an incident that occurred during the Kennedy administration. The *New York Times* was about to break the story of a plan to invade the Bay of Pigs when the President personally requested that the story be killed. The *Times* cooperated by altering its story. Later, Kennedy confided to the editor that if the original story had appeared, the invasion would have had to be canceled and error and embarrassment might have been avoided.[26] In other words, had the press sustained the tension between itself and government, rather than capitulating to the President's argument, it could have better served the public interest.

The tension between government and the media was highly visible during the 1970s over four particularly volatile issues: secret deployment and manipulation of journalists and media companies by the Central Intelligence Agency; the Pentagon Papers affair; the confidentiality of the Pike Report about misconduct by the Central Intelligence Agency; and publication of information on the hydrogen bomb.[27] In the 1980s, the Reagan administration was highly successful in maintaining secrecy, in discrediting the media, and in controlling the information that reached the public—all unwittingly abetted by the media itself.[28] *Village Voice* reporter Mark Hertsgaard wrote at the time that the neutrality concerns of the press were misplaced and overreaching.

> It is precisely this philosophy—WE DON'T TAKE SIDES—that has shaped coverage.... Reluctant to present too negative a picture of the president for fear of appearing partisan, and willing to believe that neutrality is truth and accuracy is bias, the news media made the Reagan Administration's work much easier by becoming an active participant in its own manipulation.[29]

This diagnosis by a member of the press has implications for more than the characterization of an administration's relationship with the press. The media does have the responsibility, as a mediating institution, not to take sides. But neutrality is not sufficient. On a higher plane, the media has a responsibility to take the side of democracy against the abuse of power by any party. Ensuring that good and full information is made available to all concerned helps to level the playing field. This role, when fulfilled in service to democracy, contributes to the flexible tension that dissolves impasse or corrects for imbalance between institutions.

A major question in the 1990s is whether the press pays enough of the right kind of attention to what government is doing. There is evidence of inattention. A recent study of news coverage at federal agencies, conducted by the Project on the State of the American Newspaper, finds that coverage is uneven. Coverage at the Departments of Justice and Defense, the Environmental Protection Agency and the Social Security Administration remained the same during this decade. There is decline in the coverage of eight other federal agencies, however, while coverage in seven that deal with business, finance, technology, health, and science increased.[30] To the extent that the public has insufficient information to hold political leaders accountable for the way they do their jobs, the media neglects its responsibility to democracy.

Public Opinion

A free media needs to enjoy legitimacy with the public to withstand the overweening influences of the government. Yet, the public's evaluation of the media has grown more negative in the last three decades.

- Louis Harris and Associates surveys between 1966 and 1998 show a decline from 29 to 14 percent of survey respondents with a great deal of confidence in the press. Similarly, the 41 percent who reported a great deal of confidence in TV news in 1973 shrank to 26 percent in 1998.[31]
- Downward trends of trust placed in journalists, the press, and TV news reporters are also documented since the 1970s by Gallup Polls, Roper Organization surveys, and the National Opinion Research Center.
- General beliefs about news organizations between 1985 and 1999, as reported in a recent Pew Research Center survey, show a rise in the opinion, from 34 percent to 58 percent, that news organizations do not get their facts straight. Furthermore, there were increases in the proportions of Americans who believe the press is inclined to cover up its mistakes, to be politically biased in its reporting, and not to care about how good of a job it does. Pew Research Center also found an increase in Americans who have the impression that the press is less caring about the people it reports about, is less moral, and is less professional. And, finally, the proportion of Americans who believe that the media protects democracy fell from 54 to 45 percent; those who think it hurts democracy rose from 23 to 38 percent.[32]

To summarize, the status of press freedom in the United States relies not just on the Constitutional guarantees, but also on the difficult task of striking a workable balance between freedom and governmental control. The government pushes unrelentingly for advantage and proves to be especially adept at censorship and obfuscation. Regulation helps in that it defines the rules, which are then open to deliberation and a chance for equitable mediation. In any struggle to sustain its autonomy, the press draws strength from public opinion and from its own internal moral compass. However, over the last three decades, the press became more vulnerable due to its own uncertainty and an erosion of public support.

Signs of Decentralization and Centralization

While censorship and regulation by government are manifestations of centralization of power and authority, local news sources indicate decentralization.[33] The nineteenth century was a period of evolution for the print media in which its role in community building was significant. Initially, the press was instrumental in encouraging and recruiting settlers of new communities. As settlements established themselves, local newspapers increasingly began to reflect the transition from community building to community life.[34]

Local News

Sociologist Merle Curti's choice for study of a Wisconsin frontier county settled from the 1830s to the 1850s was based partly on the abundance of materials made available by the ten newspapers that appeared during the time of settlement. Curti found that the press was an important agency of education. Local papers reported occasions of mutual helpfulness, daily community events, technological developments, different sides of debates, and crimes against persons and property. Local editors articulated behavioral standards for community members. They urged their fellow citizens

> to be thrifty, hard working, honest, decent—to observe, in effect, all the virtues of the McGuffey Readers. Games of chance, especially when sponsored by churches, were subjects of especial condemnation. And young men were urged to spend less time in stores and hotels of an evening and more time improving their minds by sound reading, for this was the path to success. Editor Luce constantly deplored the emphasis, not immoral in itself, of course, on the pursuit of gain, and urged great consideration for the cultural values, for appreciation of nature's beauty, and interest in the issues of the larger world, political, economic, and literary (121).[35]

Many newspapers openly aligned themselves with a political party and were distinctly partisan in content.[36] Curti found that "until the launching at Arcadia in 1880 of the Trempealeau *Democrat*, all the local papers were Republican in politics."[37] Partisan papers often courted government dollars in the forms of subsidy, contracts, and advertising.[38] Alternative news sources, such as the penny press, upped the competition by soliciting private advertising, claiming political independence, and reporting local news, weddings, deaths, etc. The general discourse grew more enlivened with these additional variations on the presentation of news and information.[39]

Early in the twentieth century, prolonged and continuous efforts by partisan papers to influence voters faded. Subsequent to reforms that weakened political party centrality, newspapers began to redefine their role to that of an impartial reporter of the news.[40] Conversation with readers was replaced by a disinterested approach. "As the link between press and party weakened, the newspaper voice no longer presumed even a broad political agreement with its readers. More and more, the voice of the professional newspaper was separated out from the voice of the readers," reports communications scholar Michael Schudson.[41] This principle persists as a part of the modern journalistic ethic. Recently, when Pew Research interviewed a sample of national and local media representatives, 76 percent confirmed their belief that "always remaining neutral" is a core principle of journalism.[42] This positioning of the press as a disinterested party, as well as the disappearance of independent publishers and small media organizations and continued consolidation of ownership has resulted in some thinning in the supply of what is locally relevant to Americans.

Attrition of independent and local publishers and media owners has gone on for much of this century. The number of independently owned newspapers dropped from 1,650 in 1920 to 850 in 1960 and further fell to 300 in 1998. Only fifteen of those remaining in 1998 had a circulation of at least 100,000.[43] This left many local communities without any local news organizations at all. Many of the local daily papers that remain, less than 1,500, are shaky. Within the last four years, there were 545 change of ownership transactions among them, a third of which were second, third, and fourth time turnovers.[44] The reverberations of corporate control are seen in priorities that favor profit, rather than public service. At least some large media conglomerates remain uncommitted to a journalistic ethic.[45] New cost efficiency-oriented owners follow strategies such as those that have constructed 125 major geographic concentrations of daily newspapers through buying, selling, and swapping.

> These groupings comprise papers under common ownership that are within roughly 100 miles of one another and have a daily circulation of at least 10,000. "Editorial sharing" encompasses a wide range of editorial cooperation, from a shared sports beat writer to shared features sections. Likewise, "business sharing" includes everything from a joint printing plant to combined advertising rates (80).[46]

Mergers have accelerated since the passage of the Telecommunications Act of 1996, even though the legislation was intended to remove de facto monopoly in the industry. Ever greater concentration of ownership is the result.[47] Near the end of 1998, all commercial broadcasting networks were owned by one of twelve companies. The holdings of the big twelve, so ranked by size of 1996 revenue, comprised an aggregate of power and influence. Between them, they owned 89 television stations, 600 radio stations, two major news magazines, most around-the-clock news channels, over 92 daily newspapers, all of the major motion picture studios, the producers of network entertainment broadcasting, every cable channel with more than a million viewers per week reaching 31 million cable households and over half of all subscribers, half of the basic and pay channels, twelve major trade book publishing companies, most recorded music, and over sixty magazines, plus international broadcasting and publishing interests around the world.[48] Additional mergers and buyouts occurred in 1999.[49]

This development in the industry was one subject of a recent survey conducted under the auspices of the Project on the State of the American Newspaper in which a cross-section of members of local and national media were interviewed between November 1998 and February 1999. Eighty-four percent of national media and 73 percent of the local media representatives confirmed that a core principle of journalism is "keeping the business people out of the newsroom."[50] A majority thought that buyouts—of local newspapers by large newspaper chains and of news organizations by diversified corporations with their emphasis on the bottom line—have had a negative effect on journalism.[51] Yet the nature of that negative effect is unclear. Large proportions of local and national media personnel believed corporate owners did *not* have very much influence over news coverage decisions, advertising concerns were not perceived as having much influence over these decisions, and the thinking was fairly evenly divided over whether an increased pressure to work for profit seriously hurts the quality of news coverage.[52] If these impressions from within the industry are accurate, profit-minded owner conglomerates may not be a threat to local news coverage.

We learn, directly and indirectly, that local news is important and in demand. The voice of and for the reader makes the local element of the media pertinent to the public discourse. In the experience of editor and Pulitzer Prize winner Bernard Stein, the local newspaper forges connections between Americans that are based on common concerns. Local media fills the gap between how life is seemingly represented in the national media and how it is actually lived by ordinary Americans. Too often, individuals feel isolated by problems they mistakenly judge to be private, rather than public. When the local newspaper suggests that one's concerns about the school or the neighborhood are shared by others, the feeling of isolation is replaced by a link between people that is both empowering and liberating, says Stein.[53] Indeed, the reason given most often in a 1985 Times Mirror survey, by 59 percent of a nationwide adult sample, for "following the news" was "[t]o feel more involved in what's going on in the world."[54] Involvement, mutual interests, or something as mundane as death notices, weather, and classified ads make local sources of news valuable to people.

When Gallup inquired in 1995 about the chief sources of news and information that Americans use and about their importance, local area TV, newspapers, and radio stations were among the most frequently utilized and valued. Significantly, Gallup provided respondents with eighteen ways of accessing news and information from which to select.[55] In 1999, Gallup again asked how people retrieved their news. Local TV news, local newspapers, and nightly network news programs ranked, in that order, at the top. A year earlier, Gallup asked whether people felt they could trust the accuracy of various news sources.

The greatest trust lies in local television news stations. Local newspapers, nightly network news, CNN News, TV news magazine shows, and discussions with friends and families were equally trusted sources that took second place.[56] Yet another survey question posed occasionally between 1985 and 1998 by Times Mirror and Pew Research Center gives priority to local origins of news and information. This survey asked for the overall opinion of four news sources: (a) network television news, (b) local television news, (c) the familiar daily newspaper, and (d) large nationally influential newspapers (which were never preferred by more than 12 percent of respondents). The two most immediate sources, local TV news and the familiar daily newspaper, were viewed as favorably, or more so, than the major network news. An exception occurred during the Persian Gulf War when the "very favorable" ratings for the two TV sources surged ahead of those for the newspaper. "Very favorable" ratings also fell for the three most utilized sources: 25 to 16 percent for network news; from 27 to 19 percent for local TV news; and from 25 to 18 percent for the familiar daily newspaper.[57]

The utility of local news was confirmed in the spring of 1998 by Pew Research Center when a majority of survey respondents reported they regularly watch local news more often than other kinds of TV and radio programs. Sixty-four percent regularly viewed local news programs, a proportion that outdistanced 38 percent who watched national nightly network news, the 37 percent who viewed news magazine shows like *60 Minutes*, and the 33 percent who watched the Weather Channel on a regular basis. In addition, one-half of these respondents were asked if they followed local, national, and international news closely most of the time or just when something important or especially interesting was happening. Thirty-four percent followed international news closely, 52 percent followed national news closely, and 61 percent followed local community news closely most of the time.[58] In this survey, the news topics followed most closely by the largest percentages of viewers were items with immediate impact on one's welfare: crime (36 percent), people and events in one's own community (34 percent), health (34 percent), sports (27 percent), local government (23 percent), science and technology (22 percent), news of political figures and events in Washington (19 percent), religion (18 percent), business and finance (17 percent), international affairs (16 percent), entertainment (16 percent), consumer news (15 percent), and culture and the arts (12 percent).[59]

The pattern of preference Pew found in 1998 for local news persisted in year 2000 with a noticeable difference. The portion who watched local news regularly shrank to 56 percent (from 64 percent), those watching national nightly network news fell to 30 percent (from 38 percent), and those who viewed news magazine shows fell to 31 percent (from 37 percent). When asked this time if they followed local, national, and international news closely most of the time or just when something important or especially interesting was happening, local community news was again followed most closely.[60]

Is the importance of local news on a collision course with corporate ownership hell-bent on profit? Or is it possible that the demand for local news is key to a healthy fiscal position for news organizations? Thinking that the latter may be the case, the *Miami Herald* is expanding its coverage of "extremely local news." The philosophy that the paper will be a "unifying voice for a diverse and complex community" has been abandoned in favor of some degree of decentralization, a decision driven by falling circulation. Now small communities within the *Herald*'s service area will get information in the paper about their particular "PTA meetings, zoning disputes, church fairs, etc."[61] The underlying assumption is that circulation can be revived with this alteration to content. This vision of a product with added immediate relevance to its consumers seeks the mix of local and national data desired by its audience.

Further empirical support for the hypothesis that local news, well done, can be profitable is provided by a comprehensive study of local television news broadcasts. In its first year of implementation, the Project for Excellence in Journalism engaged a large cadre of professional, scholastic, and research personnel to define quality local news, to rate two weeks of local broadcasting and 8,500 stories reported by sixty-one stations in twenty cities, and to compare these evaluations with commercial success as reflected by three years of Nielsen Media Research ratings.[62] Five of the eight stations with the highest quality of local news were rising in the Nielsen ratings. The Project definition of *good* local news broadcasting says that it "should accurately reflect their whole community, cover a wide variety of topics, cover what is significant, and balance their stories with multiple points of view, a variety of knowledgeable sources, and a high degree of community relevance." The five stations that received the highest scores on this set of criteria *and* succeeded commercially also delivered lengthier stories, greater depth in sourcing, more enterprise in reporting, stories featuring ordinary people, and community-relevant pieces about big ideas and issues. But another kind of local news also paid off, depending on the audience. Four of the seven lowest scoring stations on quality of news programming were also rising in the ratings. The researchers tentatively concluded this was because segments of the audience differ in their news presentation preferences. Some consumers prefer a tabloid-type of presentation, while others prefer the "sober, information-based approach."[63] There are other variables, such as size and diversity of the locality, that may figure into the findings but it is already apparent that local news cannot look the same everywhere.

Yet, making news coverage work well for a local area is extremely difficult with dwindling resources, thin staffing, and demands for high profit margins, sometimes as high as 40 percent.[64] Now three years into the research project, spokespersons deduce that local TV news is in trouble due to discrepancies between what viewers want *and* (1) what advertisers believe that audiences want, based on wrong ideas and poor research, and (2) profit demands. Newscasters are "selling out." As this research moves forward it increasingly confirms what Americans value, as indicated by ratings. Americans want local news, broad community coverage, longer stories, identified sources, reporters on scene, serious investigation, street interviews, and locally relevant political coverage.[65]

Flow of Advertising Dollars

Spending for advertising in periodicals multiplied six times and in newspapers by more than five times between 1909 and 1929. By 1930 twenty advertisers had placed at least a million dollars of advertising in leading periodicals. In 1929, advertising totaled about 2 percent of the national income; by 1999 it expanded to 2.9 percent. These items of information are important to this exploration because the allocation of advertising budgets naturally follows the practices and media preferences of Americans. Its trends in this century confirm (a) a continued need for local information, (b) a need for national information, and (c) a shift in sources used for news and local information.

Television, a favored source of news and information, pulls the largest share of advertising monies. In 1935, newspapers received 45 percent of the advertising dollar, magazines 8 percent, and radio 7 percent. The remaining 40 percent of spending was spread across direct mail, business papers, outdoor advertising, and miscellaneous devices. Once television ads became an option, they escalated steadily from 3 percent of the ad dollar in 1950 to 24 percent in 1999.[66] Theodore H. White, in describing how the magazine *Collier's* steadily lost advertising to television—from 1,718 pages in 1951 to 1,008 pages in 1955—reported that during 1954 the weekly circulation of *TV Guide* rose from 815,000 to 1.647 million.[67] In addition to its impact on mass circulation magazines such as *Collier's*, television advertising grabbed part of the newspapers' share. By 1999, then, television received 24 percent of the advertising dollar, newspapers 22 percent, magazines 5 percent, and radio 8 percent, while the remaining 41 percent of spending was spread across yellow pages, direct mail, business papers, outdoor advertising, and other forms.[68]

The targeting of national and local markets changed during the 1935 to 1999 time frame, as well. In 1935, 51 percent of the advertising dollar was for national advertising of products, while 49 percent went to local advertising. A small shift away from local markets occurred so that in 1999, 59 percent of the advertising dollar went to national advertising of products and 41 percent for local advertising. It implies a stronger national focus and, at the same time, a more expansive concept of what is local. But these figures do not highlight the changes in local-national advertising spending profiles within particular media. Thirty-two percent of all television advertising was spent on local TV spot ads in 1950; this was down to 26 percent in 1997, a change consistent with the overall trend favoring a national focus, although it rose to 30 percent in 1999. Advertising in newspapers, which is predominantly local, grew more local—from 80 percent in 1935 to 87 percent in 1999. And so did advertising on the radio. The local share of radio advertising expenditures increased from 31 to 78 percent. That radio and newspaper advertising became more local and TV ads less so is not only a division of media labor, but it also reiterates the need for local news and information.[69]

In synopsis, local news established itself along with the emergence of communities and, just as Tocqueville observed, the press was initially an advisor interested in talking with its readers. This interest turned to disinterest with a move away from political party alignments and adoption of an impartial stance as the reporter of news. The supply of local news coverage to local communities thinned and contracted during this century as the media industry consolidated its organization and resources. Decentralized, local news coverage is sacrificed to ownership concentration and profit-driven management in many locales. At the same time, public appreciation and demand for local news and information remains strong, evidenced by preferences for news sources and modes of presentation, topical news interests, and the markets to which media advertising dollars flow.

Connections via the Media and Communication Technology

Americans have historically adapted technology to perpetuate associational life. The newspaper, periodical, telephone, television, and the Internet each contribute to the framework of connectedness, but how they are applied and adapted, alone and in relation to each other, is a matter of continual adjustment.

The Newspaper

A decline in the number of newspapers throughout the twentieth century in the United States might suggest a disintegration of common ties. In 1999 there were 27 percent fewer daily papers listed in the *Editor and Publisher International Yearbook* than in 1921.[70] In 1921, a daily newspaper circulated for every 3.8 Americans. From 1945 to 1955, every 2.9 persons could share a daily paper if they liked. But by 1960 the per capita rate was falling, notwithstanding the effects of transportation improvements, advanced production technology, economy of scale and other management strategies. That decline steadily progressed to its lowest point ever in 1999 when one daily newspaper circulated for every 4.9 Americans.[71]

This pattern is reiterated in General Social Survey trends that reflect a drop of 26 percentage points in self-reported daily newspaper reading, from 69 to 43 percent, between 1972 and 1998. The small portion of survey respondents who never read the paper averaged 5 percent, while the proportion of respondents who paced their newspaper reading to several times a week, once a week, or less than once a week, rather than daily, grew larger.[72] A similar downward trend in daily newspaper reading reported by Pew Research Center shows that, in 2000, 46 percent of Americans read a newspaper yesterday, compared to 71 percent in 1965.[73] Early in the year 2000, 63 percent of Pew survey participants read a newspaper regularly—the lowest at any time in the previous decade.[74] Sunday papers do not follow the same pattern of decline. Per capita circulation for Sunday papers averaged 0.24 from 1970 to 1999, showing little change for a quarter of a century.[75] Yet, major metropolitan newspapers such as the *Washington Post* are now realizing erosion in Sunday paper consumption.[76]

The newspaper has not disappeared from the lives of Americans, but neither does it possess the day-to-day immediacy it once held. This change in an important, traditional means of mass communication would mean a loss of connectedness among Americans—*if* it were their only news source. The newspaper, always an important source of general news and information, loosely binds a diverse network of Americans who have at hand a variety of ways of tapping into that shared pool of information. A 1995 Gallup Poll in which respondents could refer to eighteen different sources for obtaining news and information that included headline news services, public television news programs, and talk shows emphasizes the growing assortment of choices.[77] Two recent reviews of empirical evidence about how citizens obtain political information note that individuals differ in their information requirements. Individuals selectively seek sources that meet their needs, which will vary over time.[78] At least since the arrival of radio, Americans have combined, customized, and explored the menu of media possibilities.

In response to a Roper question regarding multiple sources of news, survey respondents used an average of 1.54 sources in 1959—but only 1.38 in 1992.[79] Pew Research Center found the percentage of respondents who did *not* get news yesterday from the TV, newspaper, *or* radio doubled from 8 percent in 1994 to 15 percent in 1996.[80] These findings suggest Americans were either narrowing their selections for news input *or* diversifying them beyond the bounds of questions asked by surveyors. Although both may be true, the aforementioned Gallup poll question that itemizes eighteen news and information sources portrays a broadening array of choices. Consequently, one goes to the Internet for headline news and to the newspaper for detail; tunes in to National Public Radio while jogging; turns on network news when home; and relies on Cable News Network (CNN) to stay in touch with major events when traveling or at home. Three-fourths of respondents in a recent Pew Research Center poll agreed that they had no need to worry if they missed their news in the usual form since "there are so many ways to get the news these days."[81]

Online news is now a part of the system for sharing and co-producing news and information. In four surveys conducted by Louis Harris between August 1995 and January 1996, an average of 9 percent of American adults reported logging on to the World Wide Web for political information.[82] By 1998, 41 percent surveyed by Pew Research Center went online and 64 percent of these users used the Internet to obtain news at least once a week. Most online news users (75 percent) continued to rely primarily on print and broadcast. Sixty-three percent of online news users indicated there was no change in the rate with which they drew upon other information sources—fewer than the 75 percent who said the same in 1995, but more than the 58 percent who reported no change in year 2000.[83]

More recently, Pew found that 54 percent of Americans go online and 61 percent of these did so to obtain news—at least once each week. They seek news and information about weather, science/health, technology, business, international conditions, entertainment, sports, and politics. Eighteen percent used online services more often and alternative sources for news less often, cutting back on television (41 percent), newspapers (35 percent), radio (15 percent), and magazines (11 percent). At the same time, 10 percent of these individuals increased their use of other avenues for news, especially television (38 percent), other unidentified sources (30 percent), and newspapers (24 percent).[84] Even as the media mix continues to shift, the newspaper remains an important, if less dominant, connector for Americans.

Magazines

Periodicals reflect more particular interests of like-minded individuals and groups, often stemming from the activities of voluntary organizations.[85] Magazine circulation reinforces smaller sets of common ties that cut across distance and other barriers within the larger social context. In 1933, the Research Committee on Social Trends recognized this use of print media as a means to associate around particular interests.[86] "'House organs,' trade journals, fraternal bulletins, and publications with purposes covering the entire range of contemporary interests, have multiplied. They are important as bonds between those with common objectives."[87]

Periodicals have a somewhat different history than newspapers. This type of publication has multiplied, no matter the list examined. Titles in *The Union List of Serials* and *The International Directory of Little Magazines and Small Presses*, for example, continue to multiply annually.[88] The Ayer/Gale database, with the longest history, carried 2,869 titles in 1900 and slowly expanded to 12,036 in 1998, slipping back to 9,893 in the following year.[89]

Two contemporary databases show increases even in the short term. The *National Directory of Magazines* lists 28,105 entries in 1998, nearly doubling in ten years. *The Standard Periodical Directory* shows an increase of 34 percent between 1991, when it listed 70,383 periodicals, and 1998, when it listed 94,413.[90]

This proliferation of magazines was accompanied by adjustments in publication schedules, presumably due to market saturation. The frequency with which periodicals are published slowed, at least after 1935. Then, over half (55 percent) of the periodicals in the Ayer/Gale database were monthly publications but only 35 percent were published every month in 1999. A similar pattern occurred in weekly periodicals; 23 percent of all periodicals were weeklies in 1935, but this share-of-total fell to 4 percent by 1999. Quarterly publications accounted for 35 percent of the total, in contrast to a minuscule 8 percent sixty years earlier.[91] There is a point at which more issues do not result in more readers, one consultant in the industry explained, referring to the drop in the average annual number of issues per Standard Rate and Data Services (SRDS), from 12.2 in 1988 to 11.8 in 1993.[92] Slippage in the Ayer/Gale database back to 1996 levels, sluggish newsstand sales, an advertising slowdown, pending rises in postal rates, and a shrinking volume of technology magazines foreshadow trend change or fluctuation.[93] The long-term fate of periodicals depends on the commitment of consumers to this media.

Periodical readership is difficult to pinpoint. To get a sense of this, we must turn to several kinds of information.

- One source, using the consumer periodical population listed with SRDS, found that the average household bought 4.9 of these magazines in 1963 and 5.9 in 1988.[94]
- Time-use studies indicate that, between 1946 and 1985, at least one-fourth of Americans read magazines.[95]
- In a 1990 Gallup poll, 36 percent reported reading a magazine yesterday. [96]
- Princeton Survey Research found that nearly one-third (31 percent) of respondents in a 1995 survey reported doing the same.[97]
- In 1994, 33 percent of Pew Research survey respondents said they read a magazine yesterday. When the question was repeated in year 2000, only 26 percent had done so.[98]
- During the 1970s, several surveys suggested that 62 to 67 percent of the adult population read magazines regularly. One in 1979 found that the 61 percent who described themselves as regular magazine readers averaged 2.3 subject types of periodicals.[99]
- Two surveys in 1990 found that majorities of American adults read magazines in the previous week: 56 percent in a Roper survey and 69 percent in a Gallup survey.[100] As for how consumers read magazines,

> one 1998 survey suggests that less than a third actually read from 25 percent to none of the articles in an issue, while 28 percent read from 76-100 percent of the articles.[101]

The periodical industry's information on readership is more optimistic. In audience research results of the 1940s, 69 percent of Americans, aged fifteen and older, were regular consumers of 4.6 periodicals per reader.[102] In the 1980s, 94 percent of adults in the United States were reading, on average, 11.6 magazines per month, according to the Magazine Publishing Association.[103] Whatever the source—market research, time use studies, surveys, industry research—each implies that reading magazines is a regular part of American lives.

The subject matter of periodicals grew increasingly diverse at the same time. The United States *Census of Manufactures*, a source of partial trends in periodical consumption between 1947 and 1977, revealed some shifts in prevalent subject matter. At midcentury, a simple set of categories existed. There were business news, general news, and "other" magazines. Interest grew in specialized periodicals, women's and home services magazines, and general entertainment magazines. Circulation of farm periodicals and comics fell.[104] Not until the 1960s was there a burgeoning of the special interest magazine, fueled by rising levels of education, affluence, and leisure interests and cutting-edge technology that made niche marketing cost-effective for the first time. "[L]eisure activities merely whetted the appetite of many for more printed information about their avocational pursuits."[105]

Reader interests continue to expand and magazine titles come and go. In the space of six years, from 1988 to 1993, Standard Rate and Data Services reported 900 new titles and 760 that disappeared.[106] *The Standard Periodical Directory* demonstrates a dramatic diversification and volatility of interests. This directory listed nearly 92,000 titles in 1996, organized under 255 subjects. Some subject categories were renamed, combined with others, or dropped between 1991 and 1996. Nineteen completely new subject categories appeared during that period. Approximately half of the total number of publications each year could be found in categories that contained more than 800 different titles. The number of subject categories with 800 or more titles grew from seventeen to twenty-nine during the six-year period. Some subjects, like religion, education, and sports remained among the largest of categories—a relatively stable set of priorities and interests that underlie periodical consumption. The size ranking of other subject categories, such as environment and genealogy proved more transitory, rising or falling markedly within this short span of time.[107]

New forms of periodicals continually materialize. A recent phenomenon is the very small, homemade publication termed the 'zine, "an outlet for the eccentric preoccupations of the people who publish them."[108] An example is

Office and Art Supply Junkie, one of thousands of 'zine titles collected by one source by mid-1997. 'Zines are a variation on the mimeographed sheet of earlier times, made so much easier with the computer. In yet another variation of the periodical, the large electronic online magazine, sometimes called a webzine, makes interaction among writers, editors, and readers possible. More than 8,300 readers dropped in to post messages, send e-mail, or chat online on the first day of the electronic edition of *Time Online*. The editor's comments a year later are noteworthy:

> Most gratifying has been the improvement in the quality of discussion since the days when the message boards were dominated by Lizard NC and the Gun Guys. We've become a gathering place for thousands of literate, well-informed, plugged-in readers who can also write. Painful as it has been at times, I think being so directly accountable to our online readers has made us better journalists—and Time a better magazine.[109]

Electronic magazines thus forge new avenues of connectedness, enliven the discourse, and reinvigorate the associational infrastructure. In whatever form they take, periodicals loosely connect people who share (a) particular, as well as general, interests and (b) constant, as well as fleeting, interests. This is a medium that is diverse, innovative, and expanding in form and substance. It adds a dimension to the loose overlay of social connectedness made possible by sources that report general news and information, such as television, newspapers, and radio.

The Telephone

The telephone is a basic element of associational infrastructure. Over one-third (35 percent) of American households had a phone by 1920. This figure rose to 41 percent in 1930, fell to 31 percent during the Great Depression, and bounced back to 42 percent by 1942. The rate continued to rise until phone service reached 94 percent of households in 1991. Household phone service saturation remains at that level.[110] With its arrival, the persistent immediacy of the telephone ring pierced insulated lifestyles. "The telephone is clearly the most obtrusive of agencies, and local calls are an accepted part of daily routine," observed the Research Committee on Social Trends in 1933.[111] In 1907 an individual received, on average, an incoming local call every three days and a toll call every fifteen days; twenty years later those intervals had shortened to 1.5 and ten days, respectively. Committee members concluded that, largely owing to the telephone, individuals were in continual contact with others: "[p]ersonal isolation—inaccessibility to the demands of others for access to one's attention—is increasingly rare, or, when desired, increasingly difficult to achieve." Recent evidence supports this early thesis about the impact of the telephone in reducing isolation. Sociologist Tom W. Smith examined the characteristics of General Social Survey respondents who did not own a telephone and discovered that, as a group, they seem more socially isolated than phone owners.

> They tend to be residentially mobile, not to read newspapers and not to have voted in the last presidential election, not to attend church nor belong to other voluntary organizations, have low confidence in banks and high social alienation, and be skeptical of human nature. While most of these associations are modest, they collectively describe the non-telephone owner as one with few ties to society in general.... In many regards, people with no telephone in their households are outsiders.[112]

In his social history of the telephone, sociologist Claude Fischer calls it a "technology of sociability."[113] The introduction of the phone brought with it the opportunity to manage the quality of contacts. Various degrees of personal distancing and gradients of social interaction were added and refined with this new technology. Face-to-face discussion was optional. The phone visit supplemented or supplanted the act of "calling," "visiting," or "dropping in."[114] Associational life spread further afield and social interaction close to home intensified with the phone. Contact via the telephone seemed to strengthen and reinforce local attitudes, behavior, and social controls.[115] This was particularly true where party lines existed.[116] I saw the party line in my childhood community foster neighborhood networks and connections, rural-town exchanges, and contacts beyond local boundaries, as well. These linkages strengthened cooperation and solidarity, and gave party line subscribers a sense of collective identity.

The continual diversification and innovation that surrounds the telephone keeps the potential for social connectedness high. Recent developments in telephone technology reflect a progressive push toward connecting with others, even as lifestyles change. When a 1992 Roper Organization survey asked respondents if they had any of twelve optional features such as call waiting, a speakerphone, memory dialing, et cetera, each feature was in use by at least a few. Five years earlier four of the listed features were not in use by any respondent—the portable cellular phone, caller ID, video telephone, and the permanent phone number.[117] And the march of new phone technologies continues. New developments include digital and video cameras in cell phones for transmitting visually to the other end of the connection.[118]

Cordless units were reportedly in the possession of one-third of the adult population in 1992, allowing freedom of movement within a certain circumference around the base unit.[119] That range of convenience and communication freedom was extended further with the cellular phone. In 1995, one-fourth of national samples owned a cell phone.[120] This proportion doubled by the year 2000.[121] The Cellular Telecommunications and Internet Association estimated 107.3 million Americans were cell phone subscribers at the end of 2000, a rapid rise from 91,600 subscribers in 1984, 55 million at the end of

1997, and 69 million in 1998.[122] An increase in working, faxing, and using computers in the home sparked new growth in the number of residential phone lines. Almost 15 percent of households had second phone lines by 1995, up from 2.7 percent in just eight years.[123] Additional lines safeguard communication access even when one is tied up with work matters or on the Internet.

Telephone use has become so well integrated into the fabric of society that it does not lend itself to definitive cataloguing of functions. We use it to "reach out and touch someone" and to provide emotional support. We organize meetings and social events via the phone. We construct phone trees to disseminate information quickly throughout a network. We recruit volunteers and charitable donations by phone and mobilize support for particular causes.[124] We also use it to manage a major resource that facilitates associational life—our time—more effectively.

Little documentation actually exists on how Americans use the phone. Fischer concluded that by the 1920s home phones were used primarily for social purposes. It was then that the phone industry began to focus its marketing on relationships with friends and family.[125] Self-reports also point to the phone as an important conduit to social connectedness. Although fewer than 5 percent of people in a 1935 time-study sample reported telephoning as an activity, reasons supplied for talking on the phone suggested, even at that early date, that 64 percent of the calls were social. Three-fourths of these conversations occurred between friends.[126]

Visiting by phone persists to the present day. A national survey of adult leisure activities in 1982 found that 45 percent of respondents spoke by phone with friends or relatives daily and another 32 percent did so once or twice a week.[127] Eighty-three percent of a national sample told Luntz Research they would choose the phone, in lieu of e-mail or letter, to convey "good or exciting news."[128] Pew Research Center reported that 52 percent of respondents surveyed in November of 1998 had called a friend or relative yesterday "just to talk."[129] A survey of cell phone users in the fall of 2000 shows that, while driving, half used the phone to keep track of family members and to chat casually, while fifty-four percent discussed business and arranged appointments.[130] Clearly, the phone has a significant role in maintaining social connectedness.

Other sources of information, in the absence of direct data, help to characterize telephone usage. The Federal Communications Commission estimates that conversation minutes per phone line averaged twenty-five minutes a day between 1980 and 1995.[131] When Gordon S. Black interviewed a national sample of adults in 1986 for *USA Today*, 46 percent reported spending an hour talking by phone every day; another 37 percent spent less time than this on the phone, and 13 percent talked for two or three hours a day.[132] Neither source says if the conversation was for business or for other purposes. However, distribution of phone capacity between homes and businesses is more heavily residential, although its exact allocation for business, household maintenance, and social purposes remains undocumented. Between 1920 and 1980 there existed, on average, 2.28 residential phones for each business phone.[133] A similar pattern of one business line to 2.03 residential lines existed in 1997.[134]

Despite the ubiquity of the phone, an individual finally has control over its intrusive nature. With the arrival of the telephone answering machine, it was no longer necessary for incoming calls to cause arbitrary disruption at an inopportune time. Only 3 percent of a national Roper Organization sample reported owning an answering machine in 1981; eight years later, 25 percent reported ownership.[135] Eight years later, only 23 percent of a national adult sample surveyed by NBC News/*Wall Street Journal*/Hart Teeter, were not in households harboring answering machines.[136] In a 1992 Roper Organization poll of answering machine owners, nearly half (48 percent) reported "frequent or often" use of the device "to listen to who is calling and then decide whether to talk to them or call them back."[137] One-fourth (26 percent) of answering machine owners in a 1996 *Washington Post*/Kaiser/Harvard poll described the answering machine as a necessity when asked if they thought of it that way or "as a luxury you could do without."[138] In 1999, an NPR/Kaiser/Harvard Technology Survey found 82 percent of a national adult sample had either an answering machine or voicemail in their household. Three out of every five of these respondents considered this technology an essential part of their lives.[139]

The telephone significantly reduces isolation, allows variation and adjustments to person-to-person distancing, provides flexibility in setting social boundaries, and permits coordination between private and public lives. The plethora of technological features attached to the telephone offers convenient, customized ways of remaining in touch with others. These features and their application reflect how Americans perpetuate associational life.

Television

Television, its influence on associational life controversial today, "was on the threshold" of American daily life in the early 1930s.[140] Introduced at the 1939 New York World's Fair, it rapidly diffused as World War II ended.[141] It entered the Middletown community in 1946 with two hours of daily programming.[142] Three decades later, Middletown had eight television channels including four that were cable. Almost everyone, 98 percent of the households, owned at least one TV set. Nationally, the household saturation rate has matched this since 1980.[143]

Viewing options have multiplied. The 862 television stations on air by 1970 grew to 1,572 by 1998.[144] The allocation of viewing share across broadcast network stations, independent stations, public television, basic cable, and pay cable became more selective. The network stations' leading share of viewer attention fell from 69 to 46 percent between 1983 and 1998; pay cable services absorbed most of this decline with a 31 percentage point increase in share, bumping network affiliates into second place. Sixty-seven percent of TV households subscribed to cable in 1998, up from 7 percent in 1970.[145] In 1999, 75 percent of households were able to use cable/satellite TV.[146] The larger portion of cable subscribers (58 percent) in 1999 could access 54 or more channels, while 33 percent had a choice of 30 to 53 channels.[147] In contrast, the average viewer in 1985 chose from only 19 channels.[148] Digital cable, recently reported to be in 12 million U.S. households, dramatically increases the choice to 150+ channels, posing interesting questions about how viewers will design their viewing agendas.[149]

Television poses two choices that leave their imprint on associational life. Both are enhanced by the diversification of technology and viewing options. One involves the use of TV as a source of general news and information that reinforces social connectedness. The other involves using TV in pursuit of leisure. This is seen in responses to a 1994 Roper-Starch national survey. The three most salient reasons for watching television programs were for information (46 percent), entertainment (47 percent), and relaxation (35 percent).[150]

The manner in which Americans gather their news and information demonstrates the importance of the information function of TV. Repeated questioning by Roper between 1959 and 1994 indicates that, in 1963, television surpassed the newspaper as a major source of news.[151] Regular news viewing outpaced newspaper reading by an average of 11 percentage points in measures taken by Times Mirror and Pew Research Center between 1990 and the spring of 2000. An average of 82 percent reported watching TV news programs regularly; an average of 71 percent said they regularly read newspapers.[152]

A smattering of single surveys confirms a long-standing preference for television news.

- Sixty percent of a national adult sample surveyed by Minnesota Opinion Research in 1984 said they would choose TV or radio to get their news in preference to a newspaper or magazine.[153]
- Kane, Parsons and Associates conducted a national survey of adults in 1987 who identified their main source of news as follows: television (56 percent), newspapers (28 percent), radio (11 percent), and magazines (2 percent).[154]
- In 1995 a Hart Teeter Research survey asked which news sources respondents used regularly. Television (87 percent) overshadowed newspapers (60 percent).[155]
- A national survey conducted by Ohio University in June of 1995 found that local and network television news took precedence over reading the daily newspaper for regular users of these media.[156]

Leisure viewing poses an additional choice between two contexts—solitary viewing or as a social activity. The personal choices exercised (or not) in the use of television, which so complements the strain of individualism in American society, cause concerns about an imbalance between private and public pursuits. If television curtails the variety of attachments of individuals to associational life in a large way, the health of a pluralistic democratic society may be at risk. Putnam is one who argues that television has indeed been a liability to associational life.[157] This resonates with many Americans' dissatisfaction with how responsibly we have used television and the choices that its use entails.

The greater part of leisure is dedicated to individual pursuits, to which television viewing is adaptable, especially with 2.4 sets per household.[158]

- Time-usage research indicates that watching television was the largest, single, free-time expenditure between 1965 and 1985.[159]
- In 1960, Gallup added watching television to a list of activities that a respondent could identify as "your favorite way of spending an evening." When that question was asked in 1938, reading received the most mentions (21 percent), but television prevailed in 1960 for 28 percent of those polled. This pattern continued in four subsequent years, although it rose and then fell: 1966 (46 percent), 1974 (46 percent), 1986 (33 percent), and 1990 (24 percent).[160]
- Television viewing was the most popular of two dozen activities in 1979 when the Roper Organization asked, "When you have free time, which of these things do you frequently do?"[161]
- A 1979 Leisure Development Center/Gallup survey asked, "How do you spend your free time? Please name as many as you like [from] the card." Of the twenty-four possibilities, the activity choice that included television, "Getting relaxed at home such as TV-watching, listening to radio or records, playing with children, just doing nothing, etc." was selected by four-fifths of the respondents.[162]
- In 1982, United Media Enterprises found that watching television and reading a newspaper were the leisure activities reported as most often engaged in during the prior year. Almost three-quarters, 72 percent, stated they had watched TV every day or almost daily while 70 percent recalled reading the newspaper that frequently.[163]
- Finally, in 1995, 1997, 1999, and 2000, Louis Harris and Associates asked national samples "What are your two or three most favorite leisure time activities?" In each year, TV watching was second only to reading.[164]

"[P]eople don't visit anymore." One resident in a rural community studied by sociologists Allen and Dillman thus explained the impact of television on the once popular activity of talking and strolling about town on a summer evening.[165] It is not self-evident, however, that a shift from the sidewalks to the television set was necessarily a retreat from associational life. On the contrary, in the rural community of my childhood, TV became an additional reason for social gatherings. My first exposure to television was in the living room of a neighbor in 1949. After several families had eaten a potluck supper together, I helped to arrange chairs in rows facing the TV set with its tiny window to other world affairs. Friends and acquaintances with television were generous in inviting the rest of us to join them. Regular meetings of the Methodist Youth Fellowship, coupled with Sunday night viewing at a group leader's home, kept carefully to the agenda so we could watch Ed Sullivan afterwards. Watching television together, especially late movies, was a teenage social event. Television stimulated conversation, as well. We were eager to discuss what we were seeing and learning as our worldview expanded through this medium. In these ways, leisure-time television viewing encouraged social connectedness.

Researchers who returned to Middletown in the late 1970s expressed astonishment to find people watching so much television (a median of twenty-eight hours per week). They also found a richer, fuller associational life than in 1935. Clubs and associations had proliferated and voluntary association membership rates were high. The ratio of churches to people had increased, along with attendance. Sports participation, reading, movie-going, and listening to the radio had grown more popular. More time was being spent with family. Unemployment was about the same.[166] So where had the time to watch television materialized?

Part of the answer was in the gain of fifteen leisure hours per week attributable to shorter work days and weeks. However, estimates suggested that viewing time far exceeded that gain. Another part of the answer was surely in time saved by the laborsaving conveniences found in most Middletown homes in 1978. Especially noteworthy, however, is the researchers' observation that homework, housework, and family conversation frequently coincided with watching television. Middletowners were "deepening" time, that is, compounding the number of tasks done simultaneously. Participants in a 1982 nationwide poll also attended to more than just the television set; less than half (41 percent) reported that they "usually pay close attention."[167]

The finding in Middletown that associational life did not lose out in favor of watching television—that folks had found a way to do both—was similar to behavior reported by United Media Enterprises in 1982. Heavy TV watchers of four hours per day tended to be involved in fewer leisure activities than light viewers of one hour per day. There was no significant difference, however, between heavy and light viewers in the amount of leisure time spent at home. Fewer heavy TV watchers were volunteers, but those who did volunteer contributed larger amounts of time each month. A little over one-fourth of heavy and light TV users alike participated once a week or more in clubs or community affairs.[168] These findings suggest that television is not necessarily anathema to associational life.

Socializing around televised sporting events and elections is commonplace. Sports bars are regular gathering places. When Roper Starch asked Americans about their motivation(s) for viewing television, 57 percent reported that spending time with family and/or friends described their motivation somewhat or very well; 46 percent said that being able to talk with others about programs motivated them to watch television. Others (36 percent) said they watched TV to get ideas for how to deal with real-life situations.[169] These rationales are not unlike the motivation for watching how-to-do-it and religious programs, participating in Oprah Winfrey's Book Club, or communicating with the broader public via televised talk shows.[170] Television programs also spark the organization of nonprofit membership organizations such as cable television associations, the Boston Society of Vulcans of Mass, the Rin Tin Tin Fan Club, and the Riverton-Fremont TV Club.[171]

Clearly, television does not inevitably detract from associational life. It does enrich and add dimensions to social experience. Worldviews and cognitive understandings expand with television, but the effects upon individual, social, and community relationships are not always clear. Historian David Thelen provides us with a vivid example, sparked by the televised Congressional hearings in 1987 on the Iran-Contra Affairs, of how television can act as a catalyst for further participation in public affairs. These hearings prompted an outpouring from Americans who joined the public debate by contacting Congressional committee members. An analysis of these communiqués indicated that Americans

> have created their own sources and authorities for fact and viewpoint by which to evaluate what appears on television.... In the course of talking about the hearings, Americans transformed themselves from television watchers into active citizens and patriots. By writing or calling a legislator, they defined citizenship in practice.[172]

The choices available in using television leave much to the discretion of the individual. On balance, it supports social connectedness more than it isolates. Frequently discussed and criticized while it remains at the core of daily life, television also acts as a catalyst for public, moral discourse. Perhaps this is one of television's more important contributions to associational life.

The "Net" and the "Web"

The Internet is a new frontier for associational life. Individuals and groups rapidly cross the Internet threshold to connect, via computer, with others throughout the world. The *Economist* recently noting the marked boost in common access to all types of information referred to "pre-Internet days (a mere five or six years ago)."[173] Less than 2 percent of Americans were using the Internet in 1994.[174] Two years later, surveys began to show that more than 35 percent of adults went online for some reason.[175] Thirty-six percent of those using the World Wide Web in 1995 learned "about new Websites to visit" from friends and relatives.[176] Early measures are not completely reliable, however, since the phenomenon is decentralized, the technology is adopted very quickly, and measures and definitions are not standardized.[177] Pew Research Center makes a persistent effort to illuminate this new frontier, however. In February 1999, Pew reported that 49 percent of adults "go online to access the Internet or World Wide Web or to send and receive e-mail."[178] Six months later, 50 percent of American adults surveyed told CBS News that they accessed the Internet.[179] When Pew repeated its question in January 2001, 61 percent surveyed went online.[180]

The new technology's suitability and potential for associational life, under exploration by online users, is implied by the terms "net" and "web." Experimentation largely centers on blending this medium into existing forms of association. We see this in developments revealed by comparing survey results that bracket a three-year period. Times Mirror interviewed a subset of online users that comprised 14 percent of a national sample in June 1995 and Pew Research Center repeated some of the questions three years later when 41 percent of Americans went online.[181]

- In 1995, almost a fourth (23 percent) had an "online buddy" they had never met. This was the same in 1998.
- More than a third (35 percent), in 1995, received an electronic news clipping or story from a friend. It was up to 42 percent by 1998.
- Almost a fourth (23 percent) communicated regularly with others via online forums, discussion lists, or chat groups at least weekly in 1995. This rose to 35 percent in April of 1998 but fell to 22 percent at the end of the year.
- One-tenth (10 percent) of 1995 users discussed politics or participated in political activity online; it was 11 percent three years later.
- In 1995, 15 percent expressed an opinion on a political or social issue to a bulletin board, online newsgroup, or electronic mail list. In 1998 it was 16 percent.[182]

Electronic mail is now a significant phenomenon. In year 2000, the Pew Internet and American Life Project found that e-mail tops online activity for Hispanic (87 percent), black (88 percent), and white (93 percent) users.[183] Nearly three-fourths (72 percent) of online users interviewed by Times Mirror in 1995 communicated with others by e-mail; the majority used it several times a week, if not daily. In 1996, 83 percent were using e-mail; at the end of 1998, it was 85 percent of online users. One-half of the e-mailers in 1995 checked their electronic mailboxes once or more every day; in 1998, it rose to

59 percent. In 1995, over two-thirds described their online mail as personal or a mix of personal and work subject matter. In 1998, 88 percent of e-mailers described it in this manner. Although a sizeable 83 percent communicated via e-mail with family and friends in 1995, in 1998 the figure increased to 93 percent of online users. In 1995, 59 percent found that access to e-mail resulted in more frequent contacts with family and friends; 61 percent said the same in 1998.[184] Obviously, early adaptations of the Internet seem to "hold" and to buttress interpersonal relationships.

Groups are also organized on the Internet. One-fourth of e-mailers in 1995 and 1998 belonged to "list servs" in which participants with a common interest simultaneously send the same message to everyone on the list. In both years, 62 percent of these "joiners" were on more than one list service.[185] Forums for continuous thematic online discussion number in the thousands. Usenet, one large cooperative electronic bulletin board service that organizes postings by subject matter, carried 50,000 newsgroups in 1998—up from 40,000 in July 1997 and from 5,000 in 1993.[186] In January 2000, Usenet group members were in decline as other web-based forums emerged.[187] Rules for communicating on the Internet pave the way for civil online interaction, via "netiquette" that relies upon "respecting the rights and desires of others, setting an example of how you want strangers to treat you, and acknowledging that the Internet is very different from face-to-face communication."[188]

Social connectedness in cyberspace interfaces with or reinforces other arenas of voluntary association. University students elicit online help from classmates, just as one might from a neighbor in the classic sense. Churches use the Web to recruit members, to publicize events, to webcast worship services, to communicate prayer requests, to stay in touch with foreign missions, and much more.[189] In an impressive example of old and new institutional blends, thousands of volunteers "met" on Net Day in California on March 9, 1996 to wire schools across the state with Internet connections. Columnist Robert Kuttner described the chain of events "as a kind of statewide high-tech barn-raising...a new way of building community support for institutions that are necessarily public."[190] An analysis of seven similar cases of grassroots political initiatives by Bonchek confirms that computer-assisted interactions cost less than more traditional methods, can provide more accurate information, and can be more efficient.[191] Net Day is an example of how computer-mediated communication reduces costs of association. It also demonstrates grassroots, ad hoc voluntary associations of the nature remarked upon by Tocqueville, who noted that greater achievement is possible when the initiatives of individuals and public officials combine.[192]

Formally organized groups help to mediate the interface of Information Age technology with society. A recent example of this role in the *Los Angeles Times* describes the problems encountered by San Francisco's New Main

Public Library. In this new high-tech facility, outraged patrons had difficulty finding books, and many books were inaccessible in closed stacks. This surge of indignation paled, however, in the shadow of public reaction to the discovery of 100,000 books culled and buried in a nearby landfill. A local chapter of a nonprofit membership association, the Gray Panthers, subsequently organized a rescue of books from the landfill and, as one member stated, is "keeping them in trust for the library until they come to their senses.... These were the books that librarians had preserved for generations."[193]

Blending new with old forms of association, the Internet offers additional choice and gradients to the quality of interaction. People are brought voluntarily into fresh combinations. How the applications of this technology will ultimately enhance or negatively influence and alter associational activity is obviously unknown. The Internet's compatibility with associational life worries some. Concerns echoing through discussions of the Internet are that connections made in this way will be "mostly meaningless, transient, fragile and unstable.... [That] without tangible bodies or enduring memories, no one can keep promises...[or] remember why they might be worth keeping."[194] Yet, fears that the Internet will produce dangerous levels of social isolation remain unrealized. Indeed, a study by Roper recently found that online users (65 percent) are more likely to invite friends over at least once a month than are nonusers (50 percent).[195] The national sample of adults interviewed by Pew Research Center at the end of 1998 was specifically asked if the "Internet is a good thing because it brings together people with similar interests" or if it is "a bad thing because it brings together small groups of people who share dangerous ideas." A majority of 54 percent replied that it was a good thing, 28 percent perceived it as bad, and 18 percent did not know. When the sample was asked "which is greater the advantage of more communication or the disadvantage of it not being face-to-face," there was little difference. Forty-three percent thought the *advantage* was greater and 46 percent that the *disadvantage* was greater.[196]

Today, the Internet sparks shared experience by a growing percentage of the American public. It inspires new ways of connecting and reinforces the familiar. New forms of association and institutional interfaces reflect an innovative spirit. While young, the Internet is already an established part of civil society infrastructure. A measure of its ability to strengthen democracy will be the extent to which this technology facilitates the crosscutting and interaction between various segments of the population. The elderly, the poor, and, to a lesser extent, ethnic groups continue to have less access and/or underutilize online opportunities.[197] Yet, an accelerating diversity of online users and activities suggest that this divide will continue to narrow.[198]

Summary and Discussion of Findings

Americans have always used communication technologies and the media to seek advice, share information, and connect with people of like interests and persuasion. The selection of technologies and media forms with which to do so continually grows more extensive and varied. Americans obtain their news and information from a mix of media forms customized to suit lifestyles, interests, and preferences. General information is complemented with sources of particular and detailed information. Social space is expanded, contracted, and social boundaries are made more permeable by the application of media and communications technology to associational life. The communication infrastructure of civil society is flexible, with room for choice and innovation. Subsequently, its diversity and density grows. This is healthy for a democratic civil society.

An ideal stream of news and information flowing through this democratic web of connectedness would be complete, objective, decentralized, representative of all different perspectives, and free of manipulation by overweening governmental forces. The degree to which this ideal is reached is another matter. Relatively speaking, the United States has a free press (media) backed by Constitutional guarantees. Regulation that defines institutional roles, the force of public opinion, and the ethics of journalism all help to fortify the press and contribute to a balance of power between it and government agencies. In practice, the press has a difficult time sustaining its autonomy in an environment where government forces push unrelentingly for advantage. It is accurate to say that the government grew adept at stymieing the press during the latter half of this century.

Other influences weakened the press, as well. Despite a clear message that the public wants local news and information, gaps developed in its supply. News and information services were centralized and delocalized by media conglomerates whose primary intent is to stretch the profit margin. An important source of support for the media is public opinion, which increasingly views its performance as less than stellar. What is most disconcerting, perhaps, is the press's own understanding of the effect of consolidated ownership on its practices and its equivocal insight into its institutional responsibility as mediator in a democracy.

Notes

1. Alexis de Tocqueville, *Democracy in America* (New York: Vintage Books, 1945), II:40-41, 119-122, 226-227, 342-343; I:195, 330.
2. Ibid., I:188-200; II:119-122, 127, 376-377.
3. Eric Foner, *The Story of American Freedom* (New York: W. W. Norton, 1998), 25-26; Michael Schudson, *The Good Citizen* (New York: Free Press, 1998), 35-36; Herbert N. Foerstel, *Free Expression and Censorship in America* (Westport,

CT: Greenwood, 1997), 239-240, 196-197; Lucas A. Powe, Jr., *The Fourth Estate and the Constitution: Freedom of the Press in America* (Berkeley: University of California Press, 1991), 8-13.

4. An Impartial Citizen, "A Dissertation Upon the Constitutional Freedom of the Press," in C. S. Hyneman and D. S. Lutz, *American Political Writing During the Founding Era 1760-1805* (Indianapolis, IN: Liberty Fund, [1801] 1983), 1126-1169.
5. Arnold S. Rice, John A. Krout, and C. M. Harris, *United States History to 1877* (New York: HarperCollins, 1991), 97; Akhil Reed Amar, *The Bill of Rights: Creation and Reconstruction* (New Haven, CT: Yale University Press, 1998), 20-26, 87-88. Foner, *The Story of American Freedom*, 43, 177, 183; Foerstel, *Free Expression and Censorship in America*, 196; Louis Edward Ingelhart, *Press and Speech Freedoms in America, 1619-1995* (Westport, CT: Greenwood, 1997), 55-60.
6. Tocqueville, *Democracy in America*, I:188-200; II:119-122.
7. Multiple judges in research at the University of Missouri School of Journalism scored countries. Charles Lewis Taylor and Michael C. Hudson, *World Handbook of Political and Social Indicators* (New Haven, CT: Yale University Press, 1972), *ix*, 151. For the criteria used, see William L. Rivers, "The Press as a Communication System" in Itheil de Sola Pool et al., eds., *Handbook of Communication* (Chicago, IL: Rand McNally, 1973), 547-549.
8. Gabriel A. Almond and G. Bingham Powell, Jr., *Comparative Politics: System, Process, and Policy*, 2d ed. (Boston, MA: Little, Brown, 1978), 150-152.
9. Twenty-eight percent of the world's countries have a partly free media and 35 percent had a media that was not free. Freedom House, "Press Freedom Survey 1999"; also see annual editions (January-February) of *Freedom Review*; Raymond D. Gastil, *Freedom in the World: Political Rights and Civil Liberties 1986-1987* (New York: Greenwood, 1987), 17-18; Raymond Duncan Gastil, "The Comparative Survey of Freedom: Experiences and Suggestions," in Alex Inkeles, ed., *On Measuring Democracy* (New Brunswick, NJ: Transaction Publishers, 1991).
10. Question: "Do you think [freedom of the press] is a major reason, a minor reason or not a reason for America's success?" Pew Research Center for the People and the Press, "1999 Millennium Survey Report," website http://www.people-press.org. N=1,546; ± 3.
11. Carl Sessions Stepp, "Access in a Post-social Responsibility Age," in Judith Lichtenberg, ed., *Democracy and the Mass Media* (Cambridge: Cambridge University Press, 1990), 192; Geneva Overholser, "Proposal for the Press: Self-Restraint," *Washington Post* (31 August 1999): A13.
12. Jeffery A. Smith, *War and Press Freedom* (New York: Oxford University Press, 1998), vii.
13. This case concerned a conflict between the right of press freedom and the investigative powers of Congress. William A. Hachten, *The Supreme Court on Freedom of the Press: Decisions and Dissents* (Ames: Iowa State University Press, 1968), 197-198.
14. Foerstel, *Free Expression and Censorship in America*, 138-147, 157-160, 171-174, 179-180, 196-205; International Centre on Censorship, *Information Freedom and Censorship World Report 1991* (Chicago, IL: American Library Association, 1991), 136-137; Jonathon Green, *The Encyclopedia of Censorship* (New York: Facts On File, 1990), 342-343; Donna A. Demac, *Liberty Denied: The Current Rise of Censorship in America* (New York: PEN American Center, 1988), 129-132; Smith, *War and Press Freedom*, 91-194; Gannet Foundation, *The*

Media at War: The Press and the Persian Gulf Conflict (New York: Gannett Foundation Media Center, 1991), 9-24; Donald Reynolds, "Words for War," in Lloyd Chiasson, Jr., ed., *The Press in Times of Crisis* (Westport, CT: Greenwood, 1995), 85-101.

15. Foerstel, *Free Expression and Censorship in America*, 143-147; Gannet Foundation, *The Media at War*, 15-20, 96-97; April Oliver, "The Wrong Lessons," *American Journalism Review* (July/August 1999): 52-55.
16. Seymour N. Siegel, "'Previous Restraint' and 'Subsequent Punishment,'" in H. B. Summers, ed., *Radio Censorship* (New York: H. W. Wilson, 1939), 60-61; Hachten, *The Supreme Court on Freedom of the Press*, 43. See Ingelhart, *Press and Speech Freedoms*, 245-290, for a chronology of significant Court cases between 1812 and 1995 that concerned press freedom.
17. Hachten, *The Supreme Court on Freedom of the Press*, 253-256.
18. Summers, *Radio Censorship*, 53-55; Louis G. Caldwell, "Program Standards Maintained by the Commission," in Summers, *Radio Censorship*, 65-66; *Nation*, "How Free is the Air?" in Summers, *Radio Censorship*, 65-66, 92-93.
19. Robert J. Landry, "Stations and Partisanship," in Summers, *Radio Censorship*, 88.
20. *Broadcasting*, "Instances of Citation of Stations," in Summers, *Radio Censorship*, 106-108; *New York Daily News*, "No Censorship by Government," in Summers, *Radio Censorship*, 246-248.
21. *Broadcasting*, "Set Owners Oppose Censorship," in Summers, *Radio Censorship*, 253.
22. *New York Times*, "Voluntary Associations for Program Scrutiny," in Summers, *Radio Censorship*, 248-249.
23. *New York Daily News*, "No Censorship by Government," 248.
24. Stuart N. Brotman, "The Bumpy Road of Regulation," *Media Studies Journal* 13:2 (Spring/Summer 1999): 112-118.
25. See John L. Hulteng, *Playing it Straight* (Chester, CT: Globe Pequot, 1981), 77-86, for codes of ethics for Associated Press Managing Editors, United Press International, the Society of Professional Journalists, and American Society of Newspaper Editors. The Hutchins Commission, convened in the 1940s by academicians and journalists and funded by *Time* publisher Henry Luce, explored the moral and social responsibilities of the media. For a complete index of Commission documents, see Frank Hughes, *Prejudice and the Press* (New York: Devin-Adair, 1950); also see Steven R. Knowlton and Patrick R. Parsons, *The Journalist's Moral Compass* (Westport, CT: Praeger, 1994), 207-227; Stepp, "Access in a Post-social Responsibility Age," 186-201; Sanford J. Ungar, "The Role of a Free Press Strengthening Democracy," in Lichtenberg, *Democracy and the Mass Media*, 368-398; Powe, *The Fourth Estate and the Constitution*, 235-259.
26. James Fallows, *Breaking the News* (New York: Vintage Books, 1997), 190-191; Carl Jensen, *20 Years of Censored News* (New York: Seven Stories, 1997), 9; Smith, *War and Press Freedom*, 180, 212; Hulteng, *Playing it Straight*, 8-9.
27. Demac, *Liberty Denied*, 131-134; Martin Shapiro, ed., *The Pentagon Papers and the Courts* (San Francisco, CA: Chandler, 1972); Ungar, "The Role of a Free Press Strengthening Democracy," 373-374; Smith, *War and Freedom*, 210-211; Nat Hentoff, *The First Freedom* (New York: Delacorte, 1980), 187-199; Daniel Schorr, *Clearing the Air* (Boston, MA: Houghton Mifflin, 1977), 192-201, 204-207, 274-280.
28. Demac, *Liberty Denied*, 136-137; Jensen, *20 Years of Censored News*, 173, 187-188, 206-208; Fallows, *Breaking the News*, 62, 196; Michael Schudson, *The Power of News* (Cambridge, MA: Harvard University Press, 1995), 125-139;

Schudson, *The Good Citizen*, 286-287; Foner, *The Story of American Freedom*, 320-321; International Centre on Censorship, *Information Freedom and Censorship World Report 1991*, 134-135.

29. Demac, *Liberty Denied*, 137.
30. John Herbers and James McCartney, "The New Washington Merry-Go-Round," *American Journalism Review* (April 1999): 50-62.
31. Question: "As far as people in charge of running [TV news] are concerned, would you have a great deal of confidence, only some confidence, or hardly any confidence at all in them?" Humphrey Taylor, "Dramatic Increase in Confidence in Leadership of Nation's Major Institutions," *The Harris Poll* 8 (11 February 1998).
32. Questions: "In general, do you think...news organizations get the facts straight, or do you think that their stories and reports are often inaccurate?"; "I'm going to read you some pairs of opposite phrases. After I read each pair, tell me which ONE phrase you feel better describes news organizations generally. If you think that NEITHER phrase applies, please say so...Care about the people they report on, or don't care about the people they report on?...Willing to admit their mistakes, or try to cover up their mistakes?...Moral or immoral?...Growing in influence, or declining in influence?...protect democracy, or hurt democracy?...Care about how good a job they do, or don't care about how good a job they do?...Highly professional, or not professional?...Stand up for America, or too critical of America?...Politically biased in their reporting, or careful that their reporting is NOT politically biased?" Pew, "News Interest Index," February 1999. N=1,203; ± 3.
33. Tocqueville, *Democracy in America*, I:192; II:120-121.
34. Schudson, *The Power of News*, 42-47; Schudson, *The Good Citizen*, 123-125; David Ramsay, "The History of the American Revolution. Philadelphia, 1789," in Hyneman and Lutz, *American Political Writing During the Founding Era 1760-1805*, 736-737.
35. Merle Curti, *The Making of an American Community: A Case Study of Democracy in a Frontier County* (Stanford, CA: Stanford University Press, 1959), 4, 114-121, 409-412.
36. Schudson, *The Good Citizen*, 121-122, 177-179; Schudson, *The Power of News*, 9, 50-51; Richard L. Kaplan, "The Press and the American Public Sphere: The Emergence of an Independent Journalism, 1865-1920," paper presented at American Sociological Association, New York, August 1996; Benjamin M. Compaine, ed., *Who Owns the Media?* (New York: Knowledge Industry, 1979), 15-16.
37. Curti, *The Making of an American Community*, 410.
38. Schudson, *The Good Citizen*, 121, 124.
39. Ibid., 119-123; Schudson, *The Power of News*, 47, 72.
40. Kaplan, "The Press and the American Public Sphere"; Schudson, *The Power of News*, 207-208; Schudson, *The Good Citizen*, 121.
41. Schudson, *The Power of News*, 50-51.
42. Question: "Please tell whether you think this a core principle of journalism, or not: Keeping the business people out of the newsroom." Pew, "Survey of Journalists," November 1998-February 1999. N=522; ± 4.5.
43. Fallows, *Breaking the News*, 70-73; James V. Risser, "Endangered Species," *American Journalism Review* (June 1998), 18-35; Compaine, *Who Owns the Media?*, 11-59.
44. Mary Walton, "The Selling of Small-Town America," *American Journalism Review* (May 1999), 58-78.
45. Neil Hickey, "Money Lust: How Pressure for Profit is Perverting Journalism," *Columbia Journalism Review* (July/August 1998): 28-36. A similar concern was

articulated in 1929 about pressures for profit and cost cutting that can impact on the integrity of journalistic content in George Seldes, *You Can't Print That! The Truth Behind the News, 1918-1928* (New York: Payson and Clarke, 1929), 12. For discussion, see Compaine, *Who Owns the Media?*, 22-26, 319-327; Dennis W. Mazzocco, *Networks of Power: Corporate TV's Threat to Democracy* (Boston, MA: South End, 1994); Ben H. Bagdikian, *The Media Monopoly*, 3d ed. (Boston, MA: Beacon, 1990), 201-202, 212, 236; Leo Bogart, *Commercial Culture* (New York: Oxford University Press, 1995), 45-60; Tom Goldstein, "Does Big Mean Bad?" *Columbia Journalism Review* (September/October 1998): 52-53.

46. Jack Bass, "Newspaper Monopoly," *American Journalism Review* (July/August 1999): 64-86.
47. Neil Hickey, "So Big: The Telecommunications Act at Year One," *Columbia Journalism Review* (January/February 1997): 23-28; Ben H. Bagdikian, "The Realities of Media Concentration and Control," *Television Quarterly* 29:3 (1998): 22-27; William F. Baker and George Dessart, "The Road Ahead," *Television Quarterly* 29:4 (1998): 2-16; Lawrence K. Grossman, "The Death of Radio Reporting: Will TV Be Next?," *Columbia Journalism Review* (September/October 1998): 61-62; Bass, "Newspaper Monopoly."
48. Baker and Dessart, "The Road Ahead."
49. Paul Farhi, "Viacom to Buy CBS, Uniting Multimedia Heavyweights," *Washington Post* (8 September 1999): A1, A7; Associated Press, "Chronology of Media Mergers Dramatizes Huge Scale of Deal," *Wall Street Journal* Interactive Edition (7 September 1999), website http://interactive.wsj.com.
50. Question: "Please tell whether you think this a core principle of journalism, or not: Keeping the business people out of the newsroom." Pew, "Survey of Journalists."
51. Question: "I'm going to read a list of things that are being talked about in journalism today. For each one that I read, please tell me whether you think this development is having a positive effect on journalism, having a negative effect on journalism, or isn't having much of an effect...Buy outs of local newspapers by large newspaper chains; Buy outs of news organizations by diversified corporations...." Seventy percent of national and 61 percent of local media respondents believed buy outs of local newspapers to have a negative effect; 73 percent of national media and 68 percent of local media believed buy outs of news organizations by diversified corporations had a negative effect. Ibid.
52. Questions: "In your opinion, to what extent do corporate owners influence news organizations' decisions about which stories to cover or emphasize?" and "In your opinion, to what extent do advertising concerns influence news organizations' decisions about which stories to cover or emphasize? A great deal; A fair amount; Not very much; Not at all," and "In your opinion, is increased bottom line pressure seriously hurting the quality of news coverage these days or is it mostly just changing the way news organizations do things?" Seventy-seven percent of national and 75 percent of local media respondents believed that advertising concerns had not very much/no influence; 69 percent of national and 61 percent of local respondents felt that corporate owners had not very much/no influence over decisions about coverage; local media were split, 45 percent and 45 percent, in thinking that profit pressures influenced news coverage; of the national media, 49 percent thought coverage was being hurt and 40 percent believed that the pressure was simply an organizational change. Ibid.
53. Bernard L. Stein, "An Ordinary Mission," *Media Studies Journal* (Spring/Summer 1999): 96.

54. Question: "Here is a list of reasons some people give for following the news. Which one of these reasons best describes why you, yourself, watch, read, or listen to the news?" Other reasons: learning about useful things (36 percent), learning about something exciting or interesting (12 percent), having something to discuss with friends (8 percent), entertainment (7 percent), passing the time (6 percent), relaxation (4 percent), to help with work (3 percent). Roper Center at University of Connecticut, Public Opinion Online, 1996 [LEXIS, Market Library, RPOLL File].
55. David W. Moore, "Americans' Most Important Source of Information: Local TV News," *Gallup Poll Monthly* (September 1995): 2-8.
56. Gallup Organization, "Media Use and Evaluation," website http://www.gallup.com.
57. Question: "Please tell which category best describes your overall opinion of what I name. Would you say your overall opinion of [network television news, local television news, large nationally influential newspapers such as the *New York Times* and the *Washington Post*, the daily newspaper you are most familiar with, cable news networks such as CNN and MSNBC] is very favorable, mostly favorable, mostly unfavorable, or very unfavorable?" Pew, "Re-Interview Survey," January 1998. N=844; ± 4. In March of 1991, during the Persian Gulf War, the network TV received 40 percent very favorable ratings, local TV news 37 percent, and the familiar daily newspaper 30 percent. When Pew added cable news networks to the 1998 inquiry, it earned a very favorable assessment from 26 percent of respondents, thus positing a developing redistribution of news consumer attention.
58. Question: "Which of the following two statements best describes you: 'I follow [local community, national, international] news closely only when something important or interesting is happening' or 'I follow [local community, national, international] news closely most of the time, whether or not something important or interest is happening'?" Pew, "Media Consumption Survey," April 24-May 11, 1998. N=3,002; ± 2.5.
59. Question: "Please tell me how closely you follow this type of news either in the newspaper, on television, or on radio...Very closely, somewhat closely, not very closely, or not at all closely?" Ibid.
60. Pew, "Biennial Media Consumption Survey, 2000."
61. David Villano, "Going More Local in Miami," *Columbia Journalism Review* (January/February 1999): 53.
62. The Project is affiliated with the University of Maryland College of Journalism, funded by Pew Charitable Trusts.
63. Tom Rosenstiel, Carl Gottlieb, and Lee Ann Brady, "Local TV News: What Works, What Flops, and Why," *Columbia Journalism Review* (January/February 1999): special insert.
64. Marya Jones, "Does Quality Cost?" *Columbia Journalism Review* (January/February 1999): special insert; Bagdikian, "The Realities of Media Concentration and Control"; Hickey, "Money Lust."
65. Tom Rosenstiel, Carl Gottlieb, and Lee Ann Brady, "Time of Peril for TV News," *Columbia Journalism Review* (November/December 2000): 84-92.
66. Robert S. Lynd and Alice C. Hanson, "The People as Consumers," in Research Committee on Social Trends, *Recent Social Trends in the United States: Report of the President's Research Committee on Social Trends* (New York: McGraw-Hill, 1933), 871-872; United States Bureau of Census, *Statistical Abstract 2000* (Washington, DC: United States Government Printing Office), 456, 579.
67. Theodore H. White, *In Search of History: A Personal Adventure* (New York: Harper and Row, 1978), 419-434.

68. United States Bureau of the Census, *Historical Statistics of the United States, Colonial Times to 1970* (Washington, DC: United States Department of Commerce, 1975), 855-856; United States Bureau of the Census, *Statistical Abstract of the United States 2000*, 579.
69. Ibid.
70. Calculated from United States Bureau of the Census, *Historical Statistics of the United States*, 809; United States Bureau of the Census, *Statistical Abstract of the United States 2000*, 576. Data for years 1945-1993 were provided by the research department of the Newspaper Association of America from annual editions of the *Editor & Publisher International Yearbook* (New York: Editor & Publisher Company).
71. Calculated with the sources in the previous note and total population figures reported by the United States Bureau of the Census, *Historical Statistics of the United States*, 10; United States Bureau of the Census, *Statistical Abstract of the United States 2000*, 7.
72. Question: "How often do you read the newspaper—every day, a few times a week, once a week, less than once a week or never?" James Allan Davis and Tom W. Smith, "General Social Surveys, 1972-1998." Cumulative Computer File. Chicago, IL: National Opinion Research Center [producer]. Ann Arbor, MI: Interuniversity Consortium for Political and Social Research [distributor], 1999, website http://www.icpsr.umich.edu /GSS/.
73. Question: "Did you get a chance to read a daily newspaper yesterday, or not?" Pew, "Media Consumption Survey," 1998.
74. Pew, "Technology Survey," October 26-December 1, 1998. N= 2000 for general public and N=1,993 for online users; ± 3.
75. United States Bureau of the Census, *Statistical Abstract of the United States 1997*, 573; United States Bureau of the Census, *Statistical Abstract of the United States 2000*, 576.
76. Michael Getler, "The Sunday Paper Habit," *Washington Post* (27 May 2001):B6.
77. Half of the sample was asked the following question: "As you know, people get their news and information from many different sources, and I would like to ask you where you get *your* news and information. I will read a list of sources, and for each one, please tell me how often you get your news from that source: very regularly, somewhat regularly, occasionally, or never." The question for the other half was the same except the gradients were "every day, several times a week, occasionally, or never." Moore, "Americans' Most Important Source: Local TV News."
78. Steven Chaffee and Stacey Frank, "How Americans Get Political Information: Print Versus Broadcast News," *ANNALS* (July 1996): 48-58; David H. Weaver, "What Voters Learn From Media," *ANNALS* (July 1996): 34-47.
79. Question: "I'd like to ask you where you usually get most of your news about what's going on in the world today—from the newspapers, or radio, or television, or magazines, or talking to people or where?" The choices were television, newspapers, radio, magazines, and people. Multiple responses were permitted. William G. Mayer, "Trends in Media Usage," *Public Opinion Quarterly* 57:4 (Winter 1993): 603.
80. Pew, "Media Consumption Survey," 1996. N=1751; ± 2.
81. Question: "Now I'm going to read a series of statements about the news. For each statement, please tell me if you completely agree with it, mostly agree with it, mostly disagree with it, or completely disagree with it....There are so many ways to get the news these days that I don't worry when I don't have a chance to read the

paper or when I miss my regular news programs." Pew, "Media Consumption Survey," 1998.

82. Questions: "Do you ever access the World Wide Web, or not?" and "Do you ever use the World Wide Web to get information about politics or political candidates or not?" David Birdsell, Douglas Muzzio, and Humphrey Taylor, "17 Million American Adults Use World Wide Web," *The Harris Poll* 11 (15 February 1996).
83. Questions: "How frequently do you go online to get news...would you say every day, 3 to 5 days per week, 1 or 2 days per week, once every few weeks, or less often?"; "Would you say you get more of your news from on-line sources, or from traditional sources such as TV news, newspapers, and magazines?"; "Since you started getting news on-line, are you using other sources of news MORE often, LESS often, or about the same as you used to?" Pew, "Technology Survey," 1998; Pew, "Biennial Media Consumption Survey," 2000.
84. Pew, "Biennial Media Consumption Survey," 2000.
85. Guidelines provided by the United Nations Educational, Scientific, and Cultural Organization (UNESCO) for its annual statistical yearbook define a periodical as a publication concerned with general or specialized subjects published in a continuous series for an indefinite period.
86. The Research Committee on Social Trends was a group of scientists appointed by President Hoover in 1932 to establish a baseline for social indicators in American society. Research Committee on Social Trends, *Recent Social Trends in the United States*, v.
87. Malcolm M. Willey and Stuart A. Rice, *Communication Agencies and Social Life* (New York: McGraw Hill, 1933), 159.
88. The *Union List of Serials* and its supplement, *New Serials Titles* (Washington, DC: Library of Congress) began in 1913 as an initiative by the American Library Association. A conservative estimate of the total universe of titles in this work, proffered by a representative of the Library of Congress, is 950,000. Now carrying over 6,000 entries, the *International Directory of Little Magazines and Small Presses* (Paradise, CA: Dustbooks Publishing) was first published in 1964 with fewer than 200 titles.
89. This is a mix of weekly, semimonthly, bimonthly, quarterly, and other U.S. and Canadian periodicals. Subject areas covered include agriculture, ethnic, fraternal, college, religious, and women's publications, general interest magazines, and trade, technical and professional serials. Willey and Rice, *Communication Agencies and Social Life*, 157; United States Bureau of the Census, *Historical Statistics of the United States*, 810; United States Bureau of the Census, *Statistical Abstract of the United States 1999*, 589.
90. Annual editions of *The National Directory of Magazines* (New York: Oxbridge Communications) lists U.S. and Canadian magazines, journals, tabloids that carry advertising, and some specific-interest newspapers. Annual editions of *The Standard Periodical Directory* (New York: Oxbridge Communications) list U.S. and Canadian publications published at least every twenty-four months. Included are directories, consumer magazines, newsletters, trade journals, scientific society transactions and proceedings, etc. I subtracted a classification for newspapers in my treatment of the data.
91. Willey and Rice, *Communication Agencies and Social Life*, 157; United States Bureau of the Census, *Statistical Abstract of the United States 1977*, 810; United States Bureau of the Census, *Statistical Abstract of the United States 1999*, 589.
92. SRDS lists approximately 2,800 titles, according to an account executive there. The magazines listed in this source rely on advertising, keep SRDS informed of

circulation information, and generally are not found on newsstands. Examples found in this database include *Readers' Digest* and *The Nation*; some not found here are *Highlights for Children* and *Guideposts*. James B. Kobak, "Magazine Trends," *Folio* 22 (Special Sourcebook Issue 1994): 235.
93. See Matthew Rose, "Magazines' Newsstand Sales Fall to Record Low 35% of Shipments," *Wall Street Journal* (15 May 2001): website http://interactive.wsj; Mike Musgrove, "Magazines Whose Time Has Gone," *Washington Post* (3 August 2001): E11.
94. James B. Kobak, "25 Years of Change," *Folio* 19 (March 1990): 82.
95. John P. Robinson, "Thanks for Reading This," *American Demographics* (May 1990): 6-7; John P. Robinson, "The Changing Reading Habits of the American Public," *Journal of Communication* 30 (Winter 1980): 147-157.
96. George Gallup, Jr., *The Gallup Poll: Public Opinion 1991* (Wilmington, DE: Scholarly Resources, 1992), 49.
97. Roper Center, Public Opinion Online, 1996.
98. Question: "Thinking about yesterday, did you spend any time reading magazines?" The portion who said yes for other years: 1997 (32 percent), 1995 (31 percent), and 1994 (33 percent). Pew, "Biennial Media Consumption Survey," 2000.
99. The Roper Organization repeated a question that asked, "On the average weekday, about how much time do you spend reading magazines?" Respondents reported amounts of time ranging from less than fifteen minutes daily up to five hours as follows: in 1973, 62 percent; in 1974, 67 percent; in 1977, 63 percent. The Institute for Survey Research conducted the 1979 national survey of adults for the National Science Foundation. Roper Center, Public Opinion Online, 1989.
100. Gallup, *The Gallup Poll: Public Opinion 1992*, 49; William G. Mayer, "The Rise of the New Media," *Public Opinion Quarterly* 58:1 (Spring 1994): 139.
101. Ogilvy Public Relations Information Resource Study conducted by National Family Opinion Research of a national adult sample of 500, ages 18 to 64. Roper Center, Public Opinion Online, 1999.
102. Theodore Peterson, *Magazines in the Twentieth Century* (Urbana: University of Illinois Press, [1964] 1975), 56.
103. William H. Taft, *American Magazines for the 1980s* (New York: Hastings House, 1982), 314.
104. Regular editions of United States Department of Commerce, *Census of Manufactures* (Washington, DC: United States Government Printing Office).
105. David Abrahamson, *Magazine-Made America* (Cresskill, NY: Hampton, 1996), 25-27, 74, 77.
106. Kobak, "Magazine Trends," 236.
107. Marcella Ridlen Ray, "Technological Change and Associational Life," in Theda Skocpol and Morris Fiorina, eds., *Civic Engagement in American Democracy* (Washington, DC: Brookings Institution and Russell Sage Foundation, 1999), 304-306.
108. Ed Brown, "Extreme Publishing: Supply Room Confidential," *Fortune* (12 May 1997): 26.
109. Philip Elmer-DeWitt, "Beyond Shovelware," *Folio* 23:17 (1994): 54-55.
110. United States Bureau of the Census, *Historical Statistics of the United States*, 776, 783; United States Bureau of the Census, *Statistical Abstract of the United States 2000*, 567.
111. Malcolm M. Willey and Stuart A. Rice, "The Agencies of Communication," in Research Committee on Social Trends, *Recent Social Trends in the United States*, 201.

112. Tom W. Smith, "Phone Home? An Analysis of Household Telephone Ownership," GSSDIRS Methodological Report 50, 1990, website http://www.icpsr.umich.edu/GSS.
113. Claude S. Fischer, *America Calling* (Berkeley: University of California Press, 1992), 266.
114. Robert S. Lynd and Helen Merrell Lynd, *Middletown: A Study in American Culture* (New York: Harcourt, Brace, 1929), 140, 275; Willey and Rice, *Communication Agencies and Social Life*, 134-154.
115. Willey and Rice, *Communication Agencies and Social Life*, 151.
116. John C. Allen and Don A. Dillman, *Against All Odds* (Boulder, CO: Westview, 1994), 30, 180.
117. Mayer, "The Rise of the New Media," 132.
118. "Say Cheese to Your Cell Phone?" *Wall Street Journal* (26 August 1999): B6.
119. Mayer, "The Rise of the New Media," 132.
120. According to a survey by Times Mirror Center for the People and the Press, "Technology in the American Household: Americans Going Online...Explosive Growth, Uncertain Destinations," news release, 16 October 1995, Washington, DC.
121. According to surveys conducted by Gallup, Princeton Survey Research Associates, and Roper Starch Worldwide.
122. See CTIA's Semi-Annual Wireless Industry Survey Results, website http://www.wow-com.
123. Federal Communications Commission, "Trends in Telephone Service," Industry Analysis Division, Common Carrier Bureau, Washington, DC, 1997, 27.
124. Having received a phone solicitation was very or somewhat important to 23 percent of charitable contributors in a recent Independent Sector survey. Independent Sector, "Giving and Volunteering in the United States: Findings From a National Survey," Washington, DC, 1996, 105.
125. Fischer, *America Calling*, 75, 253.
126. Pitirim A. Sorokin and Clarence Q. Berger, *Time-Budgets of Human Behavior* (Cambridge, MA: Harvard University Press, 1939), 106, 191, 197.
127. Question: "Now I'll read you a list of activities and ask how often you engaged in them during the past year. Some activities you may do only in the winter or the summer, for example. When answering how often you participate in those activities, think of how often you did them during the season: Every day or almost every day; About once or twice a week; About once or twice a month; Less than once a month; Never...Talk on the phone with friends or relatives." Watching television and reading the newspaper were choices, as well. United Media Enterprises, *Where Does the Time Go?* (New York: Newspaper Enterprise Association/United Media Enterprises, 1983), 30.
128. The national sample of 1,000 adults plus an oversample of 444 likely technology users was surveyed for *Wired Magazine* and Merrill Lynch. Roper Center, Public Opinion Online, 1998.
129. Question: "Yesterday did you call a friend or relative just to talk?" Results from previous years reveal this figure to be an anomaly or representative of a sudden drop: 1994 (63 percent), 1995 (56 percent), 1997 (65 percent), April 1998 (67 percent). Pew, "Technology Survey," 1998.
130. A nationwide sampling of 1,000 adults conducted by Roper Starch Worldwide in September 2000.
131. Federal Communications Commission, "Trends in Telephone Service," 33, 36.
132. Question: "I would like to ask you a few questions about your everyday activities. On an average day, how many hours do you...talk on the telephone?" The choice

of 0, 1, 2, or 3 hours is too imprecise to determine actual time spent on the phone. Roper Center, Public Opinion Online, 1993.

133. United States Bureau of the Census, *Historical Statistics of the United States*, 776, 783; United States Bureau of the Census, *Statistical Abstract of the United States 1980*, 584; United States Bureau of the Census, *Statistical Abstract of the United States 1984*, 560.
134. Federal Communications Commission, "Trends in Telephone Service," 27; United States Bureau of the Census, *Statistical Abstract of the United States 1999*, 583.
135. Mayer, "The Rise of the New Media," 128.
136. Roper Center, Public Opinion Online, 1996.
137. Mayer, "The Rise of the New Media," 146.
138. *Washington Post*/Kaiser Family Foundation/Harvard University, "Survey of Americans and Economists on the Economy," Menlo Park, CA: Kaiser Family Foundation, 1996, 13.
139. Nationwide survey of 1,506 adults, including a black oversample, conducted by International Communications Research. Roper Center, Public Opinion Online, 2000.
140. Frederick P. Keppel, "The Arts in Social Life," in Research Committee on Social Trends, *Recent Social Trends in the United States*, 993.
141. Mayer, "Trends in Media Usage," 594.
142. Theodore Caplow, Howard M. Bahr, Bruce A. Chadwick, Reuben Hill, and Margaret Holmes Williamson, *Middletown Families: Fifty Years of Change and Continuity* (Minneapolis: University of Minnesota Press, 1982), 22-23.
143. United States Bureau of the Census, *Statistical Abstract of the United States 2000*, 567.
144. Ibid.
145. *World Almanac and Book of Facts 2001* (Mahwah, NJ: World Almanac Education, 2000), 315; John W. Wright, ed., *The Universal Almanac 1996* (Kansas City, MO: Andrews and McMeel, 1995), 232.
146. Nielsen Media Research, "TV Viewing in Internet Households," May 1999.
147. *Television and Cable Factbook* (Washington, DC: Warren Publishing, 2000) as reported by the National Cable Television Association, website http://www.ncta.com/sitemap.html.
148. Roper Center, "Mass Communications," *The Public Perspective* (September/October 1992): 6.
149. Jim Rutenberg, "The Media Business: Cable Networks Look for Ways to Stand Out," *New York Times* (20 August 2001): C1, C9.
150. Question: "People have given us various reasons why they watch television. Here are some of them. Please tell me if you think each of them explains your use of television very well, somewhat, or hardly at all: To obtain information about what is happening in the world; To spend time with your family and/or friends; To forget about the worries of everyday life; To be entertained; To fill your spare time; For companionship when you are alone; Simply to relax; To be able to talk to others about programs; To see what happens to my favorite characters on TV; To get ideas on how to deal with real-life situations." Roper Starch Worldwide, "America's Watching: Public Attitudes Toward Television," March 31, 1995 news release, 31.
151. Question: "First, I'd like to ask you where you usually get most of your news about what's going on in the world today—from the newspapers, or radio, or television, or magazines, or talking to people or where?" Respondents could name more than one choice. Mayer, "Trends in Media Usage," 593-611. Data for 1994 were provided by courtesy of the Roper Organization.

152. Questions: "Do you happen to read any daily newspaper or newspapers regularly, or not?" and "Do you happen to watch any TV news programs regularly, or not?" Times Mirror, "Technology in the American Household," 65; Pew, "Biennial Media Consumption Survey," 2000.
153. Question: "Some people prefer to read their news in newspapers or magazines, and some people prefer to get news on TV (television) or radio. If you had to choose one way of getting news and information, would you rather read it in a newspaper or magazine, or would you rather get it on TV or radio?" Roper Center, Public Opinion Online, 1989.
154. Question: "What would you say is your main source of news...TV (television), newspapers, magazines, or radio?" Roper Center, Public Opinion Online, 1989.
155. Question: "Which of the following sources of news, if any, do you use on a regular basis—television, radio, newspapers, or news magazines?" Roper Center, Public Opinion Online, 1995.
156. Guido H. Stempel III and Thomas Hargrove, "Mass Media Audiences in a Changing Media Environment," *Journalism and Mass Communication Quarterly* 73:3 (Autumn 1996): 551-552. Regular users were those who watched or read the news four or more days each week.
157. Robert D. Putnam, "Tuning In, Tuning Out: The Strange Disappearance of Social Capital in America," *PS: Political Science and Politics* (December 1995): 664-683.
158. For data on leisure time pursuit, see John P. Robinson and Geoffrey Godbey, *Time for Life: The Surprising Ways Americans Use Their Time* (University Park: Pennsylvania State University Press, 1997), 126, 322-323; Sorokin and Berger, *Time-Budgets of Human Behavior*, 148-160, 194-195; Susan Ferge, ed., "Part III: Statistical Appendix," in Alexander Szalai, ed., *The Use of Time: Daily Activities of Urban and Suburban Populations in Twelve Countries* (The Hague: Mouton, 1972); Gabriel A. Almond and Sidney Verba, *The Civic Culture: Political Attitudes and Democracy in Five Nations* (Newbury Park, CA: Sage Publications, [1963] 1989), 209-211; Elizabeth Hann Hastings and Philip K. Hastings, eds., *Index to International Public Opinion, 1980-1981* (Westport, CT: Greenwood, 1982), 483-484, 496; United Media Enterprises, *Where Does the Time Go?*, 30-32. For the number of sets per household see United States Bureau of the Census, *Statistical Abstract of the United States 1999*, 581.
159. Robinson and Godbey, *Time for Life*, 322-323.
160. Gallup, *The Gallup Poll: Public Opinion 1987*, 104-105; Gallup, *The Gallup Poll: Public Opinion 1991*, 130.
161. Roper Center, Public Opinion Online, 1989.
162. Hastings and Hastings, *Index to International Public Opinion 1980-1981*, 483-484, 496.
163. Question: "Now I'll read you a list of activities and ask how often you engaged in them during the past year. Some activities you may do only in the winter or the summer, for example. When answering how often you participate in those activities, think of how often you did them during the season: Every day or almost every day; About once or twice a week; About once or twice a month; Less than once a month; Never...Talk on the phone with friends or relatives." Watching television and reading the newspaper were choices, as well. United Media Enterprises, *Where Does the Time Go?*, 30-31.
164. Humphrey Taylor, "Fishing, Gardening, Golf and Team Sports Are America's Most Popular Leisure Activities...Apart from Reading, TV Watching, and Spending Time with Family," *The Harris Poll* 31 (7 July 1997).
165. Allen and Dillman, *Against All Odds*, 180-181.

166. Caplow et al., *Middletown Families*, 22-25.
167. United Media Enterprises, *Where Does the Time Go?*, 55.
168. Ibid., 60-63.
169. Question: "People have given us various reasons why they watch television. Here are some of them. Please tell me if you think each of them explains your use of television very well, somewhat, or hardly at all: To obtain information about what is happening in the world; To spend time with your family and/or friends; To forget about the worries of everyday life; To be entertained; To fill your spare time; For companionship when you are alone; Simply to relax; To be able to talk to others about programs; To see what happens to my favorite characters on TV; To get ideas on how to deal with real-life situations." Roper Starch, "America's Watching: Public Attitudes Toward Television."
170. For discussion of the latter, see Joshua Gamson, *Freaks Talk Back* (Chicago, IL: University of Chicago Press, 1998).
171. *Encyclopedia of Associations* (Detroit, MI: Gale Research, 1997).
172. David P. Thelen, *Becoming Citizens in the Age of Television* (Chicago, IL: University of Chicago Press, 1996), 9.
173. "Controlling the Internet: Web Phobia," *Economist* (24 March 2001): 99.
174. Kara Swisher, "There's No Place Like a Home Page," *Washington Post* (1 July 1996): A1, A8.
175. Hart Teeter Research learned from 38 percent of a national adult sample in December 1996 that they "[r]egularly use the Internet or other online computer information services, either at home or at work." Roper Center, Public Opinion Online, 1996. In November 1997, 37 percent of those interviewed by Pew Research Center said they "use a computer at work, school or home to connect with other computers over the Internet, with the World Wide Web, or with information services such as America Online or Prodigy." Thirty-six percent reported similarly in April and May of 1998. Pew, "Biennial News Consumption Survey,"1998 and "Values Update Survey," November 1997.
176. Times Mirror, "Technology and On-Line Use."
177. Peter Lewis, "In a Recount, Cyber Census Still Confounds," *New York Times* (17 April 1996): D1.
178. Pew, "Survey of Journalists."
179. Question: "Do you personally use a computer either at home, work or school to connect to the Internet or an online service like AOL?" CBS Worldwide, "Who Uses the Internet?", website http://www. cbs.com.
180. Pew, "News Interest Index," January 2001.
181. Times Mirror, "Technology and On-Line Use"; Pew Research "Media Consumption Survey," 1998. Twenty-two percent of a national sample were online users in 1996 and by February 1999 it had risen to 49 percent according to Pew, "Survey of Journalists."
182. Times Mirror, "Technology and On-Line Use"; Pew, "Technology Survey," 1998.
183. The Pew Internet and American Life Project, March-August 2000 Poll, website http://www.pewinternet.org.
184. Times Mirror, "Technology and On-Line Use"; Pew, "Survey of Technology,"1996; Pew, "Technology Survey," 1998.
185. Times Mirror, "Technology and On-Line Use"; Pew, "Technology Survey,"1998.
186. Nancy K. Baym, "The Emergence of Community in Computer-Mediated Communication," in Steven G. Jones, ed., *Cybersociety* (Thousand Oaks, CA: Sage Publications, 1995), 138; Usenet Information Center, 1997-1998, website http:// sunsite.unc.edu /usenet.

187. Rob Pegoraro, "Is Usenet Becoming Yesterday's News?" *Washington Post* (4 February 2000): E1, E11.
188. Paul E. Hoffman, *Netscape and the World Wide Web for Dummies* (Foster City, CA: IDG Books Worldwide, 1995), 336.
189. Bill Broadway, "Flocking to the Web," *Washington Post* (18 September 1996): B7; "Wired Churches, Wired Temples," the Pew Internet and American Life Project.
190. Robert Kuttner, "Net Day: A Lesson in Logging On," *Washington Post* (19 February 1996): A25.
191. Mark S. Bonchek, "Grassroots in Cyberspace: Using Computer Networks to Facilitate Political Participation." Working Paper 95-2.2, The Political Participation Project, MIT Artificial Intelligence Laboratory. Presented at the annual meeting of the Midwest Political Science Association, Chicago, April 6, 1995.
192. Tocqueville, *Democracy in America*, I:98.
193. Mary Curtius, "Libraries Write New Chapter," *Los Angeles Times* (1 February 1997): A1.
194. Edward Mendelson, "The Word and the Web," *New York Times Book Review* (2 June 1996): 35.
195. Roper Starch Worldwide Yahoo Internet Life Study as reported by Jeremy Schlosberg, "Web Users Share a Happier Outlook," *Media Life* (13 March 2001), website http://www.medialife magazine. com.
196. Pew, "Technology Survey," 1998.
197. Melinda Patterson Grenier, "More People Have Access to Internet But Digital Divide Persists, Study Says," *Wall Street Journal* online edition (18 February 2001), website http://wsj.com.
198. Michael J. Weiss, "Online America," *American Demographics* (March 2001), website http:// www.demographics.com.

6

Autonomy: Transformed, Tentative, and Tenacious

Self-governance, with regional differences, was unmistakably a vital force throughout the United States in the 1830s. Tocqueville noted the township system, imported by English colonists and located at the core of decentralized governance, was upheld by a strong belief that local institutions were necessary conditions for power and prosperity of the nation. Municipalities and townships were self-governing, had complete authority within a particular sphere, and lent their agents to the state. Numerous citizens, rich and poor, fulfilled the tasks of governing without undue hardship. State taxes were levied and collected locally. Schools were built and financed locally. Common affairs were discussed by general assemblies of citizens.

Local autonomy was manifested in a spirit of liberty, the sovereignty of the people, and the practice of political association. It existed long before a federal power was established to look after the general interests of the nation. It was never intended that federal governmental authority interfere with, or regulate, the subordinate matters of society. Yet Tocqueville noted "[a] highly civilized community can hardly tolerate a local independence, is disgusted at its numerous blunders, and is apt to despair of success before the experiment is completed (62)." He accurately predicted that the tension between central power and local autonomy would escalate. The latter would need to defend itself against encroachment as necessary resources and assistance flowed from a central authority.

One of the best safeguards for local autonomy, Tocqueville suggested, was its embeddedness in national custom.[1] The values and traditions embodied in the form of general-purpose local governmental entities—counties, municipalities, and townships—endure to the present day (see chapter 2). Core units of local government are both in partnership with and antagonistic to central power. Their persistence demonstrates a resiliency in the face of an increasingly complex set of challenges to local communities. Yet, local education has noticeably experienced effects of centralization. Rising numbers of curriculum prescriptions by legislatures between 1903 and 1930 and conditional funds from state and federal levels marked an erosion of independence for local schools—despite strong sentiment for keeping school decisions close to home. A dramatic plummet in numbers of school districts due to widespread consolidation and annexation of schools, noted in chapter 2, clearly marks a loss of local autonomy in matters of education.[2] On the other hand, an expanding number of special districts, established under the auspices of local entities to provide services not usually provided by general-purpose government, have widened the base of self-governance and added flexibility to its repertoire.[3]

Conditions that once characterized local independence—the confidence and the ability to be strictly self-determining—disappeared around the beginning of the century, according to historian Robert Wiebe. It was then that the distinction between a community and larger society became less clear. Worldviews encompassed more than the immediate environment. Communities were increasingly buffeted by external influences.[4] Even though information about local government was scarce, the Committee on Recent Social Trends noted a progressive movement of authority from local to state to federal government during the first three decades of the twentieth century and believed that chances for a reversal were slight.[5] In 1935, sociologist J. F. Steiner wrote, "No forward-looking community now plans for its future by confining its attention to its own immediate problems.... The community is extending its borders to include its surrounding territory—a tendency that is far more marked than was the case during the 1920's."[6]

Certainly, local independence no longer exists as it was experienced prior to the infusion of isolated, self-sufficient communities with transportation and communication technologies. As social and community boundaries extended outward, local autonomy increasingly became a function of continuously negotiated and renegotiated relationships between institutions. A revolution in meaning occurred. Autonomy, as sociologist Robert Merton pointed out, is a matter of degree and of interdependency for most groups or institutions; "[t]he appearance of full autonomy...is often deceiving."[7]

The revolution in meaning of autonomy is highlighted by a comparison of governmental functions across three periods of the nation's history: 1790-1830, 1830-1900, and 1900-1960. Warner and Trimm found the list of tasks performed by each level of government grew longer and some were found at all three levels of government. Thirty-seven functions were performed in the first time period, 51 during the second, and 112 in the third. While 73 percent of these functions were performed at the federal level during the first period, all of them were by 1960. The proportion of tasks executed by localities, on the other hand, declined from 54 percent in the first period to 32 percent in 1960, although local government functions nearly doubled—from 20 to 36.[8]

Regardless of Tocqueville's enthusiasm for local autonomy in the United States, it was often hard to win and to keep. Local sovereignty appeared to grow along with a capacity to provide services and to limit state influence. Of course, containing state intervention is ultimately subject to the will of the state to which a local government legally owes its existence. Not until the late nineteenth century did state legislatures, for the most part, cease to alter aspects of municipal government at will. A dramatic example of such tinkering, sometimes at the invitation of local representatives, is the record of ninety-one modifications made to one city charter in the forty years preceding 1876.[9]

Attempts to restrain legislative intervention and abuse with various kinds of state constitutional amendments were designed to: (1) bar laws specific to a particular, local problem; (2) establish procedures through which a law affecting a particular locality could be enacted, often including local review or approval; (3) limit the classes of local government that could be established; and/or (4) authorize the legislature to only pass bills that had the same impact upon *all* local governmental units. A countermovement lobbied for granting broad, affirmative power to local government as first seen in optional charter laws. In some states, responsibility and power were enumerated and divided between local and state government. Inevitably, with this model of divided power, questions arose about where the line should be drawn. Subsequent dissatisfaction with this arrangement grew as the courts tended to rule against local government in favor of the state. A second prototype, devolution of power, generally embraced by mid-twentieth century, legislatively delegated all authority possible to the local entity, giving it the discretion to be self-governing. Conflicts that developed under this model were less likely to end in court and more likely to be resolved by legislative action.[10]

Federal government influence on local affairs, sparked by a flow of federal funds to communities for urban renewal, transportation, housing, and social services, further frustrated local autonomy in the latter half of this century.[11] Although the flow of these funds waned during the Reagan administration, the demands and contingencies that the federal government visited upon state and local government failed to slow at a concomitant rate.[12] Subsequent intergovernmental tension, aggravated by local taxpayer revolts, intensified state and local objections to the burden of federal contingencies. The Unfunded Mandates Reform Act of 1995 (UMRA) marked efforts to stem the tide, but Conlan et al. cautioned at the time that "obituaries for the era of regulatory federalism may be premature."[13] The law was meant to produce better-informed legislation sensitive to the cost impact of federal rules and regulations and to make it more difficult for Congress to generate them without accompanying funding. Federalism scholar Timothy Conlan finds that it has been relatively ineffective:

> The new law deterred Congress from mandating in a handful of instances and prompted it to modify its behavior in others. But Congress's propensity for mandating remained strong.... The policy aims had changed, but the instruments had remained the same. If a revolution occurs in intergovernmental relations, it will not be as a result of UMRA.[14]

Fiscal Autonomy for Local Government

Fiscal authority is often used to measure autonomy. Finance (in contrast to government structure, function, and personnel) is the area of least discretion for cities, counties, towns and villages as measured by an index of local discretionary authority constructed by the Advisory Commission on Intergovernmental Relations in 1981.[15] Federal government funding was a small piece of the local general revenue picture in 1902, amounting to less than half a percent (figure 6.1). A gentle rise in the federal share began around 1932, consisting of 1 to 2 percent of local budgets until the 1960s when it rose and subsequently peaked in 1977 at 8 percent. Until the late 1940s, however, most of the activity was comprised of an increasing proportionate share of state-sourced general revenue and a decline in that of local-sourced general revenue. This continued more slowly until the 1970s, with an accom-

Figure 6.1

Sources of General Revenue for Local Government, 1902-1997

Percentage of Total Revenue

	1902	1922	1927	1932	1938	1942	1948	1952	1957	1962	1967	1972	1977	1982	1987	1992	1997
Own Sources	87	85	84	79	68	65	60	60	62	62	58	56	51	51	53	54	54
State Government	6	8	9	13	21	22	25	26	25	25	28	30	30	30	28	30	31
Federal Government	0.44	0.22	0.14	0.16	2	1	2	1	1	2	3	4	8	7	4	3	3

Source: U.S. Bureau of the Census, *Historical Statistics of the United States* and the *Census of Governments*.

panying increase in general revenue for local governments from federal sources. After 1972, revenue from states remained steady, local-sourced general revenue showed a slight gain, and federal-sourced general revenue fell back to a 1967 level of 3 percent of local general revenue. Locally generated revenue remained the largest share of local government budgets throughout the century. Yet, to the extent that autonomy is equated with generating own-source general revenue, these trends show that local governmental entities experienced an overall loss of fiscal independence.[16]

The pattern of general revenue apportionment for each kind of local entity between 1967 and 1997 is shown in table 6.1. In every case, but for school districts, own-source revenue makes up the largest share of budget in each year. This suggests five out of the six kinds of local entities are successful in sustaining local autonomy. Townships were by far the most fiscally self-reliant during this time, with 70 percent of their revenue generated from own

Table 6.1

Apportionment of General Revenue Sources for Local Government, 1967, 1992, and 1997 (in percentages)

		1967	1992	1997	% Pts. Change
County	federal	1	2	2	+1
	state	37	32	32	-5
	own	58	60	59	+1
Municipality	federal	3	4	4	+1
	state	17	17	16	-1
	own	59	56	56	-3
Township	federal	1	1	1	None
	state	21	20	19	-2
	own	72	71	72	None
School District	federal	2	1	1	-1
	state	40	52	53	+13
	own	55	46	45	-10
Special District	federal	6	10	11	+5
	state	4	5	7	+3
	own	55	52	50	-5

Source: Compiled from *Census of Governments* reports issued every five years by the United States Bureau of the Census.

Notes: Miscellaneous sources of revenue not shown here: employee retirement, liquor store, utility service charges, insurance trust, and other local governments. Own source revenue includes taxes, charges for current services, and miscellaneous revenue related to general government activity.

sources. Thus, townships have retained the most fiscal independence and school districts the least.

Also shown in this detail of local units is the change that occurred in revenue structure. First, state revenue continued to grow larger and own-source revenue grew smaller for school districts, with a notable shift of decision-making authority from local to state venues.[17] Second, federal dollars assumed a larger presence in special district budgets, although the largest portion of revenue remained locally sourced. Third, the portion of state dollars in county budgets declined slightly. These changes in revenue apportionments confirm an existence of a dynamic intergovernmental tension that was most intense between counties and states and between school districts and states during this thirty-year period.

Fiscal Autonomy for Private Voluntary Associations

The likelihood that a private voluntary organization will experience a loss of autonomy also increases whenever it accepts non-self-generated revenue, especially from the government. The risks entailed in such a nonprofit revenue mix are "not less but more government involvement in the affairs of voluntary and community agencies."[18] Grønjberg found, in an analysis of the revenue profiles of Chicago area nonprofits in the 1980s, that each source of revenue represents a unique set of complex exchange relationships.[19] As origins of income multiply, so do the agendas and objectives that require coordination and mediation. Smith and Lipsky articulate the problems posed by a mix of private agency and public funds. Placed in jeopardy are unique nonprofit values and contributions, the distinction between public and private, and a direct, clear accountability for the use of tax monies. Nonprofits may, indeed, become agents of the state, depend upon government for survival, and exercise quasi-governmental authority over citizens. When that happens, "the [nonprofit] sector is significantly compromised in its ability to offer clear alternatives," a potential disadvantage to the common welfare.[20] At the same time, the government can become too distanced from its own output.[21]

The actual "crowding out" of particular agencies or the cooptation of certain groups as agents of the state may be appropriate in the dynamic processing of ideas, positions, problems, and/or solutions. A vital public dialogue requires the competition of ideas and action. When the Research Committee on Social Trends considered whether some tasks seemed uniquely suited for private agency management, it concluded that the answer was *no*, not in a permanent sense, but *yes* in the sense that private entities could experiment, take greater risks, and discover effective and efficient ways of addressing social problems. In regard to a division of labor between private social agencies and public programs, "private social agencies initiate a variety of socially necessary services, experiment with methods of administration, and seek to secure permanent financial support from tax funds when the services appear legitimate public undertakings."[22] Subsequent to this observation by the Committee, joint efforts between the private and public sector blurred and the division of labor changed. In fact, Steiner reported in 1935 that the "breakdown of private philanthropy during the financial depression" altered that division of labor so that "privately supported social agencies will not again dominate the whole field...but will regard themselves more definitely as supplementary to governmental departments of public welfare."[23]

Service agencies, in particular, have a history of working with the public sector to meet social needs in the United States, in the absence of an expansive welfare state. In two groups of cities researched during the 1920s, approximately three-fifths (60 percent) of social agency revenue came from private sources and the remainder (40 percent) from public coffers.[24] It was not uncommon by 1930 to find the private and public sectors in many large cities and in some states sharing the fiscal responsibility for social programs.[25] Segments of the population in which need was greatest—mothers with dependent children, the dependent elderly, and injured workers—were large enough to exhaust the capacity of private agencies, requiring supplemental public funding. Cities, especially, were sites of disproportionate need and relief activity. The Russell Sage Foundation found that half of the entire country's relief expenditure in 1931 went to eighty-one cities that contained less than one-third of the U.S. population.[26]

In general, public monies that went to nonprofit agencies tended to be modest in amount—until 1960.[27] Social welfare spending nearly doubled during the 1960s with a flood of funds from new categorical federal programs, research and development grants and other purchases of services.[28] The influx of federal dollars altered the mix of revenue for many voluntary social service agencies. This was clearly the case in thirteen large, traditional, community-based New England nonprofits examined by Smith and Lipsky. Only one of these agencies received a significant amount of public funding (32 percent of revenue) in 1960. Twenty years later all thirteen were receiving anywhere from 37 to 81 percent of their revenue from government funds.[29] Jacobs also found that service and revenue patterns changed for a national sample of 287 private social service agencies that accepted Community Action Program (CAP) funds. In 1964, only 21 percent of these agencies had revenue from government; within five years, half added government dollars to their income portfolios.[30]

By 1979, Nielsen wrote that nonprofits were losing control, even as they were struggling to balance their budgets and retain their integrity upon a fragile mix of charitable and religious tradition, civic spirit, public sentimentality, tax privilege and general economic conditions. In sum,

> the influence of government upon private nonprofit institutions has become immeasurably greater than ever before. It now sets the priorities for the nation's scientific laboratories, as it determines the extent of access to medical care, as it controls, through the power of its purse, that part of the income of educational and welfare institutions which decisively shapes their growth and character.[31]

Revenue profiles vary by region and by type of agency, as well as over time. The Smith and Lipsky sample, for instance, came from northeastern states where nonprofits were more numerous and per capita nonprofit expenditure rates were higher than in other regions of the country.[32] Using the nationwide Independent Sector database of charitable and social welfare organizations, commonly called 501(c)3s and 4s, we can observe variance in revenue profiles by type of organization.[33] The revenue base for five types of these nonprofits relies on four sources of revenue: private contributions, government dollars, private payments (self-generated via dues, fees, and charges), and *other* revenue (endowments, investment, church gifts, etc.). The proportionate mix of these receipts, shown in table 6.2 for 1977 and 1992, signals the kinds of negotiated relationships that challenge these groups.[34]

Organizations involved in education and research and in health services are the most independent in that these two clusters of nonprofits rely most on self-generated income. To the degree that an inverse relationship exists between the magnitudes of government funding and autonomy, civic-social-and-fraternal groups and social-and-legal service agencies must work hardest to retain their unique characteristics. To the extent that an inverse relationship exists between the size of private contributions and autonomy, art and culture groups must consider particular interests of their benefactors more than if they relied upon private pay, or self-generated, and other income. As Schiller points out, cultural centers, higher education, public libraries, and public events are increasingly aware of the interest that big business contributors may have in shaping and directing public expression, national symbolism, documentation of events, and the interpretation of history.[35]

As for changes in revenue mix during the fifteen years between 1977 and 1992, civic-social-and-fraternal organizations infused their budgets with more dollars from private pay and other revenue, reduced the dominance of government funds, and ended with a more equitable fiscal position from which to negotiate with the agendas of government and private donors. Social-and-legal service agencies exchanged revenue from private contributions and public coffers for private pay and other revenue.[36] Education and research groups grew less reliant on other revenue. Health service organizations picked up more government funds. Overall, self-generated revenue from dues, fees, and charges played an increasingly important role between 1977 and 1992. These associations increasingly shared the cost burden with users of their services, negotiating for self-control by concentrating access to service on those to whom it is affordable. As a result, direct government influence and

Table 6.2

Revenue Sources for Five Kinds of Nonprofit Associations, 1977 and 1992 (in rounded percentages)

Type of Association	Revenue Profile, 1977		Revenue Profile, 1992		% Pt. Change
Health Services	Private payment	49	Private payment	48	- 1
	Government	32	Government	41	+ 9
	Other	11	Other	7	- 4
	Private Contribution	8	Private Contribution	4	- 4
Education & Research	Private payment	53	Private payment	57	+ 4
	Government	18	Government	20	+ 2
	Private Contribution	9	Private Contribution	13	+ 4
	Other	20	Other	10	- 10
Social & Legal Services	Government	54	Government	50	- 4
	Private Contribution	32	Private contribution	20	- 12
	Private payment	10	Private payment	18	+ 8
	Other	4	Other	12	+ 8
Civic, Social, & Fraternal	Government	50	Government	33	- 17
	Private Contribution	29	Private Contribution	31	+ 2
	Private payment	12	Private payment	20	+ 8
	Other	10	Other	15	+ 5
Arts & Culture	Private Contribution	41	Private Contribution	40	- 1
	Private payment	29	Private payment	24	- 5
	Other	18	Other	21	+ 3
	Government	12	Government	15	+ 3
		Total change:	Government		- 7
			Private contr.		- 11
			Private payment		+14
			Other		- 4

Source: Compiled from Hodgkinson and Weitzman, *Nonprofit Almanac 1996-1997*, 165, 172, 180, 185, 190-192. Subsectors not shown are religious organizations and foundations.

Note: Private payment = income from dues, fees, charges; Private contributions = income from individuals, foundations, corporations, fund-raising organizations; Other = income from endowments, investment, church gifts; Government = income from grants, service provision.

reliance on private contributions was somewhat lessened. The downside of this is the possibility of exclusion due to hardship for those who cannot afford user fees, but need the services.

Beyond Fiscal Autonomy

Difficulty in finding other measures of local autonomy encourages an overemphasis on fiscal resources that are visible, powerful, and easily quantified. What must not be overlooked is that local political and civil associations are part of an organized community reliant on an array of resources in addition to fiscal ones. Clark tentatively concluded from community research in the 1960s that some of the more important influences upon local autonomy and decentralization included institutional and cultural distinctiveness at the local level, the power and influence of local leaders, devolved authority, access to resources, and a differentiated social system with a variety of actors and tasks.[37] Lessons we are learning from research in sustainable development help to put these important resources into perspective. Evidence from Chicago, intergovernmental relations forums, and American rural communities is consistent with what this research says about sustaining local autonomy.

Lessons from Sustainable Development

Clark's elements of autonomy are demonstrated empirically in the sustainable development literature that finds social ties and networks do provide the means for exchanging and sharing resources—goods, information, services, demands and supports, human energy, and technologies.[38] Resources, however, cannot be counted on to "flow evenly or randomly in a social system with its asymmetric ties and bounded network clusters."[39] The manner of distribution of resources depends on institutional relationships and their reciprocity.

Esman and Uphoff, researchers in rural developmental activity for over three decades, have identified local organizations as significant agents in mobilizing and distributing resources for higher productivity and an improved quality of life. Regular and reliable two-way interaction and resource exchange between local organizations and central government produced a balance of power that correlated well with productivity.[40] Without these vertical links, localities were isolated and without access to developmental resources. Without reciprocal vertical interaction, the central authority was in total control and development activity was not productive. Minus the links and interactions, central government failed to comprehend the local situation and the local community was unable to adequately inform the central authority. The most productive relationships existed where central governmental authority gained relevant insights about the people, local goals, soil, climate, settlement patterns, ethnic traditions, norms and values. It meant, too, that central authority approached the relationship with respect, commitment to building local capacity over the long term, and dedication to enhancing the legitimacy of local organizations.

Reciprocal, horizontal relationships were also necessary for workable development of local areas: "Local institutional development is itself a strategy of decentralization to create capacities at several local levels for handling authority and responsibility."[41] Multiple parallel organizations, levels, and approaches, all working in different ways and directions towards the same end increased the "carrying capacity" of joint effort.[42] It meant more of everything: points of access, ideas, information, influence, skills, and alternatives in case of blockages, failures, or monopolies. Thus, local organizations with a high degree of interaction and reciprocity amongst themselves contributed effectively to vertical relationships with authorities beyond the local community.

Conditions that facilitated horizontally linked local organizations for community development were several: (1) participation that generated cooperation and self-help, expressed grievances, and enhanced legitimacy of local groups; (2) leadership that was committed and accountable to the community consensus; (3) arenas for making competing claims, regulating, and resolving conflict; and (4) institutionalization over time that made local activity and performance regular and predictable.[43] Specifically, in one comparative study of local capacity from 1954 to 1974, Esman and Uphoff established that those locales with the strongest capacity to invest in both vertical and horizontal relationships saw the highest gains in three agricultural productivity measures, in technological adaptation and innovation, in welfare conditions (nutrition, health, education), in safety and security, and in employment rates.[44]

Similarly, among the factors credited for long-term survival of commonly pooled resource (CPR) institutions studied by Ostrom, the mobilization and distribution of resources were guided by local conditions and by attributes of the shared resource itself. External authorities recognized the CPR institution's right to organize and govern its own resource. Participants themselves made and changed the rules. Monitoring and sanctioning was done by local participants rather than by external authority. Mechanisms for conflict-resolution were ready and easy to use. In large systems, multiple layers of nested activities were organized and coordinated.[45] The basic design of successful CPR institutions thus exhibited the vertical *and* horizontal linkages of the sort discovered by Uphoff and Esman. Cernea also found these institutional design features missing among failed development projects supported by the World Bank. Without local people at the center of an approach and linkages to the needed resources, both vertical and horizontal, there were no lasting development effects.[46]

Evidence in Chicago

Results in sociologist Albert Hunter's study of Chicago communities in the late 1960s are consistent with the sustainable development research findings discussed above and with Tocqueville's hypothesis that sentiment for the local community protects autonomy. The Chicago communities demonstrated horizontal and vertical relationships that produced, strengthened, and perpetuated local identity and autonomy. Hunter documented connections between voluntary participation in associations, local sentiment, and community autonomy. He found that membership in local voluntary organizations was related to a clear cognitive image of the immediate community, to a positive evaluation of the local area, and to expressions of attachment to the local area.[47] Also, community residents who had friends inside their local area were more likely to belong to voluntary associations, suggesting a positive relationship between formal and informal association.

These small organizations at the block and neighborhood level were oriented to local community interests, helping to give definition to the local area. Multiple levels of horizontal community organization existed and overlapped in terms of *my* area, *your* area, and *our* area. Over half of the groups were affiliated with various federated organizations that covered larger areas of the city, a number that had grown since 1948. Hunter found as many as four levels of federation that had originated from existing local community associations. These federations, in turn, had generated more local groups. Thus, Hunter found the production of two-way interactions, in horizontal and vertical directions, within the community.

The smaller independent groups were "oriented to *individuals within* the community in hopes of *maintaining* some valued characteristic of the area (167)." They rewarded involvement and provided "social control and public surveillance (171)." The federation provided "an integrative link between the local community and its citizens and the higher levels of urban government (169)." Frequently, federation activity was an organized response to the impact of bureaucratic practices and policies by government agencies that provided services to the local community. This response was sometimes adversarial, but there were vertical negotiations characterized by cooperation, particularly when it came to obtaining public monies for neighborhood improvements. Large federations effectively represented their communities on an equal level with larger outside bureaucracies. In Hunter's words, these federations pursued "goals through specific activities which are oriented to *groups external* to the community in the hope of bringing about community *change* (167)."

Evidence in Intergovernmental Relations

The history of intergovernmental relations is a dynamic one of vertical relationships between local and central influences. Samuel Beer speaks of "three great waves of centralization: the Lincolnian, the Rooseveltian, and the Johnsonian."[48] Walker's account is one of progression from dual, to cooperative, to an overloaded and dysfunctional federalism.[49] Wright described seven different modes of intergovernmental relations during this century, each shaped by unique problems and strategies.[50] Elazar illuminated the diversity in patterns of localism and centralism that are traditionally maintained by civil communities and states.[51] Peterson traced an evolution in which each level of government tended toward its area of competence, influenced by the political needs of legislators.[52]

However described, the ebb and flow in the configuration of power sharing between local and central forces is often pushed and pulled by crises and inadequate resources. Two excellent examples are seen in Steiner's 1935 analysis of traditional community organization in the United States. One situation did not end in a balanced exchange of resources, while the other did—for the duration of an emergency. The first was prompted by the unemployment that accompanied the Great Depression, overwhelming local community relief capacity. State and federal subsidies, accompanied by central authority programs and requirements, filled the breech. Local responsibility for unemployment relief was handed-off to arbitrary federal control with little or no effort to modify national policy to local conditions. This was a missed opportunity, Steiner observed: The "crisis, which might have been expected to strengthen local community solidarity, has in reality been working to a large degree in the opposite direction." In contrast to this outcome, the national war effort fostered a sense of reciprocity via a division of labor in which local communities were cast as contributors and "builders of national strength" while the federal government organized and coordinated the forthcoming resources, applying them to the war effort.[53]

The balance of tension between centralism and localism can seem to be irrevocably lost at a particular point in time. In Middletown (Muncie, Indiana), Walker's assessment at the end of the 1970s was that "intergovernmentalization of nearly all aspects of Muncie's public life suggest the triumph of vertical functional (and regulatory) forces over the traditional horizontal and territorial."[54] Yet the nature of the affairs and politics of the day, such as the following bulleted items, mark a constant process of vertical *and* horizontal negotiations in the United States.

- Innovative designs for self-governing communities, including dual private-public governments and gated communities are tried, tested, and revised.[55]
- Community goal-setting projects that elicit broad citizen input in charting the future of communities are conducted around the country.[56]
- Between 1992 and 1994, newspaper articles on unfunded federal mandates multiplied dramatically as negotiations intensified over adjustments in the relationship between state and local versus federal governments.[57]
- Communities continue to experiment with public-private partnerships, hoping to get it right function-by-function.[58]

- City mayors, in light of recent devolution initiatives, are "enjoying the increased influence they have as spokesmen for their regions."[59]
- Pagano and Bowman identified a number of policy issues in 1994-95 that were catalysts for negotiating vertical relationships. Struggles surged around health care, voter registration, federal mandates, state mandates, gun-control enforcement, environment, civil rights, block grants, welfare reform, immigration, military base closings, housing, community development, transportation, Congressional term limits, gun-free school zones, redistricting, tax and regulatory policies, management of local fiscal affairs, First Amendment rights, school desegregation and affirmative action. All community levels and all three branches of government were involved in this multitude of "challenges to a rebalanced federalism."[60]

The variety of public issues apparent in this discourse cuts across public opinion in a myriad of ways. It is produced by numerous exchanges, both horizontal and vertical. Although we are often dissatisfied with the qualitative input and content of public discourse, the process is vital and malleable.

Evidence in American Rural Communities

Flora and Flora find that a locality is most likely to respond to changing circumstances with agility if it possesses what they call an entrepreneurial social infrastructure. Their body of research pertaining to community structure, social relationships and economic development suggests that local autonomy is best served by being able to "exploit the strengths of community solidarity yet minimize its inherent weaknesses." The nature of local institutions and networks where such conditions exist is characterized by several elements. One is a newspaper that stimulates a comprehensive deliberation of issues and alternatives over time. Another is a variety of efforts, both individual and collective, aimed at mobilizing fiscal resources. A third is a set of inclusive and permeable linkages that extend horizontally and vertically. In their studies, Flora and Flora have also observed specific behaviors that are typical of communities like this—visits to learn from other localities, joint efforts and shared facilities, extra-community competitive events, and participation in organizations at multiple levels.[61]

Continuity of Process

We can infer continuity of process from the change, experimentation, and negotiation that occur between local and central forces. Lessons noted in rural development point to the importance of plunging in, remaining flexible, planning for contingencies, heeding what happens, and making adjustments along the way.[62] Similarly, Tocqueville thought the progressive march towards democracy needed to be faced practically, despite his personal misgivings about democracy. There was no point in wasting time and energy on nostalgia; better to "secure the new benefits which equality supplies." What men did with democratic conditions would determine "whether it will lead to servitude or freedom, to knowledge or barbarism, to prosperity or wretchedness."[63] The progression of the democratic experiment itself is a safeguard for local autonomy as long as localities invest in maintaining the tension and participate in the negotiations about who should do what and when.[64] As John Stuart Mill wrote to Tocqueville:

> one of your great general conclusions is exactly that which I have been almost alone in standing up for here, and have not as far as I know made a single disciple—namely that the real danger in democracy, the real evil to be struggled against, and which all human resources employed while it is not yet too late are not more than sufficient to fence off—is not anarchy or love of change, but... stagnation & immobility.[65]

Continuous, meaningful interaction between and among organizations and institutions is, therefore, essential for sustaining democratic tension. That it is necessarily a learning process is established empirically.[66]

Local Sentiment

Tocqueville noted that public opinion was an important safeguard for local autonomy. Not only was the township the most natural unit of self-governance springing from a group of people in proximity, it excited the "warmest of human affection." He posited it would be a rare American who thought the state had "any right to interfere in their town affairs."[67] In speaking of the power and persistence of public opinion, Tocqueville also noted the influence of custom.

> When once an opinion has spread over the country and struck root there, it would seem that no power on earth is strong enough to eradicate it . . . .As men grow more like each other, the doctrine of the equality of the intellect gradually infuses itself into their opinions, and it becomes more difficult for any innovator to acquire or to exert much influence over the minds of the people . . . It is extremely difficult to excite the enthusiasm of a democratic people for any theory which has not a palpable, direct, and immediate connection with the daily occupations of life; therefore they will not easily forsake their old opinions . . . . Democratic nations have neither time nor taste to go in search of novel opinions. Even when those they possess become doubtful, they still retain them because it would take too much time and inquiry to change them.[68]

Although Tocqueville recognized there is always resistance to opinion change, thus helping to stabilize a democracy, he also realized that "[t]ime, events, or the unaided individual action of the mind will sometimes undermine or destroy an opinion, without any outward sign of the change."[69] It is feasible that the creep of centralization would cause local self-governance to lose its saliency in the minds of Americans. Yet, when public opinion about local matters is examined today, it appears there is an abiding value for things local which helps to maintain a balance of democratic tensions. This sentiment is reflected in interest in local affairs, attitudes about involvement in local affairs, confidence in local government and leaders, attitudes about the cost of local government, and beliefs about tasks that local government should perform, as shown in the following sections.

Interest in Local Affairs

American adults sustain an interest in local affairs that supersedes interest in events elsewhere. Comparatively greater interest in indigenous matters is also evident in surveys that explore the extension of interest beyond national borders.

- In a 1996 ABC News, *Washington Post* poll, two-thirds surveyed said they were very or somewhat interested in current events *and* that their household subscribed to the local community newspaper. Moreover, nine out of ten local newspaper subscribers said they read it very or somewhat closely.[70]
- When the American Association of Retired Persons inquired of those surveyed in 1996 about the level of interest in activity at local, state, and national levels, the largest portion (42 percent) reported being very interested in local affairs, followed by 33 percent in state affairs and 31 percent in national affairs.[71]
- Local interests consistently prevail when it comes to reading newspaper articles about one's local community, other countries, or U.S. relations with other countries, according to responses to a survey question asked by Louis Harris in 1974 and 1978 and subsequently repeated by Gallup in 1982, 1986, 1990, and 1994.[72] Not only did local community news evoke the most interest in each of these years, it rose from 56 percent in 1974 to 65 percent in 1994. Smaller portions expressed the most interest in state news (51 percent), in national news (55 percent), and in news of other countries (33 percent). In 1998, Gallup found fewer (60 percent) who were very interested in local news although the pattern persisted in which just 47 percent were as interested in national news and 29 percent were as interested in news of other countries. However, news of relations of the U.S. with other countries *was* very interesting to 45 percent.[73]
- The same pattern of interest is reiterated in a year 2000 poll commissioned by Aspen Institute. More respondents in this survey reported a great deal of interest in news that is local and state (46 percent), than in national (35 percent) and international (25 percent).[74]

- Forty-six percent of survey respondents also told Gallup in 1999 that local community problems were of the greatest interest and concern. This was followed by international (27 percent), national (19 percent), and state problems (10 percent).[75]

Interest in following local politics grew stronger in the seven-year period between 1987 and 1994, according to Times Mirror. In 1994, 76 percent of Americans were completely or mostly in agreement with a statement describing themselves as "pretty interested in following local politics" up from 70 percent seven years earlier. In subsequent surveys when Pew asked about this interest in local politics, some fluctuation occurred from 68 percent in 1997, 74 percent in 1998, 66 percent in 1999, and 66 percent in year 2000.[76]

Attitudes about Involvement in Local Affairs

One half (51 percent) of Americans surveyed in 1960 in *The Civic Culture* study believed the average person should be active in local community affairs. An additional third thought it important to at least stay interested and informed about local affairs, to vote, and/or participate in church-related activities.[77] If confronted with a local regulation that seemed unfair, over three-fourths (77 percent) said they would do something about it; 59 percent would enlist the help of others, and another 18 percent would act on their own.[78]

In the latter part of the 1990s, similar attitudes are evident. "American democracy is only as strong as the virtue of its citizens" according to 83 percent of Americans in a 1996 survey regarding American political culture. The terms "community" and "civic responsibility" each evoked very positive or positive feelings from 87 percent in the same survey.[79] Fifty-nine percent of a 1997 national sample told the Institute for Social Inquiry it is very important to community life for people to give time and money to charitable organizations. Volunteering time to community service seemed absolutely essential to 20 percent of the respondents in that poll.[80] Nearly three-fourths of another nationwide study by Hart Teeter in 1997 rated "being involved in helping your community be a better place" as being of above average importance.[81] Community involvement was judged as very important by 47 percent of American adults interviewed in an NBC News/*Wall Street Journal* Poll—and somewhat important by another 47 percent.[82] A 1999 *New York Times* poll found that 35 percent of the public considered community involvement as very important; another 51 percent judged it somewhat important.[83]

This attitude extends to the role that Americans see for themselves in local affairs. In 1999, 73 percent of a national adult sample felt they possessed the knowledge and skills needed "for effective participation in the community, government, and politics."[84] Two-thirds of those interviewed by Princeton

Survey Research Associates in 1997 believed they have a big or moderate impact in making their community a better place to live.[85] Yet another national adult sample in the same year had thoughts about *how* to be involved; 69 percent believed it better to help one's community via civic activities, while only 19 percent thought it better to do so by getting involved in politics and government.[86] A felt sense of citizen responsibility is acknowledged in a 1999 survey sponsored by the Democratic Leadership Council in which 59 percent viewed participation in community decision-making meetings as a very important obligation; 91 percent agreed that with all the benefits one receives, citizens should also "give back to society through participation in the community." Significantly, 73 percent displayed a sense of efficacy in having the necessary "knowledge and skills that I need for effective participation in the community, government, and politics."[87]

Americans think that community involvement is important and seem confident in their ability to make a difference in communities. Their evaluation of public-spiritedness, as reflected in several recent surveys, can be characterized as cautiously optimistic.

- Recently, two-thirds of the public gave the country a C or a B when it comes to people's involvement in their community.[88]
- Three-fourths of the public said we were doing a good or fair job on volunteering our time to community service.[89]
- Seventy percent feel good about the morals and values of people in their community.[90]
- Eighty-nine percent of the public expresses great confidence or some confidence in the capacity of our community life, neighbors and friends to confront problems we face in the new century.[91]
- Overall, 76 percent of the public is satisfied with the way things are going in their local communities.[92]

Yet, there is a strain of self-criticism. Sixty-seven percent surveyed in 1996 by the American Association of Retired Persons said that they had *not* worked with others to try to solve some community problem within the last twelve months. Although this differs from what Americans think *should* happen, it is consistent with their ambivalence and the low priority generally, and historically, assigned to civic business in relation to other leisure pursuits. On the other hand, making the community a better place to live was the reason given by 70 percent of those who volunteered (43 percent) during the past twelve months.[93] And two-thirds (67 percent) of participants in the 1996 American Political Culture study believe the public good has greater priority when individual interests seem to conflict with the good of the larger community.[94] Americans *are* public-spirited and understand the importance of self-governance, despite the ambivalence it causes.

Confidence in Local Government

The public is more positive about local government now than earlier in the twentieth century. Some highpoints from recent survey findings illustrate the attitude.

- In 1992, 24 percent of Americans held a great deal or a lot of confidence in local government; by 1999 that increased to 33 percent.[95]
- In mid-2000, 47 percent of a nationwide sample of adults graded the overall performance of local government with an A or B.[96]
- At the end of year 2000, 22 percent of the American public thought local government was strong and working well. Another 47 percent evaluated the institution as doing only a fair job but expected that it will improve in dealing with issues important to the public.[97]
- When Louis Harris and Associates asked American adults in 1998 if their local government's ability to involve citizens in the development of priorities and solutions needed to be improved, 31 percent replied that major improvement was needed while 37 percent said that it needed only minor improvement.[98]
- A third of those interviewed in the year 2000 in a NPR/Kaiser/Kennedy School Survey said local government had a lot of impact on their daily life; 38 percent felt some impact; 24 percent recognized "just a little."[99]
- In 1998, over half (54 percent) of the public envisioned a larger influence for local government in their daily lives by the year 2025, while 38 percent felt its influence would be smaller.[100]

A variety of survey questions invite independent or comparative judgments of confidence or opinion about the several levels of government. Table 6.3 lists nineteen questions, asked on thirty-eight occasions between 1936 and 2000, which invite comparison of local with other levels of government. Little difference existed between most assessments of local and state government, blurring distinctions between local and state levels. Local-federal comparisons favored local government on twenty-four occasions. Six times the federal government elicited higher opinion ratings than did local government. Five of these were pre-Watergate (1973) and one was during the Persian Gulf War (1991), both points in time when the federal government generally evoked less criticism. This kind of differentiation in attitude between the two levels of government is illustrated by a 2000 CBS News poll in which 39 percent of a nationwide sample felt their views were "represented in the national government in Washington" while a larger 51 percent felt this was true of local government.[101]

This picture is consistent with other indications of the bent of public opinion. The 1996 Survey of American Political Culture, found 57 percent of Americans were in favor of moving many public functions from the federal level to the states.[102] About half (53 percent) interviewed by Pew Research

Table 6.3

Public Confidence in Local, State, and National Levels of Government

Year	Question	Local	State	Federal	N =	Error[1]
1936	a. Which do you think is most carefully and honestly run–your city or town government, your county government, your state government, or your national government? (The remainder of respondents thought they were all equal or that none were carefully and honestly run.) Roper for *Fortune Magazine*, Roper Report 93-8, 27.	15 9	6	18	—	—
1993	Q repeated.	29 9	8	13	—	—
•1968	b. We find that people differ in how much faith and confidence they have in various levels of government in this country. In your case, do you have more faith and confidence in the national government, in the government of this state, or in the local government around here? Center for Political Studies, cited by William G. Mayer, *The Changing American Mind* (Ann Arbor: University of Michigan Press, 1992), 450.	23	16	39	1673	±4*
•1972	Q repeated.	26	20	40	1569*	±4*
1974	Q repeated.	28	22	25	1575*	±4*
1976	Q repeated.	31	23	26	1348	±4*
•1991	Q repeated. ABC, *Washington Post*, Roper Center, Public Opinion Online, 1991.	31	22	43	1009	±4*
1996	Q repeated. Thomas M. Guterbock and John C. Fries, *Maintaining America's Social Fabric* (Washington, DC: American Association of Retired Persons, 1997).	42	17	13	1500	±2.5
•1972	c. Overall, how much trust and confidence do you have in (the federal/your state/your local government) to do a good job in carrying out its responsibilities—a great deal, a fair amount, not very much, none at all?[2] Opinion Research Corporation for ACIR, cited in Timothy J. Conlan, "Federal, State, or Local? Trends in the Public's Judgment," *The Public Perspective*, January/February, 1993, 3-5.	64	67	74	1000*	±4*
1987	Q repeated. Gallup for ACIR, Advisory Commission on Intergovernmental Relations, *Changing Public Attitudes on Governments and Taxes* (Washington, DC: ACIR, 1988).	73	73	68	1013	±4*

Year	Question	Local	State	Federal	N =	Error
1992	Q repeated. Gallup (for ACIR) in Conlan, "Federal, State, or Local?"	60	51	42	1000*	±4*
•1973	d. Do you feel you have more, less, or same confidence in ________ government compared to five years ago? Harris and Associates for Senate Committee on Government Operations, Subcommittee on Intergovernmental Relations, *Confidence and Concern: Citizens View American Government—A Survey of Public Attitudes,* 93rd Congress, 1st session, December 3, 1973, Committee Print, parts 2, 93, 99, 105.	30	26	57	1600	±4*
1973	e. As far as you personally are concerned, do you feel that local/state/federal government has improved the quality of life in the past few years, made it worse, or not changed it much either way?" Ibid., 15-16.	28 11	27 14	23 37	1600	±4*
•1972	f. How much trust and confidence do you have in the [government of this state] [local government here in this area where you live] [our federal government] when it comes to handling [state] [local] [domestic] problems: a great deal, a fair amount, not very much, or none at all? William Watts and Lloyd A. Free, eds., *State of the Nation* (New York: Universe Books, 1973), 298.	64	67	70	524	±5
1974	Q repeated. Watts and Free, *State of the Nation 1974* (Washington, DC: Potomac Associates, 1974), 336.	72	75	51	611	±5
1976	Q repeated. Watts and Free, *State of the Nation III* (Lexington, MA: D.C. Heath, 1978), 221-222.	66	72	49	530	±5
1997	Q repeated. *Gallup Poll Monthly* (June 1997) 4.	69	68	—	935	±4
1980	g. Here is a list of groups to which some people look for leadership in handling the country's problems. For each, please tell me how much confidence you have in its leadership ability—a great deal, a fair amount, not very much, or none at all. Local governments? State governments? Federal government? Opinion Research Corporation, Roper Center, Public Opinion Online.	71	73	65	1013	±4
1986	h. Which level of government—federal, state, or local—does the best job of dealing with the problems it faces? CBS News/*New York Times*, cited by Dennis A. Gilbert, *Compendium of American Public Opinion* (New York: Facts on File Publications, 1988), 202.	34	29	19	1000*	±4*

Year	Question	Local	State	Federal	N =	Error[1]
1987	i. How much of the time do you think you can trust the government in Washington/local government here in . . . to do what is right—just about always, most of the time, only some of the time, or almost never? National Opinion Research Center, General Social Survey, Roper Center, Public Opinion Online, 1989.	56	—	36	1466	±4*
1989	j. Do you have the most confidence in the federal government in Washington/the government in your state/the government in your local community? Not sure? *Time*, Cable Network News, Yankelovich Clancy Shulman, Roper Center, Public Opinion Online, 1989.	30	32	25	1009	±4*
1995	k. I am going to read a list of institutions in American society. Would you tell me how much confidence you, yourself, have in each one—a great deal, quite a lot, some, or very little confidence? Your local or community government? Your state government? The federal government? Hart Teeter for The Council for Excellence in Government.	31	23	15	1003	±4*
1997	Q repeated.	38	32	22	1003	±4*
1998	Slightly altered: I am going to read you a list of institutions in American society. Please tell me how much confidence you, yourself, have in each one—a great deal, quite a lot, some, or very little. Gallup (for CNN, *USA Today*).	37	37	—	1035	±4*
1999	Slightly altered: I am going to read a list of institutions in American society, and I'd like you to tell me how much confidence you have in each one—a great deal, quite a lot, some, or very little confidence. Your local or community government? Your state government? The federal government? Hart Teeter (for The Council for Excellence in Government).	35	33	21	1214	±4*
2000	Q repeated. Ibid.	31	30	26	1003	±4*
2000	Q repeated. Hart Teeter (for NBC News, *Wall Street Journal*).	38	38	28	2107	±2
1996	l. Select the one word that best describes how you feel about the following institution—our national government, your local government. How do you feel about the way that it is running—enthusiastic, pleased, content, confused, worried, afraid, upset, resentful, angry, indifferent? Don't really care? Hunter and Bowman, *The State of Disunion*.	54	—	19	2047	±2
1996	m. How much of the time do you think you can trust the national government/your local government to do what is right—just about always, most of the time, only some of the time, or hardly ever? Guterbock and Fries, *Maintaining America's Social Fabric*.	47	—	26	842 833	±4.5

Year	Question	Local	State	Federal	N =	Error[1]
2000	Q repeated. International Communications Research for NPR/Kaiser/ Kennedy School.	40	38	29	1557	±4*
1997	n. Next, I'm going to read a list of institutions. For each one, please tell me whether you feel that you can trust them a lot, some, only a little, or not at all. How about your city or local government/your state government/the federal government in Washington? Pew Research Center for the People and the Press, "Social Trust Survey: National Component." February 1997, 119.	14	9	6	1003	±4
1997	o. Now, I'd like your opinion of some organizations and institutions. Do you have a very favorable, mostly favorable, mostly unfavorable, or very unfavorable opinion of the federal government in Washington/your state government/your local government? Pew Research Center for the People and the Press, "Trust in Government Survey," Sept. 25-Oct. 31.	68	66	38	1762	±3
1997	p. How much trust and confidence do you have in your state government when it comes to handling state problems/your local government when it comes to handling local problems—a great deal, a fair amount, not very much, or none at all? Gallup (in May) cited by Pew, "Trust in Government Survey."	69	68	—	1000*	±4*
1997	Q repeated. Pew, "Trust in Government Survey."	78	81	60	883 879 1762	±4 ±4 ±3
1998	Q repeated. Gallup Poll.	77	80	—	1005	±4*
2000	q. Which level of government do you currently have the most trust in—the federal government, your state government, or your local government? Hart Teeter for NBC News, *Wall Street Journal*.	36	29	25	2107	±2*
2000	r. If you had to choose, which do you think is most corrupt—the federal government, your state government, or your local government? International Communications Research for NPR/Kaiser/Kennedy School.	13	15	59	1557	±4*
2000	s. When the government in Washington decides to solve a problem, how much confidence do you have that the problem will actually be solved? How about your state government? And your local government? A lot, some, just a little, none. Ibid.	16	10	8	1557	±4*

Notes: The sampling tolerance and size was not stated in some of the sources cited. Conservative estimates, indicated by an asterisk (*), were derived using secondary sources such as the Inter-University Consortium for Political and Social Research, *Guide to Resources and Services 1994-1995* (Ann Arbor, MI: ICPSR, 1995), tables provided by Gallup in issues of *The Gallup Poll Monthly*, and guidelines provided by William Buchanan, *Understanding Political Variables*, 4th ed. (New York: Macmillan, 1988), 96-104. Response percentages are reported for the reply gradients underlined in the questions. A bullet (•) indicates an occasion on which federal government elicited more favorable opinion than local government.

Center in 1997 thought that the "federal government is interfering too much in state and local matters," up from 40 percent in 1964.[103] Yet, when asked in 1997 if their recommendation to the federal government would be to grow smaller, more effective, or give state and local governments more responsibility, about half (54 percent) were in favor of making it more effective. More responsibility for state and local governments was favored by 31 percent of those interviewed.[104] Significantly, support for local government is sustained, while an appreciation for both local and central forces is also shown in these results.

Opinion about Local Officials

Favorable endorsement of local officials is as strong, or more so, than it was thirty years ago. Within this context, 41 percent of the public thinks that quite a few government officials are crooked.[105] Local leaders fare better than state or federal level officials in comparative ratings of honesty, ethics, or confidence evoked. For example, when Gallup solicited an assessment of the *dis*honesty of state and local officials in 1986, 38 percent of Americans thought almost all or quite a few local officials were crooked. Yet a larger 51 percent held that view about state officials.[106] The following year, more Americans surveyed by the Advisory Commission on Intergovernmental Relations (ACIR) trusted people running local government (37 percent) than those running state (22 percent) or federal (19 percent) government.[107] And in 1989, ACIR asked "On the whole, who do you think are the most honest?" Local officials received the nod three times as often as state and federal officials.[108]

Attitudes continue to be relatively more positive about local government representatives. In 1996 the University of Virginia and Gallup found about half (53 percent) of the American public was pleased or contented with local elected officials. This was three times greater than the 17 percent who felt the same about elected officials in Washington, DC.[109] Pew Research Center found a similar result in 1997 when 70 percent of their respondents had very or most favorable thoughts about state and local officials, in contrast to the 57 percent who held similarly favorable opinions about elected officials at the federal level.[110] Again in 1999, local elected officials were trusted more than twice as often as Congress or politicians in Washington to do what is right for "you or your community."[111] Local officials were seen as community problem-solvers by 43 percent of Americans interviewed by Pew in 2000, while only 28 percent perceived federal officials in the same say.[112]

A backward glance at ratings of ethical and moral practices of government officials in polls taken by Opinion Research Corporation (ORC) in 1964 reveals excellent or good ratings for federal officials from 47 percent of respondents. Fewer (40 percent) state/local officials were regarded this well. This order of higher approval for federal officials was reversed by 1973.

Ratings fell for both groups, but more so for federal officials. By 1973, only 26 percent of Americans judged the ethical behavior of federal officials as excellent or good while a larger 32 percent believed this of state/local officials. In several subsequent repetitions of the question, the latest by Pew Research Center, assessments of federal officials consistently trail those of state or local status. Federal officials received excellent or good ratings from 31 percent of survey participants in 1997, in contrast to the 43 percent who rated state or local officials the same way (figure 6.2).[113] Additionally, state or local officials regained the favor accorded them in 1964, and enjoyed a higher regard than did federal officials.

Honesty and ethics ratings in annual Gallup polls for local officeholders surpassed ratings of federal officeholders (senators and congressmen) during the last decade. The differences in honesty and ethics ratings among sets of leaders were not large, however. In 1977, local officeholders received very high or high assessments from 14 percent of Americans polled. Senators and congressman were viewed in a slightly more positive light with very high or high ratings in honesty and ethics by 19 and 16 percent surveyed. Twenty years later, senators and congressmen were rated this well by only 14 and 12 percent, respectively. Local officeholders, however, were rated very highly or highly by 20 percent of survey participants, an increase of six percentage points between 1977 and 1997 (figure 6.2).[114] This pattern of regard for local

Figure 6.2

Public Opinion about Local Officeholders

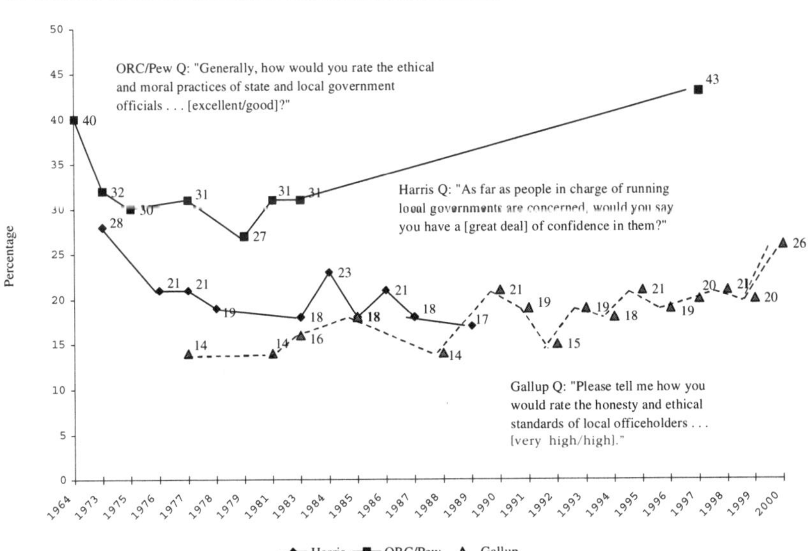

officeholders held for the final three years of the century, with an upswing in year 2000 that extended to officeholders at every level of government.[115]

A trend in Louis Harris Polls from 1973 to 1989 bridges and overlaps the ORC/Pew and the Gallup trends.[116] From 1973 to 1989, the percentage of Americans who reported a great deal of confidence in people running local government fell from 28 to 17 percent (figure 6.2). This trend reiterates the faltering of confidence in local officials during the 1970s, illuminated by ORC and the gentle fluctuation in the 1980s shown by Gallup data. Both Gallup and ORC/Pew Research Center data reflect a subsequent rise in confidence in local officials.

Division of Labor

What should local government do? Times Mirror and Pew Research Center documents a consistent pattern between 1987 and 1999 in which three-fourths or more of American adults completely or mostly agree that "The federal government should run ONLY those things that cannot be run at the local level."[117] *Time*/CNN/Yankelovich found majorities in favor of devolution from the federal to the state level of government in 1994 when the question was asked "Would you favor or oppose having your state government assume many of the governmental powers and functions now exercised by the federal government in Washington?" Fifty-nine percent were in favor. Again in 1995, 75 percent were in favor when asked "Turning to policy issues, do you favor or oppose having the states take over more responsibilities now performed by the federal government?"[118] In 1997, 67 percent of Americans thought it would be very or fairly effective if certain federal government functions were shifted to state and local governments.[119]

Notwithstanding a bias for things local, a division of labor among levels of governmental entities makes sense to the public and many tasks are thought to be the purview of state and federal, not local, government. Indeed, when Hart Teeter asked in 1997 what people's "main message to the federal government" would be, a majority of 54 percent chose "to make government more effective through better management" in contrast to the smaller number, 31 percent, who preferred to "give state and local governments more responsibility."[120] However, Americans who have been asked about this indicate that local governments and communities are responsible, or as responsible as other entities, for certain tasks. Table 6.4 lists some such functions and problems for which the public has viewed localities as responsible or most capable of handling. Expected responsibilities for localities are found in the areas of education, safety and public order, infrastructure and basic services, land use and environment, social services, culture and recreation, and leadership in issues of equity and morality.

Table 6.4

In the Public's Opinion: Whose Responsibility?

Education

a. ensure every American can afford to send children to college[1] (1962*): local (39%).
b. finance a college education[3] (1996): individuals (30%); state (27%); federal (28%).
c. ensure every American can afford to send children to college[1] (1997*): community groups (38%); state & federal (35%).
d. improve public schools[2] (1973): local (51%); state (50%).
e. improve schools in your community[16] (2000): local & state (74%).
f. racial integration in education[2] (1973): local (32%); state (36%); federal (39%).
g. set academic standards for public school[1] (1997): local (50%).
h. early education to low-income children[8] (1997): local (32%); state (39%).

Safety & Public Order

a. reduce juvenile delinquency[1] (1962*): local (44%); community groups (39%).
b. reduce juvenile delinquency[1] (1997*): community groups (58%).
c. security at big rock concerts[2] (1973): local (53%).
d. police protection[2] (1973): local (91%).
e. traffic congestion[2] (1973): local (69%).
f. security at radical demonstrations[2] (1973): local (36%); state (34%); federal (37%).
g. law enforcement[4] (1995): local (45%).
h. law enforcement[17] (2000): local (44%).
i. law enforcement[18] (2000): local (36%).
j. fight crimes and drugs[5] (1996): local (31%); state (32%); federal (30%).
k. fight crime[8] (1997): local (42%).
l. decide when smoking is permissible in public[3] (1996): local (29%); state (25%); federal (26%).

Infrastructure & Basic Services

a. keep streets clean[2] (1973): local (96%).
b. collect garbage[2] (1973): local (95%).
c. maintain streets[10] (1986): local (73%).
d. maintain parks and pools[10] (1986): local (68%).
e. garbage[10] (1986): local (53%).
f. ambulance[10] (1986): local (52%).
g. parking[10] (1986): local (48%); private (42%).
h. hospitals[10] (1986): local (45%); private (46%).
i. regulate use of pesticides on home lawns, public grounds in community[14] (1992): local (52%).

Land Use, Environment

a. zoning for housing[2] (1973): local (68%).
b. environmental protection[19] (2000): local (28%); state (30%); EPA (34%).

Equity & Morality

a. racial integration in housing[2] (1973): local (31%); state (35%); federal (38%).
b. promote honesty, stronger morals[1] (1962*): community groups (71%).
c. promote honesty, stronger morals[1] (1997*): community groups (76%).
d. restrict access to violent entertainment[20] (1999): local (38%); parents (59%); federal (38%).

Social Services

a. help homeless[6] (1989): local (27%); state (26%); federal (28%).
b. child care[13] (1990): local (29%); state (34%).
c. regulate location and building of low-income housing in communities throughout the country[14] (1992): local (72%).
d. deal with homelessness[9] (1996): local (30%); state (28%).
e. safety net, or basic necessities of shelter, food, and emergency health care[12] (1996): local (31%); state (38%).

Culture & Recreation

a. run cultural facilities, such as libraries, concerts and museums[4] (1995): local (53%).
b. pay for cultural facilities, such as libraries, concerts and museums[4] (1995): local (46%).
c. financial support for orchestras, theaters, arts[15] (1995): community organizations (48%).
d. fund arts groups[11] (1996): local (67%); state (63%).

(*) designates questions asked in 1962 and repeated in 1997.

Notes:

1. Q: "In your opinion, who should be primarily responsible for [____]? The federal government, state and local government, private industry, or individuals and community groups?" Question asked by Opinion Research Center in January 1962 (N = 1000; ±4 est.) and again by Pew in 1997. N = 879 for the academic standards item and N = 883 for the juvenile delinquency item; ± 4.
2. Q: "Now I want to read you a list of problems. For each, tell me what level or levels of government you feel can best handle that problem—local government, state government, or federal government?" Senate Committee on Government Operations, Subcommittee on Intergovernmental Relations, "Confidence and Concern: Citizens View American Government—A Survey of Public Attitudes," 93rd Congress, 1st session, December 3, 1973, Committee Print, pt. 1, 169-170; pt. 2, 237-62. Survey conducted by Louis Harris Associates. N = 1600; ±4 est.
3. Q: "Since our founding, different levels of our government have had different responsibilities. For each of the following, I want you to tell me whether you think it should be mainly the responsibility of the federal government in Washington, the

state government in [____], your local government, or private organizations. Or do you think it should be mainly left up to individuals?" James Davison Hunter and Carl Bowman, directors, *The State of Disunion: 1996 Survey of American Political Culture* (Ivy, VA: In Medias Res Educational Foundation, 1996). N = 2047; ± 2.

4. Q: "Which level of government do you think should be the most responsible for [running] [paying for] — federal government, state government, or local government?" Survey conducted by Hart Teeter for the Council for Excellence in Government, March 1995. N = 1003; ± 4 est.
5. Q: "Now I would like to read you a list of issues facing the country. Please tell me, for each one, which level of government that can best deal with ...." Survey by *U.S. News & World Report*, November 1996, reported in "Federal, State, Local, or Private Action?" *American Enterprise* (November/December 1997): 94.
6. Q: "To the extent that government may be involved, in which level of government do you have the most trust and confidence to handle each of the following problems most effectively: federal, state, or local?" Advisory Commission on Intergovernmental Relations, *Changing Public Attitudes on Government and Taxes–1989* (Washington, DC: ACIR, 1989), 9. N = 1029; ± 4.
7. Q: "Is the problem of homelessness more the responsibility of local communities or more of a national problem that should be dealt with by the federal government?" NBC News, *Wall Street Journal.* N = 1002; ± 4 est. Roper Center at University of Connecticut, Public Opinion Online, 1995.
8. Q: "In which level of government do you have the most trust and confidence to handle [____]?" Pew Research Center, January 1997, reported in "Federal, State, Local, or Private Action."
9. Q: "Who[m] do you think should be mainly responsible for dealing with the problem of homelessness? Federal government, state government, local government, nobody in particular, churches or religious organizations, themselves (the homeless), someone else, not sure." Louis Harris and Associates, April 25-29, 1996. N = 1005; ± 4. Roper Center, Public Opinion Online, 1996.
10. Q: "Would the following services be more efficiently produced/delivered by private companies or your local government? Parking facilities, street maintenance, hospitals, parks and swimming pools, garbage collection, ambulance service." Advisory Commission on Intergovernmental Relations, *Changing Public Attitudes on Government and Taxes–1986.*
11. Harris Poll reported by Jacqueline Trescott, *Washington Post* (12 June 1996): C04.
12. Q: "Now I would like to read you a list of issues facing the country. Please tell me, for each one which level of government that can best deal with ...?" *U. S. News & World Report*, November 1996. Reported in "Federal, State, Local or Private Action."
13. Q: "To the extent that government may be involved, in which level of government do you have the most trust and confidence to handle each of the following problem most effectively?" Advisory Commission on Intergovernmental Relations, *Changing Public Attitudes on Government and Taxes–1990.*
14. Q: "Should the federal government regulate..., or should each local government regulate...?" Advisory Commission on Intergovernmental Relations, *Changing Public Attitudes on Government and Taxes–1992.*

15. Q: "Many people want to see the arts flourish. There's disagreement, though, about who's responsible for that. In your opinion, is financial support for orchestras, theaters, and the like mainly the responsibility of individuals who attend such performances, the responsibility of local community organizations, or the responsibility of the federal government?" Conducted by Institute for Social Inquiry for *Reader's Digest*, February-March 1995. N = 1031.
16. Q: "Do you think improving schools in your community is something the federal government can do much about or is improving schools in your community mostly up to your state and local government?" CBS News, *New York Times* Poll, September 27-October 1, 2000. N=1462.
17. Q: "When it comes to law enforcement, in which level of government do you have the most confidence—federal, state, or local?" NPR/Kaiser/ Kennedy School Attitudes Toward Government Survey, May 26-June 25, 2000. N=1557.
18. Q: "When it comes to law enforcement, do you have more confidence in the FBI (Federal Bureau of Investigation), your state police, or your local police?" Ibid.
19. Q: "When it comes to environmental protection, do you have more confidence in the Environmental Protection Agency (EPA), your state's environmental agency, or your local environmental agency?" NPR/Kaiser/ Kennedy School Attitudes Toward Government Survey.
20. Q: "Please indicate how much responsibility you think local government should have for restricting children's access to violent entertainment—the most responsibility, a major responsibility along with others, little responsibility, or no responsibility." Gallup for Cable News Network, *USA Today,* June 1999. N=1022.

Two matters of public concern poignantly illustrate a change in what is expected of local government (table 6.4). One demonstrates a change in opinion concerning the reduction of juvenile delinquency. In 1962, a majority of Americans felt local government was responsible for reducing delinquency; in 1997, a larger majority considered it the responsibility of community groups. In another example, in 1962, a majority believed it was local government's job to ensure that every American could afford to send their children to college. By 1996 and 1997, local government was no longer seen as a principal agent in this objective. Instead, public opinion became more diffused, suggesting individuals, community groups and state and federal government must all share in the responsibility for funding education. Thus we observe a shift in opinion, moving the charge from private to public to shared arenas, and vice versa.

The public sees a need for multiple levels of cooperation, sometimes in horizontal and sometimes in vertical directions. One indication that this is so is seen in inquiries about who should set national educational standards. A majority, 60 percent, of registered voters in 1997 favored an approach for developing these standards with a commission of representatives from state and local government, business, parent groups, teachers, and school administrators. Yet, 62 percent also agreed that the Federal Department of Education should be eliminated to save wasteful spending and that control of schools ought to be returned to the local level.[121] Finding a workable relationship between levels of authority on an issue like education, where significant loss of local autonomy has occurred, is sensitive. Half (49 percent) of Americans interviewed in 1997 for a NBC News, *Wall Street Journal* Poll was concerned the federal government will not be sufficiently involved in doing what is necessary to improve the schools and meet the country's educational needs. Nearly that many (44 percent) felt the federal government would become excessively involved.[122] Reading between the lines, we might conclude the public would prefer that federal education dollars be spent as local and state authorities think best.

The sentiment for local control emerged in an education survey by University of Maryland in the summer of 2000. In this case, the public was asked what, if national testing were carried out, should be done with the results? The majority, 52 percent, felt the state and local school board should receive the information and make any necessary decisions. A smaller 30 percent felt direct federal involvement would be appropriate. Only 13 percent favored the federal government withholding funds to pressure schools to improve.[123] However, when it comes to making decisions about community schools, a national sample in 2000 was not largely dissatisfied with the distribution of responsibility between local school boards, the states, and the federal government. Half (49 percent) felt that local school boards held just about the "right amount of say," although the same proportion felt the federal government had too much and 43 percent felt the state had too much say. A majority, 61 percent, preferred that the federal government have less influence in the future in determining the educational programs of local public schools.[124] Thus, the issue of education illuminates the complexities and uncertainties in determining which institutions, and in what combinations, are most suited to supply resources and set agendas. Nevertheless, local decision makers clearly have an important role, in the opinion of the public.

Cost of Local Government

Six of every ten Americans think "people in the government waste a lot of money we pay in taxes." Another three believe there is some waste.[125] In this context, public opinion regarding the cost effectiveness of local government has not eroded but seems to have grown more positive in recent years. Two questions from annual surveys conducted between 1972 and 1994 by the Advisory Commission on Intergovernmental Relations (ACIR) tap public opinion about taxes at each level of government and about the level of government perceived as giving the most for one's money. Of four taxes—local property, state sales, state income, and federal income—the local property and the federal income tax consistently evoked the most unfavorable reaction.[126] A pattern suggested by years in which we see significant differences in the perception of local versus federal government costs has three features shown in table 6.5. First, 1972 was a year when the largest portion of respondents, 45 percent, named the local property tax as least fair—significantly different from the 19 percent who believed the federal income tax was least fair. Second, between 1972 and 1978 the federal government was seen as giving the most for the money by larger numbers of Americans. Third, from 1979 to 1986 the local property tax was less unpopular than the federal income tax.

During the eighties, neither the local nor federal government stood out as giving the most for the money, except in 1984. When ACIR began to ask, in 1989, which level of government gave the *least* for the money, a difference in perception of federal and local governments did emerge (table 6.5).[127] Then, over one-third (36 percent) said federal government gave the least for the dollar, while a smaller one-fourth (25 percent) held similar views about local government. The gap widened by 1994, when 46 percent thought the least return came from federal government and only 19 percent said local government gave the least. In yet another question, asked thrice between 1989 and 1993, three to five times as many Americans regarded local government as the wiser spender of tax monies.[128] The outlier year of 1972 reflects an earlier period when federal government costs seemed less troublesome than local ones.

The Roper Organization found that 22 percent of a 1936 national sample considered city or town government as the most expensive level of government, followed by state (17 percent), county (13 percent), and national (13 percent) government.[129] At that time, the threshold for payment of federal income taxes excluded most Americans.[130] Perceptions differed by 1993 when Roper repeated the question. National government now seemed the most costly to 41 percent of respondents, in contrast to state (14 percent) and local entities—city or town (12 percent) and county (5 percent) governments.[131] This sentiment is consistent with ACIR's more recent findings (table 6.5) and with one by Hart Teeter in 1995. The largest plurality of those surveyed by Hart Teeter believed that tax monies are spent most prudently by local government (50 percent), followed by state (24 percent), and, finally, federal government (10 percent).[132] In a similar vein, a larger portion of Americans believe they pay more than their fair share of federal taxes (55 percent), in contrast to those who feel they must pay more than is equitable in local (39 percent) and state (40 percent) taxes.[133]

The majority of a national sample interviewed by Louis Harris and Associates in 1996 reported their biggest concern was not the amount of taxes, nor the fairness of the taxes, but the effectiveness of how tax money was spent.[134] The public's bias in favor of the cost of government closest to home is prob-

Table 6.5

Change in Perceptions of Local and Federal Government Cost (in percentages)

	Least Fair Tax	Government Offers Most for $s	Government Offers Least for $s	Government Spends Tax $s Wisely
1972	**Local Property 45** Federal Income 19	**Federal 39** Local 26		
1973		**Federal 35** Local 25		
1975		**Federal 38** Local 25		
1976		**Federal 36** Local 25		
1977		**Federal 36** Local 25		
1978		**Federal 35** Local 26		
1979	**Federal Income 37** Local Property 27			
1980	**Federal Income 36** Local Property 25			
1983	**Federal Income 35** Local Property 26			
1984		**Federal 35** Local 24		
1985	**Local Property 44** Federal Income 38			
1986	**Federal Income 37** Local Property 28			
1989			**Federal 36** Local 25	**Local 36** Federal 11
1990			**Federal 41** Local 21	
1991				**Local 35** Federal 12
1992			**Federal 49** Local 18	
1993	**Federal Income 36** Local Property 26	**Local 38** Federal 23		**Local 35** Federal 7
1994			**Federal 46** Local 19	

Source: Compiled from annual editions of the Advisory Commission on Intergovernmental Relations, *Changing Public Attitudes on Governments and Taxes.*

Notes: N = 1000-1500; ± 4, except in 1985 and 1990 when it was ± 3. Annual differences are significant.

ably not based upon management efficiency in the narrow sense, however. In 1995, when Hart Teeter asked survey respondents to select one of three statements about devolving federal responsibility to state and local government, just 26 percent replied that state and local government managed more efficiently at less cost. Thirty-three percent believed that state and local governments do a better job in addressing individual needs and problems of local communities. Another third (33 percent) saw state and local government as more likely to put an end to wasteful government activity.[135] Government waste and cost efficiency is an important issue but not the whole story for Americans; the other piece is that local concerns, when feasible, are best handled locally.

Summary and Discussion of Findings

A long-standing custom of self-governance in the United States survived a remarkable transformation during the twentieth century. With the expansion and increased permeability of social space made possible by communication and transportation technologies, local communities were no longer independent, but increasingly had to learn to negotiate their relationships with other entities. The required kind of relationship was one of reciprocity and interdependence characterized by Kant:

> every substance...must contain in itself the causality of certain determinations in another substance, and, at the same time, the effects of the causality of that other substance, that is, substances must stand in dynamical communion, immediately or mediately, with each other.[136]

Achieving this is a continuous process in which self-governance remains vulnerable to infringement from government and corporate interests who push for advantage, control, and centralization. Localities are reliant on resources accessible through these overweening entities. To obtain needed resources while resisting cooptation, i.e., to be successful in these vertical negotiations, voluntary associations and local communities must have the wherewithal to withstand encroachment. This encompasses a broader resource base than that provided by dollars, although the paucity of money can easily undo a negotiated balance. Less tangible resources such as identity, innovation, information, and legitimacy are also quite necessary.

Sustainable development research tells us that horizontal networking builds capacity for effective vertical relationships that, in turn, supports horizontal linkages. Sustaining autonomy thus requires sensitivity and a capacity to flex with change, to refocus horizontal and vertical relationships as they evolve, and to adjust divisions of labor accordingly. Clearly, conserving autonomy is much more demanding and complex now than at the beginning of the century when independence was simple. But every voluntary association, every unit of local government, and every community in existence is evidence of some success. A recent rise in confidence in local government also implies success in negotiating local autonomy. Could the attainment be greater? Undoubtedly. The process of experimenting, learning, and working out relationships, both vertically and horizontally, was visible and constant, however, throughout the past century. At one extreme, there was little concern for autonomy since local entities were quite independent. As that changed, the balance of power tipped to one heavily weighted with a federal influence. Today, a better balance of tension is sought between local and central forces.

One safeguard that Tocqueville predicted would be important remains in place. Public opinion supports and mediates the tension between centralism and localism. A tenacious and positive local sentiment coexists in the minds of Americans along with an awareness that other authorities also contribute to the overall effort. Care about local affairs grows and overrides, without precluding, interest in events beyond local perimeters. The public's preference is that government be local *if* the task can be done there. However, as the nature of necessary tasks and capacities change, so may the public's idea of which agency should perform what public task. Such changes in attitude reflect an ability to flex with the times and conditions, which bodes well for civil society.

Notes

1. Alexis de Tocqueville, *Democracy in America* (New York: Vintage Books, 1945), I:29, 42, 61-101.
2. Charles H. Judd, "Education," in Research Committee on Social Trends, *Recent Social Trends in the United States* (New York: McGraw-Hill, 1933), 362-370; Carroll H. Wooddy, "The Growth of Governmental Functions," in Research Committee on Social Trends, *Recent Social Trends in the United States*, 1302-1303.
3. Eighty-nine special districts of a wide variety were noted in 1933. Wooddy, "The Growth of Governmental Functions," 1316-1317.
4. Robert H. Wiebe, *The Search for Order, 1877-1920* (New York: Hill and Wang, 1966), 2-12, 44-48, 133.
5. Leonard D. White, "Public Administration," in Research Committee on Social Trends, *Recent Social Trends in the United States*, 1393-1402. Also see Wooddy, "The Growth of Governmental Functions," 1315-1321.
6. Jesse Frederick Steiner, "Community Organization," *American Journal of Sociology* XL (May 1935): 791.
7. Robert K. Merton, *Social Theory and Social Structure* (Glencoe, IL: Free Press, [1949] 1957), 322-323.
8. W. Lloyd Warner and John H. Trimm, "The Rise of Big Government," in W. L. Warner, ed., *The Emergent American Society: Large-Scale Organizations* (New Haven, CT: Yale University Press, 1967), 577-580. Also see Wooddy, "The Growth of Governmental Functions," 1274-1330.
9. Nancy Burns, *The Formation of American Local Governments* (New York: Oxford University Press, 1994), 45-53.
10. Advisory Commission on Intergovernmental Relations, "Measuring Local Discretionary Authority," Information Report M-131 (Washington, DC: November 1981),

11-21. For a discussion of intergovernmental relations paradigms, see Deil S. Wright, "Models of National, State, and Local Relationships," in Laurence J. O'Toole, Jr., *American Intergovernmental Relations: Foundations, Perspectives, and Issues* (Washington, DC: Congressional Quarterly, 1993), 75-88.

11. Burns, *The Formation of American Local Governments*, 61-64.
12. Timothy Conlan, *From New Federalism to Devolution: Twenty-five Years of Intergovernmental Reform* (Washington, DC: Brookings Institution, 1998), 258-260; Harold A. Hovey, *The Devolution Revolution: Can the States Afford Devolution?* (New York: Century Foundation, 1999); Marcella Ridlen Ray and Timothy J. Conlan, "At What Price: Costs of Federal Mandates Since the 1980s," *State and Local Government Review* 28:1 (Winter 1996): 7-16.
13. Timothy J. Conlan, James D. Riggle, and Donna E. Schwartz, "Deregulating Federalism? The Politics of Mandate Reform in the 104th Congress," *Publius* 25:3 (Summer 1995): 5.
14. Conlan, *From New Federalism to Devolution*, 269-272.
15. Joseph F. Zimmerman, "The Discretionary Authority of Local Governments," *Urban Data Service Reports* 13:11 (November 1981), Washington, DC: International City Management Association, 7, 11.
16. United States Bureau of the Census, *Historical Statistics of the United States: Colonial Times to 1970* (Washington, DC: United States Department of Commerce, 1975), 1133, and United States Bureau of the Census, *Census of Governments* (Washington, DC: United States Department of Commerce, Economics and Statistics Administration, 1967-1992 editions). The same data, for years 1962-1984, were also used by Deil S. Wright to develop a local government fiscal dependency index found in *Understanding Intergovernmental Relations*, 3d ed. (Pacific Grove, CA: Brooks/Cole, 1988), 165. I extended the time period, using data from United States Bureau of the Census, *Historical Statistics of the United States*, 1133, and United States Bureau of the Census, *Census of Governments*. This measure of local fiscal dependency rose from 0.07 in 1902 to a high of 0.75 in 1977, and fell to 0.60 in 1992.
17. For discussion of the more visible developments of this shift, see David R. Berman, "Takeovers of Local Governments: An Overview and Evaluation of State Policies," *Publius* 25:3 (Summer 1995): 59-60, 64-68.
18. Steven Rathgeb Smith and Michael Lipsky, *Nonprofits for Hire* (Cambridge, MA: Harvard University Press, 1993), 5.
19. Kirsten A. Grønjberg, *Understanding Nonprofit Funding* (San Francisco, CA: Jossey-Bass, 1993), 53-68.
20. Smith and Lipsky, *Nonprofits for Hire*, 11-14, 207. See Nathan Glazer, "Towards a Self-Service Society?" *The Public Interest* 70 (Winter 1983): 79-85 for discussion of how the efforts of voluntary groups wishing to provide social services are sometimes subverted.
21. H. Brinton Milward, "Nonprofit Contracting and the Hollow State," *Public Administration Review* 54:1 (January/February 1994): 73-77.
22. Sydnor H. Walker, "Privately Supported Social Work," in Research Committee on Social Trends, *Recent Social Trends in the United States*, 1196.
23. Steiner, "Community Organization," 792-794. Also see Michael FitzGibbon, "Accountability Misplaced: Private Social Welfare Agencies and the Public in Cleveland, 1880-1920," *Nonprofit and Voluntary Sector Quarterly* 26:1 (March 1997): 27-40.
24. Walker, "Privately Supported Social Work," 1195-1215.
25. Ibid., 1168-1223; Smith and Lipsky, *Nonprofits for Hire*, 47-50; Lester M. Salamon, "Partners in Public Service: The Scope and Theory of Government-Nonprofit

Relations," in Walter W. Powell, ed., *The Nonprofit Sector* (New Haven, CT: Yale University Press, 1987), 99-101.

26. Leo Wolman and Gustav Peck, "Labor Groups in the Social Structure," in Research Committee on Social Trends, *Recent Social Trends in the United States*, 826-827; Walker, "Privately Supported Social Work," 1214-1215.
27. Smith and Lipsky, *Nonprofits for Hire*, 47-53; Grønjberg, *Understanding Nonprofit Funding*, 78-81; Bruce Jacobs, *The Political Economy of Organizational Change* (New York: Academic, 1981), 76-77.
28. Smith and Lipsky, *Nonprofits for Hire*, 53-57; United States Department of Treasury, "Social Welfare and the Economy Highlights," *Social Security Bulletin, Annual Statistical Supplement* (1996): 157-160; Grønjberg, *Understanding Nonprofit Funding*, 78-81.
29. Smith and Lipsky, *Nonprofits for Hire*, 234-237.
30. Jacobs, *The Political Economy of Organizational Change*, 83, 88.
31. Waldemar A. Nielsen, *The Endangered Sector* (New York: Columbia University Press, 1979), 8-21.
32. Salamon, "Partners in Public Service," 107.
33. Virginia Ann Hodgkinson and Murray S. Weitzman, et al., *Nonprofit Almanac 1996-1997: Dimensions of the Independent Sector* (San Francisco, CA: Jossey-Bass, 1996), 155-192.
34. These five clusters of nonprofit organizations garnered 85 percent of all revenue in the Independent Sector database. Private payments accounted for 38 percent in 1977 and 39 percent of total revenue in 1992. Private contributions accounted for 26 percent in 1977 and 18 percent in 1992. Government dollars accounted for 27 and 31 percent. *Other* revenue accounted for 10 percent and 11 percent.
35. Herbert I. Schiller, *Culture, Inc.: The Corporate Takeover of Public Expression* (New York: Oxford University Press, 1989). Also see Paul Farhi, "A Joke That Rang True: Ad Claiming Liberty Bell Purchase Angers Public," *Washington Post* (2 April 1996), E1, E3.
36. The Independent Sector includes legal, individual and family, job training, child day care, residential care, and *other* services in this category.
37. Terry Nichols Clark, "The Structure of Community Influence," in Harlan Hahn, ed., *People and Politics in Urban Society* (Beverly Hills, CA: Sage Publications, 1972), 283-314; Terry Nichols Clark, "Community Autonomy in the National System: Federalism, Localism, and Decentralization," in Terry Nichols Clark, *Comparative Community Politics* (New York: John Wiley, 1974).
38. Norman T. Uphoff and Milton J. Esman, "Comparative Analysis of Asian Experience with Local Organization and Rural Development," in Norman T. Uphoff, ed., *Rural Development and Local Organization in Asia: South East Asia* (Delhi: MacMillan India, 1983), 338, 317; Michael J. Esman and Norman T. Uphoff, *Local Organizations: Intermediaries in Rural Development* (Ithaca, NY: Cornell University Press, 1984); Norman T. Uphoff, *Rural Development and Local Organization in Asia: Introduction and South Asia* (Delhi: Macmillan India, 1982); Elinor Ostrom, *Governing the Commons: the Evolution of Institutions for Collective Action* (Boston, MA: Cambridge University Press, 1990), 30-43, 92-93; Michael M. Cernea, "The Sociologist's Approach to Sustainable Development," *Finance and Development* (December 1993): 11-13; Michael M. Cernea, ed., *Putting People First: Sociological Variables in Rural Development* (New York: Oxford University Press, 1985).

39. Barry Wellman, "Network Analysis: Some Basic Principles," in Randall Collins, *Sociological Theory 1983* (San Francisco, CA: Jossey-Bass, 1983), 176-179.
40. Esman and Uphoff, *Local Organizations*, 93, 152.
41. Norman Uphoff, *Local Institutional Development: An Analytical Sourcebook with Cases* (West Hartford, CT: Kumarian, 1986), 221. The importance of horizontal networks is also documented in Robert D. Putnam with Robert Leonardi and Raffaella Y. Nanetti, *Making Democracy Work: Civic Traditions in Modern Italy* (Princeton, NJ: Princeton University Press, 1993), 175-176.
42. Uphoff, *Rural Development* (1983), 311. For a discussion of competition and cooperation among voluntary groups, see James Q. Wilson, *Political Organizations* (Princeton, NJ: Princeton University Press, [1974] 1995), 261-280.
43. Uphoff and Esman, "Comparative Analysis," 263-399; network theory explains that "incumbency of a structural position...determines access to other resources." Wellman, "Network Analysis: Some Basic Principles," 176-179.
44. Uphoff, *Rural Development* (1982), 22-27.
45. Ostrom, *Governing the Commons*, 88-102.
46. Cernea, "The Sociologist's Approach to Sustainable Development," 11-13.
47. Albert Hunter, *Symbolic Communities: The Persistence and Change of Chicago's Local Communities* (Chicago, IL: University of Chicago Press, 1974), 95-116, 129, 152-155, 162-172.
48. Samuel H. Beer, "The Idea of the Nation," in Laurence J. O'Toole, Jr., ed., *American Intergovernmental Relations* (Washington, DC: Congressional Quarterly, 1993), 357.
49. David B. Walker, *Toward a Functioning Federalism* (Cambridge, MA: Winthrop, 1981).
50. Wright, *Understanding Intergovernmental Relations*, 65-118.
51. Daniel J. Elazar, *American Federalism: A View from the States* (New York: Thomas Y. Crowell, 1972), 198-205.
52. Paul E. Peterson, *The Price of Federalism* (Washington, DC: Brookings Institution, 1995).
53. Steiner, "Community Organization," 789-790.
54. Walker, *Toward a Functioning Federalism*, 255-256.
55. Andrew Stark, "America, The Gated?" *Wilson Quarterly* (Winter 1998): 58-79; Richard Moe and Carter Wilkie, *Changing Places: Rebuilding Community in the Age of Sprawl* (New York: Henry Holt, 1997); Edward J. Blakely and Mary Gail Snyder, *Gated Communities in the United States* (Washington, DC: Brookings Institution/Lincoln Institute of Land Policy, 1997); Christina A. Samuels, "'Cohousing' Village Breaks Ground in Virginia," *Washington Post* (19 July 1999): B7.
56. Bruce W. McClendon and John A. Lewis, "Goals for Corpus Christi: Citizen Participation in Planning," *National Civic Review* (February 1985): 72-80; Sy Adler and Gerald F. Blake, "The Effects of a Formal Citizen Participation Program on Involvement in the Planning Process: A Case Study of Portland, Oregon," *State and Local Government Review* (Winter 1990): 37-43; Craig M. Wheeland, "Citywide Strategic Planning: An Evaluation of Rock Hill's Empowering the Vision," *Public Administration Review* 53:1 (1993): 65-72; Frank J. Smith and Randolph T. Hester, Jr., *Community Goal Setting* (Stroudsburg, PA: Hutchinson Ross, 1982); Ronald K. Vogel and Bert E. Swanson, "Setting Agendas for Community Change: The Community Goal-Setting Strategy," *Journal of Urban Affairs* 10:1 (1988): 41-61; Michael McGuire, Barry Rubin, Robert Agranoff, and Craig Richards, "Building Development Capacity in Nonmetropolitan Communities,"

Public Administration Review 54:5 (September/October 1994): 426-433; "Progress '90," *Pensacola News-Journal* (24 March 1985): Section H; Peter T. Johnson, "How I Turned a Critical Public into Useful Consultants," *Harvard Business Review* (January/February 1993): 56-66. For a collection of examples and observations discussed in the media, see National Civic League, "The Landscape of Civic Renewal," 1999, Denver, CO.

57. Conlan, Riggle, and Schwartz, "Deregulating Federalism?," 27.
58. For example, the management of tennis centers in the city of Dallas, Texas, described in Jere R. Mills, "Partnerships Providing Service," *Parks and Recreation* 29:5 (May 1994): 32-34. For discussion of other experiments and some of the issues and pressures to be addressed in public-private initiatives, see Arnold H. Raphaelson, ed., *Restructuring State and Local Services* (Westport, CT: Praeger, 1998).
59. "Mayor-Power," *The Economist* (19 June 1999): 24-26.
60. Michael A. Pagano and Ann O'M. Bowman, "The State of American Federalism, 1994-1995," *Publius* 25 (Summer 1995): 1-21.
61. Cornelia Butler Flora, Jan L. Flora, Jacqueline D. Spears, and Louis E. Swanson, *Rural Communities: Legacy and Change* (Boulder, CO: Westview, 1992), 57-78, 231-247; Jan L. Flora, Jeff Sharp, Cornelia Flora, and Bonnie Newlon, "Entrepreneurial Social Infrastructure and Locally Initiated Economic Development in the Nonmetropolitan United States," *Sociological Quarterly* 38:4 (1997): 623-645.
62. Norman Uphoff, Milton J. Esman, and Anirudh Krishna, *Reasons for Success: Learning from Instructive Experiences in Rural Development* (West Hartford, CT: Kumarian, 1998), 20-34.
63. Tocqueville, *Democracy in America*, II:349-352.
64. See National Civic League, "The Civic Index," 1998, Denver, CO, a guide for communities that wish to "undertake a self-evaluation of their civic infrastructure" and to enhance their "capacity to deal with critical issues."
65. John Stuart Mill, "Letter to Alexis de Tocqueville," in Francis E. Mineka, ed., *The Earlier Letters of John Stuart Mill 1812-1848* (Toronto: University of Toronto Press, 1840), 433-434.
66. Uphoff, Esman, and Krishna, *Reasons for Success.*
67. Tocqueville, *Democracy in America*, I:62, 68-69.
68. Ibid., II:271-276.
69. Ibid., II:276.
70. Questions: "Do you or does someone in your household subscribe to your local community newspaper, or not? Yes; No." "How closely would you say you read your local paper—very closely, somewhat closely, not too closely or not closely at all?" N=1,005. Roper Center at University of Connecticut, Public Opinion Online, 1996 [LEXIS, Market Library, RPOLL File]. It is noted that this is according to self-report and that responses may be influenced by normative expectation.
71. Questions: "How interested are you in national affairs? Are you very interested, somewhat interested, only slightly interested, or not at all interested?" "Thinking about the state where you live, how interested are you in state affairs?" "Thinking about [local area name], how interested are you in local affairs?" Thomas M. Guterbock and John C. Fries, "Maintaining America's Social Fabric: The AARP Survey of Civic Involvement," Washington, DC, American Association of Retired Persons, December 1997, 101-102. N=1,500; ± 2.5. National sample of adults, one-half of whom were 50 years of age or older.
72. Question: "When you pick up a newspaper these days, how interested are you in reading articles relating to news about the following: local community, other coun-

tries, US relations with other countries. Very interested, somewhat interested, or hardly interested at all?" "Wanted: An Activist US," *The Public Perspective* (August/September 1997): 10.

73. Question: "When you follow the news these days, how interested are you in reports about the following: [News about your state?] [News about other countries?] [News about your local community?] [National news?] Very interested, somewhat interested, hardly interested at all." Survey conducted by Gallup for The Chicago Council on Foreign Relations, October 7-24, 1994. N=1,492. Repeated for the same sponsor in "Attitudes of the American Public Related to Foreign Policy." October 15-November 10, 1998. N=1507. Roper Center, Public Opinion Online, 1995 and 1999.
74. Question: "How much attention do you pay to news in each of the following areas: a great deal, a fair amount, just some, not very much, or none at all?" Roper Center, Public Opinion Online, 2000. N=2201.
75. Question: "Which of these four kinds of problems…international, national, state, or local problems—would you say you usually feel the most interested in and concerned about on a day-to-day basis?" Gallup Organization, "Hopes and Fears: Happiness Survey," October 1999. N=1549. Roper Center, Public Opinion Online, 1999.
76. Times Mirror Center for the People and the Press, "The New Political Landscape," October 1994; Pew Research Center for the People and the Press, "Values Update," 1997, website http://www.people-press.org; Pew, "News Interest Index," 1998; Pew, "Values Update," 1999; Pew, "People and the Press Voter Attitudes Survey," 2000.
77. Question: "We know that the ordinary person has many problems that take his time. In view of this, what part do you think the ordinary person ought to play in the local affairs of his town or district?" Multiple responses were recorded although the percentages reported here are based on the most active type of participation mentioned per respondent. Gabriel A. Almond and Sidney Verba, *The Civic Culture: Political Attitudes and Democracy in Five Nations* (Newbury Park, CA: Sage Publications, [1963] 1989), 126-129.
78. Questions: "Suppose a law were being considered [by the most local governmental unit: town? Village? Etc. specified] that you considered to be very unjust or harmful. What do you think you could do? If you made an effort to change this law, how likely is it that you would succeed? If such a case arose, how likely is it you *would actually* try to do something about it?" in Almond and Verba, *The Civic Culture*, 140-142, 148.
79. Questions: "The public schools provide one of the most important ways for teaching our children about the American story. If you were to decide which themes the schools should include, how important would each of the following be in your lesson about America—would it be absolutely essential, very important, somewhat important, somewhat unimportant, very unimportant, or would you definitely leave it out?" and "Different words and images generate different feelings in people, both positive and negative. On a scale from plus 5 all the way down to minus 5, where plus 5 indicates a very positive feeling, minus 5 indicates a very negative feeling, and 0 indicates a neutral feeling, please rate your initial response to each of the following phrases. Does it give you a good feeling, a bad feeling, or neither? Just call off the number." James Davison Hunter and Carl Bowman, *The State of Disunion: 1996 Survey of American Political Culture* (Ivy, VA: In Medias Res Educational Foundation, 1996).
80. Institute for Social Inquiry, Roper Center, National Philanthropy Survey, March 1997. N=1010. Roper Center, Public Opinion Online, 1999.

81. Question: "On a scale from 10 down to 1, I'd like you to rate the importance to you of each one. If a particular goal is extremely important to you, pick a number closer to 10. If it is of average importance, pick a number around 5 or 6. If a particular goal is not really that important to you, pick a number closer to 1. (You can select any number between 1 and 10, depending on how strongly you feel)... Being involved in helping your community be a better place." Hart and Teeter Research for the Council for Excellence in Government, Attitudes Toward Government Survey, October 1997. N=505. Roper Center, Public Opinion Online, 1998.
82. Question: "How important is each of the following values to you personally, would you say it is very important, somewhat important, not that important, or not important at all?...Community involvement." NBC News/*Wall Street Journal* Poll, February 1998. N=2004. Roper Center, Public Opinion Online, 1999.
83. Question: "How important to you is being involved in your community—very important, somewhat important, somewhat unimportant, not very important, or not at all important?" N=1178. Roper Center, Public Opinion Online, 2000.
84. Question: "Which is closer to your view? I have the knowledge and skills that I need for effective participation in the community, government, and politics. I do not have the knowledge and skills that I need for effective participation in the community, government, and politics." Community Census Survey conducted by Penn, Schoen & Berland, February 12-14, 1999. N=509. Roper Center, Public Opinion Online, 2001.
85. Question: "Overall, how much impact do you think people like you have...A big impact in making my community a better place to live, a moderate impact, a small impact, no impact?" Princeton Survey Research Associates for the Pew Research Center, February 6-9, 1997, cited in "Volunteering in America," *The American Enterprise* (July/August 1997): 92. N=656; ± 4.
86. Question: "If someone wants to help his community is it...[Better to get involved in politics and government] [Better to volunteer for civic activities]?" Survey by Maricopa Research, Inc., April 14-16, 1997, cited in "Volunteering in America," 92. N=1,000; ± 3.
87. Community Consensus Survey.
88. Question: "If you were giving the United States a 'report card' on how we are doing when it comes to...people's involvement in their community...would you give the country an A, B, C, D, or F?" Human Rights Survey conducted by Peter D. Hart Research, November 1997. N=1004. Roper Center, Public Opinion Online, 1999.
89. Question: "Looking at it a little differently, in terms of how most Americans act, please tell me if you think we as a society are now doing an excellent job, a good job, a fair job, or a poor job. Volunteering time to community service...how good a job are we doing on that?" Institute for Social Inquiry, Roper Center, National Philanthropy Survey, March 1997. N=1010. Roper Center, Public Opinion Online, 1999.
90. Question: "We'd like to know whether or not you feel good about various things in this country and in your life. Do you feel good about...the morals and values of people in your community, or not?" Harris Poll, May 1999. N=1010. Roper Center, Public Opinion Online, 1999.
91. Question: "How confident are you in each of the following to confront problems that we face in the new century?...Great confidence (44%), some confidence (45%), little confidence (10%)...Community life, neighbors & friends." Zogby

International Real America Poll, June 1999. N=1008. Roper Center, Public Opinion Online, 1999.
92. Question: "All in all, are you satisfied or dissatisfied with the way things are going in your local community?" Gallup Poll, January 2001. N=1004. Roper Center, Public Opinion Online, 2001.
93. Guterbock and Fries, "Maintaining America's Social Fabric."
94. Question: "Sometimes when people pursue their individual interests it is good for everyone, as is true when someone paints a beautiful landscape or discovers a cure for a disease. But sometimes what individuals want to do is harmful to the larger community. Then we have to decide which takes priority...personal freedom or the public good. When you personally compare the importance of individual freedom and the public good, which takes priority in your mind? Individual freedom has much greater priority; Individual freedom has greater priority; The public good has much greater priority; The public good has greater priority; Both have equal priority." Hunter and Bowman, *The State of Disunion.*
95. Serial editions of the Independent Sector report, "Giving and Volunteering in the United States."
96. NPR/Kaiser/Kennedy School, Attitudes Toward Government Survey, May-June 2000. N=1557. Roper Center, Public Opinion Online, 2000.
97. NBC News/*Wall Street Journal* Poll, December 7-10, 2000, conducted by Hart Teeter Research. N=2107. Roper Center, Public Opinion Online, 2001.
98. Health Research and Education Trust Community Health Survey, October 14-20, 1998. N=1013. Roper Center, Public Opinion Online, 1999.
99. NPR/Kaiser/Kennedy School, Attitudes Toward Government Survey.
100. Gallup, *U.S.A. Today* Poll, September 30-October 1, 1998. Roper Center, Public Opinion Online, 1998.
101. CBS News Poll, February 6-10, 2000. N=1499. Roper Center, Public Opinion Online, 2000.
102. Question: "I'm going to read you some proposals that are now being discussed nationally. As I read each one, please select the number that best expresses how much you favor or oppose it. If you don't really care about the issue, please say so.... Shifting many government functions from the Federal level to the states." Hunter and Bowman, *The State of Disunion.*
103. Pew, "Deconstructing Distrust."
104. Hart Teeter Research, Attitudes Toward Government Survey, February 1997. Roper Center, Public Opinion Online, 1998.
105. National Election Studies 1948-1998 Cumulative Data File, Ann Arbor: University of Michigan, Center for Political Studies, 2001, website http://www.umich.edu/~nes.
106. Question: "Just your best guess... How many people [running the government of this state] [running your local government] do you think are dishonest or crooked—almost all, quite a few, not very many, or none at all?" Error rate of ± 6 percentage points. George Gallup, Jr., "Despite Recent Campaign, Politics Has Cleaner Image Today Than in 1983." November 27, 1986 press release.
107. Question: "In which of the following people in government do you have the most trust and confidence: The people in charge of [running the federal government], [your state government], [your local government]?" Advisory Commission on Intergovernmental Relations, "Changing Public Attitudes on Governments and Taxes" (Washington, DC: ACIR, 1988), 54.
108. Local, 35 percent; state, 11 percent; federal, 13 percent. Advisory Commission on Intergovernmental Relations, "Changing Public Attitudes on Governments and Taxes" (Washington, DC: ACIR, 1989), 20.

109. Hunter and Bowman, *The State of Disunion*.
110. Question: "Generally speaking, what is your opinion of [elected federal officials] [state and local government officials]? Is it favorable, mostly favorable, mostly unfavorable, or very unfavorable?" Pew, "Trust in Government," September 25-October 31, 1997. The entire sample of 1,762 was asked about elected federal officials (± 3); one half (N=879; ± 4) asked about state and local officials.
111. Princeton Survey Research for Kaiser Family Foundation, Race, Ethnicity, and Medical Care Survey, July-September 1999. N=3884. Roper Center, Public Opinion Online, 1999.
112. Richard Morin, "Nonprofit, Faith-Based Groups Near Top of Poll on Solving Social Woes," *Washington Post* (1 February 2001): A19.
113. Question: "Generally, how would you rate the ethical and moral practices of [federal] [state and local] government officials? Would you give them an excellent, good, only fair or poor rating?" Ibid.
114. Gallup asks "Please tell me how you would rate the honesty and ethical standards of people in these different fields—very high, high, average, low, or very low?... [Local officeholders], [state officeholders], [Senators], [Congressmen]?" N=1000-1500; ± 3. Leslie McAneny and Lydia Saad, "Honesty and Ethics Poll," *The Gallup Poll* online, public release December 13, 1997, website http// :www.gallup.com/poll/news.
115. Gallup Organization, Gallup/CNN/*USA Today* Poll, October 1998, N=1013; Gallup Poll, November 1999, N=1011; Gallup Poll, November 2000, N=1028. Roper Center, Public Opinion Online, 2001.
116. Harris Polls has a trend from 1973 to 1989 based on the following question: "As far as people in charge of running...[local governments], [state governments], [the executive branch of the federal government], [Congress]...are concerned, would you say you have a great deal of confidence, only some confidence, or hardly any confidence at all in them?" N=1200-1500; ± 3. Louis Harris and Associates, "Public Confidence Declines in 11 of 16 Key Institutions," *The Harris Poll*, news release of July 9, 1989.
117. Times Mirror Center for The People and The Press, "The New Political Landscape"; Princeton Survey Research for Pew, "Values Update Survey 1999."
118. Time, CNN, Yankelovich Partners Poll, January 25-26, 1995. N=800. Roper Center, Public Opinion Online, 1995.
119. Hart Teeter Research for The Council for Excellence in Government, Attitudes Toward Government Survey, February 1997. Roper Center, Public Opinion Online, 1998.
120. Hart Teeter Survey Research for The Council for Excellence in Government. A third response choice was "to make government smaller by cutting programs," which 8 percent favored.
121. Question: "Many people agree that we need to set national education standards for teaching and student achievement. Some people say these standards should be set by the Department of Education in conjunction with Congress and the national teacher's unions. Other people say these standards should be set by a commission of people from state and local governments along with representatives of business, parents groups, teachers and school administrators in all 50 states. Still others say that local schools and parents should be autonomous from national standards of any kind and be allowed to set their own standards. Which of these approaches do you favor?" The American Viewpoint National Monitor Poll surveyed 1,000 registered voters who said they will definitely/probably vote in the 1998 elections; ±4 (est.). Roper Center, Public Opinion Online, 1997.

122. Hart Teeter Research for NBC News, *Wall Street Journal*, March 1997. Roper Center, Public Opinion Online, 1997.
123. Program on International Policy Attitudes, University of Maryland, Education Survey, June 2000. Roper Center, Public Opinion Online, 2000.
124. Gallup Organization for Phi Delta Kappa, Attitudes Towards the Public Schools, June 2000. Roper Center, Public Opinion Online, 2000.
125. National Election Studies, 1998.
126. Questions: "Which do you think is the worst tax, that is the least fair—federal income tax, state income tax, state sales tax, local property tax?" and "From which level of government do you feel you get the most for your money—federal, state, or local?" Advisory Commission on Intergovernmental Relations, "Changing Public Attitudes on Governments and Taxes," S-23 and "Public Attitudes on Governments and Taxes 1994," 29-30 (Washington, DC: ACIR, 1994), 4, 7.
127. Question: "From which level of government do you feel you get the *least* for your money—federal, state, local?" Advisory Commission on Intergovernmental Relations, "Changing Public Attitudes," 6.
128. Question: "Which level of government do you think spends your tax dollars most wisely—federal, state, or local?" Advisory Commission on Intergovernmental Relations, "Changing Public Attitudes on Governments and Taxes" S-22 (Washington, DC: ACIR, 1993), 5, 20.
129. Question: "Which do you find most costly to you…Your city or town government, your county government, your state government, your national government?" Reported by Roper Starch Worldwide and cited in "Disillusionment with Washington," *The American Enterprise* (March/April 1995): 101.
130. United States Internal Revenue Service, *IRS Historical Fact Book: A Chronology* (Washington, DC: United States Department of the Treasury, 1993).
131. "Disillusionment with Washington."
132. Question: "Which of the following levels of government do you think spends your tax money most wisely—the federal government, state government, or local government?" Hart Teeter Survey Research for The Council for Excellence in Government, March 16-18, 1995.
133. NPR/Kaiser/Kennedy School, Attitudes Toward Government.
134. While 19 and 20 percent were most concerned about the amount or the fairness of taxes they pay, 59 percent were most concerned about the effectiveness with which tax monies are spent. Harris Poll, December 12-16, 1996. N=1004. Roper Center, Public Opinion Online, 1996.
135. Question: "Let me read a few reasons some people think it would be better to give state and local governments responsibility for programs now carried out by the federal government. After I've read all three statements, I'd like you to tell me which comes closest to your opinion…. State and local governments can [do a better job of addressing the individual needs and problems of local communities], [can manage programs more efficiently and at less cost to the taxpayer than the federal government], [are more likely than the federal government to terminate unnecessary and wasteful policies and programs]." Ibid.
136. Immanuel Kant, *Critique of Pure Reason* (Garden City, NY: Anchor, Doubleday, [1781] 1966), 167.

7

Mediation: Necessary Nurturance of Democratic Tensions

"Human societies always contain tensions that make them vulnerable to possible dissolution," sociologist Dennis Wrong writes in his exploration of what unites and divides society.[1] These tensions require continual balancing at more than one level. Overall symmetry is necessary between the ideas, interests, authorities, and freedoms exercised by individuals and groups in a democratic civil society and the powerful forces of government. *Within* a democratic civil society, individuals fulfill seemingly incompatible responsibilities—to be independent and self-actualizing while also striving collectively for democratic objectives. Yet, both responsibilities are necessary to maintain a mediated, nurtured tension within and between the institutions of civil society and the overweening power of government.[2] Mediation does not resolve all differences. It is, rather, an adjustment of tension that surmounts debilitating amounts of uncertainty or imbalance and allows constructive interplay.

Tocqueville understood that a resilient, mediated democratic order is increasingly difficult to sustain as gains toward the democratic objective of equality accrue. Equality, he explained, perpetuates itself by creating repugnance for privilege, as well as desire for even greater equality. Progress toward conditions of equality would intensify democratic tensions, thus challenging tolerance and respect for the interests and rights of fellow citizens. Furthermore, as members of society enjoy the benefits of fortune and intellect more equitably, Tocqueville expected that pursuit of private interests would hold greater appeal than the pursuit of commonly shared interests. It followed that the natural inclination of citizens would be to allow the administrative state to take care of matters. The state, in turn, would find it increasingly convenient to treat all citizens uniformly without acknowledging differences, personal rights, and freedoms. These developments would make it difficult to achieve a working balance of power in the horizontal and vertical relationships among and between citizens and government.

Administrative convenience for the state thus dovetails with convenience for individuals, but at some price to individual freedom.[3] The bottom line seems to be that preserving tension between sovereign and the sovereignty of the people cannot happen easily in a democracy. As Tocqueville put it, "in the democratic ages which are opening upon us, individual independence and local liberties will ever be the products of art… centralization will be the natural government."[4]

The Progression of Equality and Freedom

Historical markers imply progress in reaching the democratic objective of equality.[5] The Bill of Rights, passed in 1791, established a formal basis for protecting the individual from federal governmental action. Slavery and involuntary servitude were prohibited by the 13th Amendment (1865). The 14th Amendment (1868) defined as citizens all who were born or naturalized in the United States, affirmed the right of due process, and extended equal protection of the law to all. Racial, sexual, economic, and age barriers to voting were eliminated with the 15th, 19th, 24th, and 26th Amendments to the Constitution. Supreme Court decisions have set aside the white primary, shortened residency requirements for voting, set aside literacy requirements and poll taxes in *any* election, and upheld redistricting that safeguards the right to an equal vote.[6] Civil rights legislation of the 1950s and 1960s brought many disenfranchised into the political mainstream for the first time. Voter registration services are more readily available to the mobile, the poor, the disabled, overseas citizens, and members of the military.[7]

From a cross-national perspective, the United States is one of the sixty-five nations with a rating of "1" in the Comparative Survey of Freedom, based upon the civil and political rights exercised by its citizens. A rating of "1" on a scale of 1 to 7 means that, comparatively, citizens have full participation in the political process and are guaranteed the freedom to "develop views, institutions and personal autonomy apart from the state."[8] Other attempts to gauge relative freedom compare the United States favorably in recent decades with such countries as Canada, the United Kingdom, West Germany, and France, but to a less favorable degree in the 1950s through the 1970s—prior to the civil rights movement.[9]

Although the Comparative Survey of Freedom is an annual measure, and has been for a quarter of a century, Gastil glanced backwards to see how the nation might have rated earlier in its history. This retrospective extension of an assessment of freedom suggests that, at the beginning of its history, the United States would have been considered only "partly free" and has subsequently made progress toward equality. Political rights would have merited a rating of "4" in the 1790s, Gastil concludes, since most white male property owners could vote, but slaves, women, and the propertyless could not. Many civil rights were respected in the pre-Revolutionary war era long before legislators or the judiciary specified them, leading Gastil to assign a rating of "3" for the status of civil rights in 1790. But not until a broadening awareness and understanding of the First Amendment was reached by the early 1970s could the United States have received the highest assessment of its civil and political freedoms on this instrument.[10]

Considering this progression of equality and freedom and Tocqueville's expectation that such progress would make it harder to sustain democratic tensions, this chapter explores change in the mediating functions of two important institutions—the political party system and the Supreme Court.

Political Association as Mediator

Civil and political associations mediate between conflicting interests and activity in a context of freedom. Noting that the two kinds of association stimulated each other, Tocqueville described civil association as more intimate, involving fewer people, and requiring investment of personal resources. Political association, on the other hand, was less particular in nature and included larger numbers of individuals and groups. Its advantages were clear. It imparted the strength of numbers and unity; it penetrated divisions and barriers; it entailed little or no risk to personal resources; and it offered collective action experience. Tocqueville spoke of at least two important ways in which political parties, in particular, fostered the maintenance and mediation of political tension. First, political parties were catalysts for articulating, differentiating, and aggregating public views and opinion. Second, the two major parties were sufficiently competitive in their capacity to win elections and thus to share governance equitably.[11] Political parties exemplify the institutionalized mediating structures that Berger and Neuhaus describe as vital in a democracy for "standing between" private and public life.[12]

Political Parties as Catalyst

A manifestation of political interest and association that transcends divisions, barriers, and differences among Americans is their tendency to identify with one of the two major political parties. Party identification is resistant to change over the long term, although some argue that short-term influences continuously have an impact on partisanship.[13] Key explained that party identification "makes the same persons allies on some questions and opponents on others."[14] The result is mediation of democratic tension via the crosscutting of diverse individuals and voluntary groups. Tocqueville was among the first to observe that political party affiliation served this process by crossing class lines and representing loose ties among many individuals who do not live together, are not close, and might not even like one another.[15]

Lipset and Rokkan used the phrase "united in their great hostility" to explain the resulting cohesion.[16] A broad diversity of Americans has thus sustained a two-party system that nurtures democratic tension (see chapter 4).

Developments since mid-century, however, suggest a weakening of the aggregative capacity of political parties. The National Election Studies reflects a decline in the proportion of Americans who describe themselves as strong or weak partisans—from 75 percent in 1952 to 63 percent in 1998. There is a comparable gain in the proportions who describe themselves as "leaning Independents" but also think of themselves as closer to one of the two major parties. Six percent unequivocally declared themselves as Independent in 1952, which climbed to 11 percent by 1998.[17] "Leaners" voted in the same proportion as weak partisans in presidential elections between 1952 and 1994, however, lending support to the hypothesis that they will make their votes count in a two-party system.[18]

Split-ticket voting also points to a loosening of loyalty to political party. The portion of voters who said they cast ballots for presidential and Congressional candidates of different parties rose from 12 percent in 1952 to a high of 30 percent in 1972, and fell to 17 percent in 1996. Split-ticket voting increases the likelihood that a party will fail to win a majority over the House, the Senate, and the Presidency. Divided government has occurred throughout American governmental history, but has been on the rise in the last half of this century at both the state and national levels.[19]

Political scientist Martin Wattenberg concluded that both political parties increasingly failed to have much of relevance to say about issues and policy between 1952 and 1980. The media reinforced linkages between candidates and parties less frequently. Issues became more closely associated with the candidates who discussed them and less with party platforms. Wattenberg posits that the disconnect between parties and candidates encourages a view of parties as inconsequential to electoral and governing processes.[20] In 1981, political sociologist Seymour Martin Lipset noted influences that contribute to this perception of parties: "crosspressures from differential commitments to economic and social values have reduced the saliency of loyalty to parties, tied largely to the structural sources of cleavage—class, ethnicity, religion, region."[21] More recently, Lipset notes that ideology plays a larger role in party alignment.[22] This is illustrated in table 4.2, which also shows that conservative and liberal ideologies became more powerful catalysts for party identification between 1952 and 1994.

The effect of a diminished role of the political party as intermediary is apparent in the moment of decision for voters in presidential elections. Once the central role of parties in electoral campaigns weakened, nominations no longer necessarily relied on party organization. Participants in the American National Election Studies who reported making their voting decision during or after party conventions fell from 53 percent in 1952 to 30 percent in 1996.

Half the respondents in 1996 reported they knew all along for whom they would vote, or from when the presidential candidate announced, in contrast to only 36 percent of the electorate in 1952 who decided at such an early point in the election process.[23]

Party Competitiveness

Tocqueville observed that American political parties maintained just enough similarity and difference to be able to share political power, monitor one another's use of political power, and to wrest majority support away from one another. He saw a two-party system that worked without large disruptions, despite frequent elections, because the difference in the two major parties was of small, rather than large, proportion. This close kind of competitiveness perpetuated hope: "In America the citizens who form the minority associate in order, first, to show their numerical strength and so to diminish the moral power of the majority...for they always entertain hopes of drawing over the majority to their own side and then controlling the supreme power in its name."[24]

In the long term, the major parties have been competitive and have shared power equitably over the entirety of American election history. Presidential victories divided evenly between the major parties during the period of 1900 to 1996. The Republicans won thirteen presidential elections and the Democrats won twelve. Length of time in power by party varied from one to five terms but the total number of years each party had control of the presidency during the twentieth century is equitable, with fifty-two years for Republicans and forty-eight years for Democrats. Fifty Congresses convened over the same time period. The Democratic Party had the majority in the House of Representatives two-thirds of the time and held the Senate majority 58 percent of the time. Although this party was in power more often, the majority changed hands eight times in the House of Representatives and ten times in the Senate. Yet an imbalance existed despite the number of turnovers, as Democrats held the majority in the House for a record-breaking length of time—from 1955 until 1995 when the Republicans finally gained control.[25]

A measure of competitiveness between parties is reflected in the difference in popular vote historically won by each party in presidential elections. Between 1828 and 1900, that difference averaged 6.9 percentage points. The gap widened in the twentieth century with an average of 12.6 percentage points for the twenty-four elections held between 1904 and 1996. If a narrow difference suggests greater party competitiveness, this was a century in which competition was somewhat blunted. Larger differences in the popular vote were recorded in the first half, with an average of 14.8 percentage points between 1904 and 1948; after 1952, the average difference narrowed to 10.4 percentage points.[26] Does this mean that competition increased in the last half of the century? This seems unlikely. Political parties simply became less influential in commanding voter registration and turnout. Since 1952, the portion of respondents to the American National Election Studies who "think there are any important differences in what the Republicans and Democrats stand for" increased from 50 percent in 1952, to 63 percent in 1996, and to 56 percent in 1998.[27] Yet, at the same time, the percentage of voters who registered as Independents or third-party voters increased from 2 percent in 1964 to 15 percent in 1996.[28] These developments imply a dulling of competition between the parties.

Party reforms early in the century established a precedent for the attenuation of party influence on elections. Direct primaries caught on as an antidote for local corruption and excessive politicization of local matters. By 1913, California filled most local offices via nonpartisan primaries.[29] Between 1929 and 1959, the portion of municipalities of over 30,000 in population with nonpartisan elections grew from 57 to 62 percent.[30] Today, most cities with a population of 2,500 and three-fourths of larger cities hold nonpartisan elections. Furthermore, 60 percent of these cities hold at-large elections; another 30 percent have a mix of at-large and district seats.[31] Unfortunately, this reform defeats an important function of partisan elections. Partisan campaigning helps to clarify and differentiate between issues, ideas, and policies. Without this definition and mediation of political issues that are immediate, participation in nonpartisan elections drops.[32]

Analysts of erosion in political party relevance and influence point to multiple contributing factors. Aldrich brings attention to the instrumental use and abuse of the political party by politicians. [33] Thus, political leaders fail to protect the integrity of the party system as a mediating institution. Not least is how media and communication technologies contributed to its deterioration. Candidate-centered organizations and direct appeal to the public through the media took center stage.[34] In his work, Schier traces an evolution in party strategies during the twentieth century in which competition for large numbers of supporters shifted to narrow targeting of particular segments of the voting population. The outcome excludes, rather than includes, many citizens.[35] Milkis also observes that parties are not competing for the attention of voters. Rather, he notes, their focus is on national government to the neglect of political association and self-governance.[36]

Nevertheless, neither party has distinguished itself as being especially adept at governing. The proportion of Americans who perceive little difference in the two parties' ability to handle the most important problem in the country climbed from 42 to 56 percent between 1972 and 1998.[37] Americans who express satisfaction with divided government as a solution may, inadvertently, be supporting impasse and gridlock in government for two reasons. First, party leadership is not necessarily effective in managing the tension left electorally unresolved, nor does it necessarily know how to strengthen party governance.[38] Second, balanced give and take between governing and opposition parties is not only a source of productivity, but of stability, as well.[39] Other risks in the failure of electoral competitiveness are described in an independent institutional assessment of Congress conducted by the American Enterprise Institute and the Brookings Institution in the early 1990s. This report remarked on the long tenure of Democrats in the House mentioned above and describes an imbalance not unlike examples one finds in Machiavelli's *History of Florence*:

> In the past, with more frequent party turnover, each party had some experience running the chamber, and some experience as the opposition...In recent years the near-permanent majority status of the Democrats and near-permanent minority status of the Republicans have led to increasingly hardened and corrosive attitudes on both sides of the aisle: an irresponsibility on the part of many members of the minority, with no stake in governance or institutional maintenance, combined with smugness, a patronizing viewpoint, and arrogance on the part of many in the majority. In the Senate, where both parties have recently experienced both the responsibilities of majority status and the frustrations of minority status, partisan tensions and their effects have been much more subdued.[40]

In summary, the two major political parties have shared power equitably over the long term. They continue to evoke nominal loyalty and to split the popular vote within a narrow range of difference. In that sense, the political party system remains the formal mechanism for aggregating and differentiating political views and opinions. The mediating role of political parties in the development of public opinion has nonetheless weakened. Although the majority of Americans continue to identify with one of the two major parties, the involvement of parties is less essential to the campaign process and to forging relationships between candidates and voters. The political party system is, subsequently, less effective as a catalyst and a mediator of political ideas, conflict, and consensus. The close results of the 2000 presidential election in which the Republican candidate won 47.87 percent and the Democratic candidate won 48.38 percent of the popular vote reflects this weakness.[41]

The Supreme Court: In Service to Mediation

Tocqueville predicted that gains in equality would intensify democratic tensions and, in turn, give the judiciary an increasingly crucial role in their management. The value of this involvement is that the judiciary "can oblige [people] not to disobey their own enactments and not to be inconsistent with themselves."[42] Therefore, the United States Supreme Court is a mechanism for adjusting or recalibrating the balance of tensions in accordance with the rule of law. The Court is especially equipped, both by training and institutional position, to consider how constitutional values adapt to modern circumstances. One of its valuable functions is to think both retrospectively and prospectively in order to sustain continuity and balance in a dynamic system.

In this way it is part of the political process.[43] Although the Court has an arbitration function, it also serves the cause of mediation over the long term by breaking impasses, clarifying meaning, providing correction, and alleviating excessive tension—which allows the democratic process to continue.

Procedural, legal and political factors influence the nature of the case selections made by the Court from several thousand petitions each year. Actual selections illuminate the tensions that demand and command Court attention.[44] Issues that can be dealt with at other institutional or judiciary levels have no need to reach the Supreme Court. However, those strains that emanate from relationships among Americans and with their government are increasingly brought to the Court, confirming the accuracy of Tocqueville's prediction of growing tension. Pacelle's analysis of Supreme Court decisions by major public policy area shows a rise from 7.8 percent to 56.9 percent in civil liberty cases, while a drop in economic ones occurred between the periods of 1933-37 and 1983-87.[45] Epstein et al. also found a mounting number of First Amendment and civil rights cases argued before the Court from 1946 to 1994 and a concomitant drop in cases concerning economic issues. These researchers established that 10 percent of the Court opinions in 1946 were First Amendment and civil rights cases, a share that more than doubled to 22 percent by 1994.[46] Individual rights and freedoms simply did not demand much Court attention before this time. Previously, relationships of "nation to state, state to state, and government to business" dominated the agenda.[47]

The use of amicus curiae briefs documents broader participation in matters brought to the Court.[48] This is a significant change. Amicus participation occurred in 6 percent of noncommercial, nongovernmental, and noncriminal cases decided by the Court between 1928 and 1940, a figure that rose to 63.8 percent during the decade of the 1970s.[49] A sample of 116 religious freedom cases selected by Epstein and Walker also shows expanding amicus participation of interested parties. In contrast to the 21 percent of their sample that attracted briefs during 1941-52, that portion grew to 44 percent in 1953-66, to 63 percent during the 1970s, and to 100 percent by 1986-92.[50] Approximately three-fourths of all Supreme Court cases in the last decade prompted briefs filed by interested parties wishing to influence Court decisions.[51] The profile of the groups who file such briefs also changed. Citizen, advocacy, and public interest groups were filing 17 percent of amicus curiae briefs in 1960 while corporations, trade associations, and labor unions filed the remainder. Three decades later this profile was reversed. Citizen, advocacy, and public interest groups were responsible for 51 percent of these briefs, reflecting a trend away from an emphasis on market to matters of civil society.[52]

A shift in the Supreme Court agenda towards civil liberty and First Amendment cases shows that its role in mediating democratic tensions has expanded. At the same time there is a widening mobilization of interested parties around this type of Supreme Court case. These developments are consistent with

Tocqueville's expectation that an escalation of tension would accompany gains in equality and democratic objectives.[53] Further evidence of these conditions is shown in the rise of Supreme Court cases that address the autonomy of institutions recognized as strong mediators of democratic tensions in the United States—religion, the press, and other voluntary associations. Their ability to serve as mediating institutions relies on remaining free and autonomous. If democratic conditions make the balancing of tensions more challenging, one would expect the Court's role in helping to sustain the autonomy of the voluntary association, the press, and religion would grow. This happened. Decisions by the Court that addressed the separation of church and state and religious freedom accrued at an accelerated rate after 1940. A roster of 171 Supreme Court opinions dating from 1896 to 1995, concerning freedom of religion or worship, shows a sharp rise in the incidence of such cases (figure 7.1).[54]

The rise began in the 1940s and continued to climb until the mid-1980s. Freedom of press cases also rose markedly after 1935 (figure 7.1). The twenty

Figure 7.1

Rise in Selected Supreme Court Cases

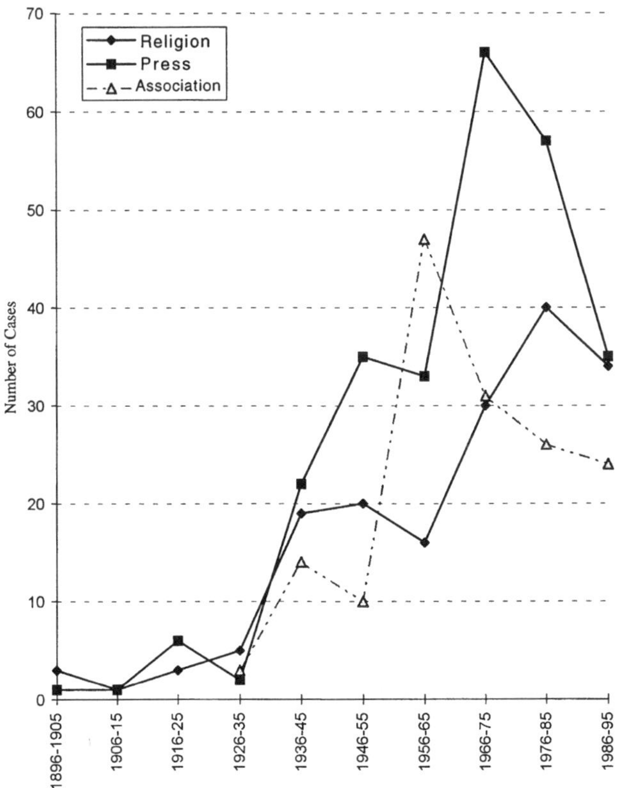

years between 1966 and 1985 were a particularly intense time of work on safeguarding a free press.[55] While the First Amendment failed to specify the right of association, a series of Supreme Court decisions in the 1950s and 1960s surrounding anti-subversive and anti-civil rights legislation reflect a struggle to affirm association freedom.[56] Supreme Court Justice White explicitly recognized this in *United States v. Robel, 389 U.S. 258 (1967)*:

> The right of association is not mentioned in the Constitution. It is a judicial construct appended to the First Amendment rights to speak freely, to assemble, and to petition for redress of grievances. While the right of association has deep roots in history and is supported by the inescapable necessity for group action in a republic as large and complex as ours, it has only recently blossomed as the controlling factor in constitutional litigation; its contours as yet lack delineation.[57]

Court opinions pertaining to freedom of association follow a pattern similar to that for cases concerning religious and press freedoms. The incidence with which the Court heard freedom of association cases rose during the early 1930s and peaked during the 1960s (figure 7.1).[58]

The incidence of each type of case—freedom of religion, the press, and association—rose dramatically. Challenges to the autonomy of these intermediary institutions signaled growing strain and required Supreme Court attention. At the same time, the meanings of these freedoms broadened, as demonstrated by the diversity of these cases.[59] Freedom of religion cases were about public and private education, aid to church-related schools, taxation, conscientious objection, labor relations, government interference in religious matters, religious organizations acting as a government agency, solicitation, Sunday closing laws, unequal government treatment of religious groups, and religious tests for public service or benefits.[60] Cases pertaining to the autonomy of the press address reporter privilege, governmental secrecy, access to information, prior restraint of expression, regulation and governmental control of media content, and libel.[61] Likewise, the variety of issues subsumed under the topic of associational freedom—group membership, patronage, group activities, intimate and expressive association, employment security and opportunity, loyalty oaths, and political affiliation—is extensive. The scope and reach of these subjects describes a range of issues that grew more diverse and complex during the century. This diversity and the rise in incidence of these cases signal an expanded role for the Court in facilitating the processes of a democratic civil society.

Summary and Discussion of Findings

The two major political parties still aggregate Americans and still help to process conflict and consensus, but the role of the political party system as mediator has become less effective. Three developments point to this conclusion. First, there is less of a competitive edge between the major parties. A rise in the perception that there are important differences in what Republicans and Democrats symbolize makes the competition less close. Lessened competition is also suggested by a rise in percentage of Americans who see little difference in the parties' ability to handle important problems of the country and by an increase in Independents who identify with neither major party. Second, there is a greater disconnect between party and electoral candidate. Candidates are more often self-selected, raise their own campaign funds, appeal directly to voters, and use the established party organization as a convenience, rather than being selected and promoted by the party. Third, a decline in strength of partisanship, an increase in split-ticket voting, a decline in voter turnout, and a rise in divided government all point to a weaker relationship between party and voter. Subsequently, political parties, the largest and most inclusive of voluntary political associations, are now less effective in aggregating voters and mediating political conflict through the electorate. Although the potential for political party influence remains significant, as demonstrated most poignantly by the persistence of political identification discussed in chapter 4, it seems to lie fallow. Political mediation is increasingly abdicated to divided government, where the balancing of tensions is less flexible.

The U.S. Supreme Court, as a failsafe to democratic processes, acquired a much more active role in keeping mediation processes vital to civil society from foundering. The cases heard by the Court that relate to freedom and autonomy of religion, of the press, and of association ballooned and diversified. Amicus participation in these cases also grew as groups participating in the balancing of democratic tension sought to inform the Court and sought alliances in these efforts. The Court furthers the cause of mediation of these matters by breaking impasses, helping to clarify meaning, providing correction, and allowing the democratic process to continue. Our reliance on the Court to facilitate this process was recently showcased by the controversy triggered by its actions in the 2000 presidential election. As Stephenson noted in his research on the Court's rare entanglements with electoral campaigns, its credibility depends on how persuaded the public is that the Constitution, rather than private interest, guides a decision.[62] The question lingers in the case of the latest election.

In summary, twentieth-century developments in both the political party system and in Supreme Court involvement attest to a dynamic process of mediating democratic tensions. This mediation grew increasingly essential, but difficult, as gains in equality and freedom were realized. The challenge clearly recommends improved understanding of this important process that characterizes democratic civil society. We must learn to nurture the articulation and mediation of democratic tension.

Notes

1. Dennis H. Wrong, *The Problem of Order* (New York: Free Press, 1994), 3-13.
2. William Kornhauser, *The Politics of Mass Society* (Glencoe, IL: Free Press, 1959).
3. Alexis de Tocqueville, *Democracy in America* (New York: Vintage Books, 1945), II:344.
4. Ibid., I:7, 48-56; II:178-80, 304-313.
5. See Derek Bok, *The State of the Nation* (Cambridge, MA: Harvard University Press, 1996), 295-312; Michael M. Gant and Norman R. Luttbeg, *American Electoral Behavior: 1952-1988* (Itasca, IL: F. E. Peacock, 1991), 93; William C. Kimberling, *Federal Election Law 96* (Washington, DC: Office of Election Administration, Federal Election Commission, 1996); Joan Biskupic and Elder Witt, *The Supreme Court and Individual Rights*, 3d ed. (Washington, DC: Congressional Quarterly, 1997), 1-15, 111-139.
6. Applicable cases include *Smith v. Allwright, 321 U.S. 649 (1944), Dunn v. Blumstein 405 U.S. 330 (1972), Harper v. Virginia State Board of Elections, 383 U.S. 120 (1966), Baker v. Carr, 369 U.S. 186 (1962)*; Kimberling, *Federal Election Law 96*; also see Lawrence Baum, *The Supreme Court* (Washington, DC: Congressional Quarterly, 1998), 258-260, for discussion of interaction between the Court, Congress, and the administrative branch regarding civil rights legislation.
7. "The Voting Accessibility for the Elderly and Handicapped Act of 1984," "The Uniformed and Overseas Citizens Absentee Voting Act of 1986," and "The National Voter Registration Act of 1993," in Kimberling, *Federal Election Law 96.*
8. For further methodological detail and the checklists of rights and liberties used in the survey, see Joseph E. Ryan, "Survey Methodology," *Freedom Review* (January-February 1995): 10-14; Freedom House, "1999 Press Freedom Survey," website http://freedomhouse.org and annual January-February editions of *Freedom Review.*
9. See Jan-Erik Lane, David McKay, and Kenneth Newton, *Political Data Handbook: OECD Countries* (New York: Oxford University Press, 1997), 120-121; Bok, *The State of the Nation,* 464.
10. Raymond D. Gastil, " A Historical Survey of Freedom in America," in R. D. Gastil, ed., *Freedom in the World: Political Rights and Civil Liberties 1984-1985* (Westport, CT: Greenwood, 1985), 145-167.
11. Tocqueville, *Democracy in America*, II:123-128; I:140, 180-187, 198-205, 213.
12. Peter L. Berger and Richard John Neuhaus, *To Empower People: From State to Civil Society*, ed. Michael Novak, 2d ed. (Washington, DC: American Enterprise, 1996), 157-164.
13. Angus Campbell, Philip E. Converse, Warren E. Miller, and Donald E. Stokes, *The American Voter* (Chicago, IL: University of Chicago Press, [1960, John Wiley] 1980), 120; V. O. Key, Jr., *Public Opinion and American Democracy* (New York: Alfred A. Knopf, 1963), 243-244; Russell J. Dalton, *Citizen Politics: Public Opinion and Political Parties in Advanced Industrial Democracies* (Chatham, NJ: Chatham House, 1996), 199-204; Martin P. Wattenberg, *The Decline of American Political Parties 1952-1996* (Cambridge, MA: Harvard University Press, 1998), 9-17; Richard G. Niemi and Herbert F. Weisberg, *Classics in Voting Behavior* (Washington, DC: Congressional Quarterly, 1993), 214-217; see Jeane Kirkpatrick, "Why We Don't Become Republicans," *Commonsense* 2 (Fall 1979): 33.
14. V. O. Key, Jr., *Public Opinion and American Democracy*, 176; also see Seymour M. Lipset and Stein Rokkan, "Cleavage Structures, Party Systems, and Voter Alignments: An Introduction," in Lipset and Rokkan, eds., *Party Systems and*

Voter Alignments (New York: Free Press, 1967), 9-13, 23-26, for discussion of the dimensions of cleavage, which were usually cultural and religious in the United States.

15. Tocqueville, *Democracy in America,* I:199; II:124.
16. Lipset and Rokkan, "Cleavage Structures, Party Systems, and Voter Alignments," 6.
17. Question: "Generally speaking, do you usually think of yourself as a Republican, a Democrat, an Independent, or what?" If the response was Republican or Democrat, "Would you call yourself a strong or a not very strong __?" If the response was Independent or Other or No preference, "Do you think of yourself as closer to the Republican or Democratic party?" National Election Studies, Cumulative Data File, 1948-1998. Ann Arbor: University of Michigan, Center for Political Studies, 2001, website http://www.umich.edu/~anes.
18. Wattenberg, *The Decline of American Political Parties 1952-1996*, 25. Seventy-eight percent of strong partisans, 65 percent of weak partisans, and 64 percent of leaning Independents voted between 1952 and 1994, according to the National Election Studies.
19. Ibid., 19-23; Harold W. Stanley and Richard G. Niemi, *Vital Statistics on American Politics* (Washington, DC: Congressional Quarterly, 1992), 122-125; Regina Dougherty, Everett C. Ladd, David Wilber, and Lynn Zayachkiwsky, eds., *America at the Polls 1996* (Storrs, CT: Roper Center for Public Opinion Research, 1997), 186-187; Regina Dougherty, "Divided Government Defines the Era," in Dougherty et al., *America at the Polls 1996*; also see Barry C. Burden and David C. Kimball, "A New Approach to the Study of Ticket Splitting," *American Political Science Review* 92:3 (September 1998): 533-544.
20. Wattenberg, *The Decline of American Political Parties 1952-1996*, 73-89, 92-98.
21. Seymour Martin Lipset, ed., *Party Coalitions in the 1980s* (San Francisco, CA: Institute for Contemporary Studies, 1981), 24.
22. Seymour Martin Lipset, "The Indispensability of Political Parties," *Journal of Democracy* 11:1 (January 2000): 48-55.
23. Question: "How long before the election did you decide that you were going to vote the way you did?" National Election Studies.
24. Tocqueville, *Democracy in America*, I:199-204; see Lipset and Rokkan, "Cleavage Structures, Party Systems, and Voter Alignments," 3-6, for discussion of the political party as an agent of conflict and integration.
25. Stanley and Niemi, *Vital Statistics on American Politics*, Table 3-17, 122-125; Dougherty et al., *America at the Polls 1996*, 187; United States Bureau of the Census, *Historical Statistics of the United States, Colonial Times to 1970* (Washington, DC: United States Government Printing Office, 1975), 1083; United States Bureau of the Census, *Statistical Abstract of the United States 1998* (Washington, DC: United States Government Printing Office), 287. The fifty Congresses referred to are the 56th through the 105th.
26. The average difference in popular vote won by the two major parties in presidential elections fluctuates, ranging from 0.17 to 26.13 during the period of 1904 to 1996. Calculated from John W. Wright, *The Universal Almanac 1996* (Kansas City, MO: Andrews and McMeel, 1996), 82-90 and the United States Bureau of the Census, *Statistical Abstract 1997*, 271.
27. Question: "Do you think there are any important differences in what the Republicans and Democrats stand for?" National Election Studies.
28. Data from the Committee for the Study of the American Electorate reported by Michael Grunwald, "Voters Shunning Party Identification, Loyalty," *Washington Post* (3 January 1999): A1, A4-A5.

29. Allan R. Richards, "Half of Our Century," in J. W. Fesler, ed., *The 50 States and Their Local Governments* (New York: Alfred A. Knopf, 1967), 71-74; Eugene C. Lee, *The Politics of Nonpartisanship* (Berkeley: University of California Press, 1960), 15-38, 172-185.
30. Lee, *The Politics of Nonpartisanship*, 24-25.
31. Steven Kelman, *American Democracy and the Public Good* (Fort Worth, TX: Harcourt Brace, 1996), 831.
32. John J. Harrigan, *Politics and Policy in States and Communities* (Glenview, IL: Scott, Foresman, 1988), 127; Howard D. Hamilton, "The Municipal Voter: Voting and Nonvoting in City Elections," *American Political Science Review* 65 (December 1971): 1135-1140; Willis D. Hawley, *Nonpartisan Elections and the Case for Party Politics* (New York: John Wiley, 1973); Robert L. Morlan, "Local Governments—The Cities," in Fesler, *The 50 States and Their Local Governments*, 501-504.
33. John H. Aldrich, *Why Parties?* (Chicago, IL: University of Chicago Press, 1995).
34. Wattenberg, *The Decline of American Political Parties 1952-1996*, 74-79, 104-105.
35. Steven E. Schier, *By Invitation Only* (Pittsburgh, PA: University of Pittsburgh Press, 2000).
36. Sidney M. Milkis, *Political Parties and Constitutional Government* (Baltimore, MD: Johns Hopkins University Press, 1999).
37. Question: "Which political party do you think would be most likely to get the government to do a better job in dealing with this problem—the Republicans, the Democrats, or wouldn't there be much difference between them?" National Election Studies.
38. David S. Broder, *The Party's Over: The Failure of Politics in America* (New York: Harper and Row, 1972), 14-105.
39. Lipset, "The Indispensability of Political Parties."
40. Thomas E. Mann and Norman J. Ornstein, *A First Report of the Renewing Congress Project* (Washington, DC: American Enterprise Institute for Public Policy Research and Brookings Institution, 1992), 54-55.
41. Federal Election Commission, "2000 Official Presidential General Election Results," 20 June 2001, website http://fecweb1.fec.gov.
42. Tocqueville, *Democracy in America*, I:289; II:343-344.
43. Stuart A. Scheingold, *The Politics of Rights: Lawyers, Public Policy, and Political Change* (New Haven, CT: Yale University Press, 1974), 28; David B. Truman, *The Governmental Process: Political Interests and Public Opinion* (New York: Alfred A. Knopf, [1951] 1971), 486-498.
44. Lee Epstein, Jeffrey A. Segal, Harold J. Spaeth, and Thomas G. Walker, *The Supreme Court Compendium: Data, Decisions, and Developments* (Washington, DC: Congressional Quarterly, 1996), 56; Richard L. Pacelle, *The Transformation of the Supreme Court's Agenda* (Boulder, CO: Westview, 1991), 1, 5-14, explains that the Judiciary Act of 1925 increased the Court's discretionary authority over its own agenda, in contrast to being required to hear any properly brought case. He says the Court's agenda is not unaffected by the social environment, but originates with complex interactions between institutional contexts and individual preference; Lee Epstein and Thomas G. Walker in *Constitutional Law for a Changing America: Rights, Liberties, and Justice* (Washington, DC: Congressional Quarterly, 1998), 15-19, for discussion of these factors; Baum, *The Supreme Court*, 2-3; Henry R. Glick, *Courts, Politics and Justice*, 3d ed. (New York: McGraw Hill, 1993), 419-423, describes the role of the courts in social change as one of a continual interplay

between demand for judicial action, court decisions, the impact of judicial action, social change, political action, and litigation; Scheingold, *The Politics of Rights*, 6, notes legal disputes are often manifestations of social struggle.

45. Pacelle, *The Transformation of the Supreme Court's Agenda*, 56-57, 207-209. Pacelle sorted 7,565 cases into fourteen general policy areas, guided by the classification system used in *The Supreme Court Reporter*, a West Publishing Company periodical. Economic cases fell from 47.2 to 10.4 percent of the total. Civil liberty cases include due process, substantive and First Amendment rights, and equality or civil rights cases. Also see discussion of the shift towards civil liberty concerns in Baum, *The Supreme Court*, 24-26.
46. See Table 2-9 in Epstein et al., *The Supreme Court Compendium*, 88-93.
47. Biskupic and Witt, *The Supreme Court and Individual Rights*, 1, 11, 28-29, 140-162.
48. Abram Chayes, "The Role of the Judge in Public Law Litigation," *Harvard Law Review* 89:7 (May 1976): 1310-1313, suggests that participation in litigation by interest groups needs to be considered carefully in that they are representative only of *some* interests; Donald L. Horowitz, *The Courts and Social Policy* (Washington, DC: Brookings Institution, 1977), 44, and Baum, *The Supreme Court*, 93-103, also comment on the incomplete representation by interest groups; Scheingold, *The Politics of Rights*, 138-139, 143-147, 205-209, also points out that litigation is valuable for mobilizing collective activity.
49. Karen O'Conner and Lee Epstein, "Research Note: Amicus Curiae Participation in U.S. Supreme Court Litigation: An Appraisal of Hakman's Folklore," *Law and Society Review* 16:2 (1981-82): 311-320.
50. Epstein and Walker, *Constitutional Law for a Changing America*, 160.
51. Ibid., 41; Glick, *Courts, Politics and Justice*, 193-194 and 198-200, explains there are additional reasons for filing amici curiae briefs such as the wish to counter opponent briefs, to satisfy group members, and as a means to build coalitions with other groups. Baum, *The Supreme Court*, 94, observes that others participate to share costs and legal consultation.
52. Epstein et al., *The Supreme Court Compendium*, 648.
53. Tocqueville, *Democracy in America*, I:7, 48-56; II:178-80, 304-313.
54. I compiled this list by relying on the authority of legal scholars. I included any freedom of religion or worship case mentioned by two or more of the following sources: Robert T. Miller and Ronald B. Flowers, *Toward Benevolent Neutrality: Church, State, and the Supreme Court*, 4th ed. (Waco, TX: Markham Press Fund of Baylor University Press, 1992); Donald L. Drakeman, *Church-State Constitutional Issues* (New York: Greenwood, 1991); Jesse H. Choper, *Securing Religious Liberty* (Chicago, IL: University of Chicago Press, 1995); Gregg Ivers, *Redefining the First Freedom* (New Brunswick, NJ: Transaction Publishers, 1992); Epstein and Walker, *Constitutional Law for a Changing America*, 95-224; Winnifred Fallers Sullivan, *Paying the Words Extra: Religious Discourse in the Supreme Court of the United States* (Cambridge, MA: Harvard University Press, 1994); Epstein et al., *The Supreme Court Compendium: Data, Decisions and Developments*; Laurence H. Tribe, *American Constitutional Law*, 2d ed. (Mineola, NY: Foundation Press, 1988), 1154-1301; Louis Fisher, *American Constitutional Law* (New York: McGraw-Hill, 1990), 698-722; Kermit Hall, ed., *The Oxford Companion to the Supreme Court of the United States* (New York: Oxford University Press, 1992), 299, 717-726.

    I also used the following online resources and search terms during the period of April-June 1998: (1) Lexis—freedom of religion, free exercise of religion; (2)

FindLaw (1906-1997), website http://www.Findlaw.com—free exercise of religion, freedom of worship; (3) FLITE, Villanova Center for Information Law and Policy (1937-1975), website http://www.law.vill.edu—freedom of religion, freedom of worship, free exercise of religion; (4) Oyez, Oyez, Oyez, website http://court.it-services.nwu.edu/oyez—Freedom of religion; (5) Cornell Law School, website http://www.law.cornell.edu—religion and free or establishment; (6) Info Synthesis (1953-1996), website http://www.usscplus.com—freedom of worship, freedom of religion.

55. I compiled a master list of 258 freedom of the press decisions written between 1896 and 1995. Again relying on the authority of legal scholars, I included any case mentioned by two or more of the following sources: Epstein and Walker, *Constitutional Law for a Changing America*, 323-356, 315-316, 383-384; Epstein et al., *The Supreme Court Compendium*, 563-587; William A. Hachten, *The Supreme Court on Freedom of the Press: Decisions and Dissents* (Ames: Iowa State University Press, 1968), xiii-xv; Fisher, *American Constitutional Law*, 618-635; Hall, *The Oxford Companion to the Supreme Court of the United States*, 808-816; John Lofton, *The Press as Guardian of the First Amendment* (Columbia: University of South Carolina Press, 1980), 331-332; Biskupic and Witt, *The Supreme Court and Individual Rights*, 55-82; Tribe, *American Constitutional Law,* 813-814, 856-886, 945-947, 955-977.

    The following online resources and search terms were also used: (1) Lexis—freedom of press, prior restraint and press, right to reply, candidate reply, (2) FindLaw—press freedom, prior restraint and press, reporter privilege, right to reply, candidate reply, (3) FLITE—freedom of press, reporter privilege, prior restraint, candidate right-to-reply, (4) Oyez, Oyez, Oyez—freedom of press, (5) Cornell Law School—freedom of press, (6) Info Synthesis—freedom of press. All were accessed during a period from April to June 1998.

56. Fisher, *American Constitutional Law*, 537-539; Biskupic and Witt, *The Supreme Court and Individual Rights*, 11.
57. Biskupic and Witt, *The Supreme Court and Individual Rights*, 11.
58. Relying once more on the authority of legal scholars, I compiled a master list of 155 freedom of association decisions written between 1896 and 1995. I included any case mentioned by two or more of the following sources: Epstein and Walker, *Constitutional Law for a Changing America*, 434-487; Epstein et al., *The Supreme Court Compendium*, 563-587; Fisher, *American Constitutional Law*, 537-539; Hall, *The Oxford Companion to the Supreme Court of the United States*, 51-52; Biskupic and Witt, *The Supreme Court and Individual Rights*, 140-165, 28-29; Tribe, *American Constitutional Law,* 1010-1022, 1101-1118, 1121-1126, 1136-1141, 1400-1409, 1458, 1463, 1479-1480, 1640-1641, 1660-1661.

    The following online resources and search terms were also used during a period from April to June 1998: (1) Lexis—freedom of association, (2) FindLaw—freedom of association, (3) FLITE—freedom of association, (4) Cornell Law School—freedom of association, (5) Info Synthesis—freedom of association.

59. Bok, *The State of the Nation*, 295-300. These changes resonate with Bok's observation that World War I marked the beginning of modern understanding of First Amendment freedoms. Pacelle, *The Transformation of the Supreme Court's Agenda*, 47-51, also notes that the New Deal, Roosevelt's attempt to "pack" the Court, partisan realignments, and some key Court cases at that time helped to accelerate this progression.
60. Miller and Flowers, in *Toward Benevolent Neutrality*, organized their selection of important cases according to these topics.

61. Biskupic and Witt, *The Supreme Court and Individual Rights*, 55-82; Epstein and Walker, *Constitutional Law for a Changing America*, 323-356, 315-316, 383-384; David M. O'Brien, *Constitutional Law and Politics: Civil Rights and Civil Liberties* (New York: W.W. Norton, 1991), 504-576, 446-481; Tribe, *American Constitutional Law*, 813-814, 856-886, 945-947, 955-977, 1711-1715; Joel B. Grossman and Richard S. Wells, *Constitutional Law and Judicial Policy Making* (New York: Longman, 1988), 605-652; Fisher, *American Constitutional Law*, 618-635. Regarding a recent issue, regulation of the Internet, see *Reno v. American Civil Liberties Union, 521 U.S. 844 (1997).*
62. Donald Grier Stephenson, Jr., *Campaigns and the Court* (New York: Columbia University Press, 1999).

8

The Evolution of U.S. Civil Society: Gain, Risk, and Resilience

The best sense of democratic civil society is that of a complex, intermediate, and elastic part of the social order that helps to sustain tension within a diverse population. A rich mix of diversity, communication, autonomy, mediation, and voluntary association forms a fertile basis for a healthy, or sufficiently vibrant, civil society that provides links and buffers between opposing groups and ideas. In such a state, neither those who are governed nor those who govern are directly accessible to the other for purposes of mobilization and manipulation. However, each remains accountable to the other. Power and loyalty are diffused equitably enough to prevent concentrations of authority, power imbalances, and unexpected shifts in power. At the same time, a vibrant civil society helps to constrain excessively intense or extreme views and behavior via the reciprocal influence that groups and individuals have on one another. The poet Kahlil Gibran might have described such a relationship as one with spaces in its togetherness.[1]

The idea of civil society in the U.S. has not been treated to a theoretically based, empirical analysis such as the present project. Robert Putnam's *Bowling Alone* posits decline of social capital originating in horizontal relationships within U.S. civil society.[2] *The Ladd Report* counters this claim.[3] My analysis is aimed at the larger institution, culturally embedded and comprised of multiple layers of mostly invisible horizontal and vertical relationships. This institution is complex and dynamic and must be considered in terms of its wholeness. It is imprudent to make sweeping generalizations about the health of civil society based on anything less. Doing so risks over-interpretation, omissions, ill-informed policy, and poor practices. The thesis, recently touted and too often accepted uncritically, that citizen apathy is an imminent threat to U.S. civil society is an example of this peril. Nonetheless, this thesis, and the public reaction to it, is also in the best tradition of Americans. We habitually exhort one another to be good citizens because we do understand its importance.

The threat of citizen negligence is ever present, by the very nature of democracy. Yet, Americans continue to rise above an historical reluctance to do civic chores to act on behalf of the community, as shown in chapter 3. Continued exhortation that resonates with guilt for not doing more, plus the stability and positive changes found in components of civil society over the twentieth century, imply that the potential and will to sustain civil society is healthy. This is, clearly, a cause for celebration. At the same time, it is appropriate to assess U.S. civil society in terms of its strengths and weaknesses.

Strengths

Twentieth-century developments in three components of U.S. civil society—voluntary association, diversity, and communication—especially signal strength and vitality.

Voluntary Association

Voluntary association remains embedded in American values and tradition. The volume of organized groups in relation to population growth grew at a faster rate during the last century. Rationales and interests, reflected in the subject categories of voluntary associations, multiplied, diversified, and were reconfigured as new interests and concerns unfolded. Voluntary organizations increasingly reached beyond the local to national, and international arenas. Religious congregations, an American societal mainstay, slowly multiplied in number. Grassroots initiatives, informal alliances, ad hoc enterprises, and widespread networking are too often overlooked. Informal association, where the political and apolitical interface, continues to be fundamentally important, if not increasingly so.

Further evidence of the stability of voluntary association exists. Measured levels of voluntary group membership, both nominal and active, have been stable for at least thirty years. Religious values continue to have a disproportionately large influence on the rationales, interests, and dedication expressed through associational life. Membership in religion-related voluntary organizations is higher than in other types of groups. Americans dedicate their personal resources to voluntary association at unchanging or increasing rates. Measures of volunteerism reflect a citizenry that combines efforts to get things done. Charitable giving remains a priority and rose with each decade throughout the twentieth century. Discussion of political matters with friends and neighbors grew more frequent. Americans would rather socialize than do civic chores but they also think civic duties are important. Historically, half of Americans at any point in time overcome this resistance to civic participation and get involved.

Diversity

Americans increasingly share and affiliate loosely with others different from themselves. Reasons for forming voluntary associations and for making connections across differences have markedly multiplied and diversified. With a swelling number of reasons to voluntarily associate with others in broader venues, the opportunity and motivation to tolerate or to surmount differences also expands. As Americans venture more frequently across a variety of perspectives, ideas, beliefs, and experiences to form networks of interest, association, and community, the divisive influences of demography and socioeconomics grow less powerful. Increased tolerance for practices, beliefs, and lifestyles of others augments a sense of accord. Americans appreciate unity and retain a sense of national identity even as voluntary association diversifies and diffuses loyalties.

Communication

The last century was revolutionary in terms of the innovation and compounding of communication and transportation technologies that strengthen civil society. The potential for sharing thoughts and ideas across distance and difference grew exponentially. These new technologies did more than ease formal and informal ways of associating. They helped Americans coordinate and integrate voluntary association with all of life's activity. Consequently, association became increasingly convenient, accessible, and embedded while social isolation grew less feasible.

Communication patterns now reflect the greater choice individuals have in modes of association, in what direction, at what distance, and in what parts of the social space. Americans customize their personal communication activities and, therefore, tailor the manner in which they attach to society. The outcome is continual expansion and re-elaboration of social space aided, in particular, by rapid advancements in communications technology. Consequently, social space assumes national, international and, even, cyberspatial dimensions. At the same time, an elaborating social space allows greater degrees of freedom in interaction intimacy.

Obviously, the web of communications sustained by Americans is no longer compact, impenetrable, or composed mostly of strong ties. The depth and intensity of strong ties limits their number and reach, as do real constraints on social interaction in an expanding world—time, money, and access to technology. Social space grew rapidly, became more complex, and transcended geographic and spatial barriers during the twentieth century. Much of this alteration in social space reflects an easy spread of weak ties that carry information.[4] The multiplication of weak ties, helped by technology, is a remarkable development that alters the ratio between strong and weak ties. While the two coexist and complement each other, the result is a more democratic social space.

Vulnerability and Strain

Autonomy and mediation are the components of civil society exhibiting the most vulnerability and strain as we enter a new century. Tocqueville's predictions ring true in that each became more difficult to sustain with gains in achieving equality.

Autonomy

The meaning of autonomy underwent a significant sea change during the last century. It once meant relative independence, but became a constant matter of maintaining and negotiating relationships of interdependence with other entities and authorities as social conditions changed. Local communities and other voluntary associations grew more vulnerable to encroachment by external authorities and forces of centralism after the turn of the nineteenth century. The need for a variety of resources to sustain autonomy underscores the importance of vital reciprocal relationships, both horizontally and vertically.

Autonomy now relies on successful negotiation of such relationships among institutions. It is a much more complicated, challenging existence than when autonomy consisted of contained self-sufficiency and a constricted sphere of interdependence. The intact phenomenon of voluntary association stands as evidence of success in sustaining resistance to centralizing forces. This could not have happened, however, without the Constitutional and legal safeguards that provide protection from overweening authority. Still, the autonomy of the news media, local schools, local political parties, local government, and some social service agencies has eroded. The interest of government, advertisers, and media conglomerates in controlling the content and influence of the communication and information exchange among Americans constantly counters autonomy. Thus, we see increased tension between these desires for mastery of the flow of information and its inherent power and the maintenance of an autonomous civil society. On the other hand, corrections for a level of autonomy that deter the democratic goal of equality are also necessary. It was not until excessively autonomous systems were penetrated by civil rights legislation that gains in equality were possible for some Americans. That this was a particularly difficult transition, requiring forcible federal intervention, demonstrates the power of local autonomy.

Today, an abiding value for the immediate, "local," and unique accompanies broadening worldviews. Public sentiment in favor of things local shows no inclination to weaken but has grown stronger in recent decades. This is a critical force for withstanding the encroachment of centralization. Still, the public has a pragmatic sense that multiple levels of authority are appropriate and that these roles sometimes need to change. This pragmatism implies a capacity to respond artfully and agilely to challenges, from within and from without, which is what Machiavelli saw as the surest way to sustain autonomy (see chapter 1).

Mediation

The mediation of democratic tensions is also under greater strain. It grows harder to surmount debilitating amounts of uncertainty or imbalance, to adjust levels of tension, and to allow constructive exchange. This is seemingly an unavoidable downside of progress toward democratic objectives. Added views complicate matters, as do greater varieties of relationships, culminating in higher levels of tension that must be sustained in workable balance. Not surprisingly, then, affairs that need the mediational assistance of the Supreme Court have increased in volume.

Traditionally, the two-party system is one of the more effective mechanisms for mediating political tension in the United States. Yet, the parties' ability to mediate tensions to bring political differences to a working consensus is now blunted and less effective. Shifts in electoral interest and declines in voting are especially notable in light of the disengagement of partisanship from local politics and local media. A long ago move to reform local politics distanced citizens from the immediacy of political conflict. This reform effectively eliminated active partisanship at the local level, which amounted to removal of an intermediate, autonomous force close to citizens.

Gain and Risk

American society has grown more democratic in terms of gains in achieving equality and personal freedoms. These gains are reflected in the nature of contemporary U.S. civil society, which we can characterize as more voluntary in nature, more inclusive, and less controlled by the expectations of a few. Today, Americans have greater choice and discretion in shaping associational life than ever before. They are free to choose from or to develop an ever-widening array of activities, shared interests, locales and backdrops, co-interactants, sources and types of shared information, modes of communication, and methods of transport. This also means greater freedom to make poor decisions about how to integrate private and public lives. Therein lies a significant concern.

What is the impact of this greater freedom? Might the risk entailed in poor decisions be too great a price to pay for individual choice?[5] Even as Tocqueville predicted that equality would allow individuals to focus on personal interests to the neglect of common interests, his contemporary John Stuart Mill foresaw the necessity for "a great increase of disinterested exertion to promote the good of others."[6] If, as anthropologist Mary Douglas claims, new kinds of thinking, behavior, and people emerge from the dynamics of an institution, then gains in equality and in freedom imply enlightened changes in individuals.[7] Such is the development of the modern individual living in a broadening sphere of cultural homogeneity, shared meanings, and easier communication. Gellner reminds us that modern individuals are diverse and can carry out varied tasks and roles but they also share many similarities. These contemporary individuals freely and effectively associate, and they are especially well equipped to combine for specific, ad hoc, and limited purposes. They are resourceful individualists.[8] This is not the narrow kind of individualism that Tocqueville feared on behalf of democracy in which common matters are neglected out of selfishness. Indeed, contemporary Americans exude a public-spiritedness that is reflected in an appreciable amount of evidence of "self-interest rightly understood." Seemingly unchanged, at least since midcentury, is an ambivalence about civic activities in lieu of other preferred kinds of social interaction. Yet, the accommodation made by Americans to other-oriented pursuits, as opposed to the solitary leisure that is highly valued, has remained in roughly the same proportion. I find no evidence of change in the extent to which Americans sacrifice public interests to pursue narrowly private interests. Americans continue to get involved in public matters, a practice sustained by values and custom.

The risk of narrow individuality is ever present, but there also is something in individuals, à la John Locke and the rule of reason, by which they recognize or learn that their fate intertwines with that of others. Individuals understand that, to be effective, they must combine efforts. Moreover, political philosopher and scientist Charles Taylor points out that individualism does not preclude social connectedness, but provides an incentive to enter dialogic relationships. Individualism's moral ideal of self-fulfillment and self-authenticity is only achieved through relationships and discourse. Thus, each comes to understand one's self through dialogue, expression, and experience. Each individual forms opinions, outlooks, and positions, and essentially does one's best to become and remain independent while remaining in dialogue with others. When substantive agreement on value(s), or a shared "horizon of significance" occurs, individualism and association are compatible.[9] Actions derived from this compatibility are consistent with Tocqueville's idea of "self-interest rightly understood," Locke's rule of reason, Machiavelli's *virtù*, and Burke's idea of prudence (see chapter 1). Moreover, this melding of self-interest with others' interest resonates with arguments by Mansbridge and by Ladd that the moral principle is inherent in the behavior of Americans and too often goes unrecognized (see chapter 1).

Social scientists Sears and Funk, for example, find that Americans exhibit more than self-interested behavior. These researchers tested the relationship between self-interest and policy or candidate preferences in the American electorate over several decades and found only rare instances of self-interest effects. In numerous surveys that addressed a variety of public issues, those surveyed tended to regard political issues with a "disinterested frame of mind." The exceptions to this were with issues that combined uncertainty and seriously negative outcomes, like the support for student deferments by half again as many freshman males as senior males and like public employee opposition to tax revolt, but only as it related to their own jobs and salaries.[10] These are the kind of self-preserving responses that Locke defended: "Every one as he is *bound to preserve himself*, and not to quit his Station willfully;" and he continued, "so by the like reason when his own Preservation comes not in competition, ought he, as much as he can, *to preserve the rest of Mankind....*"[11]

Princeton psychologist Dale Miller proposes that "individualistic cultures spawn social norms that induce people to follow their material self-interest rather than their principles or passions... But however strong the disposition to pursue material self-interest may be, it is likely not as strong as the prevalence of self-interested behavior in everyday life suggests."[12] The substance of daily discussion and processing of information that occurs among friends, acquaintances, and family generally escapes systematic scrutiny, although talk about politics between friends and family is rising. Since interests take shape in dialog, daily interaction is a source of insight into operational understandings of self-interest and "self interest rightly understood." This is an area ripe for research, for individual decisions about the exercise of freedom increasingly shape civil society. This development recommends that Americans need opportunities for (1) developing skills for critical thinking and good choices, (2) telling each other what is important and why, and (3) developing shared understandings and moralities through dialogic relationships.

The Bottom Line

Fortunately, the vulnerability of U.S. civil society is not pivotally attributable to apathy, indifference, or self-centeredness of the public. Rather, the greatest challenges it confronts—sustaining autonomy and effectively mediating conflict and consensus—actually stem from successes in achieving democratic goals. The evolution of U.S. civil society during the twentieth century is situated in a context of significant gains made in freedom and equality. This freedom did not lead to decline in voluntary association or social connectedness as individuals grew freer to attach or to detach from community.

Instead, we find a much wider array of activities and technological adaptations that facilitate crosscutting and connectedness. We find choice and diversity in association, an enhanced flow of information, and more versatility in communication within a context of a larger, less dense social space. The greatness and resourcefulness of more than narrow spectrums of citizens are widely available to all. Americans voluntarily shape and use modes of association according to need, interest, and social conditions, thus contributing to the elasticity of civil society. For these reasons, U.S. civil society is more democratic and flexible than ever as we enter the twenty-first century. The resilience of this institution will help to mitigate threats to autonomy, challenges to mediation, and other perils that accompany democratic progress.

Notes

1. Kahlil Gibran, *The Prophet* (New York: Alfred A. Knopf, 1969), 15.
2. Robert D. Putnam, *Bowling Alone* (New York: Simon and Schuster, 2000); "A Symposium on Robert D. Putnam, *Bowling Alone*," *Contemporary Sociology* 30:3 (May 2001): 223-230.
3. Everett Carll Ladd, *The Ladd Report* (New York: Free Press, 1999).
4. Mark Granovetter, "The Strength of Weak Ties," *American Journal of Sociology* 78:6 (1973): 1360-1380; Mark Granovetter, "The Strength of Weak Ties: A Network Theory Revisited," in Randall Collins, ed., *Sociological Theory* (San Francisco, CA: Jossey-Bass, 1983), 201-233.
5. Michael J. Sandel, *Democracy's Discontent: America in Search of a Public Philosophy* (Cambridge, MA: Belknap Press of Harvard University Press, 1996), 24-28.
6. Alexis de Tocqueville, *Democracy in America* (New York: Vintage Books, 1945), II:129-132; John Stuart Mill, *Utilitarianism, Liberty, and Considerations on Representative Government* (London: J. M. Dent, [1859] 1920), 132-133.
7. Mary Douglas, *How Institutions Think* (New York: Syracuse University Press, 1986).
8. Ernest Gellner, *Conditions of Liberty: Civil Society and Its Rivals* (New York: Allen Lane, Penguin, 1994), 5, 97-106.
9. Charles Taylor, *The Malaise of Modernity* (Concord, Ontario: House of Anansi, 1991).
10. David O. Sears and Carolyn L. Funk, "Self-Interest in Americans' Political Opinions," in Jayne J. Mansbridge, ed., *Beyond Self-Interest* (Chicago, IL: University of Chicago Press, 1990), 147-170, 326-327.
11. John Locke, *Two Treatises of Government*, ed. Peter Laslett (Cambridge, UK: Cambridge University Press, 1988), II § 7.
12. Dale T. Miller, "The Norm of Self-Interest," *American Psychologist* 54:12 (December 1999): 1053-1060.

Bibliography

Abrahamson, David. 1996. *Magazine-Made America*. Cresskill, NY: Hampton Press.

ACTION. 1975. "Americans Volunteer 1974." Washington, DC.

Adams, Rebecca G. 1998. "The Demise of Territorial Determinism: Online Friendships." In *Placing Friendship in Context*, eds. Rebecca G. Adams and Graham Allan. Cambridge: Cambridge University Press.

Adler, Sy, and Gerald F. Blake. 1990. "The Effects of a Formal Citizen Participation Program on Involvement in the Planning Process: A Case Study of Portland, Oregon." *State and Local Government Review* (Winter): 37-43.

Advisory Commission on Intergovernmental Relations. 1981. "Measuring Local Discretionary Authority." Information Report M-131. Washington, DC.

———. serial editions. "Changing Public Attitudes on Governments and Taxes." ACIR, Washington, DC.

Aldrich, John H. 1995. *Why Parties?* Chicago, IL: University of Chicago Press.

Allen, John C., and Don A. Dillman. 1994. *Against All Odds*. Boulder, CO: Westview.

Almond, Gabriel A. 1987. "Civic Culture." In *The Blackwell Encyclopaedia of Political Institutions*, ed. Vernon Bogdanor. Oxford, UK: Blackwell Reference.

Almond, Gabriel A., and G. Bingham Powell, Jr. 1978. *Comparative Politics: System, Process, and Policy*. 2d ed. Boston, MA: Little, Brown.

Almond, Gabriel A., G. Bingham Powell, Jr., and Robert J. Mundt. 1993. *Comparative Politics: A Theoretical Framework*. New York: HarperCollins.

Almond, Gabriel A., and Sidney Verba. [1963] 1989. *The Civic Culture: Political Attitudes and Democracy in Five Nations*. Newbury Park, CA: Sage Publications.

———. 1980. *Civic Culture Revisited*. Boston, MA: Little, Brown.

Amar, Akhil Reed. 1998. *The Bill of Rights: Creation and Reconstruction*. New Haven, CT: Yale University Press.

American Association of Fund-Raising Counsel Trust for Philanthropy. annual reports. "Giving USA." New York.

American Business Directories. annual editions. Omaha, NE: American Business Lists.

"Americans are Churchgoers." 1998. *Society* 35:5 (July/August): 2-3.

Andersen, Kristi. 1996. *After Suffrage*. Chicago, IL: University of Chicago Press.

Anglo, Sydney. 1969. *Machiavelli: A Dissection*. London: Victor Gollancz.

An Impartial Citizen. [1801] 1983. "A Dissertation Upon the Constitutional Freedom of the Press." In *American Political Writing during the Founding Era 1760-1805*, ed. C. S. Hyneman and D. S. Lutz. Indianapolis, IN: Liberty Fund.

Arendt, Hannah. [1951] 1968. *Totalitarianism*. New York: Harcourt, Brace and World.

Aristotle. [1946] 1952. *The Politics*, trans. Ernest Barker. Oxford, UK: Clarendon Press.

———. [1980] 1998. *The Nicomachean Ethics*, trans. David Ross. Oxford, UK: Oxford University Press.

Associated Press. 1999. "Chronology of Media Mergers Dramatizes Huge Scale of Deal." *Wall Street Journal* Interactive Edition (7 September). Website http://interactive.wsj.com.

Auerbach, M. Morton. 1968. "Edmund Burke." Pp. 464-471 in *International Encyclopedia of the Social Sciences*, vol. 9, ed. David L. Sills. Toronto: Crowell Collier and Macmillan.

Axelrod, Morris. 1956. "Urban Structure and Social Participation." *American Sociological Review* 21 (February): 13-18.

Babchuk, Nicholas, and Alan Booth. 1969. "Voluntary Association Membership: A Longitudinal Analysis." *American Sociological Review* 34 (February): 31-45.

Baer, Douglas, James Curtis, and Edward Grabb. 2000. "Has Voluntary Association Activity Declined? A Cross-National Perspective." Paper presented at American Sociological Association Annual Meeting, Washington, DC.

Bagdikian, Ben H. 1990. *The Media Monopoly*. 3d ed. Boston, MA: Beacon.

———. 1998. "The Realities of Media Concentration and Control." *Television Quarterly* 29 (3): 22-27.

Baker, William F., and George Dessart. 1998. "The Road Ahead." *Television Quarterly* 29 (4): 2-16.

Banton, Michael. 1968. "Voluntary Associations: Anthropological Aspects." Pp. 357-362 in *The International Encyclopedia of the Social Sciences*, ed. David Sills. New York: Macmillan and Free Press.

Barber, Benjamin R. 1995. "The Search For Civil Society." *The New Democrat* 7:2 (March/ April): 13-17.

Barker, Ernest. 1959. *The Political Thought of Plato and Aristotle*. New York: Dover.

Barnes, Samuel H., Max Kaase, et al. 1979. *Political Action: Mass Participation in Five Western Democracies*. Beverly Hills, CA: Sage.

Bass, Jack. 1999. "Newspaper Monopoly." *American Journalism Review* (July/ August): 64-86.

Baum, Lawrence. 1998. *The Supreme Court*. 6th ed. Washington, DC: Congressional Quarterly.

Baumgartner, Frank R., and Jack L. Walker. 1988. "Survey Research and Membership in Voluntary Associations." *American Journal of Political Science* 32:4 (November): 908-928.

Baym, Nancy K. 1995. "The Emergence of Community in Computer-Mediated Communication." In *Cybersociety*, ed. Steven G. Jones. Thousand Oaks, CA: Sage.

Beer, Samuel H. 1993. "The Idea of the Nation." In *American Intergovernmental Relations*, ed. Laurence J. O'Toole, Jr. Washington, DC: Congressional Quarterly.

Bell, Daniel. 1956. "The Theory of Mass Society." *Commentary* 22 (July): 75-83.

———. [1973] 1976. *The Coming of Post-Industrial Society*. New York: Basic Books.

Bell, Wendell, and Maryanne T. Force. 1956. "Social Structure and Participation in Different Types of Formal Associations." *Social Forces* 34:4 (May): 345-350.

———. 1956. "Urban Neighborhood Types and Participation in Formal Associations." *American Sociological Review* 21 (February): 25-34.

Bellah, Robert N. 1970. *Beyond Belief*. New York: Harper and Row.

Bellah, Robert N., Richard Madsen, William M. Sullivan, Ann Swidler, and Steven M.Tipton. 1985. *Habits of the Heart: Individualism and Commitment in American Life*. New York: Harper and Row.

Belli, Robert F., M. W. Traugott, M. Young, and K. A. McGonagle. 1999. "Reducing Vote Overreporting in Surveys." *Public Opinion Quarterly* 63 (Spring): 90-108.

Berger, Peter L. and Richard John Neuhaus. 1977. *To Empower People: The Role of Mediating Structures in Public Policy*. Washington, DC: American Enterprise Institute for Public Policy Research.

———. 1996. *To Empower People: From State to Civil Society*, ed. Michael Novak. 2d. ed. Washington, DC: American Enterprise Institute for Public Policy Research.

Berman, David R. 1995. "Takeovers of Local Governments: An Overview and Evaluation of State Policies." *Publius* 25:3 (Summer): 55-70.

Berry, Jeffrey M., Kent E. Portney, and Ken Thomson. 1993. *The Rebirth of Urban Democracy*. Washington, DC: Brookings Institution.

Beyme, Klaus von. 1991. "Post-Modernity, Postmaterialism and Political Theory." Pp. 309-331 in *Eurobarometer*, eds. Karlheinz Reif and Ronald Inglehart. New York: St. Martin's.

Birdsell, David, Douglas Muzzio, and Humphrey Taylor. 1996. "17 Million American Adults Use World Wide Web." *The Harris Poll* 11 (15 February).

Biskupic, Joan, and Elder Witt. 1997. *The Supreme Court and Individual Rights*. 3d ed. Washington, DC: Congressional Quarterly.

Black, Antony. 1987. "Civil Society." In *The Blackwell Encyclopedia of Political Thought*, ed. David Miller. New York: B. Blackwell.

Black, C. E. 1966. *The Dynamics of Modernization: A Study in Comparative History*. New York: Harper and Row.

Blakely, Edward J., and Mary Gail Snyder. 1997. *Gated Communities in the United States*. Washington, DC: Brookings Institution/Lincoln Institute of Land Policy.

Blendon, Robert J., John M. Benson, Mollyann Brodie, Drew E. Altman, Richard Morin, Claudia Deane, and Nina Kjellson. 1999. "The 60s and the 90s." *Brookings Review* (Spring): 14-17.

Bogart, Leo. 1995. *Commercial Culture*. New York: Oxford University Press.

Boggs, Carl. 2001. "Social Capital and Political Fantasy: Robert Putnam's *Bowling Alone*," *Theory and Society* 30:2, 281-297.

Bok, Derek. 1996. *The State of the Nation*. Cambridge, MA: Harvard University Press.

Bonchek, Mark S. 1995. "Grassroots in Cyberspace: Using Computer Networks to Facilitate Political Participation." Working Paper 95-2.2, The Political Participation Project, MIT Artificial Intelligence Laboratory. Presented at annual meeting of the Midwest Political Science Association in Chicago, April 6.

Broadcasting. 1939. "Instances of Citation of Stations." In *Radio Censorship*, ed. H. B. Summers. New York: H. W. Wilson.

———. 1939. "Set Owners Oppose Censorship." In *Radio Censorship*, ed. H. B. Summers. New York: H. W. Wilson.

Broadway, Bill. 1996. "Flocking to the Web." *Washington Post* (18 September): B7.

Broder, David S. 1972. *The Party's Over: The Failure of Politics in America*. New York: Harper and Row.

Brotman, Stuart N. 1999. "The Bumpy Road of Regulation." *Media Studies Journal* 13:2 (Spring/Summer): 112-118.

Brown, Ed. 1997. "Extreme Publishing: Supply Room Confidential." *Fortune* (12 May): 26.

Brunner, Edmund deS, Gwendolyn S. Hughes, and Marjorie Patten. 1927. *American Agricultural Villages*. New York: George H. Doran.

Burden, Barry C., and David C. Kimball. 1998. "A New Approach to the Study of Ticket Splitting." *American Political Science Review* 92:3 (September): 533-544.

Burke, Edmund. 1880. *The Works of the Right Honorable Edmund Burke*. 6th ed. Boston, MA: Little, Brown.

Burns, Nancy. 1994. *The Formation of American Local Government*. New York: Oxford University Press.

Bushee, Frederick A. 1945. "Social Organization in a Small City." *American Journal of Sociology* 51, 217-226.

Caldwell, Louis G. 1939. "Program Standards Maintained by the Commission." In *Radio Censorship*, ed. H. B. Summers. New York: H. W. Wilson.

Campbell, Angus, Philip E. Converse, Warren E. Miller, and Donald E. Stokes. [1960, John Wiley] 1980. *The American Voter*. Chicago, IL: University of Chicago Press.

Cantril, Hadley. 1951. *Public Opinion 1935-1946*. Princeton, NJ: Princeton University Press.

Caplow, Theodore, Howard M. Bahr, Bruce A. Chadwick, Reuben Hill, and Margaret Holmes Williamson. 1982. *Middletown Families: Fifty Years of Change and Continuity*. Minneapolis: University of Minnesota Press.

Caplow, Theodore, Louis Hicks, and Ben J. Wattenberg. 2001. *The First Measured Century*. Washington, DC: AEI Press.

Center for the American Woman and Politics. 1976. *Women in Public Office*. NewYork: R. R. Bowker.

———. 1978. *Women in Public Office*. Metuchen, NJ: Scarecrow.

———. 1997. "Women in Elective Office 1997 Fact Sheet." National Information Bank on Women in Public Office, Eagleton Institute of Politics, Rutgers University.

Cernea, Michael M., ed. 1985. *Putting People First: Sociological Variables in Rural Developmen*t. New York: Oxford University Press.

———. 1993. "The Sociologist's Approach to Sustainable Development." *Finance and Development* (December): 11-13.

Chaffee, Steven, and Stacey Frank. 1996. "How Americans Get Political Information: Print Versus Broadcast News." *ANNALS* (July): 48-58.

Chapman, Gerald W. 1967. *Edmund Burke: the Practical Imagination*. Cambridge, MA: Harvard University Press.

Chapman, John W. 1969. "Voluntary Association and the Political Theory of Pluralism." In *Voluntary Associations,* Nomos XI, eds. J. Roland Pennock and John W. Chapman. New York: Atherton.

Chayes, Abram. 1976. "The Role of the Judge in Public Law Litigation." *Harvard Law Review* 89:7 (May): 1281-1316.

Choper, Jesse H. 1995. *Securing Religious Liberty*. Chicago, IL: University of Chicago Press.

"Civic Index, The." 1998. National Civic League. Denver, CO.

Clark, Terry N. 1972. "The Structure of Community Influence." Pp. 283-314 in *People and Politics in Urban Society*, ed. Harlan Hahn. Beverly Hills, CA: Sage.

Clark, Terry Nichols. 1974. "Community Autonomy in the National System: Federalism, Localism, and Decentralization." In *Comparative Community Politics*, ed. Terry Nichols Clark. New York: John Wiley.

Cnaan, Ram A., Femida Handy, and Margaret Wadsworth. 1996. "Defining Who is a Volunteer: Conceptual and Empirical Considerations." *Nonprofit and Voluntary Sector Quarterly* 25:3 (September): 364-383.

Cobban, Alfred. 1960. *Edmund Burke and the Revolt Against the Eighteenth Century*. London: George Allen and Unwin.

Cohen, Jean L., and Andrew Arato. 1994. *Civil Society and Political Theory*. Cambridge, MA: MIT Press.

Compaine, Benjamin M., ed. 1979. *Who Owns the Media?* (New York: Knowledge Industry).

Conlan, Timothy. 1998. *From New Federalism to Devolution: Twenty-Five Years of Intergovernmental Reform*. Washington, DC: Brookings Institution.

Conlan, Timothy J., James D. Riggle, and Donna E. Schwartz. 1995. "Deregulating Federalism? The Politics of Mandate Reform in the 104th Congress." *Publius* 25:3 (Summer): 23-24.

Conlan, Timothy J. 1993. "Federal, State, or Local? Trends in the Public's Judgment," *The Public Perspective* (January/February): 3-5.

Conyers, James E., and Walter L. Wallace. 1976. *Black Elected Officials: A Study of Black Americans Holding Governmental Office*. New York: Russell Sage Foundation.

Cowan, Ruth Schwartz. 1997. *A Social History of American Technology*. New York: Oxford University Press.

Crenshaw, Albert B. 1995. "An Investing Club Seeks Funds and Friendship." *Washington Post* (15 October): H1, H6.

Crick, Bernard. 1970. "Introduction." In Niccolò Machiavelli, *The Discourses*, trans. Leslie J. Walker. London: Penguin.

Crowe, Ian. 1997. *Edmund Burke: His Life and Legacy*. Dublin, Ireland: Four Courts.

Curti, Merle. 1959. *The Making of an American Community: A Case Study of Democracy in a Frontier County*. Stanford, CA: Stanford University Press.

Curtis, James E., Edward G. Grabb, and Douglas E. Baer. 1992. "Voluntary Association Membership in Fifteen Countries: A Comparative Analysis." *American Sociological Review* 57 (April): 139-152.

Curtius, Mary. 1997. "Libraries Write New Chapter." *Los Angeles Times* (1 February): A1.

Dahl, Robert A. 1993. "Pluralism." In *The Oxford Companion to Politics of the World*, ed. Joel Krieger. New York: Oxford University Press.

———. 1996. "Thinking About Democratic Constitutions: Conclusions from Democrat Experience." In *Political Order*, ed. Ian Shapiro and Russell Hardin. New York: New York University Press.

Dalton, Russell J. 1996. *Citizen Politics: Public Opinion and Political Parties in Advanced Industrial Democracies*. Chatham, NJ: Chatham House.

Davis, James Allan, and Tom W. Smith. 1999. "General Social Surveys, 1972-1998." Cumulative Computer File. Chicago, IL: National Opinion Research Center [producer]. Ann Arbor, MI: Interuniversity Consortium for Political and Social Research [distributor]. Website http://www.icpsr.umich.edu/GSS.

De Vita, Carol J. 1997. "Viewing Nonprofits Across the States." Washington, DC: Urban Institute.

Demac, Donna A. 1988. *Liberty Denied: The Current Rise of Censorship in America*. New York: PEN American Center.

Deutsch, Karl W. [1954] 1964. "Cracks in the Monolith: Possibilities and Patterns of Disintegration in Totalitarian Systems." In *Totalitarianism*, ed. Carl J. Friedrich. New York: Grosset and Dunlap.

Diamond, Larry. 1992. "Economic Development and Democracy Reconsidered." In *Reexamining Democracy*, eds. Gary Marx and Larry Diamond. Newbury Park, CA: Sage.

———. 1993. "Civil Society and the Construction of Democracy." Speech given at Harvard University, Cambridge, MA, December 7.

———. 1994. "Rethinking Civil Society: Toward Democratic Consolidation." *Journal of Democracy* 5 (3): 5-7.

———. 1999. *Developing Democracy: Toward Consolidation*. Baltimore, MD: Johns Hopkins University Press.

"Disillusionment with Washington." 1995. *The American Enterprise* (March/April):101.

"Do That Many People Really Attend Worship Services?" 1994. *Emerging Trends* 16:5 (May): 1-3.

Dougherty, Regina. 1997. "Divided Government Defines the Era." In *America at the Polls 1996*, eds. Regina Dougherty, Everett C. Ladd, David Wilber, and Lynn Zayachkiwsky. Storrs, CT: Roper Center for Public Opinion Research.

Dougherty, Regina, Everett C. Ladd, David Wilber, and Lynn Zayachkiwsky, eds. 1997. "America at the Polls 1996." Storrs, CT: Roper Center for Public Opinion Research.

Douglas, Mary. 1986. *How Institutions Think*. Syracuse, NY: Syracuse University Press.

Drakeman, Donald L. 1991. *Church-State Constitutional Issues*. New York: Greenwood.

Eckstein, Harry. 1966. *Division and Cohesion in Democracy*. Princeton, NJ: Princeton University Press.

Edwards, Bob, and Michael W. Foley. 2001. "Much Ado about Social Capital," *Contemporary Sociology* 30:3 (May): 227-230.

Eisenstadt, Stuart N. 1995. "Civil Society." Pp. 240-242 in *The Encyclopedia of Democracy*, ed. Seymour Martin Lipset. Washington, DC: Congressional Quarterly.

Elazar, Daniel J. 1972. *American Federalism: A View from the States*. New York: Thomas Y. Crowell.

Ellis, Susan J., and Katherine H. Noyes. 1990. *By the People: A History of Americans as Volunteers*. San Francisco, CA: Jossey-Bass.

Elmer-DeWitt, Philip. 1994. "Beyond Shovelware." *Folio* 23:17, 54-55.

Encyclopedia of Associations. serial editions. Detroit, MI: Gale Research.

Epstein, Lee, Jeffrey A. Segal, Harold J. Spaeth, and Thomas G. Walker. 1996. *The Supreme Court Compendium: Data, Decisions, and Developments*. Washington, DC: Congressional Quarterly.

Epstein, Lee, and Thomas G. Walker. 1998. *Constitutional Law for a Changing America: Rights, Liberties, and Justice*. Washington, DC: Congressional Quarterly.

Erickson, Bonnie H., and T. A. Nosanchuk. 1990. "How an Apolitical Association Politicizes." *Canadian Review of Sociology and Anthropology* 27:2, 206-219.

Esman, Michael J., and Norman T. Uphoff. 1984. *Local Organizations: Intermediaries in Rural Development*. Ithaca, NY: Cornell University Press.

Etzioni, Amitai. 2001. "Is Bowling Together Sociologically Lite?" *Contemporary Sociology* 30:3 (May): 223-224.

Fallows, James. 1997. *Breaking the News*. New York: Vintage Books.

Farhi, Paul. 1996. "A Joke That Rang True." *Washington Post* (2 April): E1, E3.

———. 1999. "Viacom to Buy CBS, Uniting Multimedia Heavyweights." *Washington Post* (8 September): A1, A7.

Federal Communications Commission. 1997. "Trends in Telephone Service." Industry Analysis Division, Common Carrier Bureau, Washington, DC.

Federal Election Commission. 2001. "2000 Official Presidential General Election Results," (20 June). Website http://fecweb1.fec.gov.

Ferge, Susan, ed. 1972. "Part III: Statistical Appendix." In *The Use of Time: Daily Activities of Urban and Suburban Populations in Twelve Countries*, ed. Alexander Szalai. The Hague: Mouton.

Finke, Roger. 1989. "Demographics of Religious Participation: An Ecological Approach, 1850-1980." *Journal of the Scientific Study of Religion* 28 (1): 45-58.

Finke, Roger, and Rodney Stark. 1992. *The Churching of America, 1776-1990*. New Brunswick, NJ: Rutgers University Press.

Fischer, Claude S. 1976. *The Urban Experience*. New York: Harcourt Brace Jovanovich.

———. 1992. *America Calling*. Berkeley: University of California Press.

———. 1994. "Changes in Leisure Activities, 1890-1940." *Journal of Social History* 27:3 (Spring): 453-475.

Fisher, Louis. 1990. *American Constitutional Law*. New York: McGraw-Hill.

FitzGibbon, Michael. 1997. "Accountability Misplaced: Private Social Welfare Agencies and the Public in Cleveland, 1880-1920." *Nonprofit and Voluntary Sector Quarterly* 26:1 (March): 27-40.

Flora, Cornelia Butler, Jan L. Flora, Jacqueline D. Spears, and Louis E. Swanson. 1992. *Rural Communities: Legacy and Change*. Boulder, CO: Westview.

Flora, Jan L., Jeff Sharp, Cornelia Flora, and Bonnie Newlon. 1997. "Entrepreneurial Social Infrastructure and Locally Initiated Economic Development in the Nonmetropolitan United States." *Sociological Quarterly* 38:4, 623-645.

Foerstel, Herbert N. 1997. *Free Expression and Censorship in America*. Westport, CT: Greenwood.

Foner, Eric. 1998. *The Story of American Freedom*. New York: W. W. Norton.

Freedom House. 1999. "Press Freedom Survey." Website http://freedomhouse.org.

Fry, C. Luther. 1930. *The United States Looks at Its Churches*. New York: Institute of Social and Religious Research. Cited in Frederick A. Bushee, "The Church in a Small City," *American Journal of Sociology* XLIX:3 (November 1943): 223-332.

———. 1933. "Changes in Religious Organizations." In *Recent Social Trends in the United States: Report of the President's Research Committee on Social Trends*, Research Committee on Social Trends. New York: McGraw-Hill.

Fukuyama, Francis. 2000. "Community Matters," *Washington Post Book World* (28 May): 5.

Gale Research Group. 1997-2001. "Associations Unlimited." Website http://galenet.gale.com.

Gallaher, Art., Jr. 1961. *Plainville Fifteen Years Later*. New York: Columbia University Press.

Gallup, George, Jr. 1986-1996. *The Gallup Poll: Public Opinion*. Wilmington, DE: Scholarly Resources.

———. 1978. *The Gallup Poll: Public Opinion 1972-1977*. Wilmington, DE: Scholarly Resources.

———. 1986. "Despite Recent Campaign, Politics Has Cleaner Image Today Than in 1983." November 27 press release.

Gamson, Joshua. 1998. *Freaks Talk Back*. Chicago, IL: University of Chicago Press.

Gannett Foundation. 1991. *The Media at War: The Press and the Persian Gulf Conflict*. New York: Gannett Foundation Media Center.

Gans, Herbert J. 1967. *The Levittowners: Ways of Life and Politics in a New Suburban Community*. New York: Pantheon.

———. 1988. *Middle American Individualism: The Future of Liberal Democracy*. New York: Free Press.

Gant, Michael M., and Norman R. Luttbeg. 1991. *American Electoral Behavior: 1952-1988*. Itasca, IL: F. E. Peacock.

Gastil, Raymond D. 1985. "A Historical Survey of Freedom in America." Pp. 145-167 in *Freedom in the World: Political Rights and Civil Liberties 1984-1985*, ed. R. D. Gastil. Westport, CT: Greenwood.

———. 1987. *Freedom in the World: Political Rights and Civil Liberties 1986-1987*. New York: Greenwood.

———. 1991. "The Comparative Survey of Freedom: Experiences and Suggestions." In *On Measuring Democracy*, ed. Alex Inkeles. New Brunswick, NJ: Transaction Publishers.

Gellner, Ernest. 1994. *Conditions of Liberty: Civil Society and its Rivals*. New York: Allen Lane, Penguin.

Gerson, Kathleen, C. Ann Stueve, and Claude S. Fischer. 1977. "Attachment to Place." In *Networks and Places*, ed. Claude S. Fischer. New York: Free Press.

Getler, Michael. 2001. "The Sunday Paper Habit." *Washington Post* (27 May): B6.

Gibran, Kahlil. 1969. *The Prophet*. Alfred A. Knop.

Gilbert, Dennis A. 1988. *Compendium of American Public Opinion*. New York: Facts on File.

Gilkeson, John Shanklin Jr. 1981. "A City of Joiners: Voluntary Associations and the Formation of the Middle Class in Providence, 1830-1920." Ph.D. dissertation, Brown University. Ann Arbor, MI: University Microfilms International.

Glazer, Nathan. 1983. "Towards a Self-Service Society?" *The Public Interest* 70 (Winter): 66-90.

Glenn, Norval D. 1974. "Trend Studies with Available Survey Data: Opportunities and Pitfalls." In Survey Data for Trend Analysis: An Index to Repeated Questions in U.S. National Surveys Held by the Roper Public Opinion Research Center, ed. Jessie C. Southwick. Washington, DC: Social Science Research Council Center for Social Indicators.

Glick, Henry R. 1993. *Courts, Politics and Justice*. 3d ed. New York: McGraw Hill.

Goldstein, Tom. 1998. "Does Big Mean Bad?" *Columbia Journalism Review* (September/October): 52-53.

Gordon, C. Wayne, and Nicholas Babchuk. 1959. "A Typology of Voluntary Associations." *American Sociological Review* 24:2 (February): 22-29.

Granovetter, Mark. 1973. "The Strength of Weak Ties." *American Journal of Sociology* 78:6, 1360-1380.

———. 1983. "The Strength of Weak Ties: A Network Theory Revisited." In *Sociological Theory*, ed. Randall Collins. San Francisco, CA: Jossey-Bass.

Gray, John. 1993. *Post-Liberalism: Studies in Political Thought*. New York: Routledge.

Grazia, Sebastian de. 1962. *Of Time Work and Leisure*. New York: Twentieth Century Fund.

Greeley, Andrew. 1997. "The Other Civic America: Religion and Social Capital." *The American Prospect* (May-June): 68-73.

Green, Jonathon. 1990. *The Encyclopedia of Censorship*. New York: Facts On File.

Greenstein, Fred I., and Nelson W. Polsby, eds. 1975. *Handbook of Political Science*. Reading, MA: Addison-Wesley.

Grenier, Melinda Patterson. 2001. "More People Have Access to Internet but Digital Divide Persists, Study Says." *Wall Street Journal* Interactive Edition (18 February). Website http://interactive.wsj.com.

Grønjberg, Kirsten A. 1993. *Understanding Nonprofit Funding*. San Francisco, CA: Jossey-Bass.

Grossman, Joel B., and Richard S. Wells. 1988. *Constitutional Law and Judicial Policy Making*. New York: Longman.

Grossman, Lawrence K. 1998. "The Death of Radio Reporting: Will TV Be Next?" *Columbia Journalism Review* (September/October): 61-62.

Grunwald, Michael. 1999. "Voters Shunning Party Identification, Loyalty." *Washington Post* (3 January): A1, A4-A5.

Guterbock, Thomas M., and John C. Fries. 1997. "Maintaining America's Social Fabric: The AARP Survey of Civic Involvement." American Association of Retired Persons, Washington, DC.

Hachten, William A. 1968. *The Supreme Court on Freedom of the Press: Decisions and Dissents*. Ames: Iowa State University Press.

Hadaway, C. Kirk, Penny Long Marler, and Mark Chaves. 1993. "What the Polls Don't Show: A Closer Look at U.S. Church Attendance." *American Sociological Review* 58 (December): 741-752.

Hall, Kermit, ed. 1992. *The Oxford Companion to the Supreme Court of the United States*. New York: Oxford University Press.

Hamilton, Howard D. 1971. "The Municipal Voter: Voting and Nonvoting in City Elections." *American Political Science Review* 65 (December): 1135-1140.

Hansen, Karen V. 1997. "Rediscovering the Social: Visiting Practices in Antebellum New England and the Limits of the Public/Private Dichotomy." In *Public and Private in Thought and Practice: Perspectives on a Grand Dichotomy*, eds. Jeff Weintraub and Krishan Kumar. Chicago, IL: University of Chicago Press.

Harrigan, John J. 1988. *Politics and Policy in States and Communities*. Glenview, IL: Scott, Foresman.

Harris, H. S. 1969. "Voluntary Association as a Rational Ideal." Pp. 138-144 in *Voluntary Associations*, Nomos XI, ed. J. Roland Pennock and John W. Chapman. New York: Atherton.

Hart, Hornell. 1942. "Religion." *American Journal of Sociology* (May), 888-897.

Hastings, Elizabeth Hann, and Philip K. Hastings, ed. 1982. *Index to International Public Opinion, 1980-1981*. Westport, CT: Greenwood.

———. 1983. *Index to International Public Opinion, 1981-1982*. Westport, CT: Greenwood.

Hausknecht, Murray. 1962. *The Joiners: A Sociological Description of Voluntary Association Membership in the United States*. New York: Bedminster.

Hawley, Willis D. 1973. *Nonpartisan Elections and the Case for Party Politics*. New York: John Wiley.
Hayghe, Howard V. 1991. "Volunteers in the U.S.: Who Donates the Time?" *Monthly Labor Review* 114 (February): 17-23.
Heer, Clarence. 1933. "Trends in Taxation and Public Finance." In *Recent Social Trends in the United States: Report of the President's Research Committee on Social Trends*, Research Committee on Social Trends. New York: McGraw-Hill.
Hentoff, Nat. 1980. *The First Freedom*. New York: Delacorte.
Herbers, John, and James McCartney. 1999. "The New Washington Merry-Go-Round." *American Journalism Review* (April): 50-62.
Hermet, Guy. 1991. "The Disenchantment of the Old Democracies." *International Social Science Journal* 129 (August): 451-461.
Heuser, Uwe Jean, and Gero von Randow. 1998. "Try Cleaning Things Up." *Die Zeit* (9 October): 58. Trans. Ingrid Sandole-Staroste.
Hickey, Neil. 1997. "So Big: The Telecommunications Act at Year One." *Columbia Journalism Review* (January/February): 23-28.
———. 1998. "Money Lust: How Pressure for Profit is Perverting Journalism." *Columbia Journalism Review* (July/August): 28-36.
Hill, B. W., ed. 1975. *Edmund Burke On Government, Politics and Society*. Sussex, England: Harvester.
Hirschman, Albert O. 1970. *Exit, Voice, and Loyalty*. Cambridge, MA: Harvard University Press.
Hochschild, Arlie. 1997. *The Time Bind*. New York: Metropolitan Books/Henry Holt.
Hodgkinson, Virginia Ann, and Murray S. Weitzman. 1989. *Dimensions of the Independent Sector: A Statistical Profile*. 3d ed. Washington, DC: Independent Sector.
Hodgkinson, Virginia A., and Murray S. Weitzman, with John A. Abrahams, Eric A. Crutchfield, and David R. Stevenson. 1996. *Nonprofit Almanac 1996-1997: Dimensions of the Independent Sector*. San Francisco, CA: Jossey-Bass.
Hodgkinson, Virginia Ann, Murray S. Weitzman, Christopher M. Toppe, and Stephen M. Noga. 1992. *Nonprofit Almanac 1992-1993: Dimensions of the Independent Sector*. San Francisco, CA: Jossey-Bass.
Hodgkinson, Virginia A., Murray S. Weitzman, Stephen M. Noga, and Heather A. Gorski. 1993. *A Portrait of the Independent Sector: The Activities and Finances of Charitable Organizations*. Washington, DC: Independent Sector.
Hoffman, Paul E. 1995. *Netscape and the World Wide Web for Dummies*. Foster City, CA: IDG Books Worldwide.
Horowitz, Donald L. 1977. *The Courts and Social Policy*. Washington, DC: Brookings Institution.
Hovey, Harold A. 1999. *The Devolution Revolution: Can the States Afford Devolution?* New York: Century Foundation.
Hughes, Frank. 1950. *Prejudice and the Press*. New York: Devin-Adair.
Hulteng, John L. 1981. *Playing it Straight*. Chester, CT: Globe Pequot.

Hunter, Albert. 1974. *Symbolic Communities: The Persistence and Change of Chicago's Local Communities*. Chicago, IL: University of Chicago Press.
Hunter, James Davison. 2000. "Bowling with the Social Scientists," *The Weekly Standard* (August 28/September 4): 31-35.
Hunter, James Davison, and Carl Bowman. 1996. *The State of Disunion: 1996 Survey of American Political Culture*. Ivy, VA: In Medias Res Educational Foundation.
Huntington, Samuel P. 1981. *American Politics: The Promise of Disharmony*. Cambridge, MA: Belknap.
Hu, Patricia S., and Jennifer R. Young. 1999. *Summary of Travel Trends 1995 Nationwide Personal Transportation Survey*. Washington, DC: Federal Highway Administration.
Hyman, Herbert H. 1972. *Secondary Analysis of Sample Surveys*. Middletown, CT: Wesleyan University Press.
Hyman, Herbert H., and Charles R. Wright. 1971. "Trends in Voluntary Association Memberships of American Adults: Replication Based on Secondary Analysis of National Sample Surveys." *American Sociological Review* 36:2 (April): 191-206.
Independent Sector. serial editions. "Giving and Volunteering in the United States." Washington, DC.
———. 1999. "Giving and Volunteering in the United States, 1999: Key Findings." October information release.
———. 2000. "America's Religious Congregations: Measuring Their Contributions to Society." Washington, DC.
———. 2001. "The Nonprofit Almanac in Brief." Website http://independentsector.org.
Ingelhart, Louis Edward. 1997. *Press and Speech Freedoms in America, 1619-1995*. Westport, CT: Greenwood.
Inkeles, Alex. [1954] 1964. "The Totalitarian Mystique: Some Impressions of the Dynamics of Totalitarian Society." In *Totalitarianism*, ed. Carl J. Friedrich. New York: Grossett and Dunlap.
International City Management Association. annual editions. *The Municipal Yearbook*. Washington, DC.
International Centre on Censorship. 1991. *Information Freedom and Censorship World Report 1991*. Chicago, IL: American Library Association.
Interuniversity Consortium for Political and Social Research. 1995. *Guide to Resources and Services 1994-1995*. Ann Arbor, MI: ICPSR.
Ivers, Gregg. 1992. *Redefining the First Freedom*. New Brunswick, NJ: Transaction Publishers.
Jacobs, Bruce. 1981. *The Political Economy of Organizational Change*. New York: Academic.
Jackman, Robert W., and Ross A. Miller. 1998. "Social Capital and Politics." Pp. 47-73 in Nelson W. Polsby, ed., *Annual Review of Political Science*. Palo Alto, CA: Annual Reviews.
Janowitz, Morris. 1974. "Foreword." In *Symbolic Communities: The Persistence and Change of Chicago's Local Communities*, ed. Albert Hunter. Chicago, IL: University of Chicago Press.

Jencks, Christopher. 1987. "Who Gives to What?" In *The Nonprofit Sector*, ed. Walter W. Powell. New Haven, CT: Yale University Press.

Jenkins, Richard. 1996. *Social Identity*. London: Routledge.

Jennings, Jerry T. 1990. "The Current Population Survey of Voting and Registration: Summary and History." Pp. 1-20 in *Studies in the Measurement of Voter Turnout*. Current Population Reports, Series P-23, No. 168, United States Bureau of the Census. Washington, DC: United States Government Printing Office.

———. 1990. "Estimating Voter Turnout in the Current Population Survey." Pp. 21-18 in *Studies in the Measurement of Voter Turnout*. Current Population Reports, Series P-23, No. 168, United States Bureau of the Census. Washington, DC: United States Government Printing Office.

Jensen, Carl. 1997. *20 Years of Censored News*. New York: Seven Stories Press.

Johnson, Peter T. 1993. "How I Turned a Critical Public into Useful Consultants." *Harvard Business Review* (January/February): 56-66.

Joint Center for Political and Economic Studies. annual editions. *Black Elected Officials: A National Roster*. Washington, DC.

Jones, Marya. 1999. "Does Quality Cost? Yes, But Not in the Way You Think." *Columbia Journalism Review* (January/February): special insert.

Judd, Charles H. 1933. "Education." In *Recent Social Trends in the United States: Report of the President's Research Committee on Social Trends*, Research Committee on Social Trends. New York: McGraw-Hill.

Judkins, Calvert Jay. 1949. *National Associations of the United States*. Washington, DC: United States Department of Commerce.

Juster, F. Thomas, and Frank P. Stafford. 1985. *Time, Goods, and Wellbeing*. Ann Arbor: Institute for Social Research, University of Michigan.

Kant, Immanuel. [1781] 1966. *Critique of Pure Reason*. Garden City, NY: Anchor, Doubleday.

Kaplan, Richard L. 1996. "The Press and the American Public Sphere: The Emergence of an Independent Journalism, 1865-1920." Paper presented at annual meeting of American Sociological Association, New York.

Karges, Ken. 2001. *Encyclopedia of Associations: Regional, State, and Local Organizations*. Farmington Hills, MI: Gale Research Group.

Kateb, George. 1969. "Tocqueville's View of Voluntary Associations." Pp. 138-144 in *Voluntary Associations*, Nomos XI, eds. J. Roland Pennock and John W. Chapman. New York: Atherton.

Kaufman, Harold. 1953. "Prestige Classes in a New York Rural Community." In *Class, Status and Power*, eds. Reinhard Bendix and Seymour Martin Lipset. New York: Free Press.

Kelman, Steven. 1996. *American Democracy and the Public Good*. Fort Worth, TX: Harcourt Brace.

Keppel, Frederick P. 1933. "The Arts in Social Life." In *Recent Social Trends in the United States: Report of the President's Research Committee on Social Trends,* Research Committee on Social Trends. New York: McGraw-Hill.

Kerri, James Nwannukwu. 1976. "Studying Voluntary Associations as Adaptive Mechanisms: A Review of Anthropolitical Perspectives." *Current Anthropology* 17 (March): 23-47.

Key, V. O., Jr. 1963. *Public Opinion and American Democracy*. New York: Alfred A. Knopf.

Kiesling, L. Lynne. 2000. "Book Reviews: Bowling Alone," *Cato Journal* 20 (Spring/Summer): 131-133.

Kimberling, William C. 1996. *Federal Election Law 96*. Washington, DC: Office of Election Administration, Federal Election Commission.

Kirkpatrick, Jeane. 1979. "Why We Don't Become Republicans." *Commonsense* 2 (Fall).

Knowlton, Steven R., and Patrick R. Parsons. 1994. *The Journalist's Moral Compass*. Westport, CT: Praeger.

Kobak, James B. 1990. "25 Years of Change." *Folio* 19 (March): 82.

——. 1994. "Magazine Trends." *Folio* 22 (Special Sourcebook Issue): 235.

Kolb, J. H., and Edmund deS. Brunner. 1935. *A Study of Rural Society: Its Organization and Changes*. Boston, MA: Houghton Mifflin.

———. 1940. *A Study of Rural Society: Its Organization and Changes*. Boston, MA: Houghton Mifflin.

———. 1946. *A Study of Rural Society*. Boston, MA: Houghton Mifflin.

———. 1952. *A Study of Rural Society*. Westport, CT: Greenwood.

Kolb, John H., and Douglas G. Marshall. 1944. "Neighborhood-Community Relationships in Rural Society." Bulletin 154 (November). Agricultural Experiment Station of the University of Wisconsin.

Kolb, J. H., and R. A. Polson. 1933. "Trends in Town-Country Relations." Research Bulletin 117 (September). Agricultural Experiment Station of the University of Wisconsin and United States Department of Agriculture.

Kolb, J. H., and A. F. Wileden. 1927. "Special Interest Groups in Rural Society." Research Bulletin 84 (December). Agricultural Experiment Station, University of Wisconsin, Madison. Cited in J. H. Kolb and Edmund deS. Brunner, *A Study of Rural Society* (Boston, MA: Houghton Mifflin, 1946), 332-334.

Komarovsky, Mirra. 1946. "The Voluntary Associations of Urban Dwellers." *American Sociological Review* (December): 686-698.

Kornhauser, William. 1959. *The Politics of Mass Society*. Glencoe, IL: Free Press.

Kuttner, Robert. 1996. "Net Day: A Lesson in Logging On." *Washington Post* (19 February): A25.

Ladd, Everett C. 1996. "The Data Just Don't Show Erosion of America's 'Social Capital.'" *The Public Perspective* (June/July): 1, 5-6.

Ladd, Everett Carll. 1999. *The Ladd Report*. New York: Free Press.

Landis, Benson Y. 1935. "The Church and Religious Activity." *American Journal of Sociology* XL (May): 780-787.

Landry, Robert J. 1939. "Stations and Partisanship." In *Radio Censorship*, ed. H. B. Summers. New York: H. W. Wilson.

"Landscape of Civic Renewal, The." 1999. National Civic League, Denver, CO.

Lane, Jan-Erik, David McKay, and Kenneth Newton. 1997. *Political Data Handbook: OECD Countries*. Oxford, UK: Oxford University Press.

Laslett, Peter. 1988. "Introduction." In John Locke, *Two Treatises of Government*. Cambridge, UK: Cambridge University Press.

Lederer, Emil. [1940] 1967. *State of the Masses: The Threat of the Classless Society*. New York: Howard Fertig.

Lee, Eugene C. 1960. *The Politics of Nonpartisanship*. Berkeley: University of California Press.

———. 1963. "City Elections: A Statistical Profile." In Orin F. Nolting and David S. Arnold, eds. *The Municipal Year Book 1963*. Chicago, IL: International City Manager's Association.

Leege, David C. 1995. "Religiosity Measures in the National Election Studies: A Guide to Their Use, Part 1." *Votes & Opinions* (October/November): 6-9, 27-30.

Lerner, Max. 1943. "Introduction." In *Aristotle's Politics*, trans. Benjamin Jowett. New York: Random House.

Lewis, Peter. 1996. "In a Recount, Cyber Census Still Confounds." *New York Times* (17 April): D1.

Lippman, Walter. [1955] 1992. *The Public Philosophy*. New Brunswick, NJ: Transaction Publishers.

Lipset, Seymour Martin. 1963. *Political Man: The Social Bases of Politics*. New York: Doubleday.

———. [1963] 1967. *The First New Nation*. New York: Anchor Books, Doubleday.

———. 1981. *Party Coalitions in the 1980s*. San Francisco, CA: Institute for Contemporary Studies.

———. 1994. "The Social Requisites of Democracy Revisited." *American Sociological Review* 59 (February): 1-22.

———. 2000. "The Indispensability of Political Parties." *Journal of Democracy* 11:1 (January): 48-55.

Lipset, Seymour Martin, and Marcella Ridlen Ray. 1996. "Technology, Work, and Social Change." *Journal of Labor Research* XVII:4 (Fall): 613-626.

Lipset, Seymour M., and Stein Rokkan. 1967. "Cleavage Structures, Party Systems, and Voter Alignments: An Introduction." Pp. 1-64 in *Party Systems and Voter Alignments*, eds. Seymour Martin Lipset and Stein Rokkan. New York: Free Press.

Lipset, Seymour Martin, Martin A. Trow, and James S. Coleman. [1956] 1977. *Union Democracy: The Internal Politics of the International Typographical Union*. New York: Free Press.

Little, Kenneth L. 1965. *West African Urbanization: A Study of Voluntary Associations in Social Change*. Cambridge, MA: Cambridge University Press.

Locke, John. 1988. *Two Treatises of Government*, ed. Peter Laslett. Cambridge: Cambridge University Press.

Lofton, John. 1980. *The Press as Guardian of the First Amendment*. Columbia: University of South Carolina Press.

Louis Harris and Associates. 1989. "Public Confidence Declines in 11 of 16 Key Institutions." *The Harris Poll*. July 9 news release.

Lundberg, George A., Mirra Komarovsky, and Mary Alice McInerny. 1934. *Leisure: A Suburban Study*. New York: Columbia University Press.

Lundberg, George A., and Margaret Lawsing. 1949. "The Sociography of Some Community Relations." In *Sociological Analysis*, eds. Logan Wilson and William L. Kolb. New York: Harcourt, Brace.

Lynd, Robert S., and Alice C. Hanson. 1933. "The People as Consumers." In *Recent Social Trends in the United States: Report of the President's Research Committee on Social Trends*, Research Committee on Social Trends. New York: McGraw-Hill.

Lynd, Robert S., and Helen Merrell Lynd. 1929. *Middletown: A Study in American Culture*. New York: Harcourt, Brace.

———. [1937] 1965. *Middletown in Transition: A Study in Cultural Conflicts*. New York: Harcourt Brace Jovanovich.

Machiavelli, Niccolò. 1851. *The History of Florence, and of The Affairs of Italy, From the Earliest Times to the Death of Lorenzo the Magnificent; Together with The Prince*. London: Henry G. Bohn.

———. 1950. *The Discourses of Niccolò Machiavelli,* vols. I-II, trans. Leslie J. Walker. London: Routledge and Kegan Paul.

Madison, James. 1961. "No. 51." In *The Federalist Papers*, Alexander Hamilton, James Madison, and John Jay. New York: New American Library.

Mann, Thomas E., and Norman J. Ornstein. 1992. *A First Report of the Renewing Congress Project*. Washington, DC: American Enterprise Institute for Public Policy Research and Brookings Institution.

Mansbridge, Jayne. 1990. *Beyond Self-Interest*. Chicago, IL: University of Chicago Press.

Mansfield, Harvey C., Jr. 1965. *Statesmanship and Party Government*. Chicago, IL: University of Chicago Press.

———. 1966. *Machiavelli's Virtue*. Chicago, IL: University of Chicago Press.

———. 1984. "Selected Letters of Edmund Burke." Chicago, IL: University of Chicago Press.

Martindale, Don, and R. Galen Hanson. 1969. *Small Town and the Nation: The Conflict of Local and Translocal Forces*. Westport, CT: Greenwood.

Mayer, William G. 1992. *The Changing American Mind*. Ann Arbor: University of Michigan Press.

———. 1993. "Trends in Media Usage." *Public Opinion Quarterly* 57:4 (Winter): 603.

———. 1994. "The Rise of the New Media." *Public Opinion Quarterly* 58:1 (Spring): 139.

"Mayor-Power." 1999. *The Economist* (19 June): 24-26.

Mazzocco, Dennis W. 1994. *Networks of Power: Corporate TV's Threat to Democracy*. Boston, MA: South End.

McAneny, Leslie, and Lydia Saad. 1997. "Honesty and Ethics Poll." December 13 public release, Gallup Poll Online. Website http//:www.gallup.com/poll/news.

McClay, Wilfred M. 2001. "Community and the Social Scientist," *The Public Interest* 143 (Spring): 105-110.

McClendon, Bruce W., and John A. Lewis. 1985. "Goals for Corpus Christi: Citizen Participation in Planning." *National Civic Review* (February): 72-80.

McGuire, Michael, Barry Rubin, Robert Agranoff, and Craig Richards. 1994. "Building Development Capacity in Nonmetropolitan Communities."

Public Administration Review 54:5 (September/October): 426-433.

McKenzie, R. D. 1933. "The Rise of Metropolitan Communities." In *Recent Social Trends in the United States: Report of the President's Research Committee on Social Trends*, Research Committee on Social Trends. New York: McGraw-Hill.

McLoughlin, William G. 1978. *Revivals, Awakenings, and Reform: An Essay on Religion and Social Change in America, 1607-1977*. Chicago, IL: University of Chicago Press.

Mendelson, Edward. 1996. "The Word and the Web." *New York Times Book Review* (2 June): 35.

Merton, Robert K. [1949] 1957. *Social Theory and Social Structure*. Glencoe, IL: Free Press.

Milkis, Sidney M. 1999. *Political Parties and Constitutional Government*. Baltimore, MD: Johns Hopkins University Press.

Mill, John Stuart. 1840. "Letter to Alexis de Tocqueville." In *The Earlier Letters of John Stuart Mill 1812-1848*, ed. Francis E. Mineka. Toronto: University of Toronto Press.

———. [1859] 1920. *Utilitarianism, Liberty, and Considerations on Representative Government*. London: J. M. Dent.

Miller, Dale T. 1999. "The Norm of Self-Interest." *American Psychologist* 54:12 (December): 1053-1060.

Miller, Robert T., and Ronald B. Flowers. 1992. *Toward Benevolent Neutrality: Church, State and the Supreme Court*. 4th ed. Waco, TX: Markham Press Fund, Baylor University Press.

Mills, Jere R. 1994. "Partnerships Providing Service." *Parks and Recreation* 29:5 (May): 32-34.

Milward, H. Brinton. 1994. "Nonprofit Contracting and the Hollow State." *Public Administration Review* 54:1 (January/February): 73-77.

Mishnun, Florence. 1934. "Voluntary Associations." Pp. 283-297 in *Encyclopedia of the Social Science*, eds. Edwin R. A. Seligman and Alvin Johnson. New York: Macmillan.

Mitchell, Susan. 1995. "Birds of a Feather." *American Demographics* 17:2 (February): 40-48.

Moe, Richard, and Carter Wilkie. 1997. *Changing Places: Rebuilding Community in the Age of Sprawl*. New York: Henry Holt.

Moore, David W. 1995. "Americans' Most Important Source of Information: Local TV News." *Gallup Poll Monthly* (September): 2-8.

Morlan, Robert L. 1967. "Local Governments—The Cities." Pp. 461-504 in *The 50 States and Their Local Governments*, ed. James W. Fesler. New York: Alfred A. Knopf.

Mulgan, R. G. 1977. *Aristotle's Political Theory*. Oxford: Clarendon Press.

Murphy, Andrew R. 2001. "In a League of its Own," *The Review of Politics* 63:2, 408-411.

Musgrove, Mike. 2001. "Magazines Whose Time Has Gone," *Washington Post* (3 August): E11.

NALEAO Educational Fund. annual editions. *National Roster of Hispanic Elected Officials*. Washington, DC.

Nall, Frank C., II. 1967. "National Associations." In *The Emergent American Society*, ed. W. Lloyd Warner. New Haven, CT: Yale University Press.
Nation. 1939. "How Free is the Air?" In *Radio Censorship*, ed. H. B. Summers. New York: H. W. Wilson.
National Civic League. 1998. "The Civic Index." Denver, CO.
———. 1999. "The Landscape of Civic Renewal." Denver, CO.
National Council of the Churches of Christ in the U.S.A. annual editions. *Yearbook of American Churches*. New York.
National Directory of Magazines. Annual editions. New York: Oxbridge Communications.
National Election Studies. 2001. Cumulative Data File, 1948-1998. Ann Arbor: University of Michigan, Center for Political Studies. Website http://www.umich.edu/~anes.
———. 1999. "The Origins of ANES." Website http://www.umich.edu/~anes.
National Opinion Research Center. 1994. International Social Survey Program. RELIGION 1991 computer file. Ann Arbor, MI: Interuniversity Consortium for Political and Social Research [distributor].
Neuhaus, Richard John. 2001. *First Things* (January): 68-69.
Neumann, Franz. [1942] 1963. *Behemoth: The Structure and Practice of National Socialism 1933-1944*. New York: Octagon.
New York Daily News. 1939. "No Censorship by Government." In *Radio Censorship*, ed. H. B. Summers. New York: H. W. Wilson.
New York Times. 1939. "Voluntary Associations for Program Scrutiny." In *Radio Censorship*, ed. H. B. Summers. New York: H. W. Wilson.
Nielsen, Waldemar A. 1979. *The Endangered Sector*. New York: Columbia University Press.
Niemi, Richard G. and Herbert F. Weisberg. 1993. *Classics in Voting Behavior*. Washington, DC: Congressional Quarterly.
Nisbet, Robert. [1953] 1990. *The Quest for Community: A Study in the Ethics of Order & Freedom*. San Francisco, CA: Institute for Contemporary Studies Press.
Norris, Pippa. 2000. *A Virtuous Circle*. Cambridge: Cambridge University Press.
O'Brien, David M. 1991. *Constitutional Law and Politics: Civil Rights and Civil Liberties*. New York: W. W. Norton.
O'Conner, Karen, and Lee Epstein. 1981-82. "Research Note: Amicus Curiae Participation in U.S. Supreme Court Litigation: An Appraisal of Hakman's Folklore." *Law and Society Review* 16:2, 311-320.
Oakley, Lisa, and Thomas H. Neale. 1995. "Citizen Initiative Proposals Appearing on State Ballots, 1976-1992." Congressional Research Service, Washington, DC.
Oliver, April. 1999. "The Wrong Lessons." *American Journalism Review* (July/August): 52-55.
Olsen, Marvin E. 1982. *Participatory Pluralism: Political Participation and Influence in the United States and Sweden*. Chicago, IL: Nelson-Hall.
Ostrom, Elinor. 1990. *Governing the Commons: the Evolution of Institutions for Collective Action*. Boston, MA: Cambridge University Press.
Overholser, Geneva. 1999. "Proposal for the Press: Self-Restraint." *Washington Post* (31 August): A13.

Pacelle, Richard L., Jr. 1991. *The Transformation of the Supreme Court's Agenda*. Boulder, CO: Westview.

Pagano, Michael A., and Ann O'M. Bowman. 1995. "The State of American Federalism, 1994-1995." *Publius* 25 (Summer): 1-21.

Parsons, Talcott, with Winston White. 1960. "The Mass Media and the Structure of American Society." Pp. 277-290 in *Talcott Parsons on Institutions and Social Evolution*, ed. Leon H. Mayhew. Chicago, IL: University of Chicago Press.

Paxton, Pamela. 1999. "Is Social Capital Declining in the United States? A Multiple Indicator Assessment," *American Journal of Sociology* 105 (July): 88-127.

Pegoraro, Rob. 2000. "Is Usenet Becoming Yesterday's News?" *Washington Post* (4 February): E1.

Perel, Anthony J. 1997. "Mansfield on Machiavelli." *The Review of Politics* 59 (2), 404-407.

Peterson, Paul E. 1995. *The Price of Federalism*. Washington, DC: Brookings Institution.

Peterson, Paul E., Barry G. Rabe, and Kenneth K. Wong. 1986. *When Federalism Works*. Washington, DC: Brookings Institution.

Peterson, Theodore. [1964] 1975. *Magazines in the Twentieth Century*. Urbana: University of Illinois Press.

Pettinico, George. 1996. "Civic Participation Alive and Well in Today's Environmental Groups." *The Public Perspective* (June/July): 27-30.

Pew Research Center for the People and the Press. 1996-2001. Website http://www.people-press.org.

Pocock, J. G. A. 1975. *The Machiavellian Moment*. Princeton, NJ: Princeton University Press.

Portes, Alejandro. 1998. "Social Capital: Its Origins and Applications in Modern Sociology." Pp. 1-24 in John Hagan and Karen S. Cook, eds., *Annual Review of Sociology*. Palo Alto, CA: Annual Reviews.

Powe, Lucas A., Jr. 1991. *The Fourth Estate and the Constitution: Freedom of the Press in America*. Berkeley: University of California Press.

Powers, William F. 1995. "The Lane Less Traveled." *Washington Post* (3 February): D1-D2.

Princeton Religion Research Center. 1990. "Religion in America 1990." American Institute of Public Opinion, Princeton, NJ.

"Progress 90." 1985. *Pensacola News-Journal*. (24 March): Section H.

Pugliese, Donato J. 1986. *Voluntary Associations: an Annotated Bibliography*. New York: Garland.

Putnam, Robert D. 1993. "The Prosperous Community: Social Capital and Public Life." *The American Prospect* (Spring): 35-42.

———. 1995. "Bowling Alone: America's Declining Social Capital." *Journal of Democracy* 6 (January): 65-78.

———. 1995. "Tuning In, Tuning Out: The Strange Disappearance of Social Capital in America." *PS: Political Science and Politics* 28 (December): 664-683.

———.1996. "Robert Putnam Responds." *The American Prospect* (March-April): 26-28.

———. 2000. *Bowling Alone*. New York: Simon and Schuster.

Putnam, Robert D., with Robert Leonardi and Raffaella Y. Nanetti. 1993. *Making Democracy Work: Civic Traditions in Modern Italy*. Princeton, NJ: Princeton University Press.

Quart, Alissa. 1998. "Neo-Counterculture." *Washington Post* (7 June): C1, C4.

Rahe, Paul. 1992. *Republics Ancient and Modern*. Chapel Hill: North Carolina University Press.

Ramsay, David. [1789] 1983. "The History of the American Revolution. Philadelphia, 1789." In *American Political Writing during the Founding Era 1760-1805*, ed. C. S. Hyneman and D. S. Lutz. Indianapolis, IN: Liberty Fund.

Raphaelson, Arnold H., ed. 1998. *Restructuring State and Local Services*. Westport, CT: Praeger.

Ray, Marcella Ridlen. 1996. "Pieces to the Association Puzzle." Paper presented at annual meeting of the Association for Research on Nonprofit Organizations and Voluntary Action, New York.

———. 1999. "Technological Change and Associational Life." In *Civic Engagement in American Democracy*, eds. Theda Skocpol and Morris Fiorina.Washington, DC: Brookings Institution/Russell Sage Foundation.

———. 2000. "Out of the Shadows: An Empirical Analysis of How Civil Society in the United States Changed During the 20th Century." Ph. D. dissertation, George Mason University.

Ray, Marcella Ridlen and Timothy J. Conlan. 1996. "At What Price: Costs of Federal Mandates Since the 1980s." *State and Local Government Review* 28:1 (Winter): 7-16.

"Real, Per Capita Charitable Giving Has Continued to Rise." 1997. *The Public Perspective* (October/November): 15.

Reif, Karlheinz, and Ronald Inglehart. 1991. "Eurobarometer." New York: St. Martin's.

Reiss, Albert J., Jr. 1959. "Rural-Urban and Status Differences in Interpersonal Contacts." *American Journal of Sociology* 65 (September): 182-195.

Research Committee on Social Trends. 1933. *Recent Social Trends in the United States: Report of the President's Research Committee on Social Trends*. New York: McGraw-Hill.

Reynolds, Donald. 1995. "Words for War." In *The Press in Times of Crisis*, ed. J. Lloyd Chiasson. Westport, CT: Greenwood.

Rice, Arnold S., John A. Krout, and C. M. Harris. 1991. *United States History to 1877*. New York: HarperCollins.

Rich, Paul. 1999. "American Voluntarism, Social Capital, and Political Culture." *ANNALS* 565 (September): 15-34.

Richards, Allan R. 1967. "Half of Our Century." Pp. 71-103 in *The 50 States and Their Local Governments*, ed. James W. Fesler. New York: Alfred A. Knopf.

Risser, James V. 1998. "Endangered Species." *American Journalism Review* (June):18-35.

Rivers, William L. 1973. "The Press as a Communication System." In *Handbook of Communication*, eds. Itheil de Sola Pool et al. Chicago, IL: Rand McNally.

Rix, Sara E., ed. 1988. *The American Woman 1988-89: A Status Report*. New York: W. W. Norton.

Robin, Corey. 2001. "Missing the Point." *Dissent* 63 (Spring): 108-111.

Robinson, John P. 1980. "The Changing Reading Habits of the American Public." *Journal of Communication* 30 (Winter): 147-157.

———. 1990. "Thanks for Reading This." *American Demographics* (May), 6-7.

———. 1999. "The Time-Diary Method: Structure and Uses." In *Time Use Research in the Social Sciences*, eds. W. E. Pentland, A. S. Harvey, M. P. Lawton, and M. A. McColl. New York: Kluwer Academic/Plenum.

Robinson, John P., and Ann Bostrom. 1994. "The Overestimated Workweek? What Time Diary Measures Suggest." *Monthly Labor Review* (August): 11-23.

Robinson, John P., and Geoffrey Godbey. 1995. "Are Average Americans Really Overworked?" *The American Enterprise* (September/October): 43.

———. 1997. *Time for Life: The Surprising Ways Americans Use Their Time*. University Park: Pennsylvania State University Press.

Roniger, Luis. 1994. "Civil Society, Patronage and Democracy." *International Journal of Comparative Sociology* 35 (September-December): 207-220.

Roper Center. 1992. "Mass Communications." *The Public Perspective* (September/October), 5.

Roper Center at University of Connecticut. 1989-2001. Public Opinion Online. LEXIS, Market Library, RPOLL File.

Roper Starch Worldwide. 1995. "America's Watching: Public Attitudes Toward Television." March 31 news release.

Rose, Arnold M. 1967. *The Power Structure: Political Process in American Society*. New York: Oxford University Press.

Rose, Matthew. 2001. "Magazines' Newsstand Sales Fall to Record Low 35% of Shipments," *Wall Street Journal* Interactive Edition (15 May). Website http://interactive.wsj.

Rosenstiel, Tom, Carl Gottlieb, and Lee Ann Brady. 1999. "Local TV News: What Works, What Flops, and Why." *Columbia Journalism Review* (January/ February): special insert.

———. 2000. "Time of Peril for TV News," *Columbia Journalism Review* (November/December): 84-92.

Rotolo, Thomas. 1999. "Trends in Voluntary Association Participation," *Nonprofit and Voluntary Sector Quarterly* 28:2 (June): 199-212.

Rudney, Gabriel, and Murray Weitzman. 1983. "Significance of Employment and Earnings in the Philanthropic Sector, 1972-1982." Working Paper No. 77. New Haven, CT: Program on Non-Profit Organizations, Yale University. Cited in Virginia Hodgkinson and Murray Weitzman, *Dimensions of the Independent Sector: A Statistical Profile*. Washington, DC: Independent Sector, 1989.

Rutenberg, Jim. 2001. "The Media Business: Cable Networks Look for Ways to Stand Out," *New York Times* (20 August): C1, C9.

Ryan, Joseph E. 1995. "Survey Methodology." *Freedom Review* (January/ February): 10-14.

Salamon, Lester M. 1987. "Partners in Public Service: The Scope and Theory

of Government-Nonprofit Relations." In *The Nonprofit Sector*, ed. Walter W. Powell. New Haven, CT: Yale University Press.
———. 1992. *America's Nonprofit Sector*. New York: Foundation Center.
———. 1995. *Partners in Public Service: Government-Nonprofit Relations in the Modern Welfare State*. Baltimore, MD: Johns Hopkins University Press.
———. 1999. *America's Nonprofit Sector: A Primer*. New York: Foundation Center.
Salamon, Lester M., and Helmut K. Anheier. 1996. *The Emerging Nonprofit Sector*. Manchester, UK: Manchester University Press.
Samuels, Christina A. 1999. "'Cohousing' Village Breaks Ground in Virginia." *Washington Post*, (19 July): B7.
Samuelson, Robert J. 1996. "'Bowling Alone' is Bunk." *Washington Post* (10 April): A19.
Sandel, Michael J. 1996. *Democracy's Discontent: America in Search of a Public Philosophy*. Cambridge: Belknap Press of Harvard University Press.
"Say Cheese to Your Cell Phone?" 1999. *Wall Street Journal* (26 August): B6.
Scheingold, Stuart A. 1974. *The Politics of Rights: Lawyers, Public Policy, and Political Change*. New Haven, CT: Yale University Press.
Schervish, Paul G., and John J. Havens. 1998. "Embarking on a Republic of Benevolence? New Survey Findings on Charitable Giving," *Nonprofit and Voluntary Sector Quarterly* 27:2 (June): 237-242.
Schier, Steven E. 2000. *By Invitation Only*. Pittsburgh, PA: University of Pittsburgh Press.
Schiller, Herbert I. 1989. *Culture, Inc.: The Corporate Takeover of Public Expression*. New York: Oxford University Press.
Schlosberg, Jeremy. 2001. "Web Users Share a Happier Outlook," Media Life (13 March). Website http://www.medialifemagazine.com.
Schor, Juliet B. 1992. *The Overworked American*. New York: Basic Books.
Schorr, Daniel. 1977. *Clearing the Air*. Boston, MA: Houghton Mifflin.
Schudson, Michael. 1995. *The Power of News*. Cambridge, MA: Harvard University Press.
———. 1996. "What If Civic Life Didn't Die?" *The American Prospect* (March-April):17-20.
———. 1998. *The Good Citizen*. New York: Free Press.
Scott, John C., Jr. 1957. "Membership and Participation in Voluntary Associations." *American Sociological Review* 22 (June): 315-326.
Scruton, Roger. 1982. *A Dictionary of Political Thought*. New York: Harper and Row.
Sears, David O., and Carolyn L. Funk. 1990. "Self-Interest in Americans' Political Opinions." In *Beyond Self-Interest*, ed. Jayne J. Mansbridge. Chicago, IL: University of Chicago Press.
Selbourne, David. 1997. *The Principle of Duty*. London: Little, Brown.
Seldes, George. 1929. *You Can't Print That! The Truth Behind the News, 1918-1928*. New York: Payson and Clarke.
Selznick, Philip. 1992. *The Moral Commonwealth: Social Theory and the Promise of Community*. Berkeley: University of California Press.

Senate Committee on Government Operations, Subcommittee on Intergovernmental Relations. 1973. *Confidence and Concern: Citizens View American Government—A Survey of Public Attitudes*, 93rd Congress, 1st session, December 3.

Shapiro, Martin. 1972. *The Pentagon Papers and the Courts*. San Francisco, CA: Chandler.

Siegel, Seymour N. 1939. "'Previous Restraint' and 'Subsequent Punishment.'" In *Radio Censorship*, ed. H. B. Summers. New York: H. W. Wilson.

Sills, David L. 1959. "Voluntary Associations: Instruments and Objects of Change." *Human Organization* 18 (Spring): 17-21 .

———. 1968. "Voluntary Associations: Sociological Aspects." Pp. 362-379 in *International Encyclopedia of the Social Sciences*, ed. David L. Sills. New York: Macmillan and Free Press.

Skinner, Quentin. 1978. *The Foundations of Modern Political Thought*. Cambridge: Cambridge University Press.

Skocpol, Theda. 1996. "Unravelling from Above." *The American Prospect* (March-April): 20-25.

Smith, Bruce James. 1985. *Politics and Remembrances: Republican Themes in Machiavelli, Burke, and Tocqueville*. Princeton, NJ: Princeton University Press.

Smith, Constance, and Ann Freedman. 1972. *Voluntary Associations: Perspectives on the Literature*. Cambridge, MA: Harvard University Press.

Smith, David Horton. 1983. "The Impact of the Volunteer Sector on Society." In *America's Voluntary Spirit*, ed. Brian O'Connell. New York: Foundation Center.

———. 1993. "Public Benefit and Member Benefit Nonprofit, Voluntary Groups." *Nonprofit and Voluntary Sector Quarterly* 22 (Spring): 53-68.

———. 1994. "Determinants of Voluntary Association Participation and Volunteering: A Literature Review." *Nonprofit and Voluntary Sector Quarterly* 23:3 (Fall): 243-263.

———. 1997. "Grassroots Associations are Important: Some Theory and a Review of the Impact Literature." *Nonprofit and Voluntary Sector Quarterly* 26:3 (Fall): 269-306.

———. 1997. "The Rest of the Nonprofit Sector: Grassroots Associations as the Dark Matter Ignored in Prevailing "Flat Earth" Maps of the Sector." *Nonprofit and Voluntary Sector Quarterly* 26:2 (June): 114-131.

———. 2000. *Grassroots Associations*. Thousand Oaks, CA: Sage.

Smith, Frank J., and Randolph T. Hester, Jr. 1982. *Community Goal Setting*. Stroudsburg, PA: Hutchinson Ross.

Smith, Jeffrey A. 1998. *War and Press Freedom*. New York: Oxford University Press.

Smith, Steven Rathgeb, and Michael Lipsky. 1993. *Nonprofits for Hire*. Cambridge, MA: Harvard University Press.

Smith, Tom W. 1990. "Phone Home? An Analysis of Household Telephone Ownership." GSSDIRS Methodological Report 50. Website http://www.icpsr.umich.Edu/GSS/.

———. 1990. "Trends in Voluntary Group Membership: Comments on Baumgartner and Walker." *American Journal of Political Science* 34:3 (August): 646-661.

———. 1997. "Factors Relating to Misanthropy in Contemporary American Society." *Social Science Research* 26, 170-196.

Smith, Tom W., and Lars Jarkko. 1998. "National Pride: A Cross-National Analysis." Cross-National Report No. 19. National Opinion Research Center, Chicago, IL. Website http://www. icpsr.umich.edu/GSS/.

"Solitary Bowler, The." 1995. *The Economist* (18 February): 21-22.

Sorokin, Pitirim A., and Clarence Q. Berger. 1939. *Time-Budgets of Human Behavior*. Cambridge, MA: Harvard University Press.

Spring, Jim. 1993. "Seven Days of Play." *American Demographics* (March), 50-56.

Standard Periodical Directory. annual editions. New York: Oxford Communications.

Stanley, Harold W., and Richard G. Niemi. 1992. *Vital Statistics on American Politics*. Washington, DC: Congressional Quarterly.

Stanlis, Peter J. 1986. *Edmund Burke and the Natural Law*. Shreveport, LA: Huntington House.

Stark, Andrew. 1998. "America, The Gated?" *Wilson Quarterly* (Winter): 58-79.

Starobin, Paul. 1998. "Party Hoppers." *The National Journal* 30:6 (February 7): 276-281.

Stein, Bernard L. 1999. "An Ordinary Mission." *Media Studies Journal* (Spring/Summer): 96.

Steiner, David M. 1995. "Postmodernism." Pp. 992-993 in *The Encyclopedia of Democracy*, ed. Seymour Martin Lipset. Washington, DC: Congressional Quarterly.

Steiner, J. F. 1933. "Recreation and Leisure Time Activities." In *Recent Social Trends in the United States: Report of the President's Research Committee on Social Trends*, Research Committee on Social Trends. New York: McGraw-Hill.

Steiner, Jesse Frederick. 1935. "Community Organization." *American Journal of Sociology* XL (May): 788-795.

Stempel, Guido H., III, and Thomas Hargrove. 1996. "Mass Media Audiences in a Changing Media Environment." *Journalism and Mass Communication Quarterly* 73:3 (Autumn): 551-552.

Stengel, Richard. 1996. "Bowling Together." *Time* (2 July): 35.

Stephenson, Donald Grier, Jr. 1999. *Campaigns and the Court*. New York: Columbia University Press.

Stepp, Carl Sessions. 1990. "Access in a Post-social Responsibility Age." In *Democracy and the Mass Media*, ed. Judith Lichtenberg. Cambridge: Cambridge University Press.

Sullivan, Vickie B. 1992. "Machiavelli's Momentary "Machiavellian Moment": A Reconsideration of Pocock's Treatment of the Discourses." *Political Theory* 20 (May): 309-318.

Sullivan, Winnifred Fallers. 1994. *Paying the Words Extra: Religious Discourse in the Supreme Court of the United States*. Cambridge, MA: Harvard University Press.

Summers, H. B. 1939. *Radio Censorship*. New York: H. W. Wilson.

Swisher, Kara. 1996. "There's No Place Like a Home Page." *Washington Post* (1 July): A1, A8.

"Symposium on Robert D. Putnam's *Bowling Alone*, A." 2001. *Contemporary Sociology* 30:3 (May): 223-230.

Taft, William H. 1982. *American Magazines for the 1980s*. New York: Hastings House.

Talbot, Margaret. 2000. "Who Wants to be a Legionnaire?" *New York Times Book Review* (25 June): 11-12.

Taylor, Charles. 1991. *The Malaise of Modernity*. Concord, Ontario: House of Anansi.

Taylor, Charles Lewis, and Michael C. Hudson. 1972. *World Handbook of Political and Social Indicators*. New Haven, CT: Yale University Press.

Taylor, Charles Lewis, and David A. Jodice. 1983. *World Handbook of Political and Social Indicators, Volume 2: Political Protest and Government Change*. New Haven, CT: Yale University Press.

Taylor, Humphrey. 1997. "Fishing, Gardening, Golf and Team Sports are America's Most Popular Leisure Activities—Apart from Reading, TV Watching, and Spending Time with Family." *Harris Poll* 31 (7 July).

———. 1998. "Dramatic Increase in Confidence in Leadership of Nation's Major Institutions." *Harris Poll* 8 (11 February).

Television and Cable Factbook. serial editions. Washington, DC: Warren Publishing.

Thelen, David P. 1996. *Becoming Citizens in the Age of Television*. Chicago, IL: University of Chicago Press.

Til, Jon Van. 1988. *Mapping the Third Sector: Voluntarism in a Changing Social Economy*. New York: Foundation Center.

Tindale, Joseph A. 1999. "Variance in the Meaning of Time by Family Cycle, Period, Social Context, and Ethnicity." In *Time Use Research in the Social Sciences*, eds. W. E. Pentland, A. S. Harvey, M. P. Lawton, and M. A. McColl. New York: Kluwer Academic/Plenum.

Tiryakian, Edward A. 1993. "American Religious Exceptionalism: A Reconsideration." *ANNALS* 527 (May): 40-54.

Tocqueville, Alexis de. 1856. *The Old Regime and the Revolution*, trans. John Bonner. New York: Harper.

———. 1983. *The Old Regime and the French Revolution*, trans. Stuart Gilbert. New York: Doubleday.

———. 1945. *Democracy in America*, vols. I-II. New York: Vintage Books.

Tribe, Laurence H. 1988. *American Constitutional Law*. 2d ed. Mineola, NY: Foundation.

Truman, David B. 1959. "The American System in Crisis." *Political Science Quarterly* 74 (December): 481-497.

———. [1951] 1971. *The Governmental Process*. New York: Alfred A. Knopf.

Underwood, Kathleen Hill. 1983. "Town Building on the Frontier: Grand Junction, Colorado, 1880-1900." Ph.D. dissertation, University of California, Los Angeles.

Ungar, Sanford J. 1990. "The Role of a Free Press Strengthening Democracy." In *Democracy and the Mass Media*, ed. Judith Lichtenberg. Cambridge: Cambridge University Press.

United Media Enterprises. 1983. *Where Does the Time Go?* New York: Newspaper Enterprise Association.
United States Bureau of the Census. 1967-1995. *Census of Governments*. Washington, DC: United States Department of Commerce, Economics and Statistics Administration.
———. 1975. *Historical Statistics of the United States: Colonial Times to 1970*. Washington, DC: United States Department of Commerce.
———. annual editions. *Statistical Abstract of the United States*. Washington, DC: United States Government Printing Office.
United States Department of Commerce. serial editions. *Census of Manufactures*. United States Government Printing Office, Washington, DC.
United States Department of Labor. 1969. "Americans Volunteer." Manpower Administration, Monograph 10 (April).
United States Department of the Treasury. 1996. "Social Welfare and the Economy Highlights." *Social Security Bulletin (*Annual Statistical Supplement): 157-160.
United States Internal Revenue Service. 1969-1974. Commissioner of Internal Revenue Annual Reports. United States Department of the Treasury, Washington, DC.
———. 1993. *IRS Historical Fact Book: A Chronology*. United States Department of the Treasury, Washington, DC.
———. 1994. *Data Book, 1993-94*. United States Department of the Treasury, Washington, DC.
———. 1995. "Tax-Exempt Status for Your Organization." Publication 557 (January). United States Department of the Treasury, Washington, DC.
———. 2000. "IRS Data Book, 1995-98." No. 55B. Website http://www.irs.gov.
United States Travel Data Center. 1985-1995. "National Travel Survey." Washington, DC.
Uphoff, Norman T. 1982. *Rural Development and Local Organization in Asia: Introduction and South Asia*. Delhi: Macmillan India.
———. 1983. *Rural Development and Local Organization in Asia: South East Asia*. Delhi: Macmillan India.
———. 1986. *Local Institutional Development: An Analytical Sourcebook With Cases*. West Hartford, CT: Kumarian Press.
Uphoff, Norman, Milton J. Esman, and Anirudh Krishna. 1998. *Reasons for Success: Learning from Instructive Experiences in Rural Development*. West Hartford, CT: Kumarian Press.
Uphoff, Norman T., and Milton J. Esman. 1983. "Comparative Analysis of Asian Experience with Local Organization and Rural Development." In *Rural Development and Local Organization in Asia: South East Asia*, ed. Norman T. Uphoff. Delhi: Macmillan India.
Usenet Information Center, 1997-1998. Website http:// sunsite.unc.edu /usenet.
Valelly, Richard M. 1996. "Couch-Potato Democracy?" *The American Prospect* (March-April): 25-26.
Verba, Sidney, and Norman H. Nie. 1972. *Participation in America: Political Democracy and Social Equality*. Chicago, IL: University of Chicago Press.

Verba, Sidney, Kay Lehman Schlozman, and Henry E. Brady. 1995. *Voice and Equality: Civic Voluntarism in American Politics*. Cambridge, MA: Harvard University Press.

Vidich, Arthur J., and Joseph Bensman. [1958] 1960. *Small Town in Mass Society*. Garden City, NY: Anchor Books, Doubleday.

Villano, David. 1999. "Going More Local in Miami." *Columbia Journalism Review* (January/February): 53.

Vogel, Ronald K., and Bert E. Swanson. 1988. "Setting Agendas for Community Change: The Community Goal-Setting Strategy." *Journal of Urban Affairs* 10 (1): 41-61.

"Voluntarism and Philanthropy." 1997. *The Public Perspective* (October/November): 15.

"Volunteering in America." 1997. *The American Enterprise* (July/August): 92.

Walker, David B. 1981. *Toward a Functioning Federalism*. Cambridge, MA: Winthrop.

Walker, Leslie J. 1950. "Introduction." In *The Discourses of Niccolò Machiavelli,* vol. I. London: Routledge and Kegan Paul.

Walker, Sydnor H. 1933. "Privately Supported Social Work." Pp. 1168-1223 in *Recent Social Trends in the United States: Report of the President's Research Committee on Social Trends*, Research Committee on Social Trends. New York: McGraw-Hill.

Walton, Mary. 1999. "The Selling of Small-Town America." *American Journalism Review* (May): 58-78.

Walzer, Michael. 1991. "The Idea of Civil Society: A Path to Social Reconstruction." *Dissent* 38 (Spring): 293-304.

"Wanted: An Activist US." 1997. *The Public Perspective* (August/September): 10.

Ward, J. A., Inc. 1962. "A Nationwide Study of Living Habits." Cited in Sebastian de Grazia, *Of Time Work and Leisure*. New York: Twentieth Century Fund.

Warner, W. Lloyd. 1949. *Democracy in Jonesville: A Study in Quality and Inequality*. New York: Harper and Row.

———, ed. 1967. *The Emergent American Society*. New Haven, CT: Yale University Press.

Warner, W. Lloyd, J. O. Low, Paul S. Lunt, and Leo Srole. 1963. *Yankee City*. New Haven, CT: Yale University Press.

Warner, W. Lloyd, and Paul S. Lunt. 1941. *The Social Life of a Modern Community*. New Haven, CT: Yale University Press.

Warner, W. Lloyd, and John H. Trimm. 1967. "The Rise of Big Government." Pp. 560-605 in *The Emergent American Society: Large-Scale Organizations*, ed. W. Lloyd Warner. New Haven, CT: Yale University Press.

Washington Post/Kaiser Family Foundation/Harvard University. 1996. "Survey of Americans and Economists on the Economy." Menlo Park, CA: Kaiser Family Foundation.

Waters, M. Dane. 1999. "A Century Later—the Experiment with Citizen-Initiated Legislation Continues." *The Public Perspective* (December/January): 123-144.

Wattenberg, Ben J. 1974. *The Real America*. Garden City, NY: Doubleday.
Wattenberg, Martin P. 1998. *The Decline of American Political Parties 1952-1996*. Cambridge, MA: Harvard University Press.
———. 2001. "Getting Out the Vote," *Public Perspective* (January/February): 16-17.
Watts, William, and Lloyd A. Free, eds. 1973. *State of the Nation*. New York: Universe Books.
———. 1974. *State of the Nation 1974*. Washington, DC: Potomac Associates.
———. 1978. *State of the Nation III*. Lexington, MA: D.C. Heath.
Weaver, David H. 1996. "What Voters Learn from Media." *ANNALS* (July): 34-47.
Weiss, Michael J. 1988. *The Clustering of America*. New York: Harper and Row.
———. 2000. *The Clustered World*. Boston, MA: Little, Brown.
———. 2001. "Online America," *American Demographics* (March). Website http://www. demographics.com.
Wellman, Barry. 1983. "Network Analysis: Some Basic Principles." Pp. 155-200 in *Sociological Theory 1983*, ed. Randall Collins. San Francisco, CA: Jossey-Bass.
Wheeland, Craig M. 1993. "Citywide Strategic Planning: An Evaluation of Rock Hill's Empowering the Vision." *Public Administration Review* 53(1): 65-72.
White, Leonard D. 1933. "Public Administration." In *Recent Social Trends in the United States: Report of the President's Research Committee on Social Trends*, Research Committee on Social Trends. New York: McGraw-Hill.
White, Theodore H. 1978. *In Search of History: A Personal Adventure*. New York: Harper and Row.
Wiebe, Robert H. 1966. *The Search for Order, 1877-1920*. New York: Hill and Wang.
———. 1975. *The Segmented Society: An Introduction to the Meaning of America*. New York: Oxford University Press.
Willey, Malcolm M., and Stuart A. Rice. 1933. "The Agencies of Communication." In *Recent Social Trends in the United States: Report of the President's Research Committee on Social Trends*, Research Committee on Social Trends. New York: McGraw-Hill.
———. 1933. *Communication Agencies and Social Life*. New York: McGraw-Hill.
Wills, Garry. 2000. "Putnam's America." *The American Prospect* (July 17): 34-37.
Wilson, James Q. 1993. *The Moral Sense*. New York: Free Press.
———. [1974] 1995. *Political Organizations*. Princeton, NJ: Princeton University Press.
Wilson, John. 2001. "Dr. Putnam's Social Lubricant." *Contemporary Sociology* 30:3 (May): 225-227.

Wolfe, Alan. 1998. *One Nation, After All: What Middle-Class Americans Really Think*. New York: Penguin.

Wolman, Leo, and Gustav Peck. 1933. "Labor Groups in the Social Structure." Pp. 801-856 in *Recent Social Trends in the United States: Report of the President's Research Committee on Social Trends*, Research Committee on Social Trends. New York: McGraw-Hill.

Wood, Neal. 1967. "Machiavelli's Concept of Virtù Reconsidered." *Political Studies* XV (2): 159-172.

———. 1968. "Niccolò Machiavelli." Pp. 505-511 in *International Encyclopedia of the Social Sciences*, vol. 9, ed. David L. Sills. Toronto: Crowell Collier and Macmillan.

Wooddy, Carroll H. 1933. "The Growth of Governmental Functions." Pp. 1274-1339 in *Recent Social Trends in the United States: Report of the President's Research Committee on Social Trends*, Research Committee on Social Trends. New York: McGraw-Hill.

World Almanac and Book of Facts. annual editions. Mahwah, NJ: Funk and Wagnalls.

World Values Study Group. 2000. World Values Survey [computer file]. ICPSR version. Ann Arbor, MI: Institute for Social Research [producer]. Ann Arbor, MI: Interuniversity Consortium for Political and Social Research [distributor].

Wright, Deil S. 1988. *Understanding Intergovernmental Relations*. 3d ed. Pacific Grove, CA: Brooks/Cole.

———. 1993. "Models of National, State, and Local Relationships." In *American Intergovernmental Relations: Foundations, Perspectives, and Issues*, ed. J. Laurence O'Toole. Washington, DC: Congressional Quarterly.

Wright, John W. 1995. *The Universal Almanac 1996*. Kansas City, MO: Andrews and McMeel.

Wrong, Dennis H. 1994. *The Problem of Order*. New York: Free Press.

Wuthnow, Robert. 1991. *Acts of Compassion: Caring for Others and Helping Ourselves*. Princeton, NJ: Princeton University Press.

———. 1991. "Tocqueville's Question Reconsidered: Voluntarism and Public Discourse in Advanced Industrial Societies." In *Between States and Markets*, ed. Robert Wuthnow. Princeton, NJ: Princeton University Press.

———. 1994. *Sharing the Journey: Support Groups and America's New Quest for Community*. New York: Free Press.

Zimmer, Basil G., and Amos H. Hawley. 1959. "The Significance of Membership in Associations." *American Journal of Sociology* 65:2 (September): 196-201.

Zimmerman, Joseph F. 1981. "The Discretionary Authority of Local Governments." *Urban Data Service Reports* 13:11 (November). Washington, DC: International City Management Association.

Zuzanek, Jiri, and Brian J. S. Smale, "Life-Cycle and Across-the-Week Allocation of Time to Daily Activities." In *Time Use Research in the Social Sciences*, eds. W. E. Pentland, A. S. Harvey, M. P. Lawton, and M. A. McColl. New York: Kluwer Academic/Plenum.

Index